The Beechers

Through the Nineteenth Century

A Radio Play

BANDANNA BOOKS • 2011 • SANTA BARBARA

The Beechers Through the Nineteenth Century ISBN 978-0-942208-44-3
Copyright © 2011 Bandanna Books Cover art: Baron C. De Grimm
Dramatization based on materials from *The Autobiography of Lyman Beecher* and original research
www.bandannabooks.com

LITERARY CLASSICS FROM BANDANNA BOOKS

www.shakespeareplaybook.com

scene-by-scene storyboarding, auditions, staging diagrams, budget, publicity, costuming, set design, playbill, stage managing

Hamlet • Merchant of Venice • Twelfth Night • Richard III • Othello Taming of the Shrew • A Midsummer Night's Dream • As You Like It Romeo and Juliet • Henry V • Much Ado About Nothing • Macbeth

also: *Seven Plays with Transgender Characters, plus Hamlet*

LIT LITE

Don't Panic: Procrastinator's Guide to Writing an Effective Term Paper
The First Detective: 3 Stories. Edgar Allan Poe
Gandhi on the Gita • *The Everlasting Gospel*, William Blake
Italian for Opera Lovers • *Dante & His Circle* • *Vita Nuova*
Ghazals of Ghalib • *Gospel According to Tolstoy* • *Hadji Murad*

LIT HEAVY

Mitos y Leyendas/Myths and Legends of Mexico. Bilingual
The Beechers Through the 19th Century
Uncle Tom's Cabin, H.B. Stowe • *Frankenstein*, Mary Shelley
Aurora Leigh, Elizabeth Barrett Browning

LIT FOR TEACHERS: SUPPLEMENT EDITIONS

Areopagitica, Milton • *Apology of Socrates, & The Crito*, Plato
Leaves of Grass, Whitman • *Sappho, The Poems*
Uncle Tom's Cabin, Harriet Beecher Stowe

CONTENTS

INTRODUCTION

The original radio production of *The Beechers* on the Little Red Radio Show aired twice in its entirety on KCSB-FM, at the University of California, Santa Barbara. Over seventy-five people participated with their voices or talents. I thank them all, but especially the four cast in the major roles of Lyman Beecher (Michael Katz), Harriet Beecher Stowe (Susan Stewart Potter), Henry Ward Beecher (Dennis Holt), Catherine Beecher (Shirley Sims). I served as the Narrator (Sasha Newborn). Audio of the actual broadcasts are currently available at www.bandannabooks.com/19th/beechers.

The origin of the idea came from a question in my mind—why members of a few families sprouted so many useful and famous careers, such as the Jameses, the Adamses, the Holmeses. And the Beechers. Is it a peculiar gene? Or perhaps the family environment is somehow conducive to genius? Out of eleven (!) children, ten of the Beechers secured a national reputation in one field or another.

As I came to know them by their personal statements, I realized that their history was our United States history, not the whole of it, but a major portion of the tides of sentiment and eras of a nation abuilding. Which is how I offer it. Each radio episode started with a pertinent quotation from Henry David Thoreau:

> The earnest seeker and hopeful discoverer of this New World always haunts the outskirts of his or her time. Our history is written in the lives of such individuals.

This was followed by a musical intro, a catchy piano piece by Louis Moreau Gottschalk, an international star performer and composer of the mid-Nineteenth Century.

The original show had 28 half-hour scripts for the entire series. I would corral people walking down the hallway at KCSB to fill in the voicing for one or another minor character. Most of them never saw the others participating, except for three half-hour scripts of Beecher family reunions, when all were catching up on each other's careers. These get-togethers were taped live with six or eight speakers, and definitely show more liveliness than lone script-reading snippets.

Audio production, besides cutting and splicing pieces of audio tape, meant writing the script, adding my own narration from other research, musical intros and outros (most of them from Dvorak's New World Symphony), timing, and airing on my eclectic show. Please excuse occasional repetitions you may find toward the beginning of each chapter; these were intentional in the original script, to remind the radio listener of the continuity of the narrative from the preceding week. The audio files can be found at www.bandannabooks.com/19th/beechers/.

Whatever possessed me to do this project in the first place? I think it was to honor the Beechers and what they had done that is so little known today. Much of the Nineteenth Century, certainly the era before the War of Secession (now known as the Civil War, which it was not), is hidden history, yet these events, these people, laid the foundations for what our culture has become.

I hope you enjoy this journey, history writ small with large consequences. It has given me a new sense of the age I live in, to pay attention to the undercurrent beneath the events that hit the headlines. May it do the same for you.

Sasha Newborn
September 2011

SYNOPSES OF BEECHER FAMILY EPISODES

1. EAST HAMPTON : (1800–1810) LYMAN BEECHER begins his ministry, revivalism on Long Island, Lyman's breakdown and recovery, the first child, Aunt Mary Foote's story, more children, Roxana as wife, the private school, more on Aunt Mary, fear of Jefferson, Uncle Samuel Foote, Lyman's fiddle, childhood and discipline, Lyman's sermon on Duelling, moving to Litchfield, Connecticut.

Characters: *Lyman Beecher, Roxana, Mary Foote, Catharine, Noah Webster, Judge Reeve, Edward.*

2. LITCHFIELD : (1810–1816)—The household at Litchfield, Miss Pierce's school, no Christmas, the house, sunsets and woods, Judge Reeve, boys fishing and hunting, Uncle Samuel, Catharine's poems, piano, Roxana's letter, her death, funeral, elegy.

Characters : *Harriet, Henry, Catharine, Roxana, Lyman, Charles.*

3. FIRSTBORN : (1816–1823)—Lyman's new wife, letters to his children, Catharine's romance, young Frederick dies, Catharine's fiance Alexander Fisher dies, Lyman's letter to her, Catharine's doubt, C. writes to Edward, Lyman to E., Lyman's advice, Catharine visits Fisher's family, Catharine's letters, her decision, Lyman's help.

Characters : *Lyman, Catharine, Harriet Porter, Edward, Henry.*

4. HARTFORD : (1823–1826)—Family projects, Harriet away from home, Aunt Esther, Byron's death, Lyman's attack on Unitarianism, Harriet's conversion, Catharine's new school in Hartford, her enthusiasm, strain of teaching, Lyman accepts invitation to preach at Boston, Catharine's revival, C.'s ideas, her breakdown.

Characters : *Harriet, Catharine, Lyman.*

5. BOSTON YEARS—1 : (1826–1829)—The Unitarian controversy, Bacon's analysis, Lyman's sermon, moving to Boston, Lyman's illness, politics of religion, Channing vs. Beecher, Old

School attacks, L.'s regimen, first sermons in Boston, progress in church, Mrs. Beecher's view of Boston, William's problems, Henry's wish to go to sea, Lyman's talk with him, prayer.

Characters : *Lyman, Harriet, William, Henry, Leonard Bacon, Channing, Harriet Porter.*

6. BOSTON YEARS—2 : (1829–1832)—Lyman as revivalist preacher, Harriet's view of Lyman, attacks on Lyman, sermons printed, L.'s techniques, Catharine's revival and Lyman's reply, fiddle tunes, arranging for a church for Edward, letter to Catharine, more help for Edward, Catharine's Cherokee appeal, Mason's hymns, Garrison's reversal, Walker on Lyman's contribution to lyceums, church burned, the call West, news of Charles and William.

Characters: *Lyman, Harriet, Lowell Mason, Amasa Walker, W.L. Garrison.*

7. THE HEIR APPARENT : (1818–1834)— Edward's regimen, his schooling, his ideas, Channing on Calvinism, E. at Hartford Seminary, Lyman's advice, Catharine's letter, helping Harriet, Harriet's reply, Edward's conception of God, and of evil, his revelation, Charles comments, E. at Park Street, Catharine's comment, Garrison's address, Lyman's position, Garrison retracts, Edward in Illinois, Bryant in Jacksonville, E. on emancipation, meets Elijah Lovejoy, E.'s sermons published.

Characters : *Edward, Harriet, Lyman, Charles, Garrison, Catharine, Channing, Bryant, Lovejoy.*

8. CINCINNATI—1 : (1832–1836)—The Beechers move West, Cincinnati, Dr. Wilson's opposition, Lyman defends himself, social activities, models for Simon Legree and Topsy, cholera, Catharine's new school, the abolitionist controversy, C.'s rebuff, her New York speech, Henry comes West, Charles takes up music, William's new job, Henry's conversion, Lyman remarries again, Harriet marries Calvin Stowe, Henry patrols for Birney, Catharine on a speaking tour, C. writing with Harriet.

Characters : *Lyman, Harriet, Charles, Henry, Foote, Catharine.*

9. REUNION—1 : (1835)—First family reunion described, Henry's progress, slavery, circular letter, Mary's invitation to Isabella, Lyman's heresy trial described, Catharine's ideas, her speech.

Characters : *Lyman, Catharine, Hastings, Harriet, George, Edward, Thomas, Isabella, Mary, Charles, Henry.*

10. REUNION—2 : (1835)—The reunion continues, Lyman counsels Charles, more of Lyman's heresy trial, abolitionism, George's ordination.

Characters : *Lyman, Harriet, Charles, Henry, Edward, Catharine, George, Isabella, Thomas, William, Mary.*

11. ALTON : (1834–1837)—Charles's stories of slavery to Harriet, Garrison's challenge, abolitionism, Eliza's escape, Lovejoy's move to Alton, anti-slavery convention disrupted, Webster's view, Channing's letter, Lovejoy's fourth press, mob kills Lovejoy, Edward becomes an abolitionist leader.

Characters : *Edward, Lyman, Daniel Webster, Elijah Lovejoy, Channing, Charles, Garrison, John Quincy Adams.*

12. CINCINNATI—2 : (1836–1840)—Harriet's dictation, Henry's speaking lessons, Catharine vs. Angelina Grimke on women's rights, Henry's sermons, Peter Cartwright confronts Joseph Smith, Edward and Charles debate Catharine in theology.

Characters : *Henry, Peter Cartwright, Joseph Smith, Lyman, Volunteer, Harriet, Isabella, Angelina Grimke, Mina, Catharine.*

13. THE FORTIES : (1839–1847)—Henry in Indianapolis, Harriet studies writing, Cartwright on abolitionism, Fanny Kemble reports on slavery conditions, Garrison's editorials, Isabella discovers women's rights, James ships out, glimpses of Harriet's book to come, revivalism in Indianapolis, brothers stay with Henry.

Characters : *Harriet, Henry, Isabella, Cartwright, Catharine, Garrison, Katy Beecher, Calvin Stowe, Lyman, Blackstone.*

14. INDIANAPOLIS—1 : (1837–1843)—Henry at Lawrenceburgh, and Indianapolis, as revivalist preacher, Henry's apostolic method, Van Buren's visit, *Seven Lectures for Young Men*, Lovell's class, Charles's progress, Julia Merrill and Betty Bates, Charles's

ordination, getting him a church in Ft. Wayne, Harriet and Henry experiment with mesmerism.

Characters : *Henry, Harriet, Lyman, Julia Merrill, Charles, Thomas.*

15. THE SUICIDE : (1830–1843)—George as student, his illness, journey to Cincinnati, George's ordination, a church at Batavia, round-robin letter on George's perfectionism, Catharine visits him in Chillicothe, his suicide, Catharine's memorial volume.

Characters : *Harriet, Lyman, George, Catharine, Henry, Charles, Calvin Stowe, William.*

16. INDIANAPOLIS—2 : (1844–1847)—Henry's anti-slavery stand in Indianapolis, H.'s work habits, his involvement with Julia Merrill, offer from Brooklyn, and one from Boston, Eunice's health, Julia's mother dies, Henry leaves for Brooklyn.

Characters : *Henry, Fanny Kemble, Lyman, King, McLean, Eunice, Ketcham, Bowen, Abbott, Cutler, Merrill, Julia Merrill, Whittier.*

17. THE TURNING POINT : (1848–1850)—Catharine's book reprinted, Thomas as her speaker, her call for teachers, Slade splits off, Henry's first Brooklyn sermon, his first freedom auction, the Delia Bacon affair, Catharine alienates the family, Edward publishes, Henry's new church design, Charles is outspoken, Ch. moves to Newark, Henry in Europe, H. becomes a collector, writes Star Papers, Fugitive Slave Law passed, Harriet and Henry meet, Catharine organizes.

Characters : *Henry, Catharine, Harriet, Lyman, John C. Calhoun, Delia Bacon, Edward.*

18. THE BOOK—1 : (1850–1852)—Lyman retires at 75, Catharine helps run Harriet's household, Frederick Douglass's story, Harriet writes to him, *National Era* publishes Harriet's chapters, *Uncle Tom's Cabin* is published, letters come in, Calvin invited to teach at Andover, *Tom* dramatized, Fanny Kemble's letter, George Sand's comments.

Characters : *Harriet, Catharine, Frederick Douglass, Fanny Kemble, Garrison, Calvin Stowe, Charles, Longfellow, George Sand, Katy Beecher, Lyman, Bailey, Whittier.*

19. FAME : (1852–1853)—*Uncle Tom's Cabin* is a huge success, Edward Beecher's *Conflict of Ages* published, Charles works on

Lyman's *Autobiography*, Harriet works to bring Catharine back together with the family, Harriet accuses Joel Parker, reaction to Edward's book, Catharine's ideas in Harriet's books, Harriet writes to Garrison, Bleeding Kansas and "Beecher's Bibles," J.R. Lowell writes to Harriet.

Characters : *Harriet, Catharine, James Russell Lowell, Charles, W.L. Garrison, Jonathan Edwards, Edward, Henry.*

20. THE BOOK—2 : (1853–1856)—Harriet becomes focal point for fundraising, letter from Jenny Lind, Harriet encouraged to visit Europe, Wendell Phillips and Frederick Douglass speak, refutation of criticism of *Uncle Tom's Cabin*, Harriet, Calvin and Charles in Europe—Scotland, a dinner in London, Englishwomen's petition, H. meets Lady Byron, H. to Geneva, Harriet's appeal to American women, *Dred* published, second European trip, H. meets the Queen.

Characters : *Harriet, Henry, F. Douglass, E.B. Browning, Jenny Lind, Kingsley, Wendell Phillips, Charles, Sumner, George Sand, Cassius Clay, George Eliot.*

21. SECOND REUNION : (1855)—Lyman talks of his father, Henry asserts leadership, Henry's organist, Lyman's birth, L.'s reaction to Milton's Satan, Henry's *Star Papers* and familiar essays published, Lyman on the Revolution, Henry's preaching described, Lyman's conversion, fishing, aurora borealis, Revolutionary skirmish, Robert G. Ingersoll on the Beechers, Henry's oratory, Lyman's support at college, the buttery, meeting his first wife, Roxana.

Characters : *Lyman, Henry, Harriet, Zundel, Timothy Dwight, Catharine, Bronson Alcott, Abbott, Robert G. Ingersoll, Theodore Parker.*

22. THE POT BOILS OVER : (1854–1860)—Henry's anti-slavery views, abolitionist agitation, Stephen Douglas's Kansas-Nebraska bill passed, Republican Party organized, Buchanan elected, Catharine on water cures and women's health issues, Harriet's son drowned, H. publishes *The Minister's Wooing* modeled on Catharine's affair, Charles's resolution against Buchanan, Edward publishes *The Concord of Ages*, Lincoln elected, Southern states hold independent conventions, war is imminent.

Characters : *Harriet, Henry, Catharine, Lincoln, Isabella, Fillmore, Dr. Hodge, Greeley, Edward, Mrs. Marvyn, Charles.*

23. LAST GATHERING : (1863)—Lyman on the War of 1812, Harriet's illness, Lyman dying, Thomas's letter, Charles's anecdote of loss of faith, Henry reads Lyman's letter about Thomas, Thomas tells of telegram, Harriet reads letter of Lyman's to Taylor, Thomas reports on being the last child at home.

Characters : *Lyman, Thomas, Harriet, Charles, Isabella, Henry.*

24. AT WAR : (1861–1863)—James becomes colonel, Frederick Stowe and Henry, jr. enlist, Alexander Stephens speaks, Thomas joins as chaplain, Henry criticizes Lincoln, gets a night visitor, Harriet goes to Jersey City and sees Frederick, H. goes to Washington with Isabella to see Lincoln, then writes a reply to the Englishwomen's petition, Hawthorne congratulates her, Henry goes to Europe, meets Leopold of Belgium but rebukes him, in England Henry is persuaded to give five speeches to hostile audiences, which sway the British away from recognizing the Confederacy, H. returns home a hero.

Characters : *Henry, Harriet, Mabie, James, Lincoln, Oliver Wendell Holmes, Frederick Stowe, Alexander Stephens, Nathaniel Hawthorne.*

25. WAR AND PEACE : (1863–1869)—The women's movement abandoned by the abolitionists, Isabella's first article, Charles's heresy trial, James given a colored regiment, Charles and Edward write a reply, Henry calls on Lincoln, Isabella drawn into women's movement, James wounded, J. gives a sermon in freed territory, Henry speaks at Ft. Sumter, Lincoln assassinated, Elizabeth Cady Stanton and Susan B. Anthony take their struggle to Kansas, Henry preaches reconciliation with the South—not a popular view, H. gets out of step with the Republican Party, Theodore Tilton takes over Henry's paper, Stanton speaks out, Henry, James and Frederick Douglass reply, women's group splits, Stanton attacks Harriet, Harriet replies, Victoria Woodhull allied with Isabella, Isabella holds a convention.

Characters : *Henry, Elizabeth Cady Stanton, Isabella, Victoria*

Woodhull, Charles, Thomas, Marcy, James, Frederick Douglass, Henry James, Susan B. Anthony.

26. A NEW ERA : (1870–1886)—Thomas and Henry together, Harriet publishes *Lady Byron Vindicated*, Charles in Florida with Harriet and Calvin, Theodore Tilton becomes a radical Republican and accuses Henry of approaching his wife, James Beecher in upper New York state, *Claflin's Weekly* publishes Beecher-Tilton scandal story, Mark Twain writes in support of Thomas Beecher, Harriet on speaking tour, another Twain piece on Thomas and his huge church, Edward moves to New York, Henry on trial, Catharine comes to Elmira, James breaks down and commits suicide, Henry dies.

Characters : *Thomas, Harriet, Eastman, Charles, Henry, Edward, Julia, Ned Buntline, Mark Twain, Isabella, Beach.*

27. SPIRITUALISM : —Catharine experiments, Harriet and Henry experiment with mesmerism, Calvin Stowe reports on his unusual experiences, William's powers, Isabella's delusions of grandeur, James on family insanity, Charles writes of spiritualism in religion, Thomas on the family.

Characters: *Calvin Stowe, Isabella, Harriet, Catharine, James, Charles, Thomas, Henry, William.*

28. AFTERMATH : (1842–1907)—Thomas Beecher graduates, Lyman at home, Thomas's scientific skills, Thomas hears Horace Bushnell, Henry's and Harriet's successes, Thomas begins his ministry, T. builds the first institutional-style church, Henry becomes an evolutionist, Henry's typical day, Catharine's vision, her death, Edward's book, Harriet's birthday party with O.W. Holmes, J.G. Whittier, Henry is interviewed about politics, Henry comes out for Cleveland against the Republicans, James's suicide, Henry's death, Isabella in the women's movement, her advice to granddaughter Isabel, the last Beecher dies.

Characters : *Henry, Harriet, Whittier, Isabella, Holmes, Edward, Lowell, Catharine, George Eliot, John Ruskin.*

29. THE FAMILY TREE

EAST HAMPTON
1800-1810

When the father Lyman Beecher retired at age 75, with the intention of sitting down to write his autobiography, he found that memories slipped away from him. His keen mind was gone, and daughters Harriet Beecher Stowe and Catharine prompted him into conversations of his early days. They also added their own reminiscences and drew on the family round robin letters; Edward Beecher supplied materials, and so did the rest of the eleven Beecher children. Charles was finally designated editor, and when the two volumes of the *Autobiography of Lyman Beecher* was finally published, it was the chronicle of a remarkable family whose ideas and actions helped shape the country that we live in today. That material is the basis for what you will hear today.

So let us begin at the turn of the nineteenth century—the democrat Jefferson has just been elected, and many are worried that the democratic Terror that gripped the French Revolution just seven years before will grip America. In a remote village on the far end of Long Island, a young minister and his wife are about to begin a most remarkable family.

At the turn of the century, Lyman Beecher was 25 and fired up with ambition. He had been schooled at Yale under the thunderer Timothy Dwight, and when he received the call, he set out to bring back the Puritan revivalism of the Great Awakening of two generations before. He had boundless energy and zeal, traveling far to carry the word. A practical preacher, he measured his success by the number of converts.

LYMAN : There was a revival fever stirred the town. Oh, how I went down there I spilled over. All the old folks waked up, and when I went home, after meeting, to Aunt Phebe's, the young people flowed together there. The work went on gloriously for six weeks and shook the whole town. 80 were converted.

ROXANA : Dear sister,—Mr. Beecher is everybody's man. I will tell you a little how it has been this winter.

Mr. Beecher has preached seven or eight times a week the whole winter. Last week, for example, he preached twice in town and two lectures, besides a funeral sermon on Gardiner's Island, and five sermons to the Indians and white people down at Montauk. He every week lectures at some one of the villages adjoining Wainscott, four miles; Amagansett, three miles; Northwest, seven; the Springs, seven; and another place with an ugly Indian name. Some weeks at two or three of these places; and when not at these places, there have been meetings afternoons and evenings, and sometimes in the forenoon. I have not in the least exaggerated, and you may therefore suppose he has not had much leisure to attend to other business.

My principal business has been to prepare three meals a day, and now and then to put my house a little in order. I have spun enough for about two pairs of stockings, and almost knit them, and have mended my own and husband's clothes. This uncommon attention to religion has brought a good deal of company. Indeed, there has been somebody here the greater part of the time. We have not passed above one or two evenings without visitors since I have been here, and they commonly stay till 11 o'clock, so that I find it difficult to seize a moment to write.

NARRATOR : But the next year, this schedule proved too much for Lyman. When he was hit with fever and ague in the winter of 1801, he had a breakdown. For weeks he was unable to do anything. Gradually he began to regain his strength and spirit and he began to fish, hunt, and ride. Later he could manage physical labor—making turf fences, haying, hauling seaweed—but recovery was slow.

LYMAN : There was a long period in which I could not preach. Old Mr. Fithian one day told me he should not pay his rates any longer if I did not preach. "What is the reason," said he, "You ministers are so hungry for money?"

"I don't know," said I, "unless it is that we see our people growing covetous and going to hell, and want to get it away from them."

About September I began to preach short sermons, 15 minutes long, the deacons taking the other services. When I finished speaking, my back and the cords down to my heels were in pain. Then I had a chair made to brace me and take the weight off my feet.

Gradually I gained so that I could stand and preach, but it was about a year first.

•

NARRATOR : Catharine Esther was the firstborn of eleven children of Lyman and Roxana Beecher, born in 1800 in East Hampton, a village on the father shore of Long Island, still partly inhabited by Indians. Also in the household was Mary Foote Hubbard. Roxana's lovely and and charming sister had married a New Haven man who was a planter in the West Indies. Unfortunately, she found that he already had a mulatto family there. At the first chance, she fled in despair, and came to live with the Beechers in East Hampton. Catharine remembers her with affection.

CATHARINE : She was the poetry of my childhood.

MARY FOOTE : I wish, dear sister Esther, you would write me all the news. We get no paper, and know no more of the affairs of the world than if we were not in it. Here we are so still, so quiet, so dull, so inactive, that we have forgotten but that the world goes on the same way. We have forgotten that there are wars, murders, and violence abroad in the earth; that there are society, and friendship, and intercourse, and social affection, and science, and pleasure, and life, and spirit, and gayety, and good-humor, alive still among the sons of the earth.

All here is the unvaried calm of a—frog pond, and without the music of it. We neither laugh nor cry, sing nor dance, nor moan, nor lament; but the man that took ten steps yesterday taketh the same today, and as standing water begins to turn green, so all the countenances you meet seem to have contracted the expression indicative of the unagitated state in which they live. I wish I could procure some nitrous oxide—laughing gas—for them to inhale once a week. What do you suppose would be the effect? Suppose they would move a muscle in the face? Send me over a bottle. For my own part I am no better than an oyster, and as it is late I will creep into my shell.

NARRATOR : The household also included a housekeeper and two bound girls, Zillah and Rachel, who tended the cooking and the children. Two years after Catharine was born came William, then Edward.

CATHARINE : There was a free and easy way of living, more congenial to liberty and society than to conventional rules.

NARRATOR : Lyman's wife Roxana never fondled or caressed the children, though Lyman did. She was gentle and kind, though she did not discipline them—that was for Lyman. At least, he took it over, exacting prompt and cheerful obedience from them, enforced with severity by a quince switch. He also loved openly and always showed concern.

LYMAN : I scarcely ever saw Roxana agitated to tears. Once, soon after we had moved into our new house, the two pigs did something that vexed me; I got angry and thrashed them. She came to the door and interposed. My fire hadn't gone out. I said quickly, "Go along in" She started, but hadn't more than time to turn before I was at her side, and threw my arms around her neck and kissed her, and I told her I was sorry. Then she wept. That was the nearest to a quarrel we ever came.

•

NARRATOR : Since Lyman's salary was inadequate for his growing family, Lyman and Roxana Beecher opened a girls' school, and took in five boarders.

LYMAN : After I had been at East Hampton five or six years, and the family multiplied—for, besides Catharine and William, now we had Edward and Mary—our expenses were so increased that it became manifest that something must be done. A school was the only thing we could think of. So, without consulting the congregation, I advertised, and scholars came from towns around, and from Middle Island.

It was a select school, and your mother taught the higher English branches, besides French, drawing, painting, and embroidery. I took great interest in the school, and used to help about subjects for composition. The school prospered, and was, on the whole, profitable.

CATHARINE : I remember how mother and Aunt Mary studied Lavoisier's *Chemistry* together. Chemistry was a new science then, and a constant subject of discussion. They tried a great many experiments, too, and sometimes with most ludicrous results. I also remember several large pieces of embroidery that were done by her scholars. Embroidery was an essential accomplishment then. Mother drew flowers from nature, and made fine copies from some splendid colored engravings of birds. In landscape drawing she was less successful.

NARRATOR : Catharine's sister Harriet remembered her mother fondly.

HARRIET : Her forte was drawing likenesses on ivory. She took many of her scholars and friends, Dr. and Mrs. Woolworth, Grandma Foote, and Aunt Esther. There were about two dozen in all, which used to be kept in the family as a treasure to be shown us children when we were good.

The one she took of Aunt Esther was specially valuable as showing how she looked when a young girl. A little brunette, with clear olive complexion, keen, piercing hazel eyes, small aquiline nose, and great vivacity of expression; petite in figure, and dressed in bright crimson silk, with low neck and bare arms. Her wit was like lightning, and sometimes rather too keen. Her sayings had a peculiar neatness and point that made them apt to be repeated, and sometimes gave offense.

CATHARINE : The large room on the left, as you enter, was the sitting room, and behind it a bedroom. Father's study was a small room on the right of the front entry. The schoolroom was over the sitting room, and in the two chambers opposite were four young ladies who boarded with us. The chambers over the kitchen and bedroom were given to the housekeeper, and to Zillah and Rachel.

We took our meals in the sitting room, and some of the most vivid of my early recollections are of the discussions between father and mother and Aunt Mary at table.

They read the *Christian Observer*, conducted by Macaulay, Wilberforce, Hannah More, and such works noticed in it as they would procure.

An *Encyclopedia*, presented to Aunt Mary by an English gentleman whose two daughters boarded with us, was mother's constant resource. Here she studied perspective, and, as a specimen of her perseverance, finding a problem in which there happened to be a mistake, she did not leave it till she had substituted the true solution.

My remembrances of Aunt Mary are more vivid than those of any other friend of early life. The peculiar faculty of charming, which seemed to be her gift, was exerted as much upon children as on older people. It seemed to spring from her versatile power of throwing herself into sympathy with any associate for the time being. I was often her little nurse and attendant, and she secured my enthusiastic devotion by the high appreciation she seemed always to have of my childish services. She convinced me that I alone, of all the world, had the talent for finding the new-laid egg in the hay, that I could boil it exactly to a moment, and arrange the table and the chair, and do every service as no one else could.

Most observing and most sympathizing was she with all the little half-fledged wants and ambitions of childhood. One instance in point. I remember my imagination had been fired by hearing her read, in some poem, of the curls of some fair heroine dropped on her book; and so, one day, with great labor, I coaxed my hair into curl, and placed myself conspicuously before her, with the curls dropping on the page of an open book. She saw the artifice, and said, in her sweetest tones, "Oh, mother, come her and see these beautiful ringlets"

Aunt Mary was a beautiful reader, and I have the most vivid recollection of the impassined tones in which her favorite authors were given to the family circle. At East Hampton, when I was only eight or nine, my mind was stored with weird tales from Scott's ballads, while the *Lay of the Last Minstrel* and *Marmion* were read aloud, mingled with enthusiastic encomiums on favorite passages.

·

NARRATOR : About this time, Noah Webster spoke for many Federalists when he warned about the new democrat President, Thomas Jefferson, with his dangerous liberal ideas, such as equality —and rights that were not dependent on king or God.

NOAH WEBSTER : The truth is, many of our leading political men, during and after the Revolution, were visionary enthusiasts. The loose, undefined sense in which the words free and equal are used in some of the American constitutions has been, and will be, of immense evil to this country. The very principle of admitting everybody to the right of suffrage prostrates the wealth of individuals to the rapaciousness of a merciless gang, who have nothing to lose, and will delight in plundering their neighbors.

NARRATOR : Webster, like many of his time, distrusted democratic ideas. They pointed to France's difficulties with its Reign of Terror, and then Napoleon. At one point, Judge Tapping Reeve, founder of the Litchfield Law Academy, believed that the Union would have to be dissolved, so distressing was the possibility of four more years under Jefferson.

JUDGE REEVE : I have seen many of our friends, and all that I have seen, and most that I have heard from, believe that we must separate, and that this is the most favorable moment.

NARRATOR : Generally, Lyman Beecher avoided political discussions, though they sometimes had a way of coming to him.

CATHARINE : I remember a visit of Uncle Samuel Foote while we lived at East Hampton, in which he brought with him various literary works, and also some of the first numbers of *Salmagundi*, conducted by Irving and his literary clique, whose careers were then just commencing. These papers were read aloud in the family with great enjoyment of their fresh and piquant humor.

Uncle Samuel Foote was a man of great practical common sense, united with large ideality, a cultivated taste, and very extensive reading. With this was combined a humorous combativeness, that led him to attack the special theories and prejudices of his friends, sometimes jocosely and sometimes in good earnest.

Of course he and father were in continual good-natured skirmishes, in which all New England peculiarities of theology or of character were held up both in caricature and in sober verity.

I remember long discussions in which he maintained that the Turks were more honest than Christians, bringing very startling facts in evidence. Then I heard his serious tales of Roman Catholic bishops and archbishops he had carried to and from Spain and America, whom he affirmed to be as learned and as truly pious and devoted to the good of men as any Protestant to be found in America.

His account of the Jews in Morocco was most curious; their condition appearing, even to his skeptical mind, the strongest verification of Hebrew prophecy. Poor, ignorant, despised, abused in every way, and offered the privileges and dignity of Muslims if they would relinquish their faith, they still clung to their sacred books and their despised people with the pertinacity and heroism of martyrs.

CATHARINE : It was at this time, with his house full of young people, that father's constitutional mirthfulness developed itself more freely than ever afterward.

He had learned to play the violin while in college, and every day practiced the liveliest airs. But if any of the girls began to take a dancing step, he would make the violin give a doleful screech, and thus always ended every attempt to dance. Some of the family, very sensitive to musical defects, were particularly annoyed by a monotonous tune he sometimes played, and so, when they happened to be late in the morning, he would station himself on the stairs, and play over and over this miserable air till all the delinquents made their appearance.

Sometimes, in school-hours, when he had got tired writing, the would come out of his study and go into the sitting-room under the schoolroom, and begin the play the violin as loud as he could. Pretty soon he would hear the schoolroom door open, and a light footstep on the stairs. Mother would come into the room, quietly walk up to him—not a word said by either of them, only a funny twinkle of the eye—and would take the violin out of his hands, go upstairs, and lay it on her table in the schoolroom.

.

CATHARINE : Occasionally we children were allowed to pass a narrow plank walk across a deep marsh where cranberries grew, but where we were told, if we stepped off to get them, we should sink and be drowned in the mud.

Beyond this we came to hills of sand, covered with beach plums, and then to the hard white sand, where the ocean broke and ran up in ceaseless play. Here we used to go down with the retreating wave, and wait till we saw another coming in ready to break, and then we all scampered to escape the upward flow. Sometimes we were overtaken and drenched, and it was strife with us to see who dared to go the furthermost down to meet the waves.

As to family government, it has been said that children love best those that govern them best. This was verified in our experience. Our mother was gentle, tender, and sympathizing, but all the discipline of government was with father. With most of his children, when quite young, he had one, two, or three seasons in which he taught them that obedience must be exact, prompt, and cheerful, and by a discipline so severe that it was thoroughly remembered and feared. Ever after, a decided word of command was all-sufficient. The obedience demanded was to be speedy, and without fretting or frowns. "Mind your mother quick no crying look pleasant" These were words of command obeyed with almost military speed and precision.

This method secured such habits of prompt, unquestioning, uncomplaining obedience as made few occasions for discipline. I can remember but one in my own case, and but few in that of the younger ones at East Hampton.

This strong and decided government was always attended with overflowing sympathy and love. His chief daily recreations were frolics with his children. I remember him more as a playmate than in any other character during my childhood. He was fond of playing pranks on us, and trying the queerest experiments with us, for his amusement as well as ours.

Gradually, as I grew older, I began to share with mother in his more elevated trains of thought. He never was satisfied with his writings till he had read them over to mother and Aunt Mary or Aunt Esther. By this intellectual companionship our house became in reality a school of the highest kind, in which he was all the while exerting a powerful influence upon the mind and character of his children.

•

NARRATOR : Lyman Beecher's first claim to national attention came after he learned that Aaron Burr set out to practice shooting before he goaded Alexander Hamilton into a duel, thus killing him legally. Beecher studied the question for six months, then gave his "Sermon on Dueling," which he was asked to repeat later at Synod.

LYMAN : Dueling is a great national sin. The whole land is covered with blood. A duelist may be a gambler, a prodigal, or fornicator, an adulterer, a drunkard and a murderer and not violate the laws of honor. Ten thousand plagues stand ready to execute His wrath: conflagration, tempest, earthquake, war, famine, and pestilence wait His command only, to cleanse the land from blood.

NARRATOR : He argued with vigor, and the synod voted to print 40,000 copies. Young Lyman Beecher's reputation spread much further than East Hampton, Long Island.

LYMAN : I rose and knocked away opposing arguments and made them ludicrous. Oh, I declare if I did not switch 'em and scorch 'em and stamp on 'em. It was the center of old fogyism, but I mowed it down, and carried the vote of the house.

NARRATOR : When Lyman Beecher had a second sermon published, his growing reputation as a fire-breathing Calvinist prompted an invitation from the Congregational Church in Litchfield, Connecticut. Litchfield was a prestigious Federalist town with America's first law school, created by Judge Tapping Reeve, a friend of the family. Litchfield offered double the salary. With five children and one on the way, Lyman decided it was time to move.

LYMAN : After a visit of three weeks in Litchfield, Connecticut, I went back to Long Island. Sold my house for $1800—the only speculation I ever made in my life; it cost me some $800. We had an auction of things we did not want to carry away. I brought the family over on a sloop, and left some at Nutplains, Roxana's old home, and some at New Haven with Esther, and went up to Litchfield on horseback to purchase the place and make preparation.

Judge Allen let me take his large two-horse wagon, and I went down and brought up your mother and all the children— Catharine, William, Edward, and Mary, but George was left to be weaned.

NARRATOR : The third Beecher child, Edward, describes that trip, and his father's prophecy.

EDWARD : I remember being in the wagon with William, and when we passed through New Haven, father stopped the horses before the college, and said to William and me, "There, boys, look there There's where you've got to go one of these days."

LITCHFIELD
1810–1816

We find the Beechers at Litchfield, Connecticut, where most of the Beechers grew up. Lyman Beecher's reputation, based on his published sermons, had secured him this prestigious position, and he did not slack in his determination to save souls. An indefatigable revivalist, he seemed to have an inexhaustible source of energy. But he never allowed his workload to interfere with the time that he spent with his family, which continued to grow larger. Lyman and Roxana Beecher arrived in Litchfield from East Hampton in 1810 with five children. The Beechers' sixth child, Harriet Elizabeth, was born one year after they arrived, Henry Ward two years later, and Charles three years after that.

CATHARINE : The first five years of father's Litchfield ministry, I think, were probably a period of more unalloyed happiness than any in his whole life. Mother enjoyed perfect health, and sympathized thoroughly with him in all his tastes and employments. The children were full of health and spirits, under a wise and happy family government. Aunt Mary spent much of her time with us, and some of mother's favorite pupils, who had come to attend Miss Pierce's school, sought a home in our family. Betsy Burr, an orphan cousin, lived with us like an adopted daughter till her marriage, which took place at our house.

The kitchen department was under the care of the good and affectionate Zillah and Rachel, who came with us from Long Island, and completed the home circle.

Mother was of that easy and gentle temperament that could never very strictly enforce any rules; while Father, you know, was never celebrated for his habits of system and order. Of course there was a free and easy way of living, more congenial to liberty and sociality than to conventional rules. As I look back to those days, there is an impression of sunshine, love, and busy activity, without any memory of a jar or cloud.

CHARLES : The Litchfield residence consisted at first of a square house with a hipped roof and an L, constituting the back part of the structure. After three or four years an enlargement was thought desirable, and a portion with a gable roof was added.

There was no boarding house connected with Miss Sarah Pierce's school, and as it brought many young ladies into the place, they were obliged to be distributed in the families of the town. It was ever a great object with Miss Pierce to secure places for her pupils in the best families, who should have a good influence in forming their characters. Mrs. Beecher was already celebrated for her success in this respect; her scholars at East Hampton were perfectly under her influence through life. Some of them had even followed her to Litchfield. This, with the hope of increasing somewhat the yearly income, led to the enlargement of the premises.

•

CATHARINE : Miss Sarah Pierce was a woman of more than ordinary talent, sprightly in conversation, social, and full of benevolent activity. She was an earnest Christian, and, being at the head of a large school of young ladies, found frequent occasions for seeking counsel and aid from her pastor. In return, she gave gratuitous schooling to as many of our children as Father chose to send, for occasionally young boys found admission.

Her school-house was a small building of only one room, probably not exceeding 30 feet by 70, with small closets at each end, one large enough to hold a piano, and the others used for bonnets and overgarments. The plainest pine desks, long plank benches, a small table, and an elevated teacher's chair, constituted the whole furniture. When I began school there she was sole teacher, aided occasionally by her sister in certain classes, and by her brother-in-law in penmanship.

At that time the higher branches had not entered female schools. Map-drawing, painting, embroidery, and the piano were the accomplishments sought, and history was the only study added to geography, grammar, and arithmetic. In process of time, her nephew, Mr. John Brace, became her associate, and introduced a more extended course. At the time Father came, the reputation of Miss Pierce's school exceeded that of any other in the country.

Thus, while Judge Reeve's law school attracted the young men from all quarters, the town was radiant with blooming maidens both indigenous and from abroad.

CHARLES : The ground floor of the new part of the house was occupied by a large parlor, in which memory recalls ministers' meetings, with clouds of tobacco-smoke, and musical soirées, with piano, flute, and song. Over this were rooms for boarders, and in the attic was the study, the window of which looked out upon a large apple tree.

NARRATOR : The Beecher children had a full life, never guessing until later that other households may have had a more traditional Christmas. Henry recalls.

HENRY : Singing carols at church choir practice was about all I knew of Christmas in my younger days. I never heard anybody speak of it. It was not known in the house of my father, for a Puritan of the Puritans was he.

CHARLES : In the old part of the house was the dining room, with a large window, and a bedroom adjoining, and two east front rooms, separated by the old hall with staircase. In the dining room was built a famous Russian stove, so constructed as to warm six rooms—three below and three above. The large window of the dining room was partially covered by a honeysuckle trained upon the side of the house.

In the long, low ell was the kitchen and well-room, and on the end of this a long, low shed, containing the wood-house and carriage-house. In front of these, and separated from the street by a stone wall, was the vegetable garden in summer, and the wood-pile in winter; for at wood-spell, as it was called, when all the teams of the parish came hauling vast loads of wood for the pastor, nearly the whole space was covered with immense logs, piled up in rows eight or ten feet high.

Behind the house was an orchard; and on the east a narrow yard filled with tamaracks, elms, maples, and other trees, separated it from the main street. The house faced south onto a side street, while the old part of the house fronted on the east.

HARRIET : My earliest recollections of Litchfield are those of its beautiful scenery, which impressed and formed my mind long before I had words to give names to my emotions, or could analyze my mental processes. I remember standing often in the door of our house and looking over a distant horizon, where Mount Tom reared its round blue head against the sky, and the Great and Little Ponds, as they were called, gleamed out amid a steel-blue sea of distant pine groves.

To the west of us rose a smooth-bosomed hill called Prospect Hill; and many a pensive, wondering hour have I sat at our playroom window, watching the glory of the wonderful sunsets that used to burn themselves out, amid voluminous wreathings, or castellated turrets of clouds—vaporous pageantry proper to a mountainous region.

Litchfield sunsets were famous, perhaps because watched by more appreciative and intelligent eyes than the sunsets of other mountain towns around. The love and notice of nature was a custom and habit of the Litchfield people; and always of a summer evening the way to Prospect Hill was dotted with parties of strollers who went thither to enjoy the evening.

Seated on the rough granite flagsteps of the east front door with some favorite book—if by chance we could find such a treasure—the book often fell from the hand while the eye wandered far off into those soft woody depths with endless longings and dreams—dreams of all those wild fruits, and flowers, and sylvan treasures which some Saturday afternoon's ramble had shown us lay sheltered in those enchanted depths. There were the crisp apples of the pink azalea—honeysuckle apples we called them—there were scarlet wintergreen berries; there were pink shell blossoms of trailing arbutus, and feathers of ground pine; there were blue, and white, and yellow violets, and crowsfoot, and bloodroot, and wild anemone, and other quaint forest treasures.

•

CATHARINE : Father had another home, of which we must give some account, for some of the happiest hours of his life were spent there. Judge Reeve, who resided at the other end of town, was his chief counselor and friend, while Mrs. Reeve was no less intimate with Mother.

Judge Reeve was an eminently pious man, and entered with the deepest sympathy into all father's parochial plans and cares; so a call at Judge Reeve's was the usual completion of evening meetings and preaching excursions. On the other hand, Mrs. Reeve, who mainly depended on a chaise for locomotion, was almost as frequent a visitor at our house. She and Mother used to read aloud to each other.

HARRIET : How well I remember Judge Reeve's house—wide, roomy, and cheerful—where we spent our first few nights in Litchfield. It used to be the Eden of our childish imagination. I remember the great old-fashioned garden, with broad alleys, set with all sorts of stately bunches of flowers. It used to be my reward, when I had been good, to spend a Saturday afternoon there, and walk up and down among the flowers, and pick currants off the bushes.

CATHARINE : Up to the age of 16 my conceptions of religion were about these: that God made me and all things; that he knew all I thought and did; that because Adam and Eve disobeyed him once only, he drove them out of Eden, and then so arranged it that all their descendants would be born with wicked hearts; and that, though this did not seem either just or good, it was so; that I had such a wicked heart that I could not feel or act right in anything till I had a new one; that God only could give me a new heart; that if I died without it, I should go to a lake of fire and brimstone.

HARRIET : My father was fond of excursions with his boys into the forests about for fishing and hunting. At first I remember these only as something pertaining to Father and the older boys, they being the rewards given for good conduct. I remember the regretful interest with which I watched their joyful preparations for departure. They were going to the Great Pond—to Pine Island—to that wonderful blue pine forest which I could just see on the horizon, and who knew what adventures they might meet. Then the house all day was so still; no tramping of laughing, wrestling boys—no singing and shouting; and perhaps only a long seam on a sheet to be oversewed as the sole means of beguiling the hours of absence.

And then dark night would come down, and stars look out from the curtains, and innuendoes would be thrown out, of children being sent to bed, and my heart would be rent with anguish at the idea of being sent off before the eventful expedition had reported itself.

And then what joy to hear at a distance the tramp of feet, the shouts and laughs of older brothers; and what glad triumph when the successful party burst into the kitchen with long strings of perch, roach, pickerel, and bullheads, with waving blades of sweet-flag, and high heads of cattail, and pockets full of young wintergreen, of which a generous portion was bestowed always upon me. These were the trophies, to my eyes, brought from the land of enchantment.

And then what cheerful hurrying and scurrying to and fro, and waving of lights, and what cleaning of fish in the back shed, and what calling for frying pan and gridiron, over which Father solemnly presided; for to his latest day he held the opinion that no feminine hand could broil or fry fish with that perfection of skill which belonged to himself alone, as king of woodcraft and woodland cookery.

I was always safe against being sent to bed for a happy hour or two, and patronized with many a morsel of the supper which followed, as father and brothers were generally too flushed with victory to regard very strictly dull household rules.

Somewhat later, I remember, were the expeditions for chestnuts and walnuts in the autumn, to which all we youngsters were taken. What fun it was, in those golden October days, when Father dared William and Edward to climb higher than he could, and shake down the glossy chestnusts. To the very last of his life, he was fond of narrating an exploit of his climbing a chestnut tree that grew up fifty feet without branches slantwise over a precipice, and then whirling himself over the abyss to beat down the chestnuts for the children below. "That was a thing," he said, "that I wouldn't let any of the boys do." I verily believe that he valued himself more on some of those exploits than even his best sermons.

·

CATHARINE : After we moved to Litchfield, Uncle Samuel came among us, on his return from each voyage, as a sort of brilliant genius of another sphere, bringing gifts and wonders that seemed to wake new faculties in all. Sometimes he came from the shores of Spain, with mementoes of the Alhambra and the ancient Moors; sometimes from Africa, bringing Oriental caps or Moorish slippers; sometimes from South America, with ingots of silver, or strange implements from the tombs of the Incas, or hammocks wrought by the Southern Indian tribes. With these came exciting stories of his adventures, and of the interesting persons of various lands whom he had carried as passengers on his ship on such foreign shores.

Whenever he came to Litchfield he brought a stock of new books, which he and Aunt Mary read aloud. This was the time when Scott, Byron, Moore, and that great galaxy of contemporary authors were issuing their works at intervals of only a few months, all of which were read and reread in the family circle.

HARRIET : One of my most decided impressions of the family as it was in my childish days was of a great household inspired by a spirit of cheerfulness and hilarity, and of my father, though pressed and driven with business, always lending an attentive ear to anything in the way of life and social fellowship.

My oldest sister, whose whole life seemed a constant stream of mirthfulness, was his favorite and companion, and he was always more than indulgent toward her pranks and jokes. Scarcely anything happened in the family without giving rise to some humorous bit of composition from her pen, either in prose or verse, which would be read at table, and passed round among the social visiting circles which were frequently at our house. Among these I remember one written to cover the retreat of a terrified domestic, who was overwhelmed by the misfortune of having broken the best dish in the minister's new service of crockery:

> Come all, and list a dismal tale
> Ye kitchen muses, do not fail,
> But join our sad loss to bewail.
> High mounted on the dresser's side,
> Our brown-edged platter stood with pride;
> A neighboring door flew open wide,
> Knock'd out its brains, and straight it died.
> Come kindred platters, with me mourn;
> Hither, ye plates and dishes, turn;
> Knives, forks, and carvers all give ear,
> And each drop a dish-water tear.
> No more with smoking roast-beef crown'd
> Shall guests this noble dish surround;
> No more the buttered cutlet here,
> Nor tender chicken shall appear;
> Roast pig no more here show his visard,

Nor goose, nor even goose's gizzard;
But broken-hearted it must go
Down to the dismal shades below;
While kitchen muses, platters, plates,
Knives, forks, and spoons upbraid the Fates;
With streaming tears cry out, "I never
Our brown-edged platter's gone forever"

and this epitaph for Tom Junior:

Here died our kit
Who had a fit
And acted queer.
Shot with a gun,
Her race is run,
And she lies here.

CATHARINE : Dramatic writing and acting became one of the nothings about which I contrived to be busy and keep others so. Various little dramas were concocted and acted between the school sessions in wintry weather, when dinners were brought. And after a while, when nearly grown up, we got up in the family, very privately, quite an affair of this kind.

I turned Miss Edgeworth's *Unknown Friend* into a drama, and for some weeks all the children old enough to take part, and several schoolgirls boarding with us, were busy as bees preparing for a rehearsal. It was kept a profound secret till the appointed evening, when Father and Mother wondered who built a fire in the large parlor, and then, still more, how it happened that so many neighbors and students called at once. Then suddenly the dining room door was opened, and all invited in, while a mysterious curtain was descried at the farther end. The curtain rose, and forthwith the actors appeared, and completed the entertainment amid thunders of applause. The next day, however, as we expected, we were told that it was very well done, but we must not do so any more.

HARRIET : Father was very fond of music, and very susceptible to its influence; and one of the great eras of the family, in my childish recollection, is the triumphant bringing home from New Haven a fine-toned upright piano, which a fortunate accident had brought within the range of a poor country minister's means. The ark of the covenant was not brought into the tabernacle with more gladness than this magical instrument into our abode.

My older sisters had both learned to play and sing, and Father soon learned to accompany the piano with his violin in various psalm tunes and Scotch airs, and brothers Edward and William to perform their part on the flute. So we had often domestic concerts, which, if they did not attain to the height of artistic perfection, filled the house with gladness.

NARRATOR : Very few of Lyman Beecher's wife Roxana's letters remain. This note is one of her last—a caring mother instructs her sister about her distant child. In 1816, Catharine, the oldest, was sixteen, Harriet was five, and Charles, the youngest, was less than a year old.

ROXANA : Dear sister Harriet, I have not sent for little Harriet on account of the joiner's work we are going to have about soon; but if any circumstance unknown to me makes it expedient she should come home, you must send her with Mr. Beecher. I should have sent her a flannel slip if I could have found an opportunity, but it is now too late in the spring. You must get shoes for her, and Mr. Beecher must pay for them; and if he should forget it, I will remember.

Write me an account of all matters and things respecting both yourselves and little Harriet, whom you must tell to be a good girl, and not forget her mamma, and brothers, and sisters. I hope to come for her sometime in the summer or autumn.

•

NARRATOR : But in 1816, Roxana Beecher died of tuberculosis. As with many wives in the nineteenth century, she was worn out. She left eight children behind, and one who had died at birth.

LYMAN : It is past. At a quarter past three this morning she fell asleep. In the course of the day she had two or three short turns of distress, but for the last six or eight hours she breathed more freely, and died without a struggle. About four hours before her death she had a lucid interval, in which I conversed with her for 20 minutes. Her state of mind was heavenly, and I have no doubt that her sorrow is turned into joy.

HARRIET : I remember a time when everyone said she was sick; when, if I went into the street, everyone asked me how my mother was; when I saw the shelves of the closets crowded with delicacies which had been sent in for her, and how I used to be permitted to go once a day into her room, where she sat bolstered up in bed, taking her gruel. I have a vision of a very fair face, with a bright red spot on each cheek, and a quiet smile as she offered me a spoonful of her gruel; of our dreaming one night, we little ones, that mamma had got well, and waking in loud transports of joy, and being hushed down by someone coming into the room. Our dream was indeed a true one. She was forever well; but they told us she was dead, and took us in to see what seemed so cold, and so unlike anything we had ever seen or known of her.

Then came the funeral. Henry was too little to go. I remember his golden curls and little black frock, as he frolicked like a kitten in the sun in ignorant joy.

I remember the mourning dresses, the tears of the older children, the walking to the burial ground, and somebody's speaking at the grave, and the audible sobbing of the family; and then all was closed, and we little ones, to whom it was so confused, asked the question where she was gone, and would she never come back?

They told us at one time that she had been laid in the ground, at another that she had gone to heaven; whereupon Henry, putting the two things together, resolved to dig through the ground and go to heaven to find her; for, being discovered under sister Catharine's window one morning digging with great zeal and earnestness, she called to him to know what he was doing, and, lifting his curly head with great simplicity, he answered, "Why, I'm going to heaven to find Ma."

The following lines, written by her eldest daughter, Catharine, then a girl of sixteen, were a tribute offered to her memory. We knew them by heart in our childhood, and have often repeated them with tears.

CATHARINE : The busy hum of day is o'er,
        The scene is sweet and still,
    And modest eve, with blushes warm,
        Walks o'er the western hill.
    The great, the good, the rich, the wise,
        Lie shrouded here in gloom;

And here with aching heart I view
  My own dear mother's tomb.
Oh, as upon her peaceful grave
  I fix my weeping eyes,
How many fond remembrances
  In quick succession rise.
Far through the vista of past years
  As memory can extend,
She walked, my counselor and guide,
  My guardian and friend.
From works of science and of taste,
  How richly stored her mind;
And yet how mild in all her ways,
  How gentle, meek, and kind.
Religion's bless'd and heavenly light
  Illumined all her road;
Before her house she led the way
  To virtue and to God.
Like some fair orb, she bless'd my way
  With mild and heavenly light,
Till, called from hence, the opening heav'n
  Received her from my sight.
Now left in dark and dubious night,
  I mourn her guidance o'er,
And sorrow that my longing eyes
  Shall see her face no more.
Father in heaven, my mother's God,
  Oh grant before thy seat,
Among the blessed sons of light,
  Parent and child may meet.
There may I see her smiling face,
  And hear her gentle voice;
And, gladden'd by thy gracious smile,
  Through endless years rejoice.

HARRIET : At Nutplains, our mother, lost to us, seemed to live again. We saw her paintings, her needlework, and, though the place was lonely, yet scarcely ever without agreeable visitors. The lonely little white farmhouse under the hill was such a paradise to us, and the sight of its chimneys after a day's ride were like a vision of Eden. To us, every juniper bush, every wild sweetbriar, every barren sandy hillside, every stony pasture spoke of bright hours of love, when we were welcomed back to Nutplains as to our mother's heart.

THE FIRST-BORN
1816–1823

When Lyman Beecher's wife Roxana died at 41 of tuberculosis in Litchfield, Connecticut, Catharine, the oldest of eight Beecher children, was sixteen. With Aunt Esther's help, she took charge of arranging family matters. For a year, she learned much and quickly about running a household—an experience that in later years would shape her career.

In 1817, Lyman Beecher married Harriet Porter, who came from a prominent Maine family that had produced two congressmen and a governor. The second Mrs. Beecher was somewhat resistant to Lyman's Calvinist vision. Once, while Dr. Beecher was reading aloud a Jonathan Edwards sermon, "Sinners in the Hands of an Angry God," she ran out of the room, crying out—

HARRIET PORTER : Dr. Beecher, I shall not listen to another word of that slander on my Heavenly Father

NARRATOR : His wife's response, among other things, led Dr. Beecher to lean toward New School Calvinism—less hell-fire and more compassion. The driving force of his life was simply to save souls, beginning with his children.

LYMAN : February 6, 1819

My dear William—While I am successful as most ministers in bringing the sons and daughters of others to Christ, my heart sinks within me at the thought that every one of my own dear children are without God in the world, and without Christ, and without hope. I have no child prepared to die; and, however cheering their prospects for time may be, how can I but weep in secret places when I realize that their whole eternal existence is every moment liable to become an existence of unchangeable sinfulness and woe.

A family so numerous as ours is a broad mark for the arrows of Death. I feel afraid that one or more of you may die suddenly, and I be called to mourn over you without hope. I do not know how I can bear it.

LYMAN : May 4, 1819

Dear Catharine—I perceive, on writing your name, that I have never written a letter to you. This, then, is the beginning of a long correspondence.

My soul is moved within me that so many of the temples in Boston and around should be only splendid sepulchers, where the spiritually dead sleep, never to awake till they meet at the judgment seat that Savior whose divinity and atonement they deny.

We shall soon attempt a journey, though whether young Frederick can come is doubtful. If possible, I would bring him, that they may see down East what children they have in Old Connecticut.

Edward has just returned to college, with every prospect of making a first-rate scholar.

Charles fell against the bedstead the other day, and cut a gash over one eye, which is healed. But before it was well he fell and cut a gash over the other eye, in precisely the same relative position, which had been well ere there had he not a few days ago fallen again, and renewed the cut in the same place.

In the meantime he stood before the vent of a gun, from which the flash and powder flew into his face and burned it, and blew it full of powder.

LYMAN : April 17, 1819

Edward—We are not gone to Salem yet, and still your letters have gone unanswered for about forty reasons. I had no money to send you. Could not find time to go to the collector and get some. Could not get any when I did go.

George and I have weeded the parsnips and beets, which have come up badly, and kept the north and south garden clean. Then I helped Mr. Taylor plant potatoes up in the orchard. Then two days plowing yard, and carrying out the stones which paved the bottom.

And now the yard waves with corn, cabbage, canteloupes, and pumpkins. Was there ever such a yard. You would not know where you were if you could not see the house. Then next I attacked the barn, the east end, which included the horse-stable, and in about two hours sawed it in two, and let it down on old Culver's head. He was taking up the stable-floor, and would not get out of the way, from the persuasion that it would fall over into the garden. I asked him if he had lived long enough. He said yes, unless she behaved better.

After which, half a dozen strokes of the saw cut off the plate, and down roof and all fell instantly, and buried him beneath the ruins. We lifted up the roof, and he crept out bleeding, with his head cut to the bone about three inches. He is, however, now recovered. But the greatest thing is yet to come. Yesterday the barn itself, having acquired an unusual understanding, moved off obliquely to Mr. Wolcott's corner, cracking and racking as it went with the noise of twenty teams and their drivers.

It commenced its movement precisely at eight o'clock in the morning, and in two hours went six rods, and stopped to move no more till it tumbles down with age, it being, as I learn, about eighty years old now.

NARRATOR : At nineteen, Catharine Beecher began preparing herself to be a teacher, concentrating on piano, painting, and poetry. Some poems in the *Christian Spectator* had already attracted the attention of Alexander Metcalf Fisher, a mathematical genius, and at twenty-five a full professor at Yale. A relationship between Catharine and Fisher blossomed. Even Horace Mann, at the time a law student in Litchfield, noticed the romance.

Frederick Beecher, young Fred, was Harriet Porter Beecher's first child, Lyman's ninth.

CATHARINE : June 20, 1820

—We are all anxious and troubled at home. Frederick has had the canker, or scarlet fever, very badly. For two or three days we have despaired of his life. Last night he nearly suffocated with the phlegm; but this morning he is much better, and we hope his greatest danger is over.

Last night Harriet was seized violently with the same disease, and we know not how it will terminate.

CATHARINE : June 23

—Disease and death have visited our house. The scarlet fever has prevailed here, and little Freddy was seized, and this morning,

38

without much struggling, breathed his last.

> We laid him in his infant grave,
>   The fairest form of earthly mould;
> Death ne'er could choose a sweeter flower
>   To deck his bosom cold.

NARRATOR : About this time, Edward was graduating valedictorian at Yale. He reports on the changes in the family:

EDWARD : Aunt Esther discharges the duties of her station with her usual fidelity and discretion. Mary is qualifying herself to take Catharine's place in the school at New London, in music and drawing. George is qualifying himself to take my place in college, which he will never do unless he studies more than he does now. Harriet reads everything she can lay hands on, and sews and knits diligently. Henry and Charles go to school—Henry as sprightly and active, and Charles as honest and clumsy as ever.

NARRATOR : Catharine was twenty-two, and was engaged to Alexander Fisher. Fisher and Catharine had developed a deep mutual respect for each other, and their friendship had deepened into a love affair. They became engaged, and a summer wedding was planned, but first Fisher was to go to England to give a paper. On his return, they would be married. Fisher had religious doubts, and Catharine shared some of them, as she confesses to her brother Edward.

CATHARINE : March 7, 1822

Edward—Last Sunday was sacrament day, and thirty-six were admitted to the Church, and ten or twelve baptized. It was very solemn. The revival is going on still, though not powerful. I fear it will pass over like others, and none of our family feel its influence.

I know it is what our dear father and mother most earnestly desire and pray for, but as yet their prayers remain unanswered. I feel as much as anyone can the necessity of a change, and still cannot feel sorrow for sin, and it sometimes seems to me I never shall.

LYMAN : April 1, 1822

—Catharine has been sick three days, the first in acute distress. I had been addressing her conscience not twenty minutes before. She was seized with most agonizing pain. I hope it will be sanctified.

•

NARRATOR : And then came a shock. Lyman Beecher's letter to Catharine two months later held bitter news.

LYMAN : New Haven, May 30, 1822

My dear child—On entering the city last evening, the first intelligence I met filled my heart with pain. It is all but certain that Professor Fisher is no more.

On that which will force itself on your pained heart with respect to the condition of his present existence in the eternal state, I can only say that many did and will indulge the hope that he was pious, though without such evidence as caused him to indulge hope.

And now, my dear child, what will you do? Will you turn at length to God, and set your affections on things above, or cling to the shipwrecked hopes of earthly good? Will you send your thoughts to heaven and find peace, or to the cliffs, and winds, and waves of Ireland, to be afflicted, tossed with tempest, and not comforted?

NARRATOR : Alexander Fisher's ship had crashed on the Irish coast. Catharine was grief-stricken, and in need of comfort. Lyman Beecher offered little. He saw it as a warning that, unlike Fisher, she could still save her soul. He spent most of the next year trying to convert her. Catharine's retreat and spiritual crisis affected all the Beecher children, who saw their father's theology fail to comfort and fail to convert Catharine, who could not achieve a religious experience. Eventually, every one of Lyman's children would find Calvinism unsatisfactory, and each found a personal solution.

HENRY : The tragedy has broken up and destroyed all the religious teachings of her life. The doctrines she had learned did not sustain her.

CATHARINE : It was as though I were surrounded by the motion and constant noise of the ever whirling machinery and wheels of a great manufactory, and all at once every sound and motion ceased and all was still as the grave—not a thread, not a circle or circumstance, for the eye or heart to rest upon.

CATHARINE : June 4, 1822

—Oh, Edward, where is he now? Are the noble faculties of such a mind doomed to everlasting woe, or is he now with our dear mother in the mansions of the blessed?

When I think of the scene of her death-bed there is a mournful pleasure. She died in peace, and the eyes that were closing on earth were to open in heaven. But when I think of the last sad moments of his short life—the horrors of darkness, the winds, the waves, and tempest, of his sufferings of mind when called to give up life and all its bright prospects, and be hurried alone, a disembodied spirit, into unknown, eternal scenes, oh, how dreadful, how agonizing

My dear brother, I am greatly afflicted. I know not where to look for comfort. The bright prospects that turned my thoughts away from heaven are all destroyed, and now that I have nowhere to go but to God, the heavens are closed against me, and my prayer is shut out.

The help of man faileth. The dearest friends can only stand and look on; it is God alone that can help.

CATHARINE : Litchfield, July, 1822

—Dear Brother—when I began to write to you on the subject which now occupies my thoughts, it was with a secret feeling that you could do something to remove my difficulties. But this feeling is all gone now.

It is the feeling of entire guilt, willful and inexcusable, which gives all the consistency and excellency to the Gospel. Without this the justice of God is impaired, His mercy is destroyed, the grace and condescension of Jesus Christ is veiled, and the aid of the Blessed Spirit made void.

This feeling I can not awaken in my heart, nor is my understanding entirely convinced that it ought to exist. I give the assent which a shortsighted, fallible creature ought to give to Omniscience, but it is an assent to authority, not to conviction.

If all was consistent and right in the apprehension of my understanding, there would be no such temptation to skepticism as I feel growing within me. I feel all the time as if there was something wrong—something that is unreasonable. There have been moments when I have been so perplexed and darkened as to feel that no one could tell what was truth from the Bible.

LYMAN : August 2, 1822

—Edward, Catharine's letter will disclose the awfully interesting state of her mind. There is more movement than there ever existed before, more feeling, more interest, more anxiety, and she is now, you perceive, handling edge-tools with powerful grasp.

I have at times been at my wit's end to know what to do. But I conclude nothing safe can be done but to assert ability, and obligation, and guilt upon divine authority, throwing in, at the same time, as much collateral light from reason as the case admits of, and taking down the indefensible positions which depravity, and fear, and selfishness, and reason set up. In other words, I answer objections and defend the ways of God.

LYMAN : September 25, 1822

—Dear Catharine—That your mind has found a kind of composure which prevents your repining at what is past, or wishing to change the present, and leaves alive only the desire to find happiness in God, though not religion, is a state of mind more propitious, I should hope, than that which has preceded it.

The cessation of restless impatience, of that desperate importunity to be delivered soon, or to cast away the irksome thoughts of religion, is also a favorable change. And yet I am startled at the tranquillity produced by your reading of John Newton. I fear only because it is precisely the effect always produced by such directions as Dr. Dwight used to give to awakened sinners, and as the English divines still give. Now, who are right, the Old or New England divines?

Which mode of exhibition is, on the whole, most evangelical and most successful, is as manifest from the facts as facts can make manifest. Look at the revivals which are filling our land with salvation; they do not prevail in England. In this country they are confined almost exclusively to the New England manner of exhibiting the truth. Mr. John Newton himself said, "I know not how it is, but we are obliged to be content with catching now and then a fish with a hook, while you in New England, like the apostles of old, drag to shore your seines full."

This is the difference which God makes between telling sinners to pray and wait, and telling them, in God's name, to repent and believe.

LYMAN : October 27, 1822

—My dear Catharine—I shall follow you, step by step, in your comfortless way. You apprehend that your mind is differently constituted from others, and that no one was ever troubled with a heart so inconsistent and ungovernable.

This, my dear child, is the complaint which I hear from the lip of every sinner who is awakened, and so much enlightened by the Spirit as to see and feel what God requires of the heart. This is conviction of sin. The commandment coming, and sin reviving, and the sinner dying.

The Bible had told you that your heart is deceitful, is desperately wicked, but you felt it not while it wandered and was allowed to wander; but now that you hold it bound to be conformed to the law, or even to the Gospel, and begin to draw the reins, and bring it and bind it to its duty, you find it, like the bullock unaccustomed to the yoke, impatient of restraint, violent, wayward, and ungovernable.

All who are convinced of sin make the same discoveries and utter the same complaints.

It is not improbable that some portion of capricious feeling may be the vibration of nervous excitement produced by conversation, with care, anxiety, and sorrow; on this account you must attend to your bodily health, especially to daily exercise, and regular habits of body and hours of rest.

NARRATOR : In grief, Catharine visited Fisher's family in Franklin, and discovered that before his trip, he too had been unable to achieve conversion, and had turned to science. Catharine's crisis was to be resolved—she would accept neither Lyman's nor her brother Edward's arguments. Alexander Fisher wrote in one of his last journals: "The heart must have something to rest upon, and if it is not God, it will be the world." Fisher also left two thousand dollars and his books to Catharine in his will, which he had made out just before he left on his last voyage.

LYMAN : November 5, 1822

—My dear afflicted Child—Until your last sad letter, I had
thought you strangely exempted from the temptation to murmur
and repine; but the renewal of your sorrows by so many touching
associations as you find at Franklin has brought a flood of temptation.

You, I fear, are now more than tempted, and while I behold you
imparting the darkness and desolation of your pained heart to all
around you, and veiling even "the mercy, and justice, and goodness of God," my heart bleeds, and my eyes are full.

CATHARINE : Franklin, New Year, 1823

—I had all along looked forward to the time of my arrival in
Franklin as the period when (if I was to be brought into the kingdom by suffering and sorrow) my heart would find in God that
comfort and peace which was nowhere else to be found; and if
I did not then obtain religion, I felt that my heart would, almost
from necessity, return to the world to receive its dregs of happiness for a portion, an unsatisfying portion, indeed; but the heart
must have something to rest upon, and if it is not God it will be
the world.

When I arrived here it was all as I had anticipated. Every sor-
rowful remembrance was recalled, every pang renewed, and it
seemed as if my heart could endure no more, and as if my sorrow
was as great as I could bear.

In addition to this were the mournful contemplations awakened
when I learned more of the mental exercises of him I mourned;
whose destiny is forever fixed, alas I knew not where. I learned
from his letters, and in other ways, probably as much as I should
have learned from his diary. I found that, even from early childhood, he had ever been uncommonly correct and conscientious,
so that his parents and family could scarcely remember of his ever
doing anything wrong, so far as it relates to outward conduct.

It was about the time I wrote to Edward that the commotion
in my mind seemed to be at its crisis. I then felt that I was created a miserable, helpless creature; that I and all my fellow-men
were placed under a severe law which we were naturally unable
to obey, and threatened with everlasting despair for violating one
of its precepts. It seemed to me that my lost friend has done all

that unassisted human strength could do; and often the dreadful thought came over me that all was in vain, and that he was wailing that he had ever been born, in the dark world where hope never comes, and that I was following his steps to that dreadful scene.

It was under the influence of such feelings as these that, when retired to the same room, and in the same place where I fancied his tears and supplications were offered in vain, I have felt that I could not bend the knee, nor open my lips to pray to a Being whose character, to my blinded eyes, was so veiled in darkness and gloom.

But such dreadful feelings did not continue long. Soon the conviction that God was just and merciful, and would ever do right, which I scarcely ever before questioned, returned, and I resolved that I would not believe anything that obscured these perfections, and gradually my feelings were brought to be something of this kind.

If I cannot be a Christian, I will try to be as near like one as I can. I must believe that there is something in the Bible to encourage us to hope for that aid of the Blessed Spirit which can help our infirmities, and that in due time we shall find that he is a rewarder of those who diligently seek him.

It is impossible that I should ever again take the course I have the past summer, unless the judgments of God should again make me desolate, and cut off every interest and employment in this world.

It was by withdrawing my thoughts and attention from everything else, and by a continued exertion to continue that vacuity and emptiness of soul which is felt when there is nothing to stimulate or interest, that I succeeded in confining my attention exclusively to the subject of religion; and I knew that whenever I did allow my feelings again to become interested in other things, unless some other stimulus was applied, all would be lost; and it seems to me now, if there is nothing in the Bible to encourage me to seek religion, there is nothing anywhere.

I hope you will answer this speedily, and in all its particulars, just as you would in conversation.

EDWARD : I think you are in danger of speculating too much. I do not expect to throw light on this dark spot, so as to make all things clear; nor ought you to expect to be entirely unembarrassed, where none within the range of my knowledge are free from perplexity.

CATHARINE : February 15, 1823

—My dear Father—The question of my entire ability to keep the law of God can never be settled, even to the conviction of my understanding, unless by supernatural interference. Should arguments equally powerful with those advanced by you and Edward, and ten thousand times more so, be advanced to prove that I had physical strength to move the everlasting hills, it would be to no purpose. Consciousness would be that brow of iron that would resist them all. Now, which is easier to abandon, confidence in my own consciousness or in your interpretation of the Bible?

I shall return next week to Boston, where God is now granting his Spirit. Once more I will agonize to enter in at the strait gate, and while I remain there will take no rest day nor night.

But if I leave there with this wayward, hard, and sinful heart, I have no hope that I shall persevere in seeking religion. My own experience these last nine months forbids all such expectation; and if I do not then obtain religion, the world will soon engross my thoughts, and I shall receive its pittance as my portion.

As to my future employment, I wish to consult you. Generally speaking, there seems to be no very extensive sphere of usefulness for a single woman but that which can be found in the limits of a school-room; but there have been instances in which women of superior mind and acquirements have rised to a more enlarged and comprehensive boundary of exertion, and by their talents and influence have accomplished what, in a more circumscribed sphere of action, would have been impossible.

My employments this winter have led to the inquiry whether there is not a course that might be pursued leading to a more extended usefulness.

I have always supposed that the distinguishing characteristics of my own mind were an active and inventive imagination, and quick perceptions in matters of taste and literature; yet I think there is reason to believe that in more solid pursuits there is no deficiency. My memory is quick and retentive, and all the reason my mind is not stored with knowledge is the neglect of the past. All the knowledge I have has, as it were, walked into my head.

When I was in Hartford, Mr. Hawes lamented the want of a good female school. This and your advice have led me to wish to commence one there.

LYMAN : Litchfield, March 2, 1823

—My dear Child—It is time, now, that you open your eye upon a phenomenon of the human heart which has evidently escaped your notice. It is the existence in the heart of what some have called disposition, but which may be more properly denominated generic volition—a stated, habitual, and all-powerful choice, opposed often, indeed, by specific volitions, regrets, resolutions, and efforts of a subordinate character.

In other words, a man may, all things considered, choose to hold on in a course which he fears to tread, and regrets to tread, and resolves and strives to turn from, but with resolutions and choice inferior to the generic volition which bears him on.

Do you ask, If this generic aversion is so powerful, why should I be so unconscious of its existence?

This calls you to regard another fact in the history of the mind. Nothing is more common than the unperceived influence of a generic volition. Should I resolve today to come to Boston, that volition, unrepeated and perhaps not perceived again, would bring me thither. It is a common thing for men to be actuated by motives they do not suspect, and by evil passions and affections of whose existence they are unconscious.

And what is confessedly true in the intercourse of life, the Scriptures declare to be true in our intercourse with God. The heart is desperately wicked, yet so deceitful that who can know it

Were I to depart from my implicit confidence in God, I could find as many difficulties and ask as many unanswerable questions as you do.

But I know that what God says is true, and what he does is right; and here I rest my faith, and desire you to rest yours, and if I have plunged into deep waters in this letter, it is not because I prefer to wade in them, but to rescue from drowning my own dear child, who is attempting to lay among the billows the foundations of her hope and confidence toward God.

LYMAN : Hartford, March 21, 1823

—I came here Tuesday evening, and began my inquiries next day about opening a school, and, having been pushing them as fast as such matters can be pushed until now, the point is, I think, well settled that such a school is greatly needed, and that scholars enough can be obtained to justify opening.

It will not, however, answer for you to engage in it listlessly, expecting yourself to superintend and do a little, and have the weight of the school come on others. I should be ashamed to have you open, and keep only a commonplace, middling sort of school. It is expected to be of a higher order; and, unless you are willing to put your talents and strength into it, it would be best not to begin.

HARTFORD
1823–1826

We now arrive at the mid-1820s in Litchfield, Connecticut. Catharine, as a result of her spiritual crisis, is turning her brilliant mind to the problems of women's education. She has left for Hartford to investigate prospects for opening a new school for girls. Edward has graduated at the top of his class at Yale, and has come home to relax. Harriet suggests that home life at the Beechers was more often hectic than relaxing.

HARRIET : My father was famous for his power of exciting family enthusiasm. Whenever he had a point to carry or work to be done, he would work the whole family up into a pitch of fervent zeal, in which the strength of each one seemed quadrupled. For instance, the wood of the family used to be brought in winter on sleds, and piled up in the yard, exactly over the spot where father wished in early spring to fix his cucumber and melon frames; for he always made it a point to have cucumbers as soon as Dr. Taylor, who lived in New Haven, and had much warmer and drier land; and he did it by dint of contrivance and cucumber frames.

Of course, as all this wood was to be cut, split, and carried into the woodhouse before an early garden could be started, it required a miracle of generalship to get it done, considering the immense quantity required in that climate to keep an old windy castle of a house comfortable. How the axes rung, and the chips flew, and the jokes and stories flew faster; and when all was cut and split, then came the great work of wheeling in and piling; and then I, sole little girl among so many boys, was sucked into the vortex of enthusiasm by father's well-pointed declaration that he "wished Harriet were a boy, she would do more than any of them."

I remember putting on a little black coat which I thought looked more like the boys', casting needle and thread to the wind, and working almost like one possessed for a day and a half, till in the afternoon the wood was all in and piled, and the chips swept up.

Then father tackled the horse into the cart, and proclaimed a grand fishing party down to Little Pond. And how we all floated among the lily-pads in our boat, christened the Yellow Perch, and every one of us caught a string of fish, which we displayed in triumph on our return.

NARRATOR : In the autumn, the entire family would work on making a whole barrel of apple butter, which would remain frozen in the milk room, to be cut into chunks when needed. Baskets of apples and quince in the kitchen would go into the apple peeler, and then into a huge brass kettle in the fireplace. Lyman and George would relate the stories of Walter Scott's newest novels—and this marked a real change for Dr. Beecher. Ever since Catharine had brought home the books and effects of Alexander Fisher, Lyman had decided, on looking them over, that Scott wasn't such a bad fellow after all.

LYMAN : George, you may read Scott's novels. I have always disapproved of novels as trash, but in these is real genius and real culture.

NARRATOR : At times, the large family had to be spread around among relatives. Harriet in particular lived for months at a time at Nutplains, her mother's home. Catharine writes her the news of Isabella's birth.

CATHARINE : Harriet, I suppose you will be very glad to hear you have a little sister at home. We have no name for her yet.

We all want you home very much, but hope you are now where you will learn to stand and sit straight, and hear what people say to you, and sit still in your chair, and learn to sew and knit well, and be a good girl in every particular; and if you don't learn while you are with Aunt Harriet, I am afraid you never will.

Old Puss is very well, and sends his respects to you, and Mr. Black Trip has come out of the barn to live, and says if you ever come into the kitchen he will jump up and lick your hand, or pull your frock, just as he serves the rest of us. Henry and Charles love to play with him very much.

NARRATOR : George and Hattie were the real readers of the family, and they grew up, not on children's books, but on the *Arabian Nights*, Cotton Mather's collection of Indian raids, witches and damnation, Don Quixote, Shakespeare, *The State of the Clergy during the French Revolution.*

HARRIET : One of father's favorite resorts was Aunt Esther's room, about half a minute's walk from our house. How well I remember that room. A low-studded parlor, looking out on one side into a front yard shaded with great elm trees, on the other, down a green sidehill. This room, always so quiet, so spotlessly neat, was a favorite retreat of all us children who were allowed, as a reward for good behavior, to go and pass an hour or two with Aunt Esther.

Aunt Esther herself, with her sparkling hazel eyes, her keen, ready wit, and never-failing flow of anecdote and information, interested us even more than the best things she could produce from her closet. She had read on all subjects—chemistry, philosophy, physiology, but especially on natural history, where her anecdotes were inexhaustible. I once heard a child say, "Only think Aunt Esther has told me nineteen rat stories all in a string." In fact, we thought there was no question we could ask her that she could not answer.

It was in Aunt Esther's room that I first found a stray volume of Lord Byron's poetry, which she gave me one afternoon to appease my craving for something to read. It was *The Corsair.* I shall never forget how it astonished and electrified me, and how I kept calling to Aunt Esther to hear the wonderful things that I found in it, and to ask what they could mean. "Aunt Esther, what does it mean—"

One I never loved enough to hate—?

"Oh, child, it's one of Byron's strong expressions."

I went home absorbed and wondering about Byron; and after that I listened to everything that father and mother said at the table about him, such as the account of his separation from his wife.

NARRATOR : At thirteen, Harriet heard her father say at dinner to his wife:

LYMAN : My dear, Byron is dead—gone. Oh, I'm sorry that Byron is dead. I did hope he would live to do something for Christ. What a harp he might have swept.

HARRIET : I looked up into the blue sky and thought of that

great eternity into which Byron had entered, and wondered how it might be with his soul

NARRATOR : Doctor Beecher's next sermon distinguished between some poems of Byron's that would prove as imperishable as brass, and other works with impurities, as in Sterne and Swift, that would doom them to oblivion. He closed with a most eloquent lamentation over the wasted life and misused powers of the great poet.

LYMAN : I wish I could have seen him. If Byron could only have talked with Taylor and me, it might have got him out of his troubles.

•

NARRATOR : About this time, Dr. Beecher struck out in a new direction, with a sermon that would launch him on a new career. The danger that he denounced was a new theology in Boston called Unitarianism. It threatened the very heart of New England Calvinism with its openness and democratic spirit. William Ellery Channing's defense of reason in religious matters roused Beecher to the attack.

LYMAN : From the time Unitarianism began to show itself in this country, it was a fire in my bones. I had watched the whole progress of the Unitarian controversy, and read with eagerness everything that came out on the subject. My mind had been heating, heating, heating. Now I had a chance to strike. Their power of corrupting the youth of the commonwealth by means of Cambridge is silently putting sentinels in all the churches, legislators in the halls, and judges on the bench, and scattering everywhere physicians, lawyers and merchants.

NARRATOR : Though young Harriet usually found her father's sermons unintelligible, there was one spontaneous sermon that led her to believe she was experiencing what her father always hoped and watched for—religious conversion.

HARRIET : Forgetting all his hairsplitting distinctions and dialectic subtleties, he spoke in direct, simple and tender language of the great love of Christ and his care for the soul. He pictured him as patient with our errors, compassionate with our weaknesses, and how he was ever near us, comforting our sorrows with a love unchilled by ingratitude, till at last he should present us faultless before the throne of his glory with exceeding joy.

I sat intent and absorbed. Oh how much I needed just such a friend, I thought to myself. Then the awful fact came over me that I had never had any conviction of my sins, and consequently could not come to him. I longed to cry out "I will," when Father made his passionate appeal, "Come then, and trust your soul to this faithful friend." Like a flash it came over me that if I needed conviction of sin, he was able to give me even this also. I would trust him for the whole. My whole soul was illumined with joy, and as I left the church to walk home, it seemed to me as if Nature herself were hushing her breath to hear the music of heaven.

As soon as Father came home and was seated in his study, I went up to him and fell in his arms, saying, "Father, I have given myself to Jesus, and he has taken me." I never shall forget the expression on his face as he looked down into my earnest, childish eyes; it was so sweet, so gentle, and like sunlight breaking out upon a landscape. "Is it so?" he said, holding me silently to his heart. "Then has a new flower blossomed in the kingdom this day."

•

NARRATOR : Catharine's tragic love affair ending with the death of her fiance, Alexander Metcalf Fisher, had left her in a deep depression. Even with the counsels of her father and brother Edward, she was unable to achieve spiritual conversion. Fisher had written her into his will before he left on his fatal voyage, and by reading his papers, Catharine found the same religious doubts that she had experienced, and an inner strength to go on. If not God, then she would serve the world.

As soon as he saw her decision, Lyman Beecher immediately supported Catharine, and made efforts to help her in her plan to establish a school at Hartford.

LYMAN : Catharine arrived Friday, and left all well at Hartford. Her examination was royal, and all her prospects of a school and of great usefulness are exceeding good.

NARRATOR : The Hartford Female Seminary opened in 1823. Catharine set up house in Hartford and shared it with her sister Mary. Later Harriet and the unteachable Henry came down to attend her school. Three years after opening, the school had a hundred pupils. yet even with a fully functioning school, Catharine would often go back home to Litchfield.

CATHARINE : You know how happy it makes us to be with father. His society seems always to give a new impulse to the affection of the heart and to every intellectual power. I never hear anybody preach that makes me feel as Father does; perhaps it may be because he is Father. But I cannot hear him without its making my face burn and my heart beat.

HARRIET : Catharine has been here, and we have all been thoroughly metaphysicated. At breakfast we generally have the last evening's argument hashed through and warmed over, indeed they serve us with an occasional nibble through the whole day. One of Bishop Butler's arguments lasted us for nearly three meals.

NARRATOR : At her school, Catharine kept up a like intensity with her pupils.

CATHARINE : Students, the time may come to some of you, even now in the morning of life, when instead of the gay colors that adorn each scene, every object will be inscribed with "mourning and lamentation and woe." Seek something that will endure when earthly expectations fail. You cannot now realize and I pray you may never experience how bereft, how lonely, how desolate is a heart that has no portion in heaven, when the hopes of this world pass away, when the bright visions of life are shrouded in darkness, when the midnight pillow is bathed in tears of lonely bitterness, and the dawn of day brings no light to the soul.

NARRATOR : That same year, 1823, Catharine joined her father's church. She now felt that she could ally herself with Lyman Beecher.

CATHARINE : If I cannot be a Christian, I will try to be as near like one as I can.

NARRATOR : Meanwhile, Lyman Beecher extended his campaign to combat Unitarianism by founding the *Connecticut Observer*. Catharine was his strong support.

CATHARINE : Father is much animated with the success of the paper. There is nothing makes me feel so happy as to be with him, and nothing so stimulates my intellect as his conversation.

NARRATOR : In these years Catharine developed her ideas on education into a little book called *Suggestions Respecting Improvements in Education*, and she began to teach a course in mental and moral philosophy.

When Harriet was barely fourteen, Catharine brought her down to her Female Seminary, for one year as a student, and then as a teacher. Hattie became aware of the writings of the "sweet singer of Hartford," Lydia Huntley Sigourney, and started writing a Byronic tragedy in blank verse—until sister Catharine advised her to use the time more profitably by studying Joseph Butler's *Analogy of Religion*. In the fall, Catharine had her teaching Butler's book in a class.

Madame de Staël's novel *Corinne*, the story of an emotionally liberated woman, made the rounds at Catharine's school, and it made a strong impression on Harriet.

HARRIET : I have felt an intense sympathy with many parts of that book, with many parts of her character. But in America feelings vehement and absorbing like hers become still more deep, morbid, and impassioned by the constant habits of self-government which the rigid forms of our society demand. They are repressed, and burn inward till they burn the very soul, leaving only dust and ashes. It seems to me the intensity with which my mind has thought and felt on every subject presented to it has had this effect. It has withered and exhausted it.

All that is enthusiastic, all that is impassioned in admiration of nature, of writing, of character, in devotional thought and emotion, or in the emotions of affection, I have felt with vehement and absorbing intensity—felt till my mind is exhausted, and seems to be sinking into deadness. Half of my time I am glad to remain in a listless vacancy, to busy myself with trifles, since thought is pain, and emotion is pain.

NARRATOR : Despite her new role as educator, Catharine found that she was not fond of teaching, or even of administration. Time spent away from the school on her own intellectual development became increasingly important to her.

CATHARINE : The only pleasant recollection of that first year was that of my own careful and exact training under my most accurate and faithful brother Edward.

I was never driven to mental effort till affliction came, but except for the comforts of religion and of friendship I find no so pure and interesting a source of earthly good as the exercise of the mind in acquiring and communicating knowledge. The exercise of the mind makes us realize the high faculties and immortal destinies of our nature.

NARRATOR : When she expressed doubts about continuing the school past its first year, Lyman told her—

LYMAN : It will not answer for you to leave that school. You must not think of it.

NARRATOR : By September 1824, Catharine had decided to put off marriage indefinitely. Edward returned to the seminary at Andover. Now Catharine was on her own, and responsible for four younger brothers and sisters. Her school at Hartford had become the second Beecher outpost.

She arranged to teach in the mornings while Mary taught in the afternoons. She organized Saturday evening social gatherings, and cultivated friendships with Hartford's leaders, including Miss Lydia Sigourney, who had run her school for young ladies until 1819.

•

NARRATOR : In December 1825, Catharine asked her father whether she ought to rent a house of her own—it would mean giving up the idea of marriage for good. Lyman agreed with the idea.

CATHARINE : I have pretty much concluded not to take a matrimonial home.

LYMAN : The strong hand with which God has turned back your family course may and it may not indicate his purpose as to the way in which he intends to resolve your service.

NARRATOR : Lyman Beecher's campaign against Unitarianism led him to accept a move to Boston, the heart of the new ideas.

LYMAN : It is in Boston that New England is to be regenerated, the enemy driven out of the temple they have usurped and polluted, the college to be rescued, the public sentiment to be revolutionized and restored to evangelic tone.

NARRATOR : Returning from a visit to Lyman's new church in Hanover Street, Boston, Catharine instigated a revival in her own school in Hartford. She started with prayer meetings in her new house, and worked with her students—despite the fact that she herself was unconverted.

Perhaps fifteen students were involved—but the Reverend Joel Hawes of Hartford ignored Catharine's revival to attend to one in Northampton. But in its third week, Catharine could report eight or ten townspeople involved. She wrote to Edward and to Lyman for help. But Lyman's response was not what Catharine expected.

LYMAN : Your last letters, giving an account of the state of things in your school, have been read with deep interest and much thanksgiving, though not without some solicitude. The very high state of excited feeling, though extremely natural among young Christians, and powerful in its effects while it lasts, is too hazard-ous to health to be indulged, and necessarily too short-lived to answer in the best manner the purpose of advancing a revival. You must instantly put yourselves upon a different system or you will all be prostrate.

NARRATOR : Once her revival was over, Catharine knew that she could lead people, but that her father's methods were not appro-priate for her. Increasingly, she acted and wrote and published as an educator. The school was expanded into a full seminary. And within two years, Catharine developed her class in "Mental and Moral Philosophy" into a discipline that could carry her own ideas forward.

Catharine, Mary, and Harriet joined Joel Hawes' church, the oldest in Hartford and the one which prominent and wealthy citi-zens attended. Catharine, now a leader of the community, could ask leading citizens to serve as trustees in her fund-raising—many of their daughters were in her school, many of their wives attended her social Saturdays.

CATHARINE : This was my first experience of the moral power and good judgment of American women, which has been my chief reliance ever since.

NARRATOR : But Catharine's new seminary was not to give sim-ply a refined education to young women, as had Lydia Sigourney's academy. Catharine had more serious motives in mind. In an article in the *American Journal of Education*, she wrote:

CATHARINE : A lady should study, not to shine, but to act. To come out in conduct, education must shape a young woman's principles and the formation of her habits. Public sentiment has advanced so much on the subject of female culture that a course of study very similar to that pursued by young men in our public institutions is demanded for young ladies of the higher circles. But facilities and teaching techniques are vastly inferior in girls' schools.

The proper education of a man decides the welfare of an individual; but educate a woman and the interests of the whole family are secured.

·

NARRATOR : In 1831, Catharine published her seminal book, *The Elements of Mental and Moral Philosophy, Founded upon Experience, Reason and the Bible.* Catharine published it at her own expense—at first anonymously, and in some cases she cut out the heretical pages, before giving copies away.

In it, Catharine insists that, with or without God, morality exists, and that moral educators can change people's behavior.

The central role of the woman in the family now becomes the vision that Catharine Beecher was to pursue with intelligence and energy.

Thus she became a reformer. She had taken one step further than Lyman Beecher ever did—he believed in saving souls, but not by changing the world. Catharine had found her career; out of her own struggles of conscience, she had first pieced together a life, and then built the foundations for a profound change in modern society.

Her contribution to Common Sense philosophy, or the Scottish school, turned the traditional female virtues of submission for the general good and self-sacrifice into strong engines for social progress. By emphasizing the family, Catharine elevated the position of the woman. In her school, she worked to reconcile evangelical and upper class ethics. Her later career was no easy road, but the direction was now clear.

When Catharine decided that morality could be taught, she

realized that only a boarding school would do. But this last step, requiring her to raise an additional $20,000 for expansion, was too much. Catharine Beecher had carved out a career—now she faced her own physical limits. Her commitment to service brought on a nervous breakdown.

CATHARINE : I thought that if I exercised two hours a day and took eight hours of quiet sleep, and a proper time for meals, I might then work all the rest of the time without danger. And so I kept my mind under pressure of responsibility and mental effort for ten successive years. At the end of that time, without a day's warning of danger, I found the entire fountain of nervous energy exhausted. I could not read a page or write a line, or even listen to conversation without distress. The evil was irretrievable and I never again could assume the duties that wore me down.

THE BOSTON YEARS: 1
1826–1829

The Beecher family prepared for the move to the cultural capital of New England—Boston. Catharine Beecher had established her school for women at Hartford just two years before. The eminent Doctor Lyman Beecher had made a national reputation on the basis of his attacks on the new tendency called Unitarianism. In consequence, he received an invitation to be pastor at Boston's Hanover Street Church. It would mean leaving rural Litchfield, Connecticut, the family home for sixteen years, for the rough and tumble of America's premier seaport and intellectual center.

Meanwhile, the rest of the Beecher household was in flux. Edward, George, and William studied for the ministry, while Catharine's Hartford school employs Mary, and sometimes Harriet—even Henry is sent to Hartford briefly, to try the backward lad in a new educational setting. Charles, Isabella, and Thomas are still children at home. And Lyman Beecher mulls over his decision.

LYMAN : From the time Unitarianism began to show itself in this country, it was as fire in my bones. I watched it, even at East Hampton, and read everything that appeared on the subject.

The minister of King's Chapel was the first that broached it. None else dared. Nor did they preach it. They used orthodox terms for a spell, ceasing to urge awakening truth, and left the old to die out, and the young to grow up Unitarians.

Then Channing came forward, and preached his famous sermon at Baltimore. He was their idol.

My farewell sermon at East Hampton seven years before had led me to give an outline of a theological system. In Litchfield I rewrote and enlarged it, and preached it in Boston.

1817 was the first time I had ever been in Boston. The sermon was long, but clear. I was not afraid, but took sight and struck on all points. The Unitarians were out. The interest grew to the last as blow after blow hit every nail on the head.

Come to go out, the old men were all in a glorification talking and chatting. Went to their dining-place, and there old Dr. Jones, not given to praising, let out. You see there had been no such attack on Unitarianism. The sensation all over the city was great. It was a perfect victory.

NARRATOR : Dr. Leonard Bacon, a supporter of Beecher's, gives his account of the situation:

LEONARD BACON : The Unitarian defection was then at the height of its power and in the full tide of its progress, and a mind like his, ever watching for the signs of the times, could not be indifferent. Already he had found one opportunity of making himself heard at the center of that great defection from evangelical truth. His sermon, *The Bible a Code of Laws,* was a most telling argument against the Unitarian system, striking it where it is most defenseless.

Four years later, in 1823, he preached at Worcester, where I had the privilege of hearing his great sermon *The Faith Once Delivered to the Saints.* That sermon, I do not hesitate to say, was one of the most effective publications in the Unitarian controversy of the time.

Stuart had published his *Letters to Channing,* which remained unanswered. Woods, the Abbott Professor at Andover, on the one side, and Ware, the Hollis Professor at Harvard, on the other, had completed their debate, each to the general satisfaction of his own friends.

But the sermon on *The Faith Once Delivered to the Saints* was like a huge bomb thrown right into the camp of the adversaries. The Worcester sermon, by its clear, fresh statement of the two systems in their contrast, and by its ingenious, intelligible, and effective demonstration that the so-called liberal system could not possibly be the faith once delivered to the saints, put that system to the awkward work of defending itself.

LYMAN : Are the doctrines of the liberal system contained in the text, according to its most direct and obvious meaning? Do they receive the sanction of approbation from the most devout persons, and the sentence of condemnation from the irreligious and vicious? Does the liberal system produce the same objections which the faith delivered to the saints produced? Do the doctrines of the liberal system occasion the same fears and anxieties about a future state, the same deep conviction of sin, and the same joyful and often sudden conversion to God, as are manifested under evangelical preaching and in revivals of religion? Do the doctrines of the liberal system produce revivals of religion at all?

•

NARRATOR : At the end of 1825, Lyman Beecher accepted the invitation to the Hanover Street Church in Boston. His campaign against Unitarianism should be conducted at the enemy's door, he felt. He began his Boston pastorate in April 1826, although his health and spirits were not good, as his eldest son William reports.

WILLIAM : I spent a week in Boston at Father's installation. He was quite unwell with dyspepsia; he suffered much from fear, and does still. I never knew him more cast down. He felt as though his course was finished. He had serious thoughts of sending for you, and had even written the letter, but concluded to wait and see how he got over the Sabbath. This was Friday.

He took a chair, and turned it down before the fire and laid down. "Ah, William," said he, "I'm done over, I'm done over" Mother told me he had often thought so before, and yet in two days had been nearly well again.

"Yes, but I never was so low before. It's all over with me. I only want to get my mind composed in God—but it is hard to see such a door of usefulness set open and not able to enter." You may be sure I felt this deeply. He seemed so sure that I almost feared it was so. I never saw him so low before.

But we at length succeeded in cheering him some, and on Saturday I rode with him to Marblehead, and he was very much better, and preached on the Sabbath quite well, without much fatigue; on Monday I left, and he has continued, with much fear and trembling, to preach since.

The house where he preaches is crowded, and the vestry meetings also. He has twenty or twenty-five inquirers; and there seems to be a revival spirit in the churches. They board at Deacon Lambert's, in Pitt Street.

HARRIET : When Dr. Beecher came to Boston, Calvinism or orthodoxy was the despised and persecuted form of faith. The strict theocracy founded by the Puritans had suffered a reaction that forced open the doors of the state. It was the dethroned royal family wandering like a permitted mendicant in the city where once it had held court, and Unitarianism reigned in its stead.

The dominant majority entered at once into possession of churches and church property, leaving the orthodox minority to go out into school-houses or town halls, and build their churches as best they could. So bitter and so strong had been the reaction of a whole generation against the bands too stringent of their fathers—but in every such surge of society, however confident and overbearing, there lies the element of a counterreaction, and when Dr. Beecher came to Boston, this element had already begun to assert itself.

NARRATOR : Dr. William Ellery Channing led the attack for the Unitarians, hitting on the real differences within Calvinism—the New-School advocates, such as Lyman Beecher, and Old-School.

CHANNING : It is a plain matter of fact that the hard features of that religious system which has been "received by tradition from our fathers" are greatly softened, and that a necessity is felt by those who hold it of accommodating their representations of it more and more to the improved philosophy of the human mind, and to the undeniable principles of natural and revealed religion. Unconditional election is seldom heard of among us. The imputation of Adam's sin to his posterity is hastening to join the exploded doctrine of transubstantiation. The more revolting representations of man's state by nature are judiciously kept out of sight, and, what is still of greater importance, preaching is incomparably more practical than formerly.

LYMAN : It is certainly an unexpected task which devolves upon me of proving that my doctrinal opinions are Calvinistic. I perceive what appears to me a settled determination in Unitarians to make the impression on the public mind that every variation in the explanation, statement, and proof of our doctrines is an abandonment of our first principles—and an approximation to Unitarianism.

But not one of the thousand trumpets which blow the fame of favored Unitarians has swelled a note in my praise, and no

Unitarian press has groaned with a second and third edition of this "anti-Calvinist" sermon for gratuitous distribution.

I have made inquiry, far and wide. But, while some differ with me on subordinate points or modes of explanation, all, without exception, have admitted that the sermon contains, substantially, a true account of the faith delivered to the saints.

•

NARRATOR : Another attack centered on Beecher's New-School doctrine of immediate repentance—the idea that a person could repent by his or her own free will. Some Unitarians claimed that that wasn't Calvinism at all, and some Calvinists agreed. A hundred years before, the Calvinist Jonathan Edwards had struggled with the same dilemma of free will, which was memorialized in this popular conundrum:

> You can and you can't
> You will and you won't
> You'll be damned if you do
> And damned if you don't

A story is told that Dr. Beecher was to exchange pulpits with an Old-School Calvinist minister. They met halfway, and the Old-School man exclaimed, "Dr. Beecher, I wish to call to your attention that before the creation of the world God arranged that you were to preach in my pulpit and I in yours on this particular Sabbath" "Is that so? Then I won't do it" retorted Beecher. And he wheeled his carriage about and drove back to his own church, to the astonishment of the other preacher.

HARRIET : He kept a load of sand in his cellar, to which he would run at odd intervals and shovel vigorously, throwing it from one side of cellar to the other, on his favorite theory of working off nervous excitement through the muscles, and his wood-pile and wood-saw were inestimable means to the same end. He had also, in the backyard, parallel bars, a single bar, ladder, and other simple gymnastic apparatus, where he would sometimes astonish his ministerial visitors by climbing ropes hand over hand, whirling over on the single bar, lifting weights, and performing other athletic feats, in which he took for the time as much apparent delight and pride as in any of his intellectual exertions.

His care of what he called regimen—diet, sleep, exercise, etc., went on with all his other cares without seeming to interrupt them. He seemed to navigate his body, as an acute mariner would work his ship through a difficult channel, with his eye intent on every spar and rope, each sail kept trimmed with the nicest adjustment.

The harsh climate of Boston, with its east winds, had long been famous for making all its literary workers dyspeptics; yet it was in this climate that his work lay; here he must conquer, notwithstanding he brought with him his life's disease. So careful was he of atmospheric influences upon the sensitive surface of the body, that he would often undress and dress again completely three or four times a day, to meet various changes of the mutable Boston weather.

LYMAN : When I commenced in Hanover Street, the first three Sabbaths the seats were free to all, and thronged above and below. Then they sold the pews, and the fourth Sabbath I preached to the Church and congregation specifically. The house was not thinned. There was a flood of young people of the middle classes that kept the congregation overflowing.

The Church had many excellent young men in it, and a fine set of women. The Church had had charge of their own affairs, property, etc., a year before I came, so that they were used to business; and, for fear it might fall into the hands of Unitarians, as other church property had done, they had a trust deed, giving it entirely and forever to the Church. It was as finely organized a church as ever trod shoe-leather. Extremely wise they were; I never knew them to make a mistake.

I remember one Sabbath, Anderson came smiling after sermon, and said with emotion, "You will overset us if you are going to preach at this rate" I never shall forget that. I knew nobody then. I took those subjects that were unquestionable; I began with prudence, because a minister, however well known at home, and however wise and successful he has been, has to make himself a character anew, and find out what material is around him.

From the beginning my preaching was attended with interest. I could take hold. There was very earnest hearing in the congregation. I felt in my own soul that the word sent forth with power. It was a happy season, hopeful and auspicious.

HARRIET : When Father was in Boston, I was more with him, and associated in companionship of thought and feeling for a longer period, than any other of my experience—and it was the most active, glowing, and successful period of his life. It was the high noon of his manhood, the flood-tide of his powers; and a combination of circumstances in the history of Massachusets brought him in to labor there just as a whole generation were on the return-wave of a great moral reaction.

LYMAN : William, it is with a deep sense of the divine goodness that I am able to say that my most distressing malady is yielding to prayer and regimen, and, I hope, passing away. I preached on fast-day two long sermons on Intemperance, attended several other meetings in the week, and at the close found myself evidently gaining strength.

The sermons on "Intemperance" struck well, and it is the wish of many that I should preach them all, which I have concluded to do.

Yesterday was a good day, though full of care and labor. Three baptisms in the morning, and the admission to the Church of five members from the world. In the afternoon the ordination of dea-cons before the congregation, and subsequently the adminstration of the sacrament. There were, besides our own, nearly a hundred communicants upon the invitation, and not many of them from the three orthodox churches; persons probably who have formed as yet no connection with any church, though some of them were known to belong to Unitarian churches. But if they will commune with us, under such instruction as I gave in the sermon, it will be an omen for good.

But, after all, the kingdom of God cometh not with observation; and I rely more on my vestry meetings on Sabbath and Tuesday eve, and on my chapel meetings on Friday eve at the North, and on my visits and labors among the middle class and the poor, than upon all the eclat of reputed talents and eloquence, and all the running to hear, and all the movements and talk from that source among the mighty and noble.

•

NARRATOR : Mrs. Beecher rather liked the metropolis, seeing how well her husband appeared to be prospering in his career.

HARRIET PORTER : I am happy to say we are beginning to be really comfortable. I know not how a minister can desire anything better than to preach the Gospel in Boston.

The four youngest children are with us. The girls are at Hartford, established as a family, with Aunt Esther at their head. Edward and George are New Haven, William at Andover. My husband's health is pretty good. He preaches a good deal, and with much encouragement.

There is a secret history of Boston which is very interesting—the history of minds and moral influence. We are at the North End, to which at first I felt reluctant. Mr. Beecher is enthusiastic in regard to this situation. This soil was pressed by the feet of the Pilgrims, and waterered by their tears, and consecrated by their prayers. Here are their tombs, and here are their children who are to be brought back to the fold of Christ.

NARRATOR : Not every Beecher child showed early promise. Henry had grown up with an enlarged palate, which made him very shy, and he was thought a dullard. William Beecher, the eldest son, had always been overshadowed by his brilliant brother Edward. He suffered from poor digestion, as his father did, and he felt himself to be the black sheep of the family.

WILLIAM : I did not know how to study and none showed me. Edward, on the contrary, learned easily. I could not learn—the fact was I had trouble in my head—a gathering and discharge from my left ear while at East Hampton—the whole outer ear was poisoned by the discharge. As I had much tooth and ear ache and my left breast bone being much smaller than the other they feared rickets. They longed to have their firstborn son a scholar and minister, and I fear they were sorrowfully disappointed. How long I stopped at home, I can't say, but the great question was, "What shall we do with William?"

NARRATOR : William tried work as a cabinet-maker's apprentice, and more than once as a store clerk. At a hardware store, William resolved to enter Andover Seminary and study theology. Lyman was happy about William's conversion, but even though he had wanted all his sons to enter the ministry—even though Roxana Beecher on her deathbed had made him promise to do so—he tried to dissuade William.

William went ahead, despite father and dyspepsia. After some time at Andover, he had to give up formal courses, and he studied with Lyman at home.

•

Noting Henry's lack of progress at school, Lyman Beecher had earlier sent him to his sister Catharine's Female Seminary in Hartford—and the next year sent him to a fellow clergyman in a town close to Litchfield. But when the Beechers moved to Boston in 1826, Henry was entered into the Boston Latin School.

Henry no longer had his fields and woods to roam in, and he found himself down at the Boston Harbor, watching the ships come in from all over the world. Finally, he decided that school was intolerable—he would go to sea! Yes, that would be the life for a misfit like himself.

Emboldened by his new plan, Henry wrote a note to one of his brothers, but then was careful to drop it where his father would be sure to find it. It was Henry's way—boldness, but cautiously.

Harriet reports the following dialogue, after Dr. Beecher called Henry to come and saw wood with him:

HARRIET : Now the wood pile was the principal debating ground and Henry felt complimented by the invitation, as implying manly companionship.

LYMAN : Let us see, Henry, how old are you?

HENRY : Almost 14.

LYMAN : Bless me how boys do grow! Why, it's almost time to be thinking what you are going to do. Have you ever thought?

HENRY : Yes—I want to go to sea.

LYMAN : To sea. Of all things Well, well. After all, why not? Of course you don't want to be a common sailor. You want to get into the Navy?

HENRY : Yes, sir, that's what I want.

LYMAN : But not merely as a common sailor, I suppose?

HENRY : No, sir, I want to be a midshipman and after that a commodore.

LYMAN : I see. Well, Henry, in order for that, you know, you must begin a course of mathematics and study navigation and all that.

HENRY : Yes sir, I am ready.

LYMAN : Well, then, I'll send you up to Amherst next week to Mt. Pleasant and then you'll begin your preparatory studies and if you are well prepared I presume I can make interest to get you an appointment.

HARRIET : And when he went up to Mt. Pleasant Collegiate Institute, his father remarked, "I shall have that boy in the ministry yet." At Amherst, he did improve in mathematics; he also studied with the remarkable John E. Lovell, an elocution teacher.

Father had not been in Boston many weeks before every leisure hour was beset by people who came to him. There seemed to be an incessant ringing of the doorbell from morning till night.

The effect of all this on my father's mind was to keep him at a white heat of enthusiasm. Within a stone's throw of our door was the old Copp's Hill burying-ground, where rested the bones of the Puritan founders; and, though not a man ordinarily given to sentiment or to visiting of graves, we were never left to forget in any prayer of his that the bones of our fathers were before our door.

His family prayers at this period, departing from the customary forms of unexcited hours, became often upheavings of passionate emotion such as I shall never forget. In hours of earnest excitement his petitions to the different persons of the Trinity would remind one of those antique, fervid invocations of the earlier Church.

LYMAN : Come, Lord Jesus, here where the bones of the fathers rest, here where the crown has been torn from thy brow, come and recall thy wandering children. Behold thy flock scattered on the countain—"These sheep, what have they done?" Gather them, gather them, O good Shepherd, for their feet stumble upon the dark mountains.

THE BOSTON YEARS: 2
1829–1832

During the time that the Beechers lived in Boston, Lyman Beecher became a rallying point for Calvinists opposed to the modern liberalism of Unitarianism. Edward and George begin their ministerial careers. William is ordained but is without church, and so stays at home. Young Henry, finally convinced of the need for education, goes to Amherst. Catharine brings Mary and Harriet down to Hartford to work at Catharine's Female Seminary. Charles, Belle—or Isabella—and Tom greet a new baby brother—James C. Beecher. He is the last of the tribe.

NARRATOR : It didn't take Dr. Beecher very long after they had moved to Boston before he decided to do what he did best—begin a revival.

LYMAN : I began to say to the Church: "I think there is a work begun. Fire in the leaves—not only among us, but in the community." I made no attack on Unitarians. I carried the state of warm revival feelings I had had in Litchfield for years. They came to hear; there was a great deal of talk about me—great curiosity.

Finally, my soul rose to it, and I preached to the Church one afternoon, explained to them the state of interest and opposition, and what an inquiry meeting was, and that they must be ready, and gave out an invitation to a long list of persons, whom I described. There were fifteen the first week, twenty the second, thirty-five the third, and the fourth time 300. The vestry was filled. Lambert met me at the door, when I came to meeting, with his eyes staring.

"It's a mistake; they've misunderstood, and think it's a lecture. You must explain."

"No," said I, "it's not a mistake; it's the finger of God!"

But I made an explanation, and only one person left.

The Baptists came in to see what was going on, and pretty soon they began to revive. When I first set up evening meetings, not a bell tingled; but, after a few weeks, not a bell that didn't tingle. The Unitarians at first scouted evening meetings; but Ware found his people going, and set up a meeting. I used to laugh to hear the bells going all round.

In this thing of revivals, you would find all these things came by showers. Each shower would increase, increase, increase; and when I saw it was about used up by conversion, I would preach so as to make a new attack on mind and conscience, varying with circumstances, and calculated to strike home with reference to other classes, and bring a new shower. The work never stopped for five years. In the revival the numbers increased so fast it was overwhelming, so I kept a record.

NARRATOR : Harriet describes the good doctor from the family's perspective.

HARRIET : The time that he spent in actual preparation for a public effort was generally not long. If he was to preach in the evening he was to be seen all day talking with whomever would talk, accessible to all, full of everybody's affairs, business, and burdens, till an hour or two before the time, when he would rush up into his study, which he always preferred should be the topmost room of the house, and, throwing off his coat, after a swing or two with the dumbbells to settle the balance of his muscles, he would sit down and dash ahead, making quantities of hieroglyphic notes on small, stubbed bits of paper, about as big as the palm of his hand.

The bells would begin to ring, and still he would write. They would toll loud and long, and his wife would say "He will certainly be late," and then would be running up and down stairs of messengers to see that he was finished, till, just as the last stroke of the bell was dying away, he would emerge from the study with his coat very much awry, come down the stairs like a hurricane, stand impatiently protesting while female hands that ever lay in wait adjusted his cravat and settled his coat collar, calling loudly the while for a pin to fasten together the stubbed little bits of paper aforesaid, which being duly dropped into the crown of his hat, and hooking wife or daughter like a satchel on his arm, away he would start on such a race through the streets as left neither brain nor breath till the church was gained.

Then came the process of getting in through the crowded aisles, wedged up with heads, the bustle, and stir, and hush to look at him, as, with a matter-of-fact, businesslike push, he elbowed his way through them and up the pulpit stairs.

LYMAN : When the time came for admission of converts to the communion, some 70 at once, it produced no small excitement. Till then all had been the butt of ridicule. The enemy had kept whist, except a few outlaws, at first, although the higher classes— the Cambridge College folks—had their spies abroad to see what was going on.

But, as the work deepened, I told my Church one of two things would come: either the revival would burst out through all these churches, or else there would be an outbreak of assault upon us such as could not be conceived. It was the latter. In one day after the seventy joined, the press belched and bellowed, and all the mud in the streets was flying at us. The upper class put mouth to ear, and hand to pocket, and said "shame on you" There was an intense, malignant enragement for a time. Showers of lies were rained about us every day. The Unitarians, with all their principles of toleration, were as really a persecuting power while they had the ascendancy as ever as ever existed. Wives and daughters were forbidden to attend our meetings; and the whole weight of political, literary, and social influence was turned against us, and the lash of ridicule laid on without stint.

As for me, I cared for it all no more than for the wind. I knew where I was, and what I was doing, and knew that I was right. All sorts of vile letters were written to me, but all this malignity did us no harm. They only rung the bell for me. It was two years before the leaders of the Unitarians began to change their tacitcs and treat me gentlemanly.

When I revised and preached my six sermons on "Intemperance," they took strong hold, and made my audience even fuller. My young men were for having them printed. Marvin did it well, and a number of editions were sold. Then the Tract Society bought the copyright. They offered $50; but I said they ought to give a hundred, and they did. These sermons made a racket all around, more than I had any idea they would.

HARRIET : As to his preaching, it consisted invariably of two parts: first, careful statement and argument addressed purely to the understanding, and second, a passionate and direct appeal, designed to urge his audience to some immediate practical result. The first part was often as dry, condensed, and clear as a series of mathematical axioms.

After this followed the scriptural argument, on which he always and unhesitatingly relied, without the shadow of a doubt that we do have, in our English translation, the authoritative, inspired declarations of God. Then came the answering of objections. Here he was conversational, sprightly, acute, and often drew a laugh. They were stirred up and enlivened, and, as a plain countryman once said, "He says it so that you feel you could have said it all yourself."

Last of all came what he considered the heart of his discourse—the application. A sermon that did not induce anybody to do anything he considered a sermon thrown away. These closing portions of his sermons were the peculiarity of his preaching. He warned, he entreated, he pleaded, urging now this motive and now that, talking as if his audience were one individual, whom he must, before he left the pulpit, persuade to take a certain step.

NARRATOR : In 1826, while Lyman Beecher was launching his Boston career, Catharine Beecher initiated her own revival at her school in Hartford, even though she herself had not experienced conversion. But once her revival spread beyond her circle of students, Catharine sought outside help from Joel Hawes, minister of the most prestigious church in Hartford. He did not encourage her activities, since she was not a minister nor formally trained in religion. So she wrote to brother Edward and to Lyman Beecher to come and help her. Lyman was cautious in his reply.

LYMAN : Your last letters, giving an account of the state of things in your school, have been read with deep interest and much thanksgiving, though not without some solicitude.

The very high state of excited feeling, though extremely natural among young Christians, and powerful in its effects while it lasts, is too hazardous to health to be indulged, and necessarily too short-lived to answer in the best manner the purpose of advancing a revival. In my early efforts I gave myself up to strong feeling, which I have since learned to economize, or I should long since have been in my grave, or been useless.

You must, therefore, all of you, instantly put yourselves upon a different system, which I will describe and hasten to send you, or you will all be prostrate, I have no doubt.

The state of feeling to be cultivated in those who superintend a revival is a mind, but constant and intense desire of heart for the awakening and conversion of sinners.

When I say intense, I do not mean agitating, but strong and steady. It is a genial warmth of heart, of steady benevolent temperature, compared with the more intense heat and flashings of holy and animal affections and passions, all boiling at once in the heart.

This is the state of heart which has carried me through all the revivals I have been in but the first, and that broke me down, and induced nervous habits which I shall never wholly retrieve.

Another thing, also, is to be carefully shut out of your soul—I mean an overpowering weight of responsibility and care. We can neither carry the world on our shoulders nor govern it, nor even govern the wants of a very small part of it, which are most immediately under our eye. Settle it in your heart, therefore, that you are to exercise your best judgment, and perform in the best manner you can your duty, and leave the whole in the hands of God. You can not be accountable for consequences.

HARRIET : After his evening services it was his custom to come directly home and spend an hour or two with his children, as he phrased it, letting himself "run down." This was our best season for being with him. He was lively, sparkling, jocose, full of anecdote and incident, and loved to have us all about him, and to indulge in a good laugh.

Often his old faithful friend the violin was called in requisition, and he would play a few antiquated contra dances and Scotch airs—"Auld Lang Syne," "Bonnie Doon," and "Mary's Dream" were among the inevitables. He aspired with ardent longings to "Money Musk," "College Hornpipe," and sundry other tunes arranged in unfavorable keys, although he invariably broke down, and ended the performance with a pshaw.

These innocent evening gala hours, like everything else, were a part of his system of regimen.

LYMAN : If I were to go to bed at the key at which I leave off preaching, I should toss and tumble all night. I must let off steam gradually, and then I can sleep like a child.

HARRIET : In fact, he was an excellent sleeper, and usually knew of but one nap, which lasted from the time his head touched the pillow till the youngest child was sent to wake him up in the morning. Great would be the pride of the little monitor, who led him at last gravely into the breakfast room, and related in baby phrase the labors of getting him up.

NARRATOR : Now that he had established a base in Boston, Lyman encouraged another Boston church to call his second son, Edward, the intellectual of the family. People in Boston were eager to see another Beecher at work.

LYMAN : Edward, I have kept up the same strain of revival preaching, with the same results, as when you were here. Fifty or sixty attend the inquiry meeting, and from two to five new cases and new hopes each week. There are probably between thirty and forty who have hope. The congregation is full and solemn, and seems to be amalgamated into a homogeneous mass of belief and solemnity by the power of truth.

Edward, just as I was about to send a letter last evening, Mr. Evarts called on me to say that the deacons of Park Street, by agreement of the committee, have written to request you to supply four Sabbaths, with a prospect, as he thinks, of their being united to give you a call.

As to the importance of the stand in Boston, as the center of extended and powerful action, I have never stood in such a place before, and do not believe that there is such another on earth. It is here that New England is to be regenerated, the enemy driven out of the temple they have usurped and polluted, the college to be rescued, the public sentiment to be revolutionized and restored to evangelical tone.

All this, under God, is to be accomplished here by intellectual power upon an intellectual people, who are captivated with vigorous intellect and powerful argument, and will come to hear it, and will be influenced by it.

You were pleased to say once that nothing brought out your mental vigor and energized your soul like my society. The effect of your society, for obvious reasons, is the same on my mind; and if it please God to place us where the action and reaction of intellectual power may be habitually experienced by us both, the public results may be great and good.

It is my hope that you will not fail to take hold of the end of the rope that is put into your hand, and pull it, till we see what is on the other end.

•

NARRATOR : Now that the family was widespread, letters became a means of continuing long-distance conversations.

LYMAN : Catharine, your letter of the 6th came duly, and awakened many recollections. I was not, however, sick when you was laid in my arms, but young, and fresh, and well. It was a year from that that I was invaded by sickness. Since then, with a constitution part of iron and part of miry clay, I have been permitted, for the most part, to preach and labor in my vocation, and to see a family of beloved and affectionate children rise up around me, some of whom, with my most beloved Roxana, are not, while most of them remain to be my crown and my comfort to this day. I am a man of many obligations daily multiplying.

I can neither speak of them nor feel them to their extent. In your life and prosperity I rejoice, being, after Aunt Esther, my nearest contemporary among the ancients of the early days. William, Edward, Mary, George, and Harriet, all in their time and place, have come to be my most affectionate companions and fellow-helpers.

NARRATOR : Lyman also continued to exert his influence to get Edward situated in Boston.

LYMAN : Edward, there is, I find, an earnest desire at Park Street Church to have you supply them. As things now stand there is no impediment, but a manifest providential indication that you should come. And my advice and my request now is that you will do it without fail. As we are not to push open doors before providence opens them, so neither are we to refuse to enter when they are opened.

Another reason is that there are the little clouds of a revival in every orthodox Church, which four weeks of exertion such as you, with myself and others, may make, might produce an overpowering shower. And the public feeling here now is such that another revival would tell wonderfully.

NARRATOR : In 1829, Cathatrine Beecher anonymously published an appeal to the "Benevolent Women of the United States," on behalf of the Cherokee Indians. The Cherokees, perhaps the most advanced tribe on the continent, who had learned farming, had schools, could read and write, were being forced by President Jackson into exile across the Mississippi, along with all other Indian tribes. The caravan followed a route called the Trail of Tears to dusty Oklahoma. This publication was only the beginning of Catharine's long career of public service.

It marked a difference of another kind, too—a difference in generations. Lyman Beecher spoke and wrote against dueling, as a matter of individual conscience, for his concern was with the soul. But he never saw matters as social problems, in which the ills to be overcome were a matter of public concern. Catharine's appeal, and many to follow from her and from her sisters and brothers, were cries for social reform, social responsibility, and even social engineering. As the crisis over slavery came closer, this division took on more and more importance in the Beecher family.

Meanwhile, Lyman Beecher was consolidating his position as a leader in Boston's religious community. He attracted fine talents to work with him, such as Lowell Mason, the musician.

LYMAN : Lowell Mason was not with me at first, but came early, and stayed while I was in Boston. he came to us from Savannah. He did good. He took young converts and trained them to sing. They drew in the unconverted, and were instrumental in their conversion. His influence was not secular, but as efficacious as preaching. Almost all who went to his classes, instead of being decoyed by it and made frivolous, were converted.

LOWELL MASON : I was accustomed to go to Dr. Beec her before the time for the commencement of the public worship on Sunday morning. He would be always short and to the point with me, but I do not remember that he ever met me with an impatient or discourteous manner. One day, it was very near the time. He looked up, and, with a smile, said:

LYMAN : I can't give you the hymns now; I don't know what I shall preach about yet, so I wish you to select any you think proper.

MASON : I went to select hymns of a general character, which answered the purpose well, as such hymns always will. After this, he would request me always to make the selection, and to send the numbers to him. The following seemed to be the result: It is better that the first and second hymns be those of direct worship, but that the last hymn sung after the sermon shall always be closely connected with the sermon, following exactly in its wake—following out and deepening, if possible, the state of mind or emotions awakened by the preacher.

LYMAN : You seem to take up the subject where I left it, and to carry it on beyond where I had the power to do.

MASON : Yes, blessed old man, but this cannot be done unless the preacher has done his work somewhat as you used to do it. I used to tell the doctor, "Sir, you laid the train, and there was nothing left for me to do but to apply the fuse."

•

NARRATOR : An ambitious young man in Lyman Beecher's congregation thought he had discovered in the reverend doctor a leader to be emulated. But William Lloyd Garrison, then in his early 20s, and at the time an advocate of gradual emancipation and of colonization, could not persuade Lyman Beecher that slavery was a national sin of overriding importance.

Then, events moved swiftly, and so did Garrison. He renounced his former opinion, which he had recently given in a speech at Edward's Park Street Church. In 1831, Nat Turner's slave revolt resulted in 61 whites being killed, and William Lloyd Garrison published the first issue of *The Liberator*, an abolitionist paper that would eventually reach an enormous circulation. Lyman Beecher's personal solutions were not enough for the headstrong Garrison, who had now become unshakable on the question of slavery.

GARRISON : I am in earnest—and I will not equivocate—I will not excuse—I will not retreat a single inch—and I will be heard.

NARRATOR : While in Boston, Lyman Beecher took the initiative in organizing groups and civic committees to combat the growing and pervasive power of the Unitarians. These groups then succeeded in prohibiting lotteries, and collectively, they gave a good start to the idea of popular lecture series and lyceums for both sexes. As these caught on in the rest of the country, the lyceums provided the platforms that launched the careers of more than one Beecher. Amasa Walker remarks on lyceums in Boston.

AMASA WALKER : It is quite difficult now to realize the great importance of this lyceum effort in changing the public taste, and in giving a higher and better tone to the public mind. The first Boston lyceum was the practical introduction of the important idea of combining popular improvement and amusement for both sexes—of furnishing some place of rational resort which the people might visit more beneficially than the theater. Ideas become impressed upon society never to be obliterated. Lyceums, however transient as organizations, have produced a social revolution in a most essential particular, and the several lecturers who now traverse the broad territory of the United States, entertaining thousands with their eloquence, have been created by the new tastes generated by the lyceum movement.

I feel that the vast influence which Dr. Beecher exerted while in Boston, through the various agencies he set in motion, is but little appreciated by the present generation. I speak not now of his denominational services, but of that great social influence which he exerted.

The results of all these great efforts to improve the moral and intellectual condition of the city, and furnish the people with rational and elevating entertainments were that in a few years the theater was in a great degree superseded. So many courses of lectures, so many interesting discussions were furnished by these various associations, that there was neither time nor taste for the entertainment of the drama, so that for some few years it nearly ceased to exist.

•

NARRATOR : In 1830, the Hanover Street Church burned. Dr. Beecher agreed to stay until the church was rebuilt, but he already had begun to map out his future in a new direction—the West.

After six years in Boston, Lyman Beecher felt that he had done what he could. He had failed to turn the tide of Unitarianism, though his Boston pulpit had given him national eminence in his field. An invitation to be president of the newly formed Lane Seminary in Cincinnati proved a catalyst for his ambitions. The

West was a vast new field to conquer, the next steppingstone of his career, to train the next generation of preachers, to win the West. Yes, it would be a fitting solution. He confides his thoughts first to his first-born. Perhaps she, too, can be persuaded of the urgency of the need.

LYMAN : Catharine, I now believe the moral destiny of our nation and all our institutions and hopes and the world's hopes turns on the character of the West, and the competition now is for that of preoccupancy in the education of the rising generation in which Catholics and infidels have got the start of us. I have thought seriously of going over to Cincinnati, the London of the West, to spend the remnant of my days in that conflict, and of consecrating to God all my children who are willing to go. If we gain the West, all is safe; if we lose it, all is lost.

NARRATOR : Catharine Beecher independently made the same decision—America was moving into the Ohio Valley, and it seemed an open promise to thousands. She arranged for her Hartford school to carry on without her, and set out for Cincinnati about the same time, with the intention of setting up another school. For her, too, it will be an important steppingstone.

Meanwhile, Charles Beecher was proving to be quite a scholar and athlete at school, like his brother Edward. He attended Boston Latin School, then Lawrence Academy, where his brother George had just been appointed principal. Just before the Beechers left Boston, Charles would depart for Bowdoin. He was 16 years old.

William Beecher, the eldest son, finally secured a parish in Newport, Rhode Island, through one of Lyman Beecher's connections. He married Katharine Edes soon after. William was built strong, like his grandfather, and when he learned that his new church, a pre-Revolutionary building, had an unsafe steeple, he pulled it down himself. But he failed at fund-raising for a new church building, and so, when he received an invitation from a Middletown, Connecticut church, he took it. Unfortunately, not long afterward, his predecessor decided to return, and William was forced to resign. So it was that William, too, traveled west with the younger Beechers, to Cincinnati, the London of the West.

THE HEIR APPARENT
1818–1834

Eeward Beecher was the second son of Lyman and Roxana Beecher, a brilliant scholar whose promise was recognized early. Though he left home early, in many ways he was a second father to several of the Beecher children. Edward is the first Beecher son to carry out his mother's deathbed wish that all her sons should become ministers. He earns his way through Yale—Lyman Beecher's old alma mater—in part, by working at Catharine's Hartford seminary.

EDWARD : I always employ at least seven hours in the school besides this I sleep seven hours, and in order to preserve my health I exercise one hour every day—this I do by cutting wood. Of course to balance all this I must take something to eat but I make my meals as short as possible, but I will allow 45 minutes for the three. Besides this I allow one and a half hours for reading the Bible and for prayer. This leaves six hours and 45 minutes. I have in the first place the translations and Latin compositions of my scholars to correct, and a thousand little things that occur every day, and I forgot to mention washing and dressing which takes me about 20 minutes every day.

NARRATOR : Edward reached Yale the year after the fire-breathing Timothy Dwight died—but Dwight's imprint had made Yale into a Calvinist stronghold ever since Lyman had attended 20 years before. Dwight's successor was his secretary, Nathaniel Taylor, Lyman Beecher's closest associate in church affairs; Edward too became close to Taylor. He also studied mathematics with the brilliant Alexander Metcalf Fisher, who was later his sister Catharine's beau, and with Benjamin Silliman, Yale's Professor of Natural Science, who saw no problems reconciling science and religion.

Edward was valedictorian of his graduating class—but it wasn't until his senior year that he had a religious experience, the one thing that Lyman Beecher most anxiously awaited for each of his children. It came about after reading certain passages of the Bible, "representing Christ as the bridegroom, and the church as the bride."

EDWARD : I felt that the exciting cause of such love must be the knowledge of his love to me and of his infinite desire to communicate his Essence to me in full and overflowing communication of love such as should affect me as should affect my whole frame until I could feel that the love of God is strong as death, that the coals thereof are coals of fire. Yea, so intensely did I desire the love of God that I felt willing that it should burn me up if it were but love, and I could rejoice to die by such a death.

•

NARRATOR : On Unitarianism, which was in his father's current view the enemy, Edward took a different, more demanding approach. He was, in fact, beginning his work of developing a new theology to resolve the inner conflict of the times.

EDWARD : Though obliged to defend the divine character from the charges of the Unitarian system, it must be without violation of charity. In pursuing an education of peculiar severity, I have felt it necessary to read everything bearing on the subject, ancient and modern; to be resolutely honest in conceding to antagonists whatever elements of truth they possess.

NARRATOR : Jonathan Edwards and other Prostestant theologians had long concerned themselves with good and evil, and the ways that an individual might seek the one while avoiding the other; saving souls, and revivals in particular, were of the utmost importance to this school of thinking, and to Lyman Beecher.

But Calvinism gave no room for discussing or solving social problems, for reform movements or change. Awareness of these issues came with the new principles of honor and right, democratic principles, principles of the Enlightenment—even God was required to act honorably and justly. Edward was willing to entertain these new notions, and if possible, to put them to work in a form more orthodox than Unitarianism, more reasonable than Calvinism. Dr. Channing, the Unitarian champion, threw down the challenge.

CHANNING : Calvinism is giving place to better views. It has passed its meridian and is sinking to rise no more. It has to contend with foes more formidable than theologians; with foes from which it cannot shield itself in mystery and metaphysical subtleties—we mean with the progress of the human mind, and with the progress of the spirit of the gospel. Society is going forward in intelligence and charity, and of course is leaving the theology of the 16th century behind it.

NARRATOR : On graduation, Edward was offered the headmastership of Hartford Academy at $500 a year—at which he spent two full years, including tutoring George, writing, teaching, studying. But then he decided to go to Andover Theological Seminary—he would become a minister, and also a theologian. He lasted less than a year, then accepted tutorship at Yale, which Catharine urged him to accept. Edward found the students too lax for his liking and so he organized Bible classes and lectured until his lecture room was filled with boys who later became known as the Yale Band, and who would subsequently invite him out to Illinois to become president of a new college. His younger brother Charles, also a formidable intellect, emulated Edward in many ways.

CHARLES : Edward is a resolute, earnest, practical man, who is determined to do his duty, and do it as perfectly as possible to humanity. His faith was so absolute, that there was never any wish to be skeptical, or to raise cavils.

•

NARRATOR : In 1826, Lyman Beecher counseled Edward to refuse a professorship at Dartmouth, and instead encouraged and promoted him toward Park Street Church, "Brimstone Corner," in Boston. Dr. Beecher himself had just recently been installed in a post at Hanover Street Church.

But Edward ws more than a model son—he was perhaps the first and certainly not the last Beecher to exhibit a tendency toward unorthodoxy that some were simply to call Beecherism. And Lyman himself contributed to it, not only with his own Taylorist New School Calvinism, but also with the remarkable family debates at dinner table or cutting wood.

LYMAN : Receive no opinions upon trust. Dare to think for yourself. Let no creed bind you because it is reputed orthodox, until you perceive its agreement with the Scriptures; but then, though everywhere spoken against it, adopt it.

NARRATOR : These principles had not helped Catharine when her fiance, Alexander Fisher, died—rather than offering consolation, Lyman offered a moral lesson. Edward made the same mistake in his letters. Catharine responded to theology with theology.

•

CATHARINE : The difficulty originates in my views of the doctrine of original sin. I feel that I am guilty, but not guilty as if I had received at birth a nature pure and uncontaminated. Is there any satisfactory mode of explaining this doctrine, so that we can perceive its consistency while the heart is unrenewed?

NARRATOR : Edward wsn't to let this question go unanswered, though it was 30 years later that he made public his doctrine of the pre-existence of souls. But for Catharine, Edward did provide sympathy, he served as executor of Fisher's effects and debts at Yale, and he provided some practical advice—Catharine should rebuild her life around service, and spend her talents in doing good for others. In fact, Edward helped her set up the Hartford Female Seminary, tutored her in sciences, and when Catharine wanted to create a course in Mental and Moral Philosophy, Edward wrote out original theological definitions for her.

Harriet came down to the Hartford Seminary at 14, and later, in Boston, Edward tried the same process with her that he had tried with Catharine—talks and letters helping her toward a conversion experience. Now, his answers were a little more sophisticated and less conventional than his correspondence with Catharine.

HARRIET : August 1828

Edward, many of my objections you did remove that afternoon we spent together. After that I was not as unhappy as I had been. I felt, nevertheless, that my views were very indistinct and contradictory, and feared that if you left me thus I might return to the same dark, desolate state in which I had been all summer.

I cannot say exactly what it is makes me reluctant to speak of my feelings. It costs me an effort to express feeling of any kind, but more particularly to speak of my private religious feelings. If anyone questions me, my first impulse is to conceal all I can.

It appears to me that if I could only adopt the views of God you presented to my mind, they would exert a strong and beneficial influence over my character. But I am afraid to accept them for several reasons. First, it seems to be taking from the majesty and dignity of the divine character to suppose that his happiness can be at all affected by the conduct of his sinful, erring creatures. Secondly, it seems to me that such views of God would have an effect on our own minds in lessening that reverence and fear which is one of the greatest motives to us for action.

•

NARRATOR : Mary Beecher also struggled with the Calvinist dogmas. She worked at Catharine's chief assistant and teacher in the Hartford school until she married a Hartford lawyer, Thomas Perkins. But Harriet was slowly forming her own conception of God, a conception that would become one of the most characteristic parts of her writing.

HARRIET : March 27, 1828

Dear Edward, I think that those views of God which you have presented to me have had an influence in restoring my mind to its natural tone. But still, after all, God is a being afar off. He is so far above us that anything but the most distant reverential affection seems almost sacrilegious. It is that affection that can lead us to be familiar that the heart needs. The language of prayer is of necessity stately and formal, and we cannot clothe all the little minutiae of our wants and troubles in it.

I wish I could describe to you how I feel when I pray. I feel that I love God—that is, that I love Christ—that I find comfort and happiness in it, and yet it is not that kind of comfort which would arise from free communication of my wants and sorrows to a friend. I sometimes wish the the Savior were visibly present in this world, that I might go to Him for a solution of some of my difficulties. Do you think my dear brother, that there is such a thing as so realizing the presence and character of God that He can supply the place of earthly friends? I really wish to know what you think of this. Do you suppose that God really loves sinners before they come to Him?

CATHARINE : When the young man came to Jesus, is it not said that Jesus loved him, though he was unrenewed?

HARRIET : Somehow or another, you have such a reasonable sort of way to saying things that when I come to reflect I almost always go over to your side. Oh, Edward, you can feel as I do; you can speak of Him. There are few, very few, who can.

•

NARRATOR : Edward in these years was evolving his picture of God, too. But the image was not that of the Calvinist God, the God of justice—rather, it was a suffering, pitying God.

EDWARD : There is a line between the true character of God, as revealed in Christ, and the Absolutist character as conceived of by even the best of men under corrupt or partially reformed systems. To deny the possibility of suffering in God is to deny that Jesus "man of Sorrows" is the express image of his person. In his pity, in his sympathy, in his agony in the garden, yea in his suffering on the cross, he expressed to us all that could be expressed of the pity, sympathy and grief of a father's heart.

NARRATOR : The doctrine of total depravity bothered Edward— how could it be that a good God had created evil or the propensity for evil?

EDWARD : Pain, sickness and death come on the human race before the development of reason. Such a constitution resembles punishment applied in anticipation of a crime. There seems to be something morally odious in the nature of every human being which is the certain cause of Sin. This, one would think, is a calamity and not a crime, a ground of pity and not of condemnation. To call total depravity voluntary seems like removing a difficulty to language only. In short, original, native, entire depravity is a hard doctrine to be explained. Why all men should tend so constantly to wickedness, against the light of Nature, and against the Christian revelation, is mysterious except on the ground that such a cause exists. And to come into being with a certainty of becoming miserable, and voluntarily so, is a great calamity.

The question is, is not the present system a malevolent one? If it reduces all things to a system of mere machinery, and of pain attached to conduct which seems voluntary, and pleasure to conduct which seems good, we land in a universe of skepticism, yet, if such is the natural consequence of reasoning, we cannot help it. Evil exists. If it does prove malevolence in God we are lost, or else must love a partial being. We cannot analyze the thing. Why has God so made men that a conviction of depravity, the most essential thing to a sense of mercy, is so hard to be obtained?

•

NARRATOR : Even Charles, doubting Charles, contributed to the debate in Edward's mind.

CHARLES : The system our father defends, does it not impugn the honor, and rectitude of God? Does it not stain the beauty of that being?

NARRATOR : The early 19th century brought to light a spirit of reform—for temperance, in education, prisons, treatment of the insane, the deaf, the blind, a peace movement, women's rights, anti-slavery, and utopian colonies. All of them were expressions of a new spirit that had also been the engine for the American and French Revolutions, romanticism, and the modern age.

EDWARD : I had been groping in some vast cathedral, in the gloom of midnight, vainly striving to comprehend its parts and relations, and suddenly before the vast arched window of the nave a glorious sun had suddenly burst forth, filling the whole structure with its radiance, and showing in perfect harmony the proportions and beautites of its parts.

NARRATOR : This revelation of Edward's was his doctrine of the pre-existence of souls—like Wordsworth's famous *Ode on Intimations of Immortality*:

> Our birth is but a sleep and a forgetting
> The Soul that rises with us, our life's Star,
> Hath had elsewhere its setting,
>   And cometh from afar:
> Not in entire forgetfulness,
> And not in utter nakedness

But Edward did not also feel that we come "trailing clouds of glory"—rather we come out of a dark cloud, our fall from grace, and the world we know is a kind of "moral hospital" in which we have a chance to make up for our pre-existent crime. So, this solves Edward's conundrum: humans are depraved, but God is not to blame.

CHARLES : Thenceforward there was something akin in Edward's experience to that of the apostle when he was caught up to the third heaven and heard things which it was not lawful to mutter. Like Moses descending from the mount—must he needs draw a veil over his countenance. Dr. Beecher had no place in his system for this new revelation—Edward must be silent, as became his youth. He must be "dead and his life hid with Christ in God." He must yield to his father's request to postpone utterance of his new views. He became, as he himself said, "Shut up to God."

Despite his two new doctrines, Edward, a young man of 23, fresh from academic life, stood side by side with his father, the leader of his denomination in the zenith of influence. He was already much honored by older men, leaders of the host; and stationed conspicuously in the focus of New England thought, intense but narrow and provincial.

NARRATOR : After two years at Park Street Church, Edward went on a much-needed vacation to Maine—but while there he gave 28 revival sermons in 26 days. Then in mid-1829, Edward made a nostalgic tour of his childhood towns—East Hampton, New Haven, Hartford. At Hartford, he poured forth his problem to Catharine, and received this reply.

CATHARINE : Your "explaining and expounding" was quite satisfactory, and I hope your inward man will soon be taught how to behave himself in all circumstances and emergencies. I wish I could catch my inward woman, and give her such an inspection and exposition, but she is such a restless thing that I cannot hold her still long enough to see her true form and outline. I am however a little afraid that in the millennium your peculiar notion not to be mentioned about a pre-existent state, will not be found in the elementary works of mental philosophy of theology.

EDWARD : How do we know that things are as they seem to be? How be certain that if God seems to be good, he really is so? Can the human imagination create ideas of glorious displays of God forever, which seem real, when there is no such reality?

•

NARRATOR : Edward married Isabella Porter Jones in 1829. Their first son was a congenital idiot, a fact that Edward never got over

On July 4, 1829, William Lloyd Garrison, a young member of Lyman Beecher's church, gave an address on slavery in Edward's Park Street Church. At this time, Garrison was anti-slavery but still a moderate; he spoke of gradualism and he supported colonization, that is, the removal of blacks to Liberia.

WILLIAM LLOYD GARRISON : The free states are constitutionally involved in the guilt of slavery. Slavery is a national sin. But the emancipation of all the slaves of this generation is most assuredly out of the question. We have not the right to use coercive measures. Moral influence, vigorously applied, is irresistible in the long run. Immediate and complete emancipation is not desirable; no rational man cherishes so wild a notion.

NARRATOR : Dr. Lyman Beecher was not far from this position, and Garrison had approached him in Boston, urging him to take a public stand. Lyman Beecher saw the question as peripheral to the business of saving souls.

LYMAN : I will make use of the current human fears, and passions, and interests, when they may be made to set in our favor, instead of attempting to row upstream against them.

I would press the consciences, so far as they have any, of the Southerners, and shake their fears, and press their interests, as the Abolitionists are doing; but then, that the pressure might avail, I would not hermetically seal their hearts by cutting off the facilities of emancipation, which might tempt them to delay it till insurrection should do the work, but offer them an easy, practicable way of doing their duty, as the Colonizationists are doing; and I can perceive no need that the two classes of philanthropists should fall out by the way.

•

NARRATOR : Two months later, Garrison changed his mind, and made a public disavowal of his Park Street Church address.

GARRISON : I admit that I had unreflectingly assented to the popular but pernicious doctrine of gradual abolition. I seize this opportunity to make full and unequivocal recantation, and thus publicly to ask pardon of my God, of my country, and of my brethren the poor slaves, for having uttered a sentiment so full of timidity, injustice, and absurdity.

I will be as harsh as truth and as uncompromising as justice. On this subject, I do not wish to think, or speak, or write, with moderation. I am in earnest—I will not equivocate—I will not excuse—I will not retreat a single inch—and I will be heard.

CHARLES : These two men, Edward and Garrison, like the pith balls on an electrical machine seemed for a time to fly apart. But for both the electricity was the same, positive.

NARRATOR : At Park Street Church, Edward Beecher showed that he was not another Lyman Beecher, not a fire-eater but an egghead. He was 23. Sentiment in the church against him grew.

He and his father worked out on gymnastic equipment in the Beecher backyard, and together they shoveled sand from one side of the cellar to the other—simply for exercise—while plotting to frustrate the opposition to Edward. They succeeded—but when he was invited by the Yale Band—a group of friends from his class at Yale—to become president of tiny Illinois College, he accepted. He left Park Street Church for Jacksonville, Illinois, in 1830. He would stay for 13 years.

•

In Jacksonville, Edward worked three years to secure a charter from the Illinois legislature, a body which included a young lawyer named Abraham Lincoln.

With Thomas H. Skinner of Philadelphia, Edward wrote a vigorous little revivalist book called *Hints Designed to Aid Christians in Their Efforts to Convert Men to God*, full of moral directives but not much theology. "Avoid everything polemic," he writes, though he himself did otherwise.

Much of Edward Beecher's energies as college president were spent in raising funds, mostly in the East. Beecher and Theron Baldwin told their audiences that the Mississippi Valley was four times larger than New England, with almost four million people, doubling every 11 years. But the role of academic beggar began to wear him down, and when the Society for the Promotion of Collegiate and Theological Education at the West was founded in 1843, Edward willingly turned to other pursuits.

The veteran editor William Cullen Bryant had occasion to stay in Jacksonville, Illinois; here is his impression:

WILLIAM CULLEN BRYANT : Jacksonville is a horridly ugly village, composed of little shops and dwellings stuck close together around a dingy square, in the middle of which stands the ugliest of possible brick courthouses, with a spire and weather-cock on its top.

NARRATOR : Edward and Isabella were community leaders in Jacksonville, one of three population centers in Illinois. A friend described him as "a great-brained and great hearted man—of earnest devotion and with the guilelessness of a child." By 1835, Edward remembered William Lloyd Garrison's statements with a more favorable eye.

EDWARD : After a careful examination of the history of experiments in abolition, I have come to agree that the doctrine of gradual emancipation is fallacious, and that of immediate emancipation is philosophical and safe. It is true that I have not participated at all in the public discussion which was so deeply exciting the nation, but have been merely an attentive and thoughtful spectator. I am dissatisfied with the spirit of much which has been written on the subject; and with the disposition so common, of pushing true principles to an extreme.

•

NARRATOR : Then Edward Beecher met the abolitionist Elijah Lovejoy at the commencement at Illinois College in 1834. Most clergymen had rejected Garrison's call for immediate abolition, as did Lovejoy.

ELIJAH LOVEJOY : We only propose that measures shall now be taken for the abolition of slavery, at such distant period of time as may be thought expedient, and eventually for ridding the country altogether of a colored population. Gradual emancipation is the remedy we propose.

NARRATOR : Meanwhile, Edward Beecher's *Six Sermons* was published—he talks of "reorganizing human society," and "certain great crises or turning points" of history. And he criticizes "the unchristian feeling exhibited in some of the great movements and discussions of the day, alike humiliating and surprising." And in 1835, a number of the clergy also were changing their minds about Garrison's principles, if not his practice.

CINCINNATI: 1
1832–1836

In 1832, most of the Beecher family moved to Cincinnati, a boom town on the Ohio River, right on the border between slavery and free soil. Dr. Beecher had decided, in his last year in Boston, that the West was the future.

LYMAN : The West is destined to be the great central power of the nation. The West is a young empire of mind, and power, and wealth, and free institutions, rushing up to a giant manhood, with a rapidity and a power never before witnessed below the sun.

NARRATOR : Even before Lyman took his family west, Edward Beecher had planted himself in Illinois. Catharine Beecher went with the family, and William and his wife Katherine Edes and child joined the caravan. Harriet and Aunt Esther managed the children—Belle, Tom, and James. Henry and Charles were off at college, and George was still principal at Lawrence Academy in Boston. Mary was well settled in Hartford with Thomas Perkins, a lawyer.

At first, the group stayed with Uncle Samuel Foote, the former sea captain, at his mansion, which was one of the social centers of the city. Catharine's prospects for founding a new school for women was good, at the outset. But Cincinnati was not homogeneous, as Hartford had been. Southerners, Yankees, and border state folk mingled easily by the expedient of not bringing up division subjects, such as slavery or abolitionism. A hard lesson for someone as outspoken as Catharine.

By the time the Beechers moved to Cincinnati in 1832, it held 30,000 people, had 60 foundries, slaughtered 120,000 hogs a year—and its factories and mills supplied much of the settled territory of the Midwest.

Frances Wright passed through Cincinnati after failing at a utopian experiment of freeing and educating slaves in backwoods Tennessee. She also spoke out for women's rights.

And Robert Dale Owen, the socialist, entered into a marathon debate about Christianity with Rev. Alexander Campbell, the man who later founded the Disciples of Christ.

After six months in a rented house, the Beechers finally moved into Walnut Hills, their permanent residence near Lane Seminary. Charles describes life there:

CHARLES : The household was replete with moral oxygen—full charged with intellectual electricity. A Kind of moral heaven, the purity, vivacity, inspiration and enthusiasm of which those only can appreciate who have lost it.

NARRATOR : A visiting member of the Foote family saw it this way:

FOOTE : Catharine has had a bilious fever. George has the dyspepsia all the time dreadfully. Mrs. Beecher is always sick and Aunt Esther is suffering from a sore mouth. And they all have nerves.

•

NARRATOR : Dr Beecher suffered an unexpected reversal when the Old School man who had invited him to Lane Seminary changed his mind, and repudiated him. But Beecher was an old pro at church politics.

LYMAN : Before I left Boston, Dr. Joshua Wilson had veered about. There had been some talk in the General Assembly some years before about a theological seminary at Cincinnati rather than near Pittsburgh when they got ready; but now, when they found it was going to be a New School affair, they vowed it should never be. All their plans would be blown up, and a mighty power exerted against them. I heard what they said.

So they wrote to Wilson a flattering letter, explaining the whole campaign, and attacking us as New England men. I had it from Wilson's own mouth that he had been accustomed to consult his particular friends at Princeton and in the Pittsburgh Synod, and, as it was their wish he should take back his invitation to me, he did so.

Besides that, Wilson fired off a 44-pounder in the New York papers, warning brethren to take heed, had it read on trail. I replied by publishing parts of his own letters to me. Wilson objected to my reception, and said he had no confidence in my doctrines. I rose and said that I was sure Dr. Wilson did not understand, and was laboring under a mistake; that I had not altered my views since he saw me years ago; and that if Presbytery would take recess and have free conversation in the vestry, I could explain.

We all went into the vestry, and I began to speak kindly (I felt kindly) and solemnly. I saw Wilson felt. Something was said about prayer, when he said, with a gentle face, waving his hand to me, "You pray"; and I did so, and we had a good season. Just then the devil in a good man jumped up and said that there had never been a man of sufficient calibre to excite Dr. Wilson's jealousy but that he opposed and drove him away. Then the fat was in the fire. I was sure I should win him. I never was more chagrined. We went up, and it was pitched battle after that.

I was able to keep down all improper feeling; treated him politely and kindly; gave him credit for honesty; but every concession contrasted with his treatment of me burnt like coals of juniper. In closing I expostulated with Dr. Wilson affectionately; stated the rising prospects of a revival in the churches, and conjured him to desist till I had furnished some better evidence of heresy than rumor, or afforded him conclusive evidence of my orthodoxy, which I had not a single doubt I should ere long be able to do.

I spoke an hour about as well as I could desire, and the verdict of public sentiment is as adverse to him, and favorable to me as I could wish. He has appealed to Synod, including items, thus giving me a more extended opportunity to defend myself and put down rumor and slang.

As it happened, Synod met at Cincinnati the very day my society had appointed to visit me in expression of welcome. I, of course, was occupied, and did not think of Synod, till suddenly I was sent for by messenger. I had no time to prepare. Wilson was speaking when I got there, and I heard the main part of his argument. I rose and made an offhand reply, as keen as ever I did, as good as I wanted. Synod decided in my favor by a large majority.

From Synod Wilson appealed to General Assembly; but they sent him back with a flea in his ear; told him if he had any case to take it up himself. He had tried to make Presbytery take it up first on common fame, and next to appoint a committee to examine my printed sermons and report. He wanted them to prosecute.

He did not want to assume the responsibility of tabling charges himself. But that Assembly happened to be very strong New School, and they would have nothing to do with him.

NARRATOR : Dr. Wilson, however, was not finished with Lyman Beecher. The test would come three years later.

•

NARRATOR : Catharine and Harriet joined the Semi-Colon Club, a literary club that included Calvin Stowe and his lovely wife Eliza, Judge James Hall, editor of the *Western Monthly*, Mrs. Peters, who later founded the Philadelphia School of Design, and Salmon P. Chase, later Lincoln's Treasury Secretary and then Chief Justice of the Supreme Court. Harriet won a $50 prize for a short story in Hall's *Western Monthly*, and from that time on decided to devote herself to writing.

HARRIET : Edward, you speak of your predilections for literature having been a snare to you. I have found it so myself. I can scarcely think, without tears and indignation, that all that is beautiful and lovely and poetical has been laid on other altars. I do not mean to live in vain. He has given me talents, and I will lay them at His feet, well satisfied if He will accept them.

NARRATOR : Catharine also participated in literary evenings at Daniel Drake's, and hobnobbed with editors and judges and their wives. Judge James Hall agreed to be one of Catharine's trustees for her new school.

A new group, the Western Literary Institute and College of Professional Teachers, allowed Catharine to participate as an observer. Lyman Beecher became a member also.

Three months after her arrival, Catharine advertised the Western Female Institute, and with Harriet, two teachers from her Hartford school, and $500, the school opened in 1833.

One of the teachers, Mary Dutton, and Harriet decided to visit Kentucky, and to meet some plantation owners. Mary remembers Harriet as a dreamy, abstracted visitor, oblivious to what was going on around her, even though these scenes would emerge later in the biggest novel of the century.

Charles Beecher for a time held a job working for a cotton factory, and in the course of his duties traveled down the Ohio and

Mississippi as far as New Orleans, the great slave-market for the Deep South. There he met a man he couldn't forget; he describes him to Harriet. Later, she would give him the name of Simon Legree.

·

CHARLES : He wasn't a big man, but he'd say, "Waal, I tell ye this yer fist has got hard as iron knocking down niggers. I never see the nigger yet I couldn't bring down with one crack. You see, I just put 'em straight through sick or well. When one nigger's dead, I buy another; and I find it comes cheaper and easier, every way."

NARRATOR : Harriet's portrait of Topsy is based on a little girl brought up from Louisiana with a number of slaves by a wealthy and cultivated family that settled near Cincinnati.

HARRIET : "Have you ever heard anything about God, Topsy?"

The child looked bewildered but grinned as usual.

"Do you know who made you?"

The idea appeared to amuse her considerably for her eyes twinkled and she added:

"I 'spect I grow'd, nobody never made me."

NARRATOR : Dr. Beecher did not see slavery as a central issue. In any case, he felt that it would disappear gradually with or without his help.

LYMAN : I am not apprised of the ground of controversy between the Colonizationists and the Abolitionists. I am myself both without perceiving in myself any inconsistency. Were it in my power to put an end to slavery immediately I would do it, but it is not. I can only pursue the measures best calculated, in my judgment, to get the slaves out of bondage in the shortest time, and best manner; and this, as I view the subject, is to make emancipation easy instead of attempting to row up-stream against them.

NARRATOR : In Dr. Beecher's first year at Cincinnati, a cholera epidemic took the lives of several Lane students.

More damaging, perhaps, to the fate of the school was the abolitionist controversy. The graduating class, under the leadership of Theodore Weld, organized an anti-slavery society while Dr.

Beecher was back East fund-raising. In his absence, the trustees decided to abolish the abolitionists, and as a consequence, the entire class withdrew. They were welcomed at Oberlin, not far away.

The stink of the affair made Lane a symbol for unwanted controversy in Cincinnati. It affected Lyman Beecher's career; it also doomed Catharine Beecher's fund-raising efforts for her school.

LYMAN : Weld was a genius. First-rate natural capacity, but uneducated. Would have made a first-rate man in the Church of God if his education had been thorough. In the estimation of the class, he was president. He took the lead of the whole institution. The young men had, many of them, been under his care, and they thought he was a god.

•

NARRATOR : Catharine's reputation as an educator opened some doors. William McGuffey, the textbook writer, invited Catharine to teach moral philosophy at a girls' school in Oxford, Ohio, about 20 miles away.

Catharine's book, *Geography for Children*, actually was suggested by her and written by Harriet, who was 22 at the time. Geography treated as a readable narrative was a novelty in itself. Catharine and Harriet collaborated on several other projects.

But the abolitionist controversy at Lane Seminary had turned Cincinnati against Lyman Beecher—and Lyman, in Boston, had made some uncomplimentary remarks about the backwardness of Westerners. When Lyman's *A Plea for the West* came out, the editor James Hall noted the discrepancy between published text and reported speeches—the offensive passages had been deleted. Hall cried foul. Daniel Drake sided with Hall.

Catharine defended her father—but then went further. She campaigned to get Hall and Drake excluded from social circles; such an action would have divided easterners from westerners. Even with her persistence, Catharine failed. Cincinnati society ran on different rules than Hartford. Edward King, an old Federalist aristocrat, and a relation, instructed his wife not to allow Catharine Beecher to run their social life; a guest in their house—and a relative at that—must act as a guest, not as a director.

For all her socializing, Catharine's ideas were not readily received either in the *Western Monthly Magazine* or by the Western Literary Institute. Her next blast at traditional methods was made at the American Lyceum in New York, a speech called *An Essay on the Education of Female Teachers.* Catharine called for the creation of an enormous corps of women teachers.

CATHARINE : The education of the lower classes is deteriorating, as it respects moral and religious restraints, and at the same time thousands and thousands of degraded foreigners, and their ignorant families, are pouring into this nation at every avenue.

In one of the best educated Western states, one third of the children are without schools. 90,000 teachers are needed, but it is chimerical to hope that enough men will become teachers when there are multitudes of other employments that will lead to wealth.

It is woman who is fitted by disposition and habits and circumstances, for such duties, who to a very wide extent must aid in educating the childhood and youth of this nation. Moral and religious education must be the foundation of national instruction.

•

HARRIET : Harriet went all the way to Amherst to attend Henry's graduation, and the two of them returned to Cincinnati together. Henry enrolled in Lane Seminary. He practiced his oratory in the woods, and taught Sunday school.

For a time, Henry served as temporary editor of the *Cincinati Journal and Western Luminary.* On his return to Lane, he roomed with Calvin Stowe. Stowe's Bible course was the only one that interested Henry.

HENRY : He led me to an examination of the Bible and to an analysis of its several portions, not as parts of a machine, formal and dead, but as a body of truth instinct with God, warm with divine and human sympathies, clothed in language adapted to their fit expressions and to be understood as similar language used for similar ends in everyday life.

NARRATOR : By 1835, Catharine's vision was unraveling. A select committee to raise $15,000 did not act. Her association with Lyman Beecher, and her own outspokenness and the campaign of ostracism that backfired, had thwarted her.

About this time, Charles returned from Bowdoin to continue his studies at Lane Seminary. He despaired of ever believing Jonathan Edwards on the will, and he feared that he must give up the idea of entering the ministry. But he was enthusiastic about music, and at Lane he began a study of church music instead. He had studied under Lowell Mason, perhaps the leading church musician of the time, at Lyman Beecher's Hanover Church. And Charles had begun teaching music. Lyman Beecher was disgusted by Charles's choice.

LYMAN : Charles has founded his determination on feeling, his plans on hopes, and his arguments on obstinacy.

NARRATOR : William secured a post at Putnam, Ohio, and he began working there, building a church and a school. He lasted at this job just a few years, resigning over a matter of principle, but a small one—a salary dispute. The pattern of William's life, paradoxically, was as principled and upright as those of his more famous brothers, yet all the Beecher qualities doomed him to failure. "What are we going to do with William?" was still asked in the Beecher house.

•

For two years, Henry, like Charles, remained a skeptic—but in his last year at Lane, Henry had a conversion experience.

HENRY : It came to me like the bursting forth of spring. It was as if yesterday there was not a bird to be seen or heard, and as if today the woods were full of singing birds. There rose up before me a view of Jesus as the Savior of sinners—not of saints, but of sinners unconverted, before they were any better—because they were so bad and needed so much; and that view has never gone from me. When I found that it was Christ's nature to lift me out of weakness to strength, out of impurity to goodness, out of everything low and debasing to superiority, I felt that I had found a God. From that hour I felt that God had a father's heart; that Christ loved me in my sin, and cared for me with unutterable tenderness. When that vision was vouchsafed to me I felt that there was no more for me to do but to love, trust, and adore.

I shall never forget the feelings with which I walked that morning. The golden pavements will never feel to my feet as then the grass felt to them; and the singing of the birds in the woods—for I roamed in the woods.

NARRATOR : And in his last months at Lane, he heard a nine-day debate between Rev. Alexander Campbell, later the founder of Disciples of Christ, and John B. Purcell, Catholic bishop of Cincinnati—and all the charges of papist plots seemed merely bigotry and prejudice. The talks showed him how religiously intolerant Calvinism had become.

•

In 1835, Harriet Porter Beecher, Lyman's second wife, and mother of Isabella, Thomas, and James, died.

In 1836, Lyman Beecher married a third time, to Mrs. Lydia Beals Jackson, who brought to the household two children, Joseph and Margaret, about James's age—and also two daughters who had already been married. Mrs. Jackson was a good organizer; her skills and energy proved useful in the busy Beecher household.

Harriet broke off a trip East when she learned that her friend Eliza Stowe died, so that she could comfort Calvin Stowe. Harriet and Calvin married in 1836. Calvin proved to be more manic-depressive than Harriet, but he was learned in Greek, Hebrew, Italian, and Arabic, a stimulating companion, as Harriet describes to Mary Dutton.

HARRIET : We are domestic as any pair of tame fowl you ever saw. And now, my dear, perhaps the wonder to you, as to me, is how this momentous crisis in the life of such a wisp of nerve as myself has been transacted so quietly. My dear, it is a wonder to myself. I am tranquil, quiet, and happy. I look only on the present and leave the future with Him who has hitherto been so kind to me.

•

NARRATOR : In mid-1836, James G. Birney, forced out of New Richmond, brought his anti-slavery weekly, *The Philanthropist*, to Cincinnati. The businessmen didn't approve; Southern buyers regularly came up during the summer, and on July 12, Birney's printer, Achilles Pugh, had his equipment damaged. Henry Ward Beecher was handling the editorship of the *Cincinnati Journal* at the time, and he printed a letter of Harriet's, under a pen name, calling for freedom of the press, but not touching on the issue of slavery.

Several prominent Cincinnatians, including Salmon P. Chase, organized a meeting, but anti-abolitionists took it over. On July 31, a mob demolished Pugh's press and threw it in the river. Mayor Davies at this point tried to disperse them, but they advanced on Franklin House, where Birney was staying. Salmon Chase raced ahead to bar the way—and he hadn't even met Birney.

Mayor Davies appeared in the doorway and said Birney wasn't there—and so the mob turned away, finally burning a few shacks in the black slums.

Next morning, when the mob reassembled, the mayor hurriedly swore in a posse authorized to shoot to kill. Henry went out with two pistols to volunteer. Harriet said, at the time:

HARRIET : For a day or two we did not know but there would actually be war to the knife, as was threatened by the mob, and we really saw Henry depart with his pistols with daily alarm, only we were all too full of patriotism not to have sent every brother we had rather than not have had the principles of freedom and order defended.

NARRATOR : Later, James G. Birney helped found the Liberty Party, and was their candidate for President in 1840 and 1844, drawing enough votes to swing at least one election.

In 1836, Catharine went on a speaking tour in the East to promote her call for teachers. She got a hundred names of missionary teachers, with promise of some funding to pay them with. Traveling agreed with her, and this new role linking East and West proved useful—because in the following year, the Cincinnati school failed. Harriet blamed Catharine for her inability to see projects through to their end; Mary Dutton also blamed her. Catharine quarreled with Harriet over small sums of money, and then left in the middle of the sale of the school property.

Catharine Beecher had a national reputation at this point, but she now had no school, and no means of starting one. For three years, she became simply a spinster aunt under the roof of Lyman Beecher. She was unable to act.

She formed a literary partnership with Harriet, and they wrote a book of moral instruction, arithmetic texts, and a book that finally gave her enough income to pursue her goals—the *Treatise on Domestic Economy*. In it, Catharine defined and elaborated on the home as the foundation of women's influence, the parlor as a podium for cultural change, the way the Beecher household always had been. Catharine Beecher had founded the new study of Home Economics.

THE FAMILY REUNION: 1
1835

The *Cincinnati Journal* of 1835 records a three-day Beecher family reunion at Walnut Hills, residence of Dr. Lyman Beecher, president of Lane Seminary and pastor of the Second Presbyterian Church of Cincinnati with his family of eleven children. Catharine, the oldest child, is 35, while James, the youngest, is 7. The occasion is Dr. Beecher's 60th birthday. A friend of the family gives his account of it:

HASTINGS : Long before Edward came out here the doctor tried to have a family meeting, but did not succeed. The children were too scattered. But—now just think of it—there has been a family meeting in Ohio. When Edward returned West, he brought on Mary from Hartford; William came down from Putnam, Ohio; George from Batavia, New York; Catharine and Harriet were here already; Henry and Charles at home too, besides Isabella, Thomas and James. These eleven The first time they all ever met together. Mary had never seen James, and she had seen Thomas but once.

Such a time as they had. The old doctor was almost transported with joy. The affair had been under negotiation for some time. He returned from Dayton late one Saturday evening. The next morning they, for the first time, assembled in the parlor. There were more tears than words. The doctor attempted to pray, but could scarcely speak. His full heart poured itself out in a flood of weeping. He could not go on. Edward continued, and each one, in his or her turn, uttered some sentences of thanksgiving. Then they began at the head and related their fortunes. After special prayer, all joined hands, and sang Old Hundred in these words:

From all who dwell below the skies.

Edward preached in his father's pulpit in the morning, William in the afternoon, and George in the evening. The family occupied the three front pews on the broad aisle. Monday morning they assembled, and, after reading and prayers, in which all joined, they formed a circle. The doctor stood in the middle, and gave them a thrilling speech. He then went round, and gave them each a kiss. They had a happy dinner.

Presents flowed in from all quarters. During the afternoon the house was filled with company, each bringing an offering. When left alone at evening they had a general examination of all their characters. The shafts of wit flew amain, the doctor being struck in several places; he was, however, expert enough to hit most of them in turn. From the uproar of the general battle, all must have been wounded.

Tuesday morning saw them together again, drawn up in a straight line for the inspection of the king of happy men. After receiving particular instructions, they formed into a circle. The doctor made a long and affecting speech. He felt that he stood for the last time in the midst of all his children, and each word fell with the weight of a patriarch's. He embraced them once more in all the tenderness of his big heart. Each took of all a farewell kiss. With joined hands they joined in a hymn. A prayer was offered; and finally, the parting blessing was spoken. Thus ended a meeting which can only be rivaled in that blessed home where the ransomed of the Lord, after weary pilgrimage, shall join in the Praise of the Lamb. May they all be there.

Truly the crown of old men is their children.

•

NARRATOR : Though the Beecher children have grown apart, often in disagreement, for these three days they set aside differences; the appearance is all of harmony.

Harriet Porter, Lyman Beecher's second wife, had recently died. Her children, the three youngest Beechers, Isabella, Thomas and James, feel a special bond among themselves. Isabella, or Belle, as she was often called, had come back from Hartford to be with her mother in her last illness—at 13, Belle is noticeably beautiful, the first beauty in the Beecher family.

Another natural grouping of Beechers is formed by the group that came from the East—Edward, who organized the caravan, Mary, a social matron in Hartford, George and William are the oldest of the male Beechers, and Catharine the eldest, who is already part of the household.

Then, there is the middle group of Beechers, the group that would yield the most famous Beechers of all—Harriet Beecher Stowe and Henry Ward Beecher, and Charles. But there is no easy way of categorizing a Beecher—of these eleven, only one, Mary, did not pursue a career of ther own. Every male Beecher eventually became a minister, and the remaining female Beechers were carving out independent lives for themselves: in education, literature, and feminism.

Henry and Harriet are the oldest still at home, except for Catharine, who is often out and around, on school business. Lyman, of course, is always busy—as seminary president and professor, as pastor, and at civic functions.

Now we listen as the Beechers catch up on the recent news.

LYMAN : I have felt and thought, and labored a great deal about each of you, you who are present in my house, and you who have established your own families elsewhere. I have pondered, argued with some of you, how your souls may be ready, even though you be far from me then, since at any moment eternity may stretch before you. Sadly, it has done so for our dear mother Harriet these past months. I know and love you all and each, more especially now that you have but one parent, and he an old man.

HARRIET : Father, you are not old.

LYMAN : I'm certainly not done with this life, not when there's so much to do. But hear me, children all. It is but a happy chance to be together again these few days—we may not see a day like this again, not a family day.

GEORGE : D'you know what they say of you in New York, Father? D'you know they say you're the father of more brains than anyone in America. Ha, ha.

LYMAN : Well, well, but it's not me they're talking about, George, it's you, all of you. I can't say how proud I am to see how well you've all turned out—George and William preaching, Catharine and Edward teaching, Henry and Charles studying—you should hear this lad Henry orate to the trees out back—do you remember, he used to be so thick of speech that Aunt Esther thought he was speaking Choctaw. Do you remember?

CATHARINE : Enlarged palate or no, the lad couldn't be stopped.

His constant prattle was a great amusement to us.

HARRIET : Oh, yes, and the catechism? The rest of us memorized readily and were brilliant reciters. But Henry was blushing, stammering, confused and hopelessly miserable. He would get stuck fast on some sand-bank of what is required or forbidden by this or that commandment, and then his mouth would choke up with the long words. He was sure to be accused of idleness or inattention and to be solemnly talked to, which made him look more stolid and miserable than ever.

HENRY : I was bashful—well, I still am, you know, I have no verbal memory at all. But even just to walk into a room where company was assembled and to do it erectly and naturally, was as impossible as it would have been to fly. My backbone grew soft, my knees lost their stiffness, and blood rushed to the head and the sight almost left my eyes.

CATHARINE : That's why you sent him to my school, wasn't it? I will confess here publicly that my teaching did him as much good as yours, Lyman Beecher.

LYMAN : Well said, dear Catharine. But listen to him now, you would not recognize him. Our Henry Ward may yet become a preacher—at least Professor Stowe is of that opinion.

HARRIET : That dear man—if any of you have a chance to meet him and his dear wife Eliza, do. He is a veritable encyclopedia of lore, knows Arabic and Hebrew, but not a bit of carpentry.

LYMAN : Charles is our student, too, aren't you, Charles?

CHARLES : Yes—after Bowdoin, Lane Seminary is quite an interesting place, even though Weld is long gone. I still have doubts, though, I...

EDWARD : Weld, isn't that Theodore Weld, the one who led the students off to Oberlin?

LYMAN : Let's get together later, Charles.

Weld? He certainly did, almost ruined the school. Weld was a genius. No doubt about that. A man about thirty, he'd followed Charles Grandison Finney—remember Finney? That's the revivalist who was grandstanding all over upstate New York, until I challenged him—told him not to cross into my territory in Connecticut or else. And he didn't. He's calmed down since those days, I hear, and is a bit more careful not to undermine the good work already done.

HENRY : I've heard him speak; he's quite powerful. Grandiloquent. Bit of a ham, I'd say.

LYMAN : Oh, your anti-slavery societies are on the whole a good idea—but Cincinnati, as we have found out, haven't we, Catharine, is on the edge, on the very edge about this whole issue. It's not New England, this Western territory. No, you just look out the window there, the southern exposure, right across the Ohio River there, that's a different proposition, Kentucky. A different proposition.

GEORGE : That's why we have to do everything we can to bring about abolition. Slavery is wrong. There's no two ways about it.

EDWARD : Let's examine this a little more closely, George. I will agree with you that slavery is wrong—and I think Father will too—am I right?

LYMAN : Right. Very right.

EDWARD : Then our duty lies in determining how best to deal with the situation.

CATHARINE : Or how best to bring about changes.

THOMAS : Colonization or Abolition.

EDWARD : Gradual or immediate emancipation.

HARRIET : Still, it does shock one to realize that it isn't like having Zillah and Rachel as "bound girls" as we did in Litchfield. Father and I've gone on little trips into Kentucky, and it's not normal.

CATHARINE : Even in Litchfield, dear Harriet, some of our Connecticut neighbors were still slave owners, though the practice was dying out. Don't forget that I remember ten years earlier than you.

HARRIET : But in Kentucky, you can be having a perfectly fine day, and then hear the most horrid dreadful, oh—they're property, people talk about them as if they were pieces of furniture or sheepdogs.

GEORGE : It's not right. It's just not right.

LYMAN : Let not your anger carry you beyond your goal, George. Year by year I see Synod become ever more divisive over this issue.

HENRY : Colonization merely moves the problem. There's no solution to slavery except freedom. We debated this my sophomore year, and I've settled my mind on it.

MARY : Endless, this discussion is endless. We came together to honor our father on his sixtieth birthday, not to wrangle among ourselves. We would do well to use the precious little time we have together more usefully.

LYMAN : Mary's right. Let us renew our ties face to face—since lately several of you have been struck by that disease of the right hand called the no-letters-home palsy. We will go round by precedence—eldest first, and ending with the one with least news—isn't that right, James? James! Where is that lad?

HARRIET : James, Jamey, dear Come in, you're wanted. He'll be along.

CATHARINE : Before we begin, Father, let me make a proposal. Now that we are so widespread across the whole country up to Louisiana Territory, and since postage is charged by the mile, let us make up a packet, each adding as it goes along the line.

EDWARD : They also charge by the sheet, sister Catharine. We may begin with a large blank folio sheet, each adding to it.

THOMAS : And when it's filled, write sideways and fill it again And your address may be to "Rev. Mr. Beecher." By next year or so, even Henry and Charles—that'll make six—will answer to that form of address.

LYMAN : Isn't he a quick study, Edward? Better watch out—you've only got 20 years on this lad. He may catch up with you, as on some days—at eleven years old—he's way ahead of me.

No, I say welcome another bright Beecher. I tell you lad, if you don't know it already, there's never enough brains wherever you turn, never enough thinking men in this country.

ISABELLA : Or thinking women, brother dear.

CATHARINE : Bravo, sister Belle. Intelligence does not grow only on one side of the family.

MARY : Nor beauty. Have any of you taken a good look at our Belle since you arrived. Belle, you were just a Hartford schoolgirl, was it only a year or two ago? How old are you, Isabella?

ISABELLA : Thirteen.

MARY : Well now, just look at you. Belle, if you came to live with me, Mr. Perkins and I could bring you out into the best Hartford society. No, I mean it.

HARRIET : I'm afraid you tried with me and failed, Mary.

MARY : Harriet, you were never interested in men, or society, not in that way. My dear Hattie, your gift is too precious to be buried in a family life. You might be another Lydia Sigourney, or Mrs. Southworth.

HARRIET : Another of the scribbling tribe of women writers, as Mr. Hawthorne puts it.

CATHARINE : It's true. She's published regularly in James Hall's *Western Monthly Magazine*. And her pieces at the Semi-Colon Club are hits.

LYMAN : Hits? My Hattie writes violence?

CATHARINE : No, they are enthusiastically received, Father. Theatrical hits; they hit the mark.

GEORGE : Say, we were going to give our news, starting with the oldest. Catharine?

THOMAS : No, there's yet one older than Catharine here, who should speak first.

LYMAN : Well, Thomas, and who is that?

THOMAS : You, Father. Tell them about your heresy trial.

EDWARD : Yes, we are anxious to hear whether or no we are sired by a heretic.

THOMAS : Are you New School or Old School heretic, Father?

GEORGE : Or is it none other than Beecherism—that one, I've heard, is pretty hard to disprove.

LYMAN : Yes, that's a devlishly difficult predicament to get out of. Fortunately for all of you, it's not been shown to be heretical—though it is incurable.

CHARLES : Then, I for one say hurrah for Beecherism But do, Father, tell them.

LYMAN : Well, it's not a short story, such as Harriet might write. I'll tell you what—I'll go in pieces, alternating with you, until the last one of you drops of incapacity to hear. Then we'll continue on the morrow. Agreed?

ALL : Agreed.

•

LYMAN : Well, as you know from reading the papers, Dr. Joshua Wilson, of the First Presbyterian Church here in Cincinnati, brought against me charges of heresy. This wasn't the first time he'd crossed my path.

When the trial came on, I took all my books and sat down on the second stair of the pulpit. It was in my church. I looked so quiet and meek my students were almost afraid I shouldn't come up to the mark. I had everything just then to weigh me down. My wife was lying at home on her death bed. She did not live a fortnight after that. Then there was all the wear and tear of the seminary and of my congregation. But when I had all my references and had nothing to do but extemporize, I felt easy. I had as much lawyer about me as Wilson and more. I never got into a corner and he never got out, though the fact is he made as good a case as could be made on the wrong side.

We had a good working majority, and the atmosphere was congenial and cordial, everything safe and smiling. We had to count noses every time there was a meeting of Presbytery or Synod, and keep a sharp lookout about absentees.

Wilson attacked me for abandoning the standards. I said no, and gave what I deemed the right exposition, subject to the revision of the General Assembly, which must be the final interpreter. Soon after, in his speech, he said I claimed a right to adopt the Creeds, and put my own construction on them. I corrected him, putting in the statement respecting General Assembly. Five minutes after he repeated it again, and I corrected him again. A third time the same thing over, and I corrected him as before. At this he scolded, and said he did not wish to be interrupted so, as it hindered him.

"Dr. Wilson," said I, "this is the third time you have misrepresented me, and I shall correct you until you put it right. You shall not go ahead from this point till you do it"; and he quailed, notwithstanding his hardihood.

He did not know what he undertook. I knew to a hair's breadth every point between Old School and New School, and knew all their difficulties, and how to puzzle with them. In Presbytery he had only inferior men on his side. He knew they were fools. There was not another man equal to Wilson on his side, nor anywhere near it. On our side the trial was as strong as possible, and everybody exulted with great exultation. So they laughed at him, even some Old Schoolish folks, and called him a dead man. Presbytery acquitted me and he appealed to Synod.

Well, so. Catharine?

•

CATHARINE : You all know of my schools—in Hartford, and here in Cincinnati—so watch out, you young Beechers, or you'll be sent to sister Catharine's.

ISABELLA : It's a good school; you learn things that matter there.

CATHARINE : I should hope so. Schools for women are extremely important—especially here in the West. Yet in the course of affairs, I have been led to spend most of my energies fund-raising. In order to build character, a school need be a boarding establishment; moral training is essential, and cannot be achieved in any other way. But the additional buildings and facilities for feeding and housing a student body simply costs a great deal of money.

GEORGE : Oh, yes, I remember the argument in your book on *Mental and Moral Philosophy.*

HARRIET : Catharine taught it as a course first.

CATHARINE : With some mighty tutoring by dear brother Edward, for which I thank him.

EDWARD : You're welcome.

GEORGE : You put forth some rather interesting propositions,

Catharine. Morality, you say, exists independently of God, and therefore it may—indeed must—be taught. That idea, applied to women's education, yields surprising conclusions, for instance, your opposition to a refined education, such as the kind that Lydia Sigourney used in her school.

CATHARINE : A woman should study, not to shine but to act. To come out in conduct, education must shape a young woman's principles and the formation of her habits. Public sentiment has advanced so much on the subject of female culture that a course of study very similar to that pursued by young men in our public institutions is demanded for young ladies of the higher circles. But facilities and teaching techniques are vastly inferior in girls' schools.

Writing has also absorbed much of my time, at the Semi-Colon Club, and on literary evenings at Daniel Drake's. I sold my story "Fanny Moreland" to one of the Christmas annuals—but Harriet takes the palm. Do you know that Harriet has earned $300 to my $30 this past year.

HARRIET : I do it for the pay.

CATHARINE : And that's the professional difference. I can see that I shall have to stick to education.

EDWARD : You might mention your theological debates via letter with myself and Charles. I don't know if you realize how seriously Charles takes these positions you take.

CATHARINE : I should hope he does.

LYMAN : By the way, Edward, did you happen to see that article on "Cause and Effect in Connection with the Doctrines of Fatalism and Free Agency"?

EDWARD : Yes, Catharine, that hit the very point you wrote to us about a few months ago. I don't know the author, but the reviewer remarked on his "sincere love of the truth, intelligence, humility, candor…"

LYMAN : *Her* love of truth.

CHARLES : That anonymous piece—yours? Catharine, no one doubts your capacity for thought, least of all myself. Yet there are limits.

CATHARINE : Talk to me of limits! Why is it that I must take a man along to give my speeches, or why I must write serious articles anonymously?

My schools will overcome those limits. And you can too—you, Edward, are president of Illinois College. When will you two hard-headed brothers recognize that the future will be no more than deterioration if we do nothing to change it?

EDWARD : Persistence, dear sister. You know that lesson already. How you manage to create such enterprises as you propose, is a mystery to me.

CATHARINE : Persistence, and a firm understanding of the true foundations of power. I'll tell you the secret of my fund-raising in Hartford: I go to the parents of the girls in my school, and to the wives of prominent men attending Joel Hawes' church, the oldest and most conservative in Hartford. It was my first experience of the moral power and good judgment of American women, and they have been my chief reliance ever since.

But I will say frankly that Cincinnati is a harder nut to crack than Hartford. The Western Literary Institute and College of Professional Teachers will let me sit but not speak, when fully half of them—all men—have nothing to say at all.

ISABELLA : Not speak? But what of your books, your New York speech, the call for female teachers?

CATHARINE : Cincinnati likes to think of itself as the "London of the West," not lacking in anything that us Yankees might have to offer.

LYMAN : Oh, how you twist my own words back on me. Did I say "London of the West," truly?

CATHARINE : Truly you did, Father.

GEORGE : What New York speech? What call? What have you been up to, Catharine?

ISABELLA : Yes, it was published in one of the papers: *Miss Catharine Beecher Speaking at the American Lyceum, an Essay on the Education of Female Teachers.* A third of the children without schools, 90,000 teachers needed. Women teachers.

EDWARD : Are you sure of your figures? 90,000 seems extreme.

CATHARINE : Edward, I do not exaggerate. Don't you recall Father's famous—"If we gain the West, all is safe; if we lose it, all is lost"? This Ohio and Mississippi Valley is filling every day with immigrants.

Oh, you're no better than the nabobs of Cincinnati, who pin the blame for anti-slavery ideas on Dr. Lyman Beecher because some of his seminary students mingled with black folk.

LYMAN : And don't forget the unexpurgated version of *Plea for the West*. What I said in Boston about Westerners' backwardness ws simply to raise money; it was one of my most telling points. No, the *Western Monthly* found me out fair and square, and reprinted all the deletions. That they take it amiss here is quite understandable, if uncomfortable for me.

HARRIET : You should all know, if no one has told you before, that you're in a hotbed of social dissension and anti-slavery propaganda, according to the current gossip. Catharine has placed herself at center-stage, as usual. As soon as Daniel Drake sided with James Hall, Catharine started her own campaign to ostracize them. It went quite the other way round.

CATHARINE : How can I not side with Father? What is it worth to be a Beecher?

LYMAN : Worthy of notice, that you can warrant. But tell them of old Edward King's letter, Cate. Priceless. That old Federalist aristocrat was unbent as stone in Catharine's storm.

CATHARINE : Belle, be a good girl and fetch the letter from the post in the kitchen, will you? Yes, you can all have a chuckle over it now, but mind you, this letter and others like it have made my job of raising enough money for the school well-nigh impossible.

HARRIET : I can vouch for that; we're dangerously low now, Cate.

CATHARINE : You'll manage. Give it a little time.

ISABELLA : Here it is, Catharine.

THOMAS : Let me read it, please, please, please.

LYMAN : All right. Now bear in mind that this man is writing to his wife—to his wife, whom he sees every day.

THOMAS : Tell Catharine Beecher that she is a guest and not a director in our home. Tell all the Beechers that if they choose to visit and partake when invited, it is well, but not as our advisors as to when and who and with whom they are to mingle at our fireside. Now our policy is to be above such matters, not even to seem to know them.

CATHARINE : All right, that's enough of me...

EDWARD : Amen.

LYMAN : And it's Amen for me, too. These old bones must lay in a heap till morn. Welcome, all, to Cincinnati. Does everyone have a place and blankets? Yes? Charles, we must put off our talk till morning. All you younger Beechers chatter till you burst. Goodnight all.

The Family Reunion: 2
1835

NARRATOR : The Beecher family reunion in Cincinnati is in full swing. All eleven children have come to help Lyman Beecher celebrate his sixtieth birthday, and his successful defense at his heresy trial.

It is early morning on the second day. Lyman Beecher is in his study, watching out the window for the sunrise. His son Charles, the doubtful one, comes to the door.

LYMAN : Come in, Charles. I've been thinking about you. Am I wrong to think that you are questioning your course of study?

CHARLES : My life, father.

LYMAN : Calvin Stowe has mentioned a certain hesitancy on your part about the ministry.

CHARLES : I'm not fit, that's all. I never will be. I'm not like you, or Edward, or George, or even William.

LYMAN : It's not the same with anyone else, Charles. We guess, we observe, we suggest—that's all. Let me tell you how it was with me.

CHARLES : All right.

LYMAN : It was not before the middle of my junior year that I was really awakened. Up to then I had only a traditionary knowledge; alive without the law; sense of sin all outward; ignorant as a beast of the state of my heart, and its voluntary spiritual state toward God. Sound familiar?

CHARLES : Yes, yes—go on.

LYMAN : One day, as we were sitting at home, Mother looked out of the window, and saw a drunkard passing, "Poor man," said she. "I hope he'll receive all his punishment in this life. He was under conviction once, and thought he had religion; but he's nothing but a poor drunkard now."

There was no perceptible effect from these words, only, after she left the room, I felt a sudden impulse to pray. It was but a breath across the surface of my soul. I was not in the habit of prayer—yes, Charles, it's true. But I rose to pray, and had not spoken five words before I was under as deep a conviction as ever I was in this life. The sinking of the shaft was instantaneous. I understood the law and my heart as well as I do now, or shall in the day of judgment, I believe. The commandment came, sin revived, and I died, quick as a flash of lightning.

"Well," I thought, "it's all over with me. I'm gone. There's no hope for such a sinner." Despair followed the inward revelation of what I had read, but never felt. I had never had any feeling of love to God, and all my affections were selfish and worldly.

After a while that entireness of despair—for I was sure I was lost, as I deserved—lessened so that I could pray without weeping; and then I began to hope I was growing good. Then my motives in praying came up before me, and I saw there was no true love in them. I then tried reformation, but seemed no better. God let down light into the dark places, and showed me there was no change of character. I turned away from this self-righteousness, and turned in, and laid hold of my heart like a giant to bring it round so as to pray aright, but could not. Couldn't make a right prayer with a wrong heart. Worked away at that till I gave up. Then Election tormented me. I fell into a dark, sullen, unfeeling state that finally affected my health.

I can see now that if I had had the instruction I give to inquirers, I should have come out bright in a few days. Mine was what I should now call a hopeful, promising case. Old Samuel Hopkins had just such an awakening, and was tormented a great while. The fact is, the law and doctrines, without any explanation, is a cruel way to get souls into the kingdom. It entails great suffering, especially on thinking minds, such as yours, Charles.

CHARLES : If I were able to attain such a state. I doubt even that.

LYMAN : Anyway, during all this struggle I had no guidance but the sermons of Dr. Dwight. When I heard him preach on "The harvest is past, the summer is ended, and we are not saved," a whole avalance rolled down on my mind. I went home weeping every step. One reason I was so long in the dark was, I was under law, was stumbling in the doctrines, and had no views of Christ. They gave me other books to read besides the Bible—a thing I have done practising long since.

For cases like mine, Brainerd's *Life* is a most undesirable thing. It gave me a tinge for years. So Edwards on the *Affections*—a most overwhelming thing, and to common minds the most entangling. The impressions left by such books were not spiritual, but a state of permanent hypochondria—the horrors of a mind without guidance, motive, or ability to do anything. They are a bad generation of books, on the whole. Divine sovereignty does the whole in spite of them. I was converted in spite of such books.

Charles, I wish I could give you my clinical theology. I have used my evangelical philosophy all my lifetime, and relieved people without number out of the sloughs of high Calvinism.

It was many months that I suffered; and, finally, the light did not come in a sudden blaze, but by degrees. I began to see more into the doctrines of the Bible. Election and decrees were less a stumbling-block. I came in by that door. I felt reconciled and resigned, yet with alternations of darkness and discouragement, and a severe conflict whether it would be right for me to preach, which extended even into my Divinity year.

Come, Charles, I hear feet stirring down below, in the kitchen. Breakfast'll be sizzling in the pan.

CHARLES : Thank you for your concern about me, Father. I appreciate everything, though at times I may seem ungrateful.

LYMAN : Let it come, Charles. There are so many ways of making it hard on yourself.

•

NARRATOR : Now Lyman Beecher and his eleven children gather around for the second day, each telling their recent histories. Catharine, the oldest, has finished her tale, and William, the eldest son, is next.

CATHARINE : So, shall we begin with William, or continue with the famous heresy trail?

LYMAN : Go ahead, William.

WILLIAM : There's not a lot to tell. I'm the new pastor at

Putnam, Ohio, which is a very small town with ambitions to become a small town. I have a wife, Katherine, and a family. We live simply. Putnam doesn't even have a church building yet, so my work is double.

GEORGE : And where were you before?

WILLIAM : Newport, Rhode Island. Middletown, Connecticut. In Middletown, the old pastor returned and asked for his post again. They gave it to him. Not much more to say.

LYMAN : Yes, William spent a little time with us here in Cincinnati before being posted to Putnam. Now that William is indeed gone from the fold, Henry is the oldest son still at home.

Let me continue on about my trial at Synod—you only heard the opening chapter last night. We've barely begun to thicken the plot.

HENRY : Ah, but before we arrive at Synod, we first must undertake to leave. Now, this might seem like a solemn day to some, but this man, our father, manages to make every day extraordinary. Picture a slightly wet day, everyone bringing down boxes and cases until all are assembled under a large beech tree.

At length we are ready to start for Synod. A trunk tumbles out of one side as Thomas tumbles in the other. At length all are aboard and Father drives out of the yard, holding the reins in one hand, shaking hands with a student with the other, giving Charles directions with his mouth—at least that part not occupied with an apple; for, since apples are plenty, he had made it a practice to drive with one rein in the right hand and the other in the left, with an apple in each, biting them alternately, thus raising and lowering the reins like threads on a loom. Away we go, Charles's horse on the full canter down the long hill, the carriage bouncing and bounding over the stones, Father alternately telling Tom how to get the harness mended, and showing me the true doctrine of original sin. Hurrah We thunder alongside the boat just in time, and we walk in the door with at least twenty minutes extra.

•

LYMAN : Anyway, when I got there and looked around, I thought the vote would run very close. My Presbytery, being appealed from, could not vote. The Old School had raked and scraped all the old dead churches where they could get an elder, and thought they might carry the day. It looked squally.

When Wilson got up and made his speech—the best he ever did make, as he misrepresented things—it made the issue look dubious. The house grew dark; it didn't look dark to me; I knew what artillery I had got; I had some letters of his as a kind of masked battery. But there was an Old School majority, and his speech made a sensation.

There was one time, though, he came near getting overset; it came near terminating the trial. Previously, in his argument before Presbytery, he had said that man has no ability of any kind to obey God's commands. At the time, I told him then he was the first man I ever knew to march boldly up to that without flinching, and I praised him for his courage.

But the fact was, that did not set well on Princeton. They wrote to him. Dr. Miller wrote—tutored him—hints, you know. He found he had gone too far; it was too rank. He undertook to change front. He went on, and changed his phraseology, and stated what he did hold. I jumped up and said, "Dr. Wilson, that is precisely what I believe; let's have no more trials; give me your hand" He was astounded—hung back. We adjourned till afternoon, and it lacked but a hair's breadth of his giving up the case.

When my turn came, I went on from one point to another, and by-the-by the tide turned; and when the time came to vote, there was a majority against him of ten to one.

They came round me like bees, some that had been on his side, as cordial as could be. The next day, when Wilson came in in the morning, he was as pale as a ghost—first time I ever saw him look down. He said he did not know what course he should take—whether to appeal to General Assembly or not; but finally he grew stronger, and appealed.

Edward, Edward, let me catch my breath. Tell us of the far West, Illinois.

•

EDWARD : As of a month ago, when I left to travel East for fundraising, my college was thriving. It's a small school, really, but abuilding.

You know, Father, I sympathize with your plight here as a target of both pro-slavery and anti-slavery elements. My position is somewhat the same. As a college president, I am expected to serve as a model for the community, but Jacksonville is so near the Mississippi that the slave trade on the river cannot but affect our whole community.

It took me all of three years to secure a charter for the school from the Illinois legislature, so unsure were they of the value or necessity for an institution of higher education.

Up to last year, I avoided direct involvement with the anti-slavery movement, while following the abolitionist debates closely. Now, I have joined Elijah Lovejoy in calling for the first Illinois state anti-slavery convention. The issue now is freedom of speech, freedom of the press.

HENRY : So, you too are an abolitionist.

GEORGE : Hurrah.

LYMAN : Now, let's not get started on that; matters of individual conscience are not to be pried into so lightly.

GEORGE : If it were only so easy as conscience.—

HENRY : Nay, it is. We shall educate and educate this nation until slavery dies away, just as it did in the North.

But let's let Mary tell her news, she's next oldest.

•

MARY : I'm not like you, Catharine; oh, I may have helped you in the Hartford school, and even tended business while you were away. But mine is no career, but a wonderful life with Thomas Clap Perkins, an outstanding attorney even in Hartford. I have four children, who take up all my time. Yet I can claim no small distinction in the circles we move in. Thomas's career has brought us into contact with prominent citizens and wealthy ones. Belle, I do not speak to boast, but I have learned so much that I could teach you. Do come back East with me; Father, may she come?

LYMAN : Mary, you should ask Isabella. So, Belle, have you slept on Mary's kind offer? We will miss you if you go, but somehow we'll manage. Isn't that right, Hattie?

HARRIET : Yes. Do tell us, Belle.

ISABELLA : Mary, I would be pleased to come to live with you in Hartford.

LYMAN : Well, then, it's settled. Bravo. You'll have some news for our next reunion, eh?

CATHARINE : Who's next? George?

•

GEORGE : I have naught to say, except I'm installed at Batavia, New York, having been ordained here not so long ago. For a short time I was principal of Lawrence Academy in Boston.

HARRIET : Now, if any of you have missed an ordination, here's your chance to hear George's.

CATHARINE : Father, this was one of Harriet's "hits" at the Semi-Colon Club, a dramatic reading of a rather dry session, you'll admit, once you hear it.

HARRIET : We'll begin in media res: We will go into the side aisle; all the body pews are engaged by the Presbytery. Do you see them all seated en masse, each one with the *Confession of Faith* by nearby, to turn to at a moment's warning?

That handsome, modest, amiable-looking young man in the chair in front of the pulpit is Brother Rankin, the moderator. He was an Old School man once; for a long time lately he has been wavering; this Presbytery he was nominated and appointed by the New School Party, and this, together with the abuse received from the other side, has fixed him, and he is now counted on as a vote. At a table sits Brother Graves, the recording secretary, with paper, pen, and ink. The meeting has not begun. Some are walking about, some talking, some reading.

At last the moderator calls the meeting to order. They proceed to business. They are to examine a candidate. The candidate is Mr. George Beecher, a New School man; but that is not the worst—a Taylorite.

Do you see, in the front pew, a tall, grave-looking man, of strong and rather harsh features, very pale, with a severe seriousness of face, and with great formality and precision in every turn and motion? Well, if you see him, that man is Dr. Wilson. His great ivory-headed cane leans on the side of the pew by him, and in his hand he holds the *Confession of Faith*.

The candidate sits on the pulpit stairs, so that he may face the Presbytery, and the examining committee are called on: Dr. Wilson, in Philosophy. Here follows, "Mr. Beecher, what is matter and what is mind, and what is the difference twixt and tween, and what is Mechanics, and Optics, and Hydrostatics, and what is Mental Philosophy, and what is Moral Philosophy, and what is right and wrong, and what is truth, and what is virtue, and what are the powers of the mind, and what is intellect, susceptibilities, and will, and conscience"—and everything else, world without end, amen After this the doctor's grave face gradually relaxes into a smile, which seems like the melting of a snow-drift as he says that he has "pursued this branch of the examination as far as might be deemed expedient."

"Mr. Moderator," says one, "I move that the examination be sustained." "I second it," says another.

The moderator then says, "Those who sustain this examination say Ay."

Now hark—"Ay ay ay"

"Those of contrary mind, No." No answer. So this is over.

Next topic is announced: "Theology" Now you may see the brethren bending forward, and shuffling, and looking wise. Over in the pew opposite to us are the students of the Lane Seminiary, with attentive eyes. There is Theodore Weld, all awake, nodding from side to side, and scarce keeping still a minute together.

"The examiner in Theology, Brother Gallagher." This is the great Goliath, whose awful brows and camp-meeting hymns used so to awe and edify me. He rises very leisurely, and gives a lunge forward, precipitating his unwieldy size into a chair without much regard to graceful disposition, and with a deep, deliberate voice begins.

The beauty of it all is that Gallagher is a warm friend to George, and of similar sentiments. The appointing him to examine was a friendly motion of the moderator. He confined his examination merely to the broad and obvious truths of Christianity, and then sat down.

But now comes the fiery trial. The moderator announces, "Any of the brethren have a right to question the candidate." You must have been before now some of them fidgeting on their seats, and waiting their turn. Then such a storm of questions rains in:

"Mr. Beecher, do you believe in the doctrine of election? Will you please to state your views on that subject?" "Mr. Beecher, do you believe in the imputation of Adam's sin?" "Mr. Beecher, do you believe infants are sinners as soon as they are born?" "Do you believe that infants have unholy natures?" "Do you believe that men are able of themselves to obey the commandments of God?" "Mr. Beecher, do you believe men are active or passive in regeneration?" "Mr. Beecher, do you make any distinction between regeneration and conversion?" "Mr. Beecher, do you think that men are punished for the guilt of Adam's first sin?" "Do you believe in imputed righteousness?"

There was George—eyes flashing and hands going, turning first to right and then to left—"If I understand your question, sir—" "I do not understand your terms, sir." "Do you mean by nature thus and so? or so?" "In what sense do you use the word imputation?" "I don't exactly understand you, sir." "Yes, sir" (to right). "No, sir" (to left). "I should think so, sir" (in front).

EDWARD : I missed this examination by a day.

HARRIET : Yes, you poked in like a ghost upon us just afterward.

LYMAN : The first that I knew of it was seeing you go by the window, and exclaiming, "There's a man looks like Edward" and the next minute there you were, standing among us.

HARRIET : And then you all had a long chat, until at last Father and Edward went down cellar to saw wood. Don't that seem natural. I heard the word "foreordination" through the parlor floor, so I knew what they were talking about. Oh, it seemed like old times.

HENRY : Hattie, why don't you finish your account? Some of us might learn something of value for the near future.

HARRIET : Someone named Henry or Charles, perhaps? Well, the examination lasted nearly two hours and a half, after which the further consideration of that subject was postponed till examination had taken place in other branches. The next day the

Presbytery were called upon to see if they had any remarks to make upon the examination thus far. Then such a war of words

The discussion lasted all day. In the evening we came, and they went at it again. All the Presbytery had finished their remarks except Father and Dr. Wilson, who, as the oldest, came last on the list. Father, as first called on, rose, and went through a regular statement of what he conceived to be the views expressed by the candidate, and a regular argument to show that they were in agreement with the *Confession of Faith*. He spoke well, clearly, and persuasively, and was occasionally a little humorous.

When Father sat down Dr. Wilson rose up, and made a speech of about half an hour, in which he stated that he believed that the candidate was not a Christian, and knew nothing experimentally about Christianity, and that he finally believed that he, and all those who held the same sentiments with him "would never see the gates of eternal bliss." Many people say that it is altogether the mildest and most temperate speech they ever heard him make.

After this speech the question was taken, though with much difficulty and opposition; and on calling the roll, the examination was sustained by a majority of 23.

About 12 o'clock at night we found ourselves once more at home and in a state of high excitement, and sat up about half an hour longer to fight over the battle to Catharine, who had not been able to go out.

GEORGE : So now you know what I've been doing. Don't everybody jump on me for saying this, but isn't it Harriet's turn?

•

HARRIET : Oh, but there's very little to say about me. I won a fifty dollar prize for writing, and I help Catharine in her school. But mostly I write.

Some projects with Catharine will be schoolbooks; I also publish in the Christmas annuals. Some sketches may go together to make a book of history.

LYMAN : The hour is getting late; you young ones ought to be getting up to bed.

THOMAS : Not until you finish the trial story—please.

LYMAN : Well, all right. Where was I? Just before the appeal to General Assembly came on at Pittsburgh, I sent two or three dozens of the report of my trial up to be distributed in the Pittsburgh Synod. When I got there they flocked round me. "Why, your doctrine is just that of our great favorite, Dr. So-and-so, and we are not going to see you hung." The third day of the session, Dr. Wilson rose and said he was prepared to prosecute the appeal, but that his friends had told him they could not sustain him, and he was willing to withdraw.

That, however, depended on my consent. I rose and said meekly that I was ready for trial, but that if Dr. Wilson wanted to cease, I supposed that, according to the Book, after being dragged through all the Church courts, I had a right to claim that my prosecutor ought to be treated as I should have been if condemned.

Dr. Wilson bounded from his seat and blazed out—he had no concessions or confessions to make.

And that is the end of the story. Your father is no heretic. Period. Now skedaddle. Up, up, up with you.

As for the rest, you may stay and talk as long as you please. This old head needs a pause in this remarkable day, in this fretful year. Good night all, and good rest.

ALL : Good night, good night, Father.

HENRY : Come into the parlor, Edward, George—you too, William— we'll get into this abolitionist affair some more. Catharine?

CATHARINE : Not I. Come, Hattie, I want to find out how the school has been progressing.

ISABELLA : Can I come, too?

HARRIET : For a time, Belle.

ALTON
1834–1837

West of Cincinnati, Edward Beecher had established himself as president of Illinois College in Jacksonville, Illinois. Events were to place Edward at the center of controversy as he and his generation faced the great question of slavery.

Most of the Beechers still lived in or near Cincinnati, where Lyman Beecher was president of Lane Seminary. Harriet had recently been married to one of Lyman's professors, the erudite Calvin Stowe, and Henry was acting editor of the *Cincinnati Journal*, and was soon to be ordained.

Slavery had simply died out in New England—the few slaves in Litchfield, where most of the Beechers had grown up, were quite old by the time the older Beecher chldren knew them. The Beecher household had included two black "bound girls" for kitchen help, but that was by negotiable contract, not involuntary servitude.

But booming Cincinnati was a border town on the great Ohio River—when the spiritual mentioned "crossing over Jordan," the Ohio was meant. Slaves were often transported down the river to the great New Orleans slavemarket serving the deep South plantations. Slavery was a fact, and merchants and consumers alike had no interest in crippling the region's economy. Abolitionists in the 1830s had to face indifference and hostility, sometimes even violence, for simply bringing up the subject. Freedom of speech was the first hurdle. Actually abolishing slavery was seen by both sides as a future possiblity, or perhaps not possible at all.

Lyman Beecher's view of slavery came mainly through church politics. In 1837, the Old School faction finally broke up the union of Presbyterians and Congregationalists. New School ministers, including the Beechers, formed a new assembly.

LYMAN : The South had generally stood neutral ... but they got scared about abolition. Rice of Virginia got his head full of that thing, and others. John C. Calhoun was at the bottom of it. I know of his doing things—writing to ministers and telling them to do this and do that. The South finally took the Old School side. It was a cruel thing—it was a cursed thing, and 'twas slavery that did it.

.

NARRATOR : The July 1837 Presbyterian General Assembly split the church, as the Old School wing cast out four abolitionist synods. Charles Beecher explains.

CHARLES : It may not be clear at first why slavery and theology should go hand in hand, in national affairs. But if we reflect that theology is but another name for the politics of the universe, or the kingdom of God, the problem becomes simple. Two systems or schools of theology were contending, called at that time Old School and New School. The former enthrones absolutism, the latter constitutionalism. According to the one, things are right because God wills them, according to others God wills them because they are right. Old School theology enthrones a great slave holder over the universe; New School enthrones a great Emancipator

NARRATOR : Those politicians who tackled the issue of slavery mainly tried to establish a middle ground between the newly articulate abolitionist movement of William Lloyd Garrison, John Greenleaf Whittier, and the New England intellectuals on the one hand, and the Southern apologists—Hayne of South Carolina, Vice President Calhoun, and others.

Calhoun had elaborated a case for the right of states to nullify acts of Congress—in 1828 he was aiming to defeat the Protectionist Tariff Bill. Hayne took up the cause, and Daniel Webster of Massachusets replied to Hayne's challenge with a resounding speech on "Liberty AND Union, now and forever." This debate settled the immediate question of nullification, but Calhoun had opened the door to secession—the idea that a state at least had the right to leave the Union. That was the point of the wedge. Webester, Clay, and the rest often forced themselves into compromises because of the threat of secession, and the South began to recognize and to use this new political leverage. When the showdown came, they would have to use it.

•

At the time of this debate, a parishioner at Lyman Beecher's church, William Lloyd Garrison, had tried to prompt Lyman into broadening his theology of immediate repentance into immediate emancipation.

GARRISON : Is not slavery a sin?

LYMAN : Yes.

GARRISON : Well, then, in accordance with your doctrine of immediate repentance is it not the duty of this nation to repent immediately of the sin of slavery and emancipate the slaves?

LYMAN : Oh, Garrison, you can't reason that way. Great economic and political questions can't be solved so simply. You must take into account what is expedient as well as what is right.

NARRATOR : In the 1820s, it was possible for a great many people to share Lyman Beecher's vague public optimism that slavery would vanish eventually without anyone lifting a finger. Even Daniel Webster said of Lyman:

WEBSTER : Lyman Beecher is the most keen-sighted, far-sighted man in the United States.

•

NARRATOR : While president of Illinois College, Edward Beecher became involved in the Illinois anti-slavery movement through Elijah P. Lovejoy. Lovejoy had recently been forced to move from St. Louis to Alton, Illinois, just a few miles from Jacksonville, the seat of Edward's college.

By 1835, the anti-abolitionist riots, the gag rule in Congress, suppression of abolitionist materials in the mail, all infringed on the Bill of Rights—freedom of speech, of assembly, of the press. In the spirit of free speech, Elijah Lovejoy in St. Louis had published the statement of principles of the American Antislavery Society, and he wrote an editorial mostly in agreement with them.

LOVEJOY : We only propose that measures shall now be taken for the abolition of slavery, at such distant period of time as may be thought expedient, and eventually for ridding the country altogether of a colored population. Gradual emancipation is the remedy we propose.

NARRATOR : A week later, he received a letter signed "Citizens of St. Louis.'"

> You are asked to pass over in silence everything connected with the subject of slavery. The right of free speech is indeed guaranteed by the Constitution, but that fact does not imply a moral right, on the part of the Abolitionists, to freely discuss the question of slavery, either orally or through the medium of the press. To do so would allow the agitation or a question too nearly allied to the vital interests of the slave-holding states. It may in fact bring ultimately a disseverment of our prosperous Union.

LOVEJOY : The heaviest blows have been those which I have received from the hands of some of my brethren, I cannot surrender my principles, though the whole world besides should vote them down—I can make no compromise between truth and error, even though my life be the alternative.

NARRATOR : At this point, Edward Beecher was willing to give Lovejoy moral support.

EDWARD : I approve the principles which you have adopted and consider them capable of an unanswerable defense. I approve also of the manner in which you have spoken as truly in accordance with the meekness and yet courage demanded in a soldier of the cross, in fighting the battles of the Lord. I see the demands of the friends of the system of slavery, and their determination to muzzle not only abolitionists, but all who are determined gradually and wisely to remove the system, whatever be their ground. I think the time for silence has gone by. I say go on. You will find as you have already that the stand you have taken will increase the number of your friends.

NARRATOR : At Alton, Lovejoy breathed on free soil again—or so he thought. Various anti-slavery men, including Edward, pushed him on toward a leadership role.

EDWARD : At last, on being again requested to bring up the subject of a state anti-slavery convention in Illinois, Lovejoy concluded to mention it in his paper, and ask for an expression of public sentiment. It became clear that there was a general and strong desire that a convention should be held.

The proposal at once aroused the hostilities of the enemies

of his sentiments, and laid a foundation for all the disastrous results which have followed. A most disgraceful and incendiary paragraph appeared in a paper in St. Louis, urging the inhabitants of Alton to eject Mr. Lovejoy as a fomenter of divisions and an enemy to the public good. Having failed to intimidate, and having no recourse in argument, they began to mature their plans for the application of force.

At this time I received a letter from Mr. Lovejoy, requesting me, if consistent with my sense of duty, to give my name to the call for a convention. I had up to this time not participated at all in the public discussion which was so deeply exciting the nation.

My views, when I came to this state, were decidedly hostile to the doctrines of immediate emancipation; and it was not until the year 1835 that I became satisfied that the doctrine of gradual emancipation was fallacious, and that of immediate emancipation was philosophical and safe. From that time I felt it to be a matter of immense importance that measures should be taken, kindly but thoroughly, to convince the slave states of the fact, and to urge the claims of duty.

At the same time I was dissatisfied with the spirit of much which had been written on the subject; and with the disposition so common, of pushing true principles to an extreme. On the whole I decidedly preferred to stand on my own ground—to join no society—and to speak as an individual, if I spoke at all. In reply to Mr. Lovejoy, I stated these facts; and added that I would join no society, unless they would assume such grounds as I could approve. In reply, he requested a full statement of all my views, which I freely gave him.

The plans of the friends of mob-law had been matured, the office of Lovejoy's *Observer* assailed, and the press destroyed. The perpetrators were then timid. Public sentiment in favor of maintaining the law might easily have prevented it, but no such public sentiment existed.

•

NARRATOR : Lovejoy called for the State Anti-Slavery Convention for November. Edward Beecher was lukewarm at first, but in August, when Lovejoy's second press was smashed, Edward proposed to open the convention to "friends of free discussion" as well as to abolitionists. This idealism of Edward Beecher brought in a lot of colonizationists, people who believed in shipping the blacks to Liberia. As soon as the convention opened, opponents packed the hall with anti-abolitionists, attacking the convention at the very outset. They were boisterous, disruptive, and intent on wrecking the meeting. Meaningful debate was impossible.

Finally, private meetings were held in homes. Beecher put forth his own particular demands, and the delegates simply nominated him as a committee of one to write the Declaration of Sentiments and to propose topics for the next convention. Thus, much of the printed material that came out of the convention was Edward's.

EDWARD : It is the object of the brethren not to admit of any exception to the idea that slavery is in all cases sinful. Nothing should weaken the power of truth on the conscience. We must so guard our language as not to bring a false accusation against any man, and not to blame anyone for not doing impossibilities.

NARRATOR : Edward's idealism had a hard go of it at the meeting itself.

EDWARD : I learned that a meeting of the Colonization Society had just been held in Upper Alton, and found that many things had been said tending to excite prejudice and odium against the friends of immediate emancipation.

On my arrival, I found a tumultuous speaker claiming seats for himself and his friends, as the patrons of free inquiry on the subject of slavery; and none of those citizens of Alton on whom I had mainly relied were there. I was also informed that some of the individuals thus claiming seats had already, by aiding or abetting the destruction of the press of the *Observer*, illustrated their views of free inquiry.

On a procedural point, the friends of free inquiry were divided in the grounds which they should assume, and it was voted to adjourn till the next day.

•

NARRATOR : The debate was going on all over the country, even in the South. In New England, Daniel Webster put forth the diplomatic view:

DANIEL WEBSTER : On the general question of slavery, a great portion of the community is already strongly excited. The subject has not only attracted attention as a question of politics, but has struck a far deeper-toned chord. It has arrested the religious feelings of the country; it has taken strong hold on the consciences of people. It is a rash person, indeed, little conversant with human nature, and especially has he a very erroneous estimate of the character of the people of this country, who supposes that a feeling of this kind is to be trifled with or despised. It will assuredly cause itself to be respected.

It may be reasoned with; it may be made willing—I believe it is entirely willing—to fulfill all existing engagements, and all existing duties: to uphold and defend the constitution, as it is established, with whatever regret about some provisions which it does actually contain. But to coerce it into silence—to endeavor to restrain its free expression—to seek to compress and confine it, warm as it is, and more heated as such endeavors would inevitably render it—should all this be attempted, I know nothing even in the Constitution or in the Union itself, which would not be endangered by the explosion which might follow.

NARRATOR : Edward Beecher read to the convention the following letter of Dr. Channing to Henry Clay.

That the cause of Republicanism is suffering abroad through the defects and crimes of our countrymen, is as true as that it is regarded with increased skepticism among ourselves. Abroad, republicanism is identified with the United States; and it is certain that the American name has not risen of late in the world. It so happens that whilst writing, I have received a newspaper from England, in which Lynch law is as familiarly associated with our country, as if it were one of our establishments. We are quoted as monuments of the degrading tendencies of popular institutions. When I visited England, fifteen years ago, republican sentiments were freely expressed to me. I should probably hear none now.

It is believed abroad that property is less secure among us, order less stable, law less revered, social ties more easily broken, religion less enforced, life held less sacred, than in other countries. The least civilized parts of the country are made to represent the whole; and occasional atrocities are construed into habits. But who does not feel that we have given cause of reproach? And shall we fix this reproach and exasperate it into indignation and hatred, by adopting a policy against which the moral sentiments of the Christian world revolt? Shall we make the name of a republic "a stench in the nostrils of all nations"?

NARRATOR : At the end of the relatively calm convention, Beecher stayed to try to persuade the local neutrals, and to help Lovejoy replace his third press, destroyed just before the convention opened.

LOVEJOY : By the help of God, I will stand. I know I am but one and you are many. My strength would avail but little against you all. You can crush me if you will; but I shall die at my post, for I cannot and will not forsake it.

Why should I flee from Alton? Is not this a free state? The mob has pursued me here, and why should I retreat again? Where can I be safe if not here? No, sir; there is no way to escape the mob, but to abandon the path of duty; and that, God helping me, I will never do.

I appeal to every individual present; whom of you have I injured? Whose family have I molested? Whose business have I meddled with? If any, let him rise here and testify against me.

You have courts, and judges and juries; they find nothing against me. Pause, I beseech you, and reflect. The present excitement will soon be over; the voice of conscience will at last be heard.

•

NARRATOR : Elijah Lovejoy's fourth press was coming by boat to Alton in the evening—but word was sent to the captain to delay arrival until 3 a.m. The ploy worked—spies for the mob left when it looked as if the press was not coming.

Meanwhile 30 supporters of the press gathered at Mr. Gilman's store. At the early morning hour, they stationed themselves to ward off any attack, and the press was safely landed. Shortly afterward, Lovejoy and Beecher went down to see.

EDWARD : The moon had set and it was still dark, but day was near; and here and there a light was glimmering from the window of some sick room, or of some early riser. The streets were empty and silent, and the sounds of our feet echoed from the walls as we passed along. Little did he dream, at that hour, of the contest which the next night would witness: that these same streets would echo with the shouts of an infuriated mob, and be stained with his own heart's blood.

We found the boat there and the press in the warehouse; we aided in raising it to the third story. All felt the crisis was over. It was thought that a small number was sufficient to guard the press afterward. Mr. Lovejoy and myself offered to take charge of the press till morning; and the rest retired.

The morning soon began to dawn; and that morning I shall never forget. Who that has stood on the banks of the mighty stream that then rolled before me can forget the emotions of sublimity that filled his heart? I thought of future ages, and of the countless millions that should dwell on this mighty stream; and that nothing but the truth would make them free. Never did I feel as then the value of the right for which we were contending: thoroughly to investigate and fearlessly to proclaim that truth.

Brother Lovejoy, too, was happy. He did not exult: he was tranquil and composed; but his countenance indicated the state of his mind. It was a calm and tranquil joy, for he trusted in God that the point was gained: that the banner of an unfettered press would soon wave over that mighty stream.

We returned to his house, and before my departure we united in prayer. Cheered by hopes I bade the Lovejoys farewell, and began my journey homeward. On my way I heard passing rumors of a meditated attack on the store; but gave them no weight.

NARRATOR : Edward Beecher did not see the final night. The group defending the press had some forewarning, and more were there than had been the night before. The attack came at ten o'clock.

At first, the mob demanded the press. Mr. Gilman refused, and he was then threatened with a pistol, and he withdrew. Stones broke several windows, and the mob fired several shots. Shot were returned from inside, and one rioter, Lyman Bishop, was killed.

At this, the mob retired, and returned with ladders lashed together, in order to set fire to the wooden roof. The mayor appeared, but he had insufficient forces with him to sway the mob.

135

They demanded that he enter the store and obtain the press for them. The mayor went in.

Gilman and the others refused the mob's request—but Gilman asked the mayor to prevent destruction of his building. The mayor said he could not, but he authorized those inside to continue to defend the property by arms.

When the mayor returned to the mob, and gave Gilman's answer, immediately men went up the ladders to fire the roof. Since the building had windows front and back, but not on the sides, the defenders had to make a difficult choice. In order to prevent the attack on the roof, they would have to go outside the building. Lovejoy was in this group.

They turned the corner, saw the ladder and fired and wounded the man trying to set the fire. The rest dispersed, but hid themselves to prevent another raid. The defenders went back inside to reload, and when they returned outside, Elijah Lovejoy took five balls in his body. He had strength enough to go inside, and climb one flight of stairs before he died.

The remaining defenders then found out that the building was on fire, and they tried to surrender, but were unable to. Finally a prominent citizen came forward out of the mob, and offered to stand between them and the mob as they ran down Water Street.

The mob then entered, and destroyed the press. By this time, a great many spectators had gathered, neither to assist nor to defend.

EDWARD : There is no tyranny on earth so exercrable as the tyranny of a mob.

•

NARRATOR : In Jacksonville, Beecher faced public attack, censure, calls for his resignation; with the support of his faculty, he weathered the storm. Edward Beecher was now a national figure in the abolitionist movement, respected even by Garrison.

An Alton jury exonerated the mob leaders, and a week later, Abraham Lincoln denounced mob lawlessness in a speech at the Lyceum in nearby Springfield. In Hudson, Ohio, John Brown consecrates himself to wiping out slavery. Owen Lovejoy, Elijah's brother, becomes a leader of the radical abolitionists. At Boston's

Faneuil Hall, young Wendell Phillips pleads for freedom of the press, and thus begins his career as the voice of abolitionism.

John Quincy Adams, the former President, spoke in the Senate.

ADAMS : The death of Elijah Lovejoy at the hands of a mob came like the shock of an earthquake to the Yankee conscience; it marks an epoch in the annals of human liberty.

NARRATOR : By January, Edward shipped his manuscript about the Alton affair to New York, but it was stolen or lost. He copied it again and sent it to Alton to be printed. His indictment of slavery and defense of freedom of inquiry and the rights of the individual is moving and eloquent.

Other books had reported many of the facts by the time Edward's saw print. But none were by an eyewitness and participant, and no other account included Edward's keen analysis of the Alton Riot.

The conclusions that he drew from the experience continued to develop in Edward Beecher's mind, crystallizing into an idea that he could finally name eight years later; he called it the "theory of organic sin." The concept was that society itself might fall into a state of sin—such as slavery. Lyman Beecher interpreted it his own way.

LYMAN : Come out in one sentence and say that Organic Sin means National Sin—make it stand out—and stop all this flummery that Phelps will make about the word.

EDWARD : If the organization of the body politic creates false and sinful permanent relations between the individuals who compose the body politic, that, and only that, as I use the term, is an organic sin.

NARRATOR : Within the abolitionist movement, Edward had to be assured by the secretary of the American Anti-Slavery Society, James G. Birney, that its own Declaration of Sentiment, written by William Lloyd Garrison, need not apply to auxiliary organizations.

According to Edward Beecher, Garrison's document contained a historical inaccuracy—the New Testament did not define slaveholder as "manstealer," but in fact some early Christians were slaveholders, though that was a time of deep moral ignorance. Also, although slaveholding was sinful, the guilt was not to be placed solely and entirely on the back of the individual slaveholder, as Garrison did. Beecher's own version, the *Illinois Declaration of Sentiment,* declared that there were grades of guilt. Dissolving the legal relationship of slave and master was a matter for the community as well as the master. This was the theory of organic sin—that the community as a whole might be guilty. So, by this document, Edward Beecher became the theoretician of conservative abolitionism.

In the campaign of 1840, conservative abolitionists were prominent in the new Liberty Party, which nominated James Birney. Edward Beecher worked with Birney and the Liberty Party organizer, Gerritt Smith. These men, together with the Tappans, John Greenleaf Whittier, Jay, and Leavitt broke away from Garrison's American Anti-Slavery Society to form a rival organization, the American and Foreign Antislavery Society.

In the late 1830s, the old Beecher home at Walnut Hills near Lane Seminary still sheltered the two youngest boys, Thomas and James. Soon after their mother died, Isabella Beecher had gone to stay with her sister Mary in Hartford. There Isabella learned the decorum and social graces that Catharine's school had not taught her. Two years later, at 15, she returned to Cincinnati, to Catharine's other school where Harriet was teaching. And at 16, she went back to Hartford for one more year of study.

ISABELLA : Father managed to send six sons to college, but never a daughter cost him a hundred dollars a year after she was 16. Yet I date my interest in public affairs from those years between 11 and 16 when our family circle was ever in discussion on the vital problems of human existence, where the United States Constitution, fugitive slave laws, Henry Clay and the Missouri Compromise alternated with free will, regeneration, heaven, hell, and "The Destiny of Man."

NARRATOR : Catharine, the oldest Beecher daughter, still lived in the household but she was more like a spinster aunt than a daughter. Rebuffed by Cincinnati society because of her outspokenness, and thwarted in her plans for expanding her school, she withdrew and busied herself with writing.

In 1836, Lyman Beecher married a third time, to Mrs. Lydia Beals Jackson, who brought to the household two children, Joseph and Margaret, about James's age; she also had two married daughters. Lydia Jackson Beecher was a good organizer; her skills and energy proved useful in the busy Beecher household.

In that same year, Harriet married Calvin Stowe, one of the Lane Seminary professors, an old friend of the family. In their first year of marriage, Calvin journeyed to Europe to study public school systems, while Harriet gave birth to twin daughters. Harriet also helped her brother edit the *Cincinnati Inquirer*. The next year she had another child. Harriet the writer had to find time when she could. Here is how a volunteer describes Harriet's new dictation methods, in actual practice.

VOLUNTEER : I am ready to write. The last sentence was: "What is this life to one who has suffered as I have?" What next?

MINA : Ma'am, shall I put in the brown or white bread first?

HARRIET : The brown first.

VOLUNTEER : "What is this life to one who has suffered as I have," I repeated. Harriet brushed the flour off her apron and sat down for a moment in a muse. Then she dictated as follows:

HARRIET : "Under the breaking of my heart I have borne up. I have borne up under all that tries a woman—but this thought— oh, Henry."

MINA : Ma'am, shall I put ginger into this pumpkin?

HARRIET : No, you may let that alone just now. "I know my duty to my children. I see the hour must come. You must take them, Henry; they are my last earthly comfort."

MINA : Ma'am, what shall I do with these egg-shells and all this truck here?

HARRIET : Put them in the pail by you.

VOLUNTEER : "They are my last earthly comfort." What next?

HARRIET : "You must take them away. It may be—perhaps it must be—that I shall soon follow, but the breaking heart of a wife still pleads, 'a little longer, a little longer.' "

MINA : How much longer must the gingerbread stay in?

HARRIET : Five minutes.

VOLUNTEER : "A little longer, a little longer," I repeated in a dolorous tone and we burst into a laugh. Then we went on, cooking, writing—and laughing till I finally accomplished taking the dictation. The piece was finished, copied and the next day sent to the editor.

·

NARRATOR : Late in 1834, Lyman, Calvin Stowe, and Harriet visited a Presbyterian synod meeting at Ripley on the Ohio River across from Maysville, Kentucky. They stayed with Rev.

John Rankin. They asked him about a lantern he placed in his window—and he revealed the fact that his house was one of the first stations of an Underground Railroad—if a slave could cross the river and reach his light, then they would be on their way to Canada.

Rankin then told them of one escape—a slave woman with a baby had had to flee even without her husband—but when she reached the river, it was still frozen, though the ice was breaking up in the spring thaw. Nevertheless, she started across, and somehow reached the other side, climbed the bluff, and found white folks to give her food and clothing, and then to take her on a little further on the long road to Canada. Her husband did escape also, followed her, and they were finally reunited. Later on, several escaped slaves each claimed that she was the original of the character of Liza that Harriet used in *Uncle Tom's Cabin*.

The Panic of 1837, as Martin Van Buren was starting his administration, almost finished Lane Seminary, but Lyman Beecher did not lose hope.

LYMAN : When I got back to the seminary, I found Stowe sick abed and all discouraged. Said 'twas all over—of no use—might just as well leave and go back East first as last. "Stowe," said I, "I've brought you 12 students. You've got no faith, and I've got nothing but faith. Get up and wash and eat bread and prepare to have a good class."

•

NARRATOR : When Henry Beecher first entered Amherst College, he began practicing public speaking almost incessantly to overcome what he believed to be an overlarge palate—though others thought it enlarged tonsils. John Lovell drilled him in posture, articulation, and gestures. Henry continued the practice at Lane with Charles and other students in the grove between the seminary and Walnut Hills, the Beecher home.

HENRY : We would make the night, and even the day, hideous with our voices, exploding all the vowels, from the bottom to the very top of our voices.

NARRATOR : When he graduated from Lane at last, his speech was clear, and he had begun to show real promise. In his first sermons, he was careful to preserve the Western prejudice for spontaneous speaking, though in fact his sermons were well thought out, sometimes entirely written out.

Even at the beginning of his career, Henry Ward Beecher was generous with money he didn't have. Though he earned a little by occasional teaching school, giving lectures, or editing the *Cincinnati Journal*, he was basically still dependent on his father. At the same time, two uncles—Samuel E. Foote and John P. Foote—were successful businessmen in the community, and the Beechers were welcome in upper class gatherings such as the Semi-Colon Club, and Daniel Drake's evenings. So it was that he attempted to live beyond his means. In March, Lyman Beecher had had to lecture him about his debts; the third Mrs. Beecher came to the rescue with an unexpected $100.

HENRY : I thank God for it. I am resolved not again to get into debt for anything. I will live within my means by living by my means and not upon credit.

NARRATOR : In the same 1837 Panic, Catharine's Cincinnati school failed, and suddenly she had no base from which to operate. She decided that fund-raising tours were more to her liking than teaching, in any case. In 1838, she published two books— *The Moral Instructor for Schools and Families*, and *Letters on the Difficulties of Religion.*

NARRATOR : Just at that time, two abolitionists, Angelina and Sarah Grimke, set out to establish women's societies for abolitionism. Catharine immediately challenged Angelina Grimke's leadership, and published an *Essay on Slavery and Abolitionsim with Reference to the Duty of American Females.* For two years the three of them fought it out in print.

The Grimkes linked women's rights to the cause of abolitionism; Catharine expanded her vision of a unified American culture centered on the family and the educated political woman. The anti-abolitionist riots at Alton and Cincinnati, she said, showed the bankruptcy of a male-dominated polity. Though the Beechers in general were anti-slavery, they were not abolitionists, and so they were caught in the middle, attacked by both sides. Catharine was seeking to broaden the issue, and to change basic cultural roles through education, not through politics. Angelina Grimke took another view.

GRIMKE : Now I believe it is woman's right to have a voice in all the laws and regulations by which she is to be governed, whether in Church or State; and that the present arrangements of society, on these points, are a violation of human rights, a rank usurpation of power, a violent seizure and confiscation of what is sacredly and inalienably hers.

NARRATOR : To which Catharine replied:

CATHARINE : Heaven has appointed to one sex the superior, and to the other the subordinate station, but while woman holds a subordinate relation in society to the other sex, it is not because it was designed that her duties or her influence should be any the less important, or all-prevading. The woman's influence should remain within the domestic and social circle, and win with kindly, generous, peaceful and benevolent principles.

Let every woman become so cultivated and refined in intellect, that her taste and judgment will be respected; so benevolent in feelings and action, that her motives will be reverenced; so unassuming and unambitious, that collision and competition will be banished; so "gentle and easy to be entreated," that every heart will repose in her presence; then, the fathers, the husbands, and the sons, will find an influence thrown around them, to which they will yield not only willingly but proudly.

•

NARRATOR : In 1837, Henry graduated from Lane, and accepted his first post—at Lawrenceburgh, Indiana, twenty miles from Cincinnati. Just as soon as he was settled there, he sent a letter back East to Eunice, the girl he had tutored at Amherst, to see whether she would join him in Ohio. And then he almost outpaced the letter himself going to see her.

HENRY : I cannot assent. What then? Preach I will, licensed or not. On that point I am determined. If I can do no better, I will go far out into the West, build a log cabin among the lumbermen and trappers, or whoever may seek employment in the forests, and devote myself to trying to interest them in religious services, far from the busy haunts of men. What will you do if this is the only course left me? Will you go with me into the wilderness?

NARRATOR : They married in the East, and returned to Lawrence-burgh, a little town on a malarial lowland of the Miami

River. The other Beechers helped them set up housekeeping, and Mrs. William Henry Harrison gave them the same bureau, brass andirons, shovel and tongs with which she had set up housekeeping 40 years before. Their boxes became bookcases.

Western life was something of a shock to Eunice, who was not altogether thrilled with the responsibility of her first child. She was also jealous of Henry's time away from home, relaxing with the men of the town. Henry, on the other hand, had never been happier in his life. When Eunice later published a novel anonymously, she did not hide her bitterness about the hardships of life in the Midwest. Her thinly veiled portrayal of Henry was not flattering, nor was her evaluation of Indiana.

The source for some of Henry's sermon topics came from books.

HENRY : I was a great reader of the old sermonizers. I read old Robert South through and through. I formed much of my style and my handling of texts on his methods. I obtained a vast amount of instruction and assistance from others of those old sermonizers, who were as familiar to me as my own name. I read Barrow, Howe, Sherlock, Butler, and Edwards particularly. I preached a great many sermons while reading these old men, and upon their discourses I often founded the framework of my own.

Nobody ever tripped me up. I had no Board of Elders ready to bring me back to orthodoxy. It was done without damage to my people, for they knew too little to know whether I was orthodox or not. They don't believe half that you say. The part that is nutritious they keep, and the rest they let alone.

NARRATOR : Though Henry wrote out his sermons, he was careful to preserve the notion that they were spontaneous. Yet he had a poor memory, even as a boy.

HENRY : The fact is, I was cheated when I was born. Hattie Stowe and George took all the memory and left me without any. I do not dare to lead in the Lord's Prayer. I couldn't repeat correctly one commandment from beginning to end. I cannot repeat a verse of any hymn in the English language.

Sometimes in preparing, I would find that after working a subject up all week, something else would take possession of me on Saturday, and I would have to preach that on Sunday to get rid of it. I felt ashamed and mortified, and began to fear I was on the way to superficiality.

NARRATOR : For a long time, Henry was so concerned with the style of delivery, the organization of his sermons that he went to bed on Sunday nights with a headache—and considered quitting the ministry altogether because of it. Sometimes he was so unsure of himself that he asked his wife Eunice not to attend church that Sunday.

Some months later, Henry went up before the Oxford Presbytery, an Old School body controlled by Scotch Presbyterians. The son of the New School leader lately come to Cincinnati was in for a close scrutiny. They voted to accept him, but first required that candidates adhere to the Old School Presbytery Assembly. On returning to his church, Henry explained that their church would be vacant if they continued under the Oxford Presbytery—and on Wednesday they voted to be independent, and to keep their new pastor.

Henry's sermons gradually improved, showing some of the fluency, the humor and homely illustrations that would mark his later style. Henry took an active role in community affairs, volunteering his church for meetings. At the time, Henry believed colonization was a way in which slavery might dwindle and disappear. In his sermons, his main topic was temperance.

Henry tried a few fire and brimstone sermons—without much effect. Then he observed Rev. John Newland Maffit, a Methodist evangelist passing through the Ohio Valley—Maffit used appeals to the imagination and passionate, even loving tones.

In another part of the Ohio Valley, another Methodist evangelist, Peter Cartwright, encountered the leader of the Mormons. Here he gives a partisan view of Joseph Smith.

•

CARTWRIGHT : After the Mormons were driven from Missouri for their infamous and unlawful deeds, they fled to Illinois, Joe Smith and all, and established themselves at Nauvoo, or the foot of the Lower Rapids, on the east side of the Mississippi. Soon afterwards, it fell to my lot to became acquainted with Joe Smith personally. On a certain occasion I fell into a free conversation with Joe Smith on the subject of religion, and Mormonism in particular. I found him to be a very illiterate and impudent desperado in morals, but, at the same time, he had a vast fund of low cunning.

In the first place, he made his onset on me by flattery, and he laid on the soft sodder thick and fast. I gave him rope, as the sailors say, and, indeed, I seemed to lay this flattering unction pleasurably to my soul.

SMITH : Indeed, if the Methodists would only advance a step or two further, they would take the world. We Latter-Day Saints are Methodists, as far as they have gone, only we have advanced further, and if you would come in and go with us, we could sweep not only the Methodist Church, but all others, and you would be looked up to as one of the Lord's greatest prophets. You would be honored by countless thousands, and have of the good things of this world all that heart could wish.

CARTWRIGHT : I then began to inquire into some of the tenets of the Latter-Day Saints. He explained. I criticized his explanation till, unfortunately, we got into high debate, and he cunningly concluded that his first bait would not take, for he plainly saw I was not to be flattered out of common sense and honesty. The next pass he made at me was to move upon my fears. He said that in all ages of the world the good and right way was evil spoken of, and that it was an awful thing to fight against God.

SMITH : Now, if you will go with me to Nauvoo, I will show you many living witnesses that will testify that they were, by the saints, cured of blindness, lameness, deafness, dumbness, and all the diseases that human flesh is heir to; and I will show you that we have the gift of tongues, and can speak in unknown languages, and that the saints can drink any deadly poison, and it will not hurt them. The idle stories you hear about us are nothing but sheer persecution.

CARTWRIGHT : I then gave him the history of an uncomfortable encounter I had in a camp meeting in Morgan County, some time before, with some of his Mormons. I ended up ejecting them to preserve the good of the meeting. When I closed, his wrath boiled over, and he cursed me in the name of his God.

SMITH : I will show you, sir, that I will raise up a government in these United States which will overturn the present government, and I will raise up a new religion that will overturn every other form of religion in this country

CARTWRIGHT : Yes, Uncle Joe; but my Bible tells me "the bloody and deceitful man shall not live out half his days"; and I expect the Lord will send the devil after you some of these days, and take you out of the way.

SMITH : No, sir, I shall live and prosper, while you will die in your sins.

CARTWRIGHT : Well, sir, if you live and prosper, you must quit your stealing and abominal whoredoms.

Thus we parted to meet no more on earth; for in a few years after this, an outraged and deeply-injured people took the law into their own hands and killed him, and drove the Mormons from the state.

NARRATOR : The appeal of Mormonism in the 1830s and 40s was that of a new revelation, complete with prophet and new sacred texts. Protestant revivals came in waves—hundreds of people meeting in the outdoors together sometimes reached pitches of enthusiasm that no church could contain. Lyman Beecher had made his earlier career on revivalism, but Henry was a failure as a revivalist, to judge by the number of new converts.

He really worked on his preaching, though, and Martha Sawyer, the woman who had first invited him to Lawrenceburgh, praised his preaching to Samuel Merrill in Indianapolis. Merrill was part of a small group which had broken away from the Old School Presbyterian Church and were just then about to form a New School church. So, on his travels, Merrill stopped by Lawrenceburgh just to hear Henry Beecher preach—and he invited the young man up to Indianapolis to give a trial sermon. The new congregation liked what they heard, and in May 1839, they invited him to be their pastor.

In the meantime, Charles Beecher had become a clerk in a cotton factor's office, and he was sent on trips downriver to New Orleans. He also worked as a church organist. In 1840, he married. The newly ordained Henry gave his brother Charles this advice about his upcoming ordination:

HENRY : Preach little doctrine except what is of moldy orthodoxy; keep all your improved breeds, your short-horned Durhams, your Berkshires, etc. away off to pasture. They will get fatter and nobody will be scared. Take hold of the most practical subjects; popularize your sermons. I do not ask you to change yourself, but for a time, while captious critics are lurking, adapt your mode so as to insure that you shall be rightly understood.

•

NARRATOR : William resigned his Putnam post over a salary dispute, and remained without a position until brother George secured him a large country church near Batavia, New York, with double his previous salary. For a few years, everything went well—but a small group in the church finally forced him out. William and Katherine now had six children.

Catharine kept herself busy mentally just as ten years before, debating her mental and moral philosophy with other Beechers. Now she discussed theological fine points with Lyman, and argued in letters with Edward at Jacksonville and with Charles, now at Indianapolis, where he was helping Henry. These serious discussions produced some intellectual heat between the participants—Charles wrote a long letter to Lyman to adjudge Catharine's claim to victory in an argument. Catharine felt that she represented the social good against the abstract reasoning of her brothers. Lyman wisely noted her need for the respect of her family.

LYMAN : Edward, Charles—omit from your letters anything that might wound Catharine too deep, for with her nervous incapacities she feels deeply any appearances of light estimation on the part of her family friends who she so sincerely loves. In her trying situation it is a happy knack of being aways in the right, demanding gratitude. For shut out from her wanted active labor, if she could not plan and correspond and keep herself in the stream of interested action for the public good, she would be exceedingly unhappy.

NARRATOR : On the other hand, Lyman soon saw that she would have to be called off; her attack on Charles was getting to be too much for him.

One of Harriet's servants was a black woman whose son served as model for "little Harry." She came fearfully one day, saying that her old master was in town looking for her. Calvin Stowe and Charles Beecher took the woman and her son to Jon Van Sant, whose house was on the Underground Railway. Van Sant had been a slave owner in Kentucky, but he had freed his slaves and moved to Ohio. He became John Van Trompe in Harriet's novel.

Harriet visited the Edward and his wife, and met the Reverend Josiah Henson, a freedman. He described seeing his father lying on the ground bruised, bleeding and dying from the blows of an overseer because he had dared pretend that the mother of his children was his wife and had tried to defend her against an assault by the overseer. She was struck by the Christlike spirit of the man even in relating such horrors. More than anyone else, he would be the model for Uncle Tom.

THE FORTIES
1839–1847

The 1840s saw the middle group of Beechers, especially Harriet and Henry, beginning their careers. It was about this time that American literature left behind its dreams, as Herman Melville and Walt Whitman found America itself an adequate—a vast—theme.

The national debate over slavery erupted into a free speech issue. Cincinnati had its own taste of mob violence. In the midst of these portentous events, Harriet Beecher, recently married to Calvin Stowe, one of her father's professors, still made time to write, as did her brother Henry.

HARRIET : Well, my dear G., about half an hour more and your old friend, companion, schoolmate, sister, etc., will cease to be Hatty Beecher and change to nobody knows who. My dear, I have been dreading and dreading the time, and lying awake all last week wondering how I should live through this overwhelming crisis, and lo it has come and I feel NOTHING AT ALL.

The wedding is to be altogether domestic; nobody present but my own brothers and sisters, and my old colleague Mary Dutton; and as there is a sufficiency of the ministry in our family we have not even to call in the foreign aid of a minister. Sister Katy is not here, so she will not witness my departure from her care and guidance to that of another.

Yesterday evening I spent scribbling for Henry's newspaper, the *Cincinnati Journal*, in this wise; "Birney's printing press has been mobbed, and many of the respectable citizens are disposing to wink at the outrage in consideration of its moving in the line of their prejudices."

I wrote a conversational sketch, in which I rather satirized this inconsistent spirit. It was designed to draw attention to a long editorial of Henry's in which he considers the subject fully and seriously. His piece is, I think, a powerful one; indeed, he does write very strongly. I am quite proud of his editorials; I think he will make a first-rate writer. Both our pieces have gone to press today, with Charles's article on music, and we have had not a little diversion about our "family newspaper."

•

NARRATOR : The same pro- and anti-slavery elements that had led to the death of Elijah Lovejoy at Alton in 1837 confronted each other again in Cincinnati. Freedom of the press was at issue—and no Beecher had any doubt about that subject.

HARRIET : The excitement about Birney continues to increase. A meeting has been convoked by means of a handbill, in which some of the most respectable men of the city are invited by name to come together and consider the quesiton whether they will allow Mr. Birney to continue his paper in the city. Many of the most respectable and influential citizens gave out that they should go.

For my part, I can easily see how such proceedings may make converts to abolitionism, for already my sympathies are strongly enlisted for Mr. Birney, and I hope that he will stand his ground and assert his rights. The office is fire-proof, and enclosed by high walls. Henry sits opposite me writing a most valiant editorial, and tells me to tell you he is waxing mighty in battle.

All the newspapers in the city, except Hammond's *Gazette* and Henry's *Journal*. were either silent or openly mobocratic. As might have been expected, Birney refused to leave, and that night the mob tore down his press, scattered the types, dragged the whole to the river, threw it in, and then came back to demolish the office.

The mayor was a silent spectator of these proceedings, and was heard to say, "Well, lads, you have done well, so far; go home now before you disgrace yourselves"; but the "lads" spent the rest of the night and a greater part of the next day, Sunday, in pulling down the houses of inoffensive and respectable blacks. The *Gazette* office was threatened, the *Journal* office was to go next; Lane Seminary and the waterworks also were mentioned as probable points to be attacked by the mob.

By Tuesday morning the city was pretty well alarmed. A regular corps of volunteers was organized, who for three nights patrolled the streets with firearms and with legal warrant from the mayor, who by this time was glad to give it, to put down the mob even by bloodshed.

For a day or two we did not know but there would actually be war to the knife, as was threatened by the mob, and we really saw Henry depart with his pistols with daily alarm, only we were all too full of patriotism not to have sent every brother we had rather than not have had the principles of freedom and order defended.

But here the tide turned. The mob, unsupported by a now frightened community, slunk into their dens and were still; and then Hammond, who, during the few days of its prevalence, had made no comments, but published simply the Sermon on the Mount, the Constitution of Ohio, and the Declaration of Independence, without any comment, now came out and gave a simple, concise history of the mob, tracing it to the market-house meeting, telling the whole history of the meeting, with the names of those who got it up, throwing on them and on those who had acted on the committee the whole responsibility of the following mob. It makes a terrible sensation, but it cuts its way and all who took other stand than that of steady opposition from the first are beginning to feel the reaction of public sentiment.

NARRATOR : In later years, James G. Birney became the Presidential candidate of the Liberty Party in the next two elections, with a vote substantial enough to affect the outcome of at least one presidential election.

About the time of the Birney incident, Cassius Clay in the Kentucky legislature was proposing a system of gradual emancipation. In 1845, he established an anti-slavery publication, *The True American*—but a mob wrecked his press and office, and he moved across the river to Cincinnati.

Though Henry Beecher was not a success even on his own terms in Lawrenceburgh, the Second Presbyterian Church in Indianapolis, and Samuel Merrill in particular, beckoned the young minister, and he left for the capital in 1839. The Indiana state capital at that time had only 4,000 residents, but it was a planned city, with wide streets radiating out from a hub. It was also malarial, and both Eunice and Henry fell ill of it. Eunice had a stillbirth.

Within months of beginning his new ministry, Henry was

writing his father that he was doing well in this larger arena. Isabella predicted a great future for him. Catharine said:

CATHARINE : I think in one year my brother Henry will make his influence felt all over the state of Indiana. I have never seen persons improve as fast morally and intellectually as my brothers since they commenced the duties of their mission.

ISABELLA : Brother Henry is working with all his might—he feels much encouraged—and writes to father in great haste (once in a while) of what he is doing—his hopes and fears. I think he is going in father's track, perhaps one day will come somewhere near him in eminence.

NARRATOR : The following year, Henry's congregation built their church, including a platform in front, at Henry's request, rather than a conventional pulpit—so that he might maintain the intimacy with his audience that gave him a certain power of communication. Henry also made another discovery.

HENRY : I can preach so as to make the people come to hear me, but somehow I can't preach them clear into the kingdom. I studied the Apostles, and found that they had sought a common ground on which the people and they stood together. Then they heaped up a large number of the particulars of knowledge that belonged to everybody, and brought it to bear upon them with all their excited heart and feelings. A sermon suceeds only if it has power on the heart.

LYMAN : Henry, though so recently established at Indianapolis, is beginning to be felt not only at home in the power of the Holy Spirit which attends his labors, but abroad as a man of piety, talents, and power, in the churches and in the capital of his state.

•

NARRATOR : Calvin Stowe was a good husband to Harriet, but he wasn't much help around the house. So, Harriet, who had been simply a daydreamer, scraped together enough money from writing to hire a "stout German girl" to do the housework, as well as Anna, the English nursemaid, to take care of three children— leaving Harriet about three hours a day in which to write. Lyman and Catharine encouraged her efforts to be a professional writer, and Calvin was very supportive. Harriet set herself to studying the formula writing of annual publications like *Affection's Gift, Token,*

Lily, and the Christmas books.

Several times Harriet and Calvin were apart for extended periods of time; often one of them retreated to a certain water-cure spa in Vermont for health reasons. They kept in touch by letter.

HARRIET : And if you see my name coming out everywhere, you may be sure of one thing—that I do it for the pay. I have determined not to be a mere domestic slave.

•

NARRATOR : When the Old School/New School schism finally came in the Presbyterian Church, Lyman, George, and Edward were leaders in organizing the New School as a separate church. Henry was against the division.

HENRY : I ask no questions about old or new school in giving my confidence. I am unwilling to be hemmed in by the narrow lines of Schools and parties—but, standing a free man in God's church, I look about to see who is most loved of God. Where there is a heart right before God there cannot be grounds for refusing fellowship and communion.

NARRATOR : Peter Cartwright, the Ohio Valley Methodist minister, saw developments in his church parallel to Lyman Beecher's experience. Slavery was becoming the topic behind all other topics.

CARTWRIGHT : Prior to the General Conference of 1826, the run-mad spirit of rabid abolitionism had broken out in some of the Eastern and Northern conferences; and Methodist preachers were found by the dozen to quit their holy callings of saving souls, and turn out and become hired lecturers against slavery. They went so far as to violently oppose colonization as a slaveholding trick.

The legislatures of the different slave states greatly embarrassed the operations of the Church by narrowing the door of emancipation, and passing unjust and stringent laws to prevent manumission.

And now, I would soberly ask, What has all this violent hue and cry of proscriptive abolitionism done for the emancipation of the poor degraded slaves? Just nothing at all; nay, infinitely worse than nothing. It has riveted the chains of slavery tighter than ever before; it has engendered prejudice; it has thrown firebrands into legislative halls; laws for the good of the people are neglected; prejudice, strife, and wrath, and every evil passion stirred up till the integrity of the union of our happy country is in imminent danger—and what has it all amounted to?

Not one poor slave set free; not one dollar expended to colonize them and send them home happy and free. Mobs are fast becoming the order of the day. Presses demolished; preachers hailing from free states are hunted down, tarred and feathered, and threatened with the rope if they do not leave in a few hours.

I believe, from more than 20 years' experience as a traveling preacher in slave states, that the most successful way to ameliorate the condition of the slaves, and Christianize them, and finally secure their freedom, is to treat their owners kindly, and not to meddle politically with slavery.

•

NARRATOR : At the other extreme was William Lloyd Garrison, the most stubborn and the most hated of the Northern abolitionists. His magazine, *The Liberator,* grew to an enormous circulation.

GARRISON : So profoundly ignorant of the nature of slavery are many persons, that they are stubbornly incredulous whenever they read or listen to any recital of the cruelties which are daily inflicted on its victims. They do not deny that the slaves are held as property, but that terrible fact seems to convey to their minds no idea of injustice, exposure to outrage, or savage barbarity.

Let it never be forgotten, that no slaveholder or overseer can be convicted of any outrage perpetrated on the person of a slave, however diabolical it may be, on the testimony of colored witnesses, whether bond or free. Hence, there is no legal protection in fact, whatever there may be in form, for the slave population; and any amount of cruelty may be inflicted on them with impunity.

•

NARRATOR : In her last year at Hartford, Isabella Beecher came to know John Hooker, a law clerk in her brother-in-law Thomas Perkins's office. They married and moved to Farmington nearby, and while John waited for his first law clients, they read Blackstone during the day, and literature at night.

But then they reached the chapter in Blackstone titled "Domestic Relations and Reciprocal Duties of Husband and Wife." Blackstone says:

> By marriage the husband and wife are one person in law, that is, the very being or legal existence of the woman is suspended during the marriage, or at least, is incorporated and consolidated into that of the husband under whose wings, protection and cover she performs everything.

ISABELLA : Is that the justice which your law furnishes to us women?

> The husband possesses the right to restrain his wife by domestic chastisement, and by whips and cudgels vigorously to punish a wife, and in certain cases to use moderate whipping for more serious domestic offenses.

NARRATOR : Isabella began a search for some defense against this legal doctrine—eventually finding it in John Stuart Mill's *On Liberty and the Subjection of Women*, and in Harriet Mill's articles on women's rights in the English magazines. Isabella wrote them both, and developed a correspondence on women's issues. But there seemed to be no scope for action.

ISABELLA : I can't write a book—nor draw pictures—nor do any other productive work. John, I have always told you that you overestimated your wife. Everywhere I go, I have to run on the credit of my relations, nowhere but at home can I lay claim to a particle of individuality, to any distinction of goodness, smartness or anything else whatever. It becomes more and more evident to me that I have great power of personal influence—family name goes a great way no doubt, but there is a magnetism of heart and eye and voice that is quite individual—oh how I wish I might exert this on a broad scale, to sweep people along on the right path.

NARRATOR : James, the youngest Beecher, was a man of action. As soon as he reached Dartmouth, he became a rebel. In his junior year, he was in debt and in disgrace: he asked his father for money so he could ship out to the Orient. Lyman refused; James left anyway. He spent five years on clipper ships, returning as an officer. He would later re-enter the fold, but always there was something wild about James.

•

In contrast, Harriet Stowe described her own life in the 1840s —surprised that anyone would bother to inquire.

HARRIET : Having reflected duly and truly on my past life, it is so thoroughly uneventful and uninteresting that I do not see how anything can be done for me in the way of a sketch. My sister, Catharine, has lived much more of a life and done more than can be told of than I whose course and employments have always been retired and domestic. The most I can think of is that I was born in Litchfield, Connecticut—was a teacher from my 15th year till my marriage, that I have been mother to seven children—six of them are now living—and that the greatest portion of my time and strength has been spent in the necessary but unpoetic duties of the family. I would say that I have never published but one book, *The Mayflower,* by Harpers.

NARRATOR : Katy Beecher, Edward's wife, encouraged Harriet to write serious pieces, not just the sentimental stories that the magazines were asking for.

KATY BEECHER : I had been nourishing an anti-slavery spirit since Lovejoy was murdered for publishing in his paper articles against slavery and intemperance when our home was in Illinois. Now, Hattie, if I could use a pen as you can, I would write something that would make this whole nation feel what an accursed thing slavery is.

NARRATOR : Harriet read this letter to her children in the front parlor, and when she came to the last words, she crushed the letter in her hand and said:

HARRIET : God helping me, I will write something. I will if I live

NARRATOR : Pondering the story of the Rev. Josiah Henson, whom she had met at Edward's, Harriet remembered the Christlike spirit of Henson's father as he was beaten to death. On returning to Brunswick, during a communion service, she suddenly had a vision of the death of Uncle Tom by the two black slave-drivers Sambo and Quimbo, of how he turned his physical defeat into a spiritual victory. At home she wrote it all out, switching to brown wrapping paper when her writing paper ran out.

Later, she found her husband weeping over some pieces of brown paper that she'd forgotten to tell him about. He said:

CALVIN : Hattie, this is the climax of that story of slavery which you promised sister Katy you would write. Begin at the beginning and work up to this and you'll have your book.

•

NARRATOR : In late 1840, Henry took Eunice back to her parents' home in Massachusetts. She had aged considerably, so that at first they didn't recognize her. Henry's congregation had noted that Eunice didn't do any of the things that a minister's wife was expected to do, that she was often absent from Sunday service, that she was moody. She was not happy with her life in the West. A visiting minister noted this of the couple.

MINISTER : Henry's greeting was hearty and sincere. I knew he meant his welcome and the invitation he extended to me to his church and his home. The latter, a neat, one-story cottage in Market Street, I soon visited, meeting his wife, a rather discontented woman, complaining constantly of chills and the unhealthy nature of the town.

NARRATOR : Henry was a moderate Whig in politics; he had known old General William Henry Harrison in Cincinnati when the old Indian-fighter had lived in nearby North Bend. About this time, Daniel Webster visited Indianapolis, and spoke on the same platform as General Harrison, Old Tippecanoe himself. Henry heard Webster give a two-hour speech on the currency in question; he listened and learned. Webster needed no ranting.

HENRY : It shows one thing plainly—that is, a promiscuous Western audience will listen attentively to plain sense and reasoning, and does not need the boisterous excitement, so prevalent and which it is said the people must have.

NARRATOR : Henry was pleased of course when Harrison won the Presidential race, despite his pro-slavery views—but a month later, Harrison died in office. Henry Beecher and Governor Samuel Bigger gave the main addresses at the memorial services in the state capitol.

Henry expanded his enthusiasm for gardening, buying two additional lots to garden in; he helped organize the Indiana Horticultural Society. Rhubarb, or as it was then called, pie-plant, was his specialty, and he sold as much as he could grow. For a few years, he edited a semi-monthly *Indiana Farmer and Gardener*, contributing articles on temperance and rowdyism as well as on vegetables.

In July 1841, Henry went East—Eunice had given birth to a son in Massachusetts—and he took along Samuel Merrill's daughter Julia, 14 years old, and her friend Betty Bates—both of whom he had taught; he'd also lived with the Merrills and was currently boarding with the Bates family. Henry may not have known it then, but Julia Merrill had a crush on the handsome young preacher.

As soon as he went away, the revival that Henry had been working on for three years began without him, first among the Methodists, then at his church and others. Lyman Beecher, now sixty-six, was filling in for Henry, and he brought Darcia Allen, one of his professors at Lane. Together they set up a rigorous schedule of meetings, sermons, and counseling. Lyman brought a dozen converts into the church. Elsewhere in Indiana, revivals broke out—and Henry helped with one in Terre Haute on his return.

In his journal of his first year in Indianapolis, Henry Ward Beecher wrote these resolutions—they explain much of his later career.

HENRY : If God will give me grace I will preach faithfully all parts of the Gospel necessary for conversion of men and perfecting them in holiness. But in his strength, I am resolved, never to become a disputant or champion on any of those points which divide truly evangelical Christians.

> 1. If I feel it a duty ever to speak of such topics, I will strive to do it so as to soften and win the feeling and promote charity rather than bitter sectarianism.

> 2. Resolve that I will strive to cherish secret feelings of love to all other churches beside my own;—to say nothing evil of them nor to desire their members;—nor their decline.

> 3. Resolved, that in public and private, I will give my

life to bringing all Christians to the work of spreading the true power of the Gospel—the love of Christ.

NARRATOR : Revivalism, mainly out of town, became very important to Henry.

HENRY : This glowing center seemed so intolerable that my whole nature and all my soul rose up in uncontrollable prayer. Through the beech woods, sometimes crying, sometimes singing, and always praying, I rode in one long controversy with God. "Slay me if Thou wilt, but do not send me home to barrenness. Thou shalt go with me. I will not be refused. I will prevail or die"—these and wilder strains went through the soul. At length the clouds rolled away. An unspeakable peace and confidence filled my soul. The assurance of victory was perfect.

NARRATOR : So he tried with his congregation for weeks. A fellow minister remembered.

MEMBER : I can see him still, in his rough brown overcoat, his trousers tucked in his heavy boots, flying around full of zeal and inspiration.

NARRATOR : And from February through April, about 90 people came to the church rolls. Then, joining a Baptist and a Methodist pastor, he held a riverside baptism on the White River, drawing two or three thousand spectators. The religious hysteria sometimes stirred up other passions too, including violence and sexuality. The minister told him:

MINISTER : Religious passion includes all other passions. You cannot excite one without stirring up the others.

NARRATOR : Younger brothers Thomas and James stayed with Henry for long periods, and brother Charles came in 1841, to serve as Henry's all-around assistant. Gradually, under Henry's influence, Charles lost his skepticism, and Henry helped him to win a pastorate in Ft. Wayne.

Henry Ward Beecher emerged from Amherst and Lane Seminary as one of the more promising Beecher sons, though his career started slowly. The Beecher family was hardly surprised at anything about Henry. He was bashful throughout his childhood, yet he also showed independence of mind, even to his father.

HENRY : I know you're plagued good at twisting. But if you can twist your creed onto the Westminster Confession you can twist better than I think you can.

LYMAN : All my children are smart, and one of them is impudent.

NARRATOR : Henry had been Lyman Beecher's constant companion on travels to Pittsburgh and all around. He'd been one of very few left at Lane when the senior class had defected over the right to speak out on slavery—after all, his father was president.

Despite his habit of rebelliousness at any constraint, Henry Ward Beecher was ordained, and he received a subsidy from the Home Missionary Society, which had sent many young men of the East into what it regarded as the spiritual desert of the Ohio Valley. His first post was Lawrenceburgh, Indiana, near Cincinnati.

HENRY : The fact is, I never had any choice about it.

NARRATOR : Lawrenceburgh was a deep disappointment to Eunice, Henry's bride—their first home was over a stable. Lawrenceburgh was also disappointed in the new minister—at one point, he resolved to give up preaching and get a farm. Often he would be out fishing or gathering driftwood by the river.

HENRY : The flock which I found gathered in the wilderness consisted of 20 persons. 19 of them were women, and the other was nothing. I remember the days of our poverty, or straitness. I was sexton of my own church at that time. There were no lamps there, so I bought some; and I filled them and lit them. I swept the church, and lighted my own fire. I did not ring the bell, because there was none to ring. I opened the church before prayer-meetings and preaching, and locked it when they were over. I took care of everything connected with the building.

NARRATOR : His early resolves set a direction for his career. He carried out all but one.

HENRY : Remember you can gain men easily if you get round their prejudices and put truth in their minds; but never if you attack prejudices.

My people must be alert to make the church agreeable, to give seats, and wait on strangers.

Secure a large congregation; let this be the first thing.

NARRATOR : On one issue, Henry's Methodist rival could claim victory.

METHODIST : Mr. Beecher could outpreach me, but I could outvisit him.

NARRATOR : When Henry was invited to a larger church in Indianapolis, he declined to answer at first. After two years of prodding, Henry reluctantly accepted the call to the Second Presbyterian Church in Indianapolis. The state capital had 4,000 people and yellow clay and malaria. The Beechers' first house was so damp that they both took sick and one child died.

Once in Indianapolis, he did reasonably well in attracting listeners. Henry's preaching once brought his new congregation to tears. An elder told him they wanted tartar, not sugar, in their sermons. His topics ranged widely to include nudity in art, agricultural chemistry, phrenology, and Macaulay's histories as well as the Gospel. But with all his success in filling the hall, Henry wanted also to change lives.

As relief from what he regarded as failure with his own congregation, Henry went on horseback to outlying congregations. Whenever possible, he rode out to wilderness camp-meetings, great gatherings of people who sought to recapture the spirit of the great Cumberland wilderness revival of 30 years before. He took back some of that enthusiasm, and roused his congregation—but not to revival pitch.

The work strained him, and he found relief in gardening, and writing for an agricultural gazette.

Just the year before, Henry and Edward Beecher had grappled intellectually in letters with the Campbellite insistence on primitive baptism. But when fellow ministers came around, Henry agreed to a grand union baptism with them, and he himself performed the sprinkling, pouring, or dunking in the White River according to the wishes of each convert. By such actions, Henry Ward Beecher won the respect of many Indiana clergymen. Through his revivals, sometimes three in one year, his fame spread to the East.

By carefully noting everything about revival meetings, he concluded that revivalism was not just a relic of the past, but a powerful expression of of people looking for a new focus of feeling and purpose. He saw that the minister's duty was to channel this energy by any means available. In his case, this meant preaching.

By 1842, he had learned the trade of revivalist preacher, and was phenomenally successful—outside of Indianapolis.

HENRY : My heart was on fire; and it rained a stream of prayer all the way home from Terre Haute to Indianapolis. It was like an Aurora Borealis, I have no doubt, ray upon ray, for that whole distance, if angels could have seen it.

LYMAN : The revival here under Henry's administration and preaching was, in the adaptation of means and happy results, one of the most perfectly conducted and delightful that I have ever known.

•

NARRATOR : He neglected his other pastoral duties to concentrate on his skills as a preacher. Doctrine didn't interest him much. He began to make a study of the preaching of the Apostles. After the revival meetings, he had a basis for understanding their methods. He would present his truths in modern Hoosier language and examples.

HENRY : First, the Apostles had a foundation of historical truth, common to them and their auditors.

Second, they presented this truth in the form of an intense personal application and appeal.

Third, they spoke simply, in the language of common life.

NARRATOR : In a sermon he gave while visiting Lyman's Cincinnati church, Henry demanded a new standard of preaching—the original disciples, he said, were like businessmen, not like scholars. They had facts to demonstrate to a skeptical audience.

HENRY : The complaint I utter against learned preaching is not that it is studious—not that it is accurate—but that it has become too dainty to walk among facts and chooses to fly among principles. The person who would work up the gospel to give it dignity is one who would tie ribbons on an oak to make it pretty, would criticize Niagara Falls to give it grace, and suggest amandments to a storm or the thunder of a raging ocean.

NARRATOR : Henry Ward Beecher's confidence that religious truth could be achieved by anyone regardless of church or doctrine led him toward the idea of awakening human consciousness. This idea was not unlike the Unitarian ideas of William Ellery Channing that earlier had influenced Edward Beecher, and that Lyman Beecher had fought against in Boston.

HENRY : We were plunged into the very center and heat of that great controversy which was raging, in which my father was an eloquent thunderer on one side, and in which Dr. Channing was an eloquent silent man on the other side. Clearly, Dr. Channing was a great man, yet humankind behind him was greater, the time was greater, and the all-informing spirit of God was greater yet.

NARRATOR : In 1842, defeated Presidential candidate Martin Van Buren came to Indianapolis on a tour of the West. Democrats and Whigs alike crowded in to see the former President. Beecher was told that Van Buren intended to come to the Methodist chapel and to the Second Presbyterian Church—his church.

HENRY : He is certainly welcome. There is plenty of room there.

CITIZEN : We thought, possibly, you might like to know that he's coming as it might make some difference.

HENRY : Oh, no, no difference. I should preach to him just as I would to any other sinner.

NARRATOR : Afterwards, Van Buren's comments were relayed to Henry.

CITIZEN : Perhaps you would like to hear what the ex-President had to say about your sermon. He said he thought your trousers didn't set too well

•

NARRATOR : Henry's habits of dress were slovenly, haphazard, and altogether for convenience, not for show. Gloves were for severe cold, a dress coat he had none. During gardening season, his knees were often stained. He wore a soft felt hat, or in summer, a straw hat.

In 1843, Henry tried a new departure in his preaching, based on a method that grew out of his own abilities and limitations. If he could not memorize books, he would memorize people.

HENRY : I never hear of the experience of others who are troubled or struggling, or groping their way, that their condition does not instantly present itself as a drama before my eyes and I do not THINK of it, but I SEE it.

NARRATOR : This sense of drama, combined with graphic realism, gave these winter sermons on gambling, dishonesty, idleness, even prostitution, a power that Indianapolis had never heard before. Nor had the rest of the country. When these sermons were published as *Seven Lectures for Young Men*, the book became a classic, and Henry Ward Beecher's reputation grew outside Indiana.

In one sermon, "Gambling and Gamblers," Henry used realistic descriptions he had gotten by cultivating the acquaintance of a gambler from whom he drew all his details. In four scenes, he graphically described the downfall of a young man. Henry's use of graphic realism led some to accuse the young pastor himself of profligacy, so accurate were his portrayals. In other sermons the crude sentimentalism of the frontier had an immediate impact on his listeners. A citizen's committee was organized, driving out of town the worst offenders. At last he was having the effect he desired.

Henry at first was reluctant to have the sermons published because he felt they were inferior, but finally he gave in. *Seven Lectures* had a large sale in England and America.

HENRY : The daydreams of indolent youth glow each hour with warmer colors and bolder adventures. Mere pleasure, sought outside usefulness, existing by itself, it fraught with poison. Beware also the artful insinuations and mischievous polish which too often lurk in literature.

Laborious occupations are avoided. Money is to be earned by genteel leisure, with the help of fine clothes, and by the soft seductions of smooth hair and luxuriant whiskers.

All your companions have jewelry; you will want a ring, a seal, or a golden watch, or an ebony cane, a silver toothpick, or a quizzing-glass. Thus item presses on item, and you lose all sense of the value of property

NARRATOR : Finally, Henry Ward Beecher had struck home. But then, as if to balance things, he delivered his *Dissuasive Against Moral Intolerance*—which decried the very system of social morality that he had been building up. He attacked narrowness in sects, by clubs, societies, even political parties.

HENRY : Their authority, usually deemed moral, may be and full often is of the most enslaving kind. Perfect emancipation is effected only when the mind is permitted to form, to express, and to employ its own convictions of truth, on all subjects, as it chooses. The United States is, I believe, the only land in which offensive opinions are MOBBED.

NARRATOR : A more unlikely child to become the forceful preacher Henry Ward Beecher might be hard to find. His sister Harriet, closest to him in age and sentiment, explains.

•

HARRIET : The childhood of Henry Ward Beecher was unmarked by the possession of a single child's toy as a gift from any older person, or a single fete.

HENRY : I had from childhood a thickness of speech arising from a large palate, so that when a boy I used to be laughed at for talking as if I had pudding in my mouth. When I went to Amherst, I was fortunate in passing into the hands of John Lovell, a teacher of elocution, and a better teacher for my purpose I cannot conceive. His system consisted in drill, or the thorough practice of inflections by the voice, of gesture, posture, and articulation. Sometimes I was a whole hour practising my voice on a word like "justice."

NARRATOR : It wasn't long in Lovell's class before Henry's progress was noticeable, and much practice enabled him to overcome his embarrassment. He began to take part in plays, and to express his emotions.

HARRIET : Henry had precisely the organization which often passes for dullness. A poor writer, a miserable speller, with thick utterance, and a bashful reticence which seemed like solid stupidity.

HENRY : At intervals I cried and prayed. There was scarcely a retired place in the garden, in the woodhouse, in the carriage-house, or in the barn that was not a scene of my crying and praying. It was piteous that I should be in such a state of mind, and that there should be nobody to help me and lead me out into the light. I do not recollect that to that day one word had been said to me, or one syllable had been uttered in the pulpit, that led me to think there was any mercy in the heart of God for a sinner like me. So I used to live in perpetual fear and dread, and often I wished myself dead.

NARRATOR : Among his influences, Henry credits a black man.

HENRY : I am not ashamed to say that my whole life, my whole career respecting the colored race was largely influenced by the effect produced on my mind, when I was between eight and ten years of age, by a poor old colored man who worked on my father's farm. He used to lie upon his humble bed (I slept in the same room with him) and read his Testament, unconscious apparently that I was in the room; and he would laugh and talk about what he read, and chuckle over it with that peculiarly unctuous throat-tone which belongs to his race. I never had heard the Bible really read before; but there, in my presence, he read it, and talked about it to himself and to God. He turned the New Testament into living forms right before me. It was a revelation and an impulse to me.

•

NARRATOR : Charles Beecher was at Lane Theological Seminary about the time Henry was—but Charles despaired of believing Jonathan Edwards on the will, and decided to pursue church music, even though Lyman was disgusted by his choice.

For a while, Charles taught music in Cincinnati, but then he took a job with a cotton factor, and traveled for him as far down the river as New Orleans, where he also played as church organist. He married at this time, and started a family—meanwhile observing the world of slavery, the world of plantations known to every black as the hell of being "sold down the river."

When he came back, he moved to Indianapolis to help brother Henry with the church music; Henry also got him teaching Sunday school. That's where he first met Julia Merrill and Elizabeth—Betty—Bates. Julia and Betty took an interest in Charles as they had in Henry. Julia had adopted Henry as her hero, while Betty was drawn to Charles, or so she told Julia.

As Henry Ward Beecher settled into his civic role in Indianapolis, he also took on more of a share in holding the family together. His influence on his brothers was generally positive. Charles Beecher had spent years of wandering in the wilderness of doubt, but through many conversations and simply by watching the example of Henry in action, Charles regained enough faith to reconsider the ministry. Thomas Beecher, after staying with brother Henry in Indianapolis, was convinced to return to Illinois College to complete his senior year; and plans were laid for James to stay with Henry.

•

Once Charles Beecher finally came out of his cloud of indecision, Henry didn't give him the time to reconsider. He scheduled Charles for a series of sermons at the Second Presbyterian on the life of Christ—in which Charles characteristically mixed history and mysticism. They were well attended. On August 11, 1843, a Presbytery at the Second Presbyterian Church examined the candidate. Charles passed scrutiny. Thomas wasn't convinced.

THOMAS : Charles's mind is not as yet quite at rest upon all points—and I prophesy that it never will be. He is, however, apparently happy and may become useful.

NARRATOR : Henry and Lyman Beecher were present at the examination of Charles as a candidate. Lyman was seen repeatedly wiping his eyes. After the trial sermon, Henry gave a sermon, and then Dr. Beecher gave the charge to Charles.

LYMAN : My son, this day, much longed for and waited for, has come. You are now a minister of the Lord Jesus Christ, and the pastor of a Church of Christ.

In the view of the coming struggle, I charge thee, before God and the Lord Jesus Christ—

Be strong in thy determined purpose.

Count the cost, and give thyself wholly to thy work.

Preach the Gospel.

Take heed to thyself, to thy body, to thy mind. Take heed to thy heart. Take heed to thy doctrine; understand it clearly.

To plant Christianity in the West is as grand an undertaking as to plant it in the Roman Empire, with unspeakably greater permanence and power.

NARRATOR : The Ft. Wayne Presbyterian Church pulpit came vacant just then—and Henry conceived the idea of installing Charles in this powerful seat. The Old School congregation sent for Hanover College's William C. Anderson to forestall Henry Beecher's efforts. Anderson arrived first, and did invite Beecher to give one sermon. But Henry then set up shop at the Courthouse, preaching twice daily, and making personal calls on everybody he thought might consider leaving the Old School church.

After two weeks, he had lured away only six—but these six asked for and received letters of dismissal. Another six joined them, and together they chartered the Second Presbyterian Church of Ft. Wayne. A month later, he saw Charles Beecher installed as pastor of the new church. On a visit to Ft. Wayne, Julia wrote to Betty.

JULIA : Do you see Henry Beecher any now, if you do give him my love, etc. Do you understand? I gave your message to Mr. Charles B. He laughed and said now he was a preacher he would try to do better.

NARRATOR : Charles began his ministry as sexton, bellringer, organist and choir leader as well as preacher. Both Henry and Lyman Beecher attended his first sermon, *The Bible a Sufficient Creed*—Charles's uncompromising remarks were widely quoted throughout the country, but wrongly attributed to Henry, whose star was known to be on the rise.

CHARLES : Liberty of opinion in our theological seminaries is a mere form. To say nothing of the thumbscrew of criticism by which every original mind is tortured into negative propriety, the whole boasted liberty of the student consists in a choice of chains—a choice of handcuffs—whether he will wear the Presbyterian handcuffs or the Methodist, Baptist, Episcopal or other Evangelical handcuffs. Hence it has secretly come to pass that the ministers themselves dare not study their Bibles.

There is something criminal in saying anything new. It is shocking to utter words that have not the mould of age upon them.

And what then is to be done? I know not what others may say, but if ever I shrink from declaring that the Bible, the whole Bible and nothing but the Bible is the perfect and thorough furniture of the Christian minister and the Christian church, then may my right hand forget her cunning and my tongue cleave unto the roof of my mouth.

NARRATOR : A few months later, Henry learned that Charles was having troubles at his new post. This prompted a serious letter to Lyman, headed by this sentence:

HENRY : Do not show this to anyone but Mother and Harriet and then burn it.

NARRATOR : Julia Merrill in Ft. Wayne reported the news as she saw it.

JULIA : Mr. Charles Beecher is pretty well liked here, though not so much as I expected. The truth is they find too much fault with him, some think he's conceited, that he knows and shows too often that he is Dr. Beecher's son. Others say he preaches too plain, that no one ever did succeed that preached the Bible. He has not enough tact, etc., etc. He seems to be common property and anyone who pleases picks at him. He does not hear all that is said, or I should think he would become disheartened.

NARRATOR : When Harriet visited her brother Henry and Eunice, who was pregnant again, for several weeks, she wrote back home to Calvin:

HARRIET : I enjoy myself very well here at Henry's. The cottage is still and quiet and I hear the clock tick with great satisfaction.

NARRATOR : During her stay, Harriet roused Henry's interest in science by suggesting that they experiment with mesmerism, a kind of hypnosis.

HARRIET : The first session he succeeded in almost throwing me into convulsions—spasms and shocks of heat and prickly sensation ran all over me, my lungs were violently constricted and my heart in dreadful commotion, and I was so frightened that I called out for quarter.

NARRATOR : Charles, too, took a great interest in spiritualism. His researches were published later as a report to the church on the possibility of some connection between modern mediums, clairvoyants, seances and the Biblical descriptions of witches and sorcerers. Spiritualism swept Europe and America like a new style in fashion, a counterweight to the almost daily discoveries of scientific marvels previously undreamed of—radio waves, electricity, radium, X-rays, new planets, new fields of mathematics, chemistry, physics. People were ready for new ideas. Most of the Beechers examined Spiritualism; for a few, including Isabella, Harriet, and Charles, it was a lifelong fascination.

THE SUICIDE
1830–1843

George Beecher was the fifth of Dr. Lyman Beecher's children, and the third male to be ordained as a minister. He was brilliant, a precocious lad of whom much was expected—perhaps too much.

The family early discovered that George and Hattie were avid readers, and when Catharine brought home many books that Alexander Fisher had bequeathed her, and Dr. Beecher had inspected them, it was George that he told.

LYMAN : George, you may read Scott's novels. I have always disapproved of novels as trash, but in these is real genius and real culture, and you may read them.

NARRATOR : And later, when the whole family was engaged in making apple butter, Lyman would challenge him to feats of memory.

LYMAN : Come, George, I'll tell you what we'll do to make the evening go off. You and I'll take turns, and see who'll tell the most out of Scott's novels.

NARRATOR : Some passages he could recite verbatim, because he'd read the book several times over.

Harriet's first writing instructor, John Brace, from Sarah Pierce's school, got George started on investigating rocks.

HARRIET : Mr. Brace was one of the most stimulating and inspiring instructors I ever knew. He was himself widely informed, an enthusiast in botany, mineralogy, and the natural sciences generally, besides being well read in English classical literature. The constant conversations which he kept up on these subjects tended more to develop the mind and inspire a love of literature than any mere routine studies.

The boys were incited by his example to set up mineralogical cabinets, and my brother George tramped over the hills in the train of his teacher, with his stone-hammer on his shoulder, for many delightful hours. Many more were spent in recounting to me the stores of wisdom derived from Mr. Brace, who, he told me with pride, corresponded with geologists and botanists in Europe, exchanging specimins with them.

NARRATOR : At 16, George was very ill, though family matters went on.

LYMAN : This has been a good day; 25 have been added to the Church, and the work of awakening and conversion moves on and increases, on the whole, both here and in Milton.

We have been this three weeks in a state of deep sympathy for George, whose distress precluded sleep, almost, for many nights, and his voice of supplication could be heard night and day. But today, and especially this evening, he seems to be very happy, and, so far as I can judge by conversation, on good grounds. He is now with the girls, singing louder than he prayed. Mary and Harriet communed today for the first time, and it has been a powerful and delightful day.

NARRATOR : Dr. Beecher always observed the state of people's souls, sick or well.

LYMAN : George seems to be one of the happiest creatures ever I saw. All this quickness and characteristic ardor seems now to be heightened by the contrast of joy with recent distress. He talks rapidly, and with much and unaffected simplicity, and is exceedingly interested now in the meetings, and begs he may stay a little longer to enjoy them.

Our family concert of prayer was held in the study, on Thanksgiving day—your mother, Aunt Esther, Henry, and Charles. It was a most deeply solemn, tender, and interesting time.

Henry and Charles have both been awakened, and are easily affected and seriously disposed now. But as yet it is like the wind upon the willow, which rises as soon as it is passed over.

NARRATOR : When the family moved to Cincinnati in 1832, George was not reluctant to leave Lawrence Academy, where he had been principal, and travel with them. Harriet reports the journey, on a new folio sheet of the Beecher's round-robin letter.

HARRIET : Well, my dear, the great sheet is out and the letter is begun. All our family are here in New York, and in good health. Mother and her tribe are at Mr. Thomas's. Father is to perform tonight in the Chatham Theater, "Positively for the last time this season." I don't know, I'm sure, as we shall ever get to Pittsburgh. Father is staying here begging money for the Biblical Literature professorship; the incumbent is to be C. Stowe.

He called yesterday on S. Van Rensselaer, and made such representations as induced him to subscribe $1,000 on the spot. They had really quite an affecting time, by all accounts.

Monday morning. Last night we had a call from Arthur Tappan and Mr. Eastman. Father begged $2,000 yesterday, and now the good people are praying him to abide certain days, as he succeeds so well. Father has been this morning in high spirits. He is all in his own element—dipping into books—consulting authorities for his oration—going around here, there, and everywhere—begging, borrowing, and spoiling the Egyptians—delighted with past success, and confident for the future.

Philadelphia, October 18. The truckman carted all the family baggage to the wrong wharf, and, after waiting and waiting on board the boat, we were obliged to start without it, George remaining to look it up. Arrived here late Saturday evening—dull, drizzling weather.

Father does not succeed very well in opening purses here. I saw today a notice in the Philadelphia about father, setting forth how "this distinguished brother, with his large family, having torn themselves from the endearing scenes of their home," etc. etc., "were going, like Jacob," etc.—a very scriptural and appropriate flourish.

Downington, Pa., October 19. Here we all are—Noah, and his wife, and his sons, and his daughters, with the cattle and creeping things, all dropped down in the front parlor of this tavern, about 30 miles from Philadelphia. If today is a fair specimen of our journey, it will be very pleasant—obliging driver, good roads, good spirits, good dinner, fine scenery, and now and then some "psalms, and hymns, and spiritual songs," for with George on board you may be sure of music of some kind. Moreover, George has provided himself with a quantity of tracts, and he and the children have kept up a regular discharge at all the wayfaring people we encountered. I tell him he is peppering the land with moral influence.

174

NARRATOR : George continues the account.

GEORGE : We had poor horses in crossing the mountains. Our average rate for the last four days to Wheeling was 44 miles. The journey which takes the mail-stage 48 hours, took us eight days. At Wheeling, we deliberated long whether to go on board a boat for Cincinnati, but the prevalence of the cholera there at last decided us to remain.

While at Wheeling, father preached eleven times—nearly every everning—and gave them the Taylorite heresy on sin and decrees to the highest notch; and what amused me most was to hear him establish it from the Confession of Faith. It went high and dry, however, above all objections, and they were delighted with it, even those in the strong Old School, since it had not been christened heresy in their hearing.

After remaining in Wheeling eight days, we chartered a stage for Cincinnati, and started next morning. At Granville, Ohio, we were invited to stop and attend a protracted meeting. Being in no great hurry to enter Cincinnati till the cholera left, we consented. We spent the remainder of the week there, and I preached five times and father four. The interest was deep and solemn each day, and when we left there were 45 cases of conversion in the town, besides those from the surrounding towns. The people were astonished at the doctrine; said they never saw the truth so plain in their lives.

From Granville we went to Columbus over corduroy roads, made of logs laid crosswise, for the benefit of dyspeptics.

We arrived safely at Cincinnati November 14th, and found our furniture had arrived the day before, so we were soon settled in our new habitation.

•

NARRATOR : George was ordained in Cincinnati, facing some of the same of the Old School who had challenged his father, including Dr. Joshua Wilson.

HARRIET : At his ordination, George was examined by Dr. Wilson. "Mr. Beecher, what is matter and what is mind, and what is the difference 'twixt and 'tween—and what is right and wrong, and what is truth, and what is virtue—and what is intellect, susceptibilities, and will and conscience—and everything else, world without end, amen"

And the other doctors present: "Mr. Beecher, do you believe in the doctrine of election?" "Mr. Beecher, do you believe infants are sinners as soon as they are born?" "Do you believe that infants have unholy natures?" "Mr. Beecher, do you think that men are punished for the guilt of Adam's first sin?"

There was George—eyes flashing and hands going, turning first to right and then to left—"If I understand your question, sir"—"Do you mean by nature thus and so? and so?" "Yes, sir" (to right). "No, sir" (to left). "I should think so, sir" (in front).

NARRATOR : George accepted a call to a church in Batavia, New York. Soon after he joined the Anti-Slavery Society.

.

Within the family, the issue of slavery was considered a political question in broad perspective, and a moral one for individual decisions. Dr. Beecher was of the opinion,, and in this he was not alone, that slavery would slowly disappear in the South as it had in New York and Connecticut just a few years before. Therefore, all the abolitionist agitation of William Lloyd Garrison and his ilk was useless and downright dangerous.

Soon after leaving the Beecher household, George was the first Beecher to make a public stand on the slavery issue. Edward Beecher in Illinois had befriended Elijah Lovejoy in Illinois, but was still trying to establish a moral neutral ground in a rapidly polarizing situation. The following year, Lovejoy's death by a mob at Alton, Illinois and Edward's book about it, catapulted Edward into the anti-slavery movement as a national leader, spokesman for conservative abolitionists.

About the same time, Lyman Beecher was married for a third time, to Lydia Beals Jackson, a fine secretary and organizer of his many activities, though not an intellectual.

When Calvin Stowe's beautiful wife Eliza died, Harriet comforted him, and soon after, married him. And George married; his wife Sarah had money of her own. Henry brought Eunice Bullard back from the East, married her, and took her to his first post, Lawrenceburgh, Indiana, just downriver from Cincinnati. Within a few short years, the Beecher family was scattered from Maine to Illinois.

Keeping in touch by mail was expensive, since letters were charged by the mile, and by the sheet. To solve this expense problem, a family circular letter was started at one end of the country on a single large folio sheet, with messages to be added by the next recipient and then sent on. When both sides of the huge paper was filled, often it would be turned sideways, and the writing continued. This was the letter in which Harriet and George reported their journey to Cincinnati.

•

On another such sheet, a controversy developed over George's presumption of the perfectionism doctrine, much discussed but little adopted by ministers. Charles comments:

CHARLES : Brother George's perfectionism is a curious matter, and lies in a nutshell. That a Christian can be perfect is evident, else God commands impossibilities. Whether they ever are or not, who can decide? Does one think oneself perfect? Amen. I hope he is not mistaken. So long as he behaves well, let the person pass for immaculate. If one does not behave properly, he deceives himself. If you ask, "Have I attained?" I say, Ask God. The more you try to decide, and the nearer you come to an affirmative, the more probable is it you are deceived. The heart is deceitful; who can know it?

NARRATOR : Henry Ward adds his advice.

HENRY : There are some signs of better things among my people; more feeling in Church and congregation, and more solemn meetings, and some cases of incipient anxiety—just that state of things that encourages, yet makes me feel most powerless.

I wish, George, you could be here a while and help me. I would, if you were here, have continuous preaching, and believe immense good could be done. I thought it possible you might be able to come. Besides, we have grown almost strangers to each other since you groped off to Rochester, and I would fain have some of our long talks again.

As to perfectionism, I am not greatly troubled with the fact of it in myself, or the doctrine of it in you; for I feel sure that if you give yourself time and prayer you will settle down right, whatever the right may be; and I rejoice, on this account, that your judgment has led you to forebear publishing, because, after we have published, if we do not hit exactly right, there is a vehement temptation not to advance, but rather to nurse and defend our published views. The treatises which have had influence in this world from generation to generation are those which have been matured, re-thought, re-cast, delayed. Apples that ripen early are apt to be worm-eaten, and decay early, at any rate; late fruit always keeps best. I have seen people by an injudicious effort run so high aground that there never was a tide high enough to float them again. They dried, shrunk, and rattled. May God never let you run ashore.

NARRATOR : Harriet, now Mrs. Calvin Stowe, adds this.

HARRIET : Well, George, it seems to be the fashion of the day to address you firstly and prime; and I, setting apart metaphysics, will enter only that interesting department of physics which your gift of flower-seeds brings to mind. Many thanks for them, hoping that you and Sarah will be here to see them in all their glory. I have a fine place laid out for them, and shall proceed with them *secundum artem.*

What is your experience with dahlias? for I was never more puzzled in my life than with the contradictory directions I hear about soil, etc. Some say the richest you can find—can't be too rich; and the other day a celebrated gardener of New York advocated dry gravel. What do you think? If you don't write pretty soon it will be too late.

NARRATOR : Catharine writes:

CATHARINE : Where is the eastern circular that started from Hartford, or ought to have started, two months since? I shall recommend that anyone who delays a circular over a week shall lose the reading of the return one, as a penalty to make them remember. I shall flit about here this summer till I find where it is best to settle next. Love to you all.

NARRATOR : And Dr. Beecher.

LYMAN : William, why do you not write to your father? Are you not my first-born son? Did I not carry you over bogs afishing, astraddle of my neck, on my shoulders, and, besides clothing and

178

feeding, whip you often to make a man of you as you are, and would not have been without? And have I not always loved you, and borne you on my heart, as the claims and trials of a first-born demand? Don't you remember studying theology with your father while sawing and splitting wood in that woodhouse in Green Street, Boston, near by where you found your wife?

Little do those know who have rented that tenement since how much orthodoxy was developed and embodied there; and now why should all this fruit of my labors be kept to yourself? Let me hear from you soon.

NARRATOR : Even Calvin Stowe was a contributor.

CALVIN : Dear Brother George,—As to Perfectionism, Brother Charles 'spresses my mind 'zactly, and I trust you will duly appreciate the patriarchal, paternal, grandfatherly, and most judicious counsel of Brother Henry. Brother Charles's advice as to faith and Brother Henry's as to works, on this perfection matter, are just the thing, according to the best judgment of your dutiful brother.

NARRATOR : To which George replies:

GEORGE : I am quite amused with the sympathy of all my brothers, and their fatherly advice touching perfectionism, as if I were on the verge of a great precipice; but I trust in God who is able to keep me from falling.

NARRATOR : And William responds to his father's plea:

WILLIAM : We received the circular, and forward it today. The Lord has been with us, and there is now a great amount of labor to be done, and great difficulties yet to be overcome. We expect to build a vestry and repair to the amount of $1,000.

•

NARRATOR : George moved to Rochester, New York to preach for a couple of years, then to Chillicothe, Ohio. In July of 1843, Catharine, on one of her many trips across the country, visited him there. He had just received the family circular letter, and had written the following, but had not sent it.

GEORGE : Dear brothers and sisters, all hail—I only wish I had you all here, and every room in my house stowed full. When, think you, Henry and Charles, shall I see your faces here? Can you not come, one or both, this summer? Our house is completed, except a little painting, and will be ready for everybody that will come in two weeks, so do make haste

NARRATOR : He then went on to list all the flowers and fruits that he had just planted for the fall and spring.

Dr. Beecher was also traveling that summer, stopping off in East Hampton for nostalgia's sake—

LYMAN : We preached and prayed, exhorted and wept. It was a solemn and joyful time. I never had a visit of such thrilling interest.

NARRATOR : But he was also on business to procure an agent and secretary, when a friend stopped him on the street.

•

LYMAN : "Have you heard the dreadful news which has come into the city this morning?" I said, "No." He said, "Your son George is dead," and handed me the paper containing the account. The shock was like that of a blow across my breast which almost suspended respiration, and left to me only the power of articulating at intervals "Oh oh oh" Tears soon came to my relief, but they were not the tears of the father which flowed first, but the tears of disappointed hope for so much and so needed usefulness in the cause of Christ cut off.

But soon busy memory flashed upon me its thousand tender recollections of feature, and person, and affection, and cooperation, and his life's history in rapid succession, and then a father's heart paid the debt of nature in a flood of tears.

I went to my place of letters immediately, and met Catharine's letter, which opened deeper the sluices of sorrow as I sympathized with you and yours in that overwhelming scene. I returned to my room through the streets of the city sighing and bathed in tears, subsiding and anon bursting out again.

NARRATOR : Catharine had stopped by George and Sarah's in the morning, on the way to a speaking tour in the East. The next morning at breakfast, she heard the news. This is Harriet's account, pieced together from eyewitnesses.

HARRIET : Noticing the birds destroying his fruit and injuring his plants, he went for a double-barreled gun, which he scarcely ever had used, out of regard to the timidity and anxiety of his wife in reference to it. Shortly after he left the house, one of the elders of his church in passing saw him discharge one barrel at the birds. Soon after he heard the fatal report and saw the smoke, but the trees shut out the rest from sight. In about half an hour after, the family assembled at breakfast, and the servant was sent out to call him. In a few minutes she returned, exclaiming, "Oh, Mr. Beecher is dead Mr. Beecher is dead."

In a short time a visitor in the family, assisted by a passing laborer, raised him up and bore him to the house. His face was pale and but slightly marred, his eyes were closed, and over his countenance rested the sweet expression of peaceful slumber.

And so it is at last there must come a time when all the most heartbroken, idolizing love can give us is a coffin and a grave All that could be done for our brother, with all his means, and all the affection of his people and friends, was just this—no more

Oh my siblings all, let this first blood shed baptize you as soldiers of Christ, to fight in the steps of him who has fallen, but who also has triumphed. Then at last,

> "We all shall meet at Jesus's feet;
> Shall meet to part no more"

NARRATOR : Every Beecher felt the shock of it. There was no going back now, no return to innocence. The official explanation of George's death was accident. Dr. Beecher never acknowledged suicide. Yet all the Beechers recognized that the intense pressures George felt were not his alone, they came with being a Beecher. Roxana Beecher's last wish in 1816 had been a promise from Lyman Beecher that every one of her sons would enter the ministry. Charles also had suffered from that wish. He graduated from Bowdoin at 19, and knew eight languages.

CHARLES : I went to college too young. Father was in a hurry to get us all through and into the ministry.

NARRATOR : William, the eldest son, had not been suited to be a preacher, had not even been encouraged by his father—yet he had followed his mother's deathbed wish. And others—Thomas, James, Charles, even Henry—had made serious plans for other careers. Yet every male in the Beecher family became ministers, and every female except Mary launched into fulltime public service careers. Beecherism, at times, was stronger than even the Beechers.

HARRIET : Our circle has begun to break up. Who shall say where it shall stop?

NARRATOR : Some feared that Catharine might be next. She was quite affected by George's death. George had become a minister to please his father, and had suffered three nervous breakdowns trying to please his congregations. Catharine read through his papers to try to find the answer. If she found one, she never said—but she never returned to the Beecher residence as a dependent again. She no longer was a loyal supporter of Lyman Beecher.

Catharine gathered up George's papers, and with Sarah's permission, edited a memorial volume—*The Biographical Remains of Rev. George Beecher.* He was 34 years old.

CATHARINE : In presenting this book to the public, I intend to awaken hope and encouragement in all who, amid similar embarrassments, are pressing forward to mark for the prize of their high calling.

NARRATOR : Then, dressed in mourning, Catharine Beecher completed an extensive tour of upper New York and western Massachusetts, renewing old acquaintances and making new friends—hearing Charles Grandison Finney preach, staying in a Shaker community. Then, with the help of Mrs. Cortlandt Van Rensselaer, Catharine set out anew on her program to educate the American West.

Slavery was dying out in the North when Eli Whitney, a New England mechanic staying in Savannah, Georgia, built a machine that separated cotton seeds from cotton fibers. The cotton gin made cotton into a very profitable crop. The value of slaves to pick cotton suddenly increased, and the practice of slavery grew in the South.

In 1820, the question of slavery seemed to be answered in the Missouri Compromise, slavery was limited to territories south of latitude 36° 30'—the line that runs between Virginia and North Carolina, between Kentucky and Tennessee, and forms most of the southern border of Missouri.

Until 1833, there was hardly an issue to discuss—but in that year, the British freed all slaves in the British West Indies. The South suddenly felt isolated. William Lloyd Garrison had begun his unrelenting attack on slavery, and he was joined by others.

When California asked for admission in 1849, and there was no counterbalancing southern territory to be admitted, the South raised a hue and cry. Henry Clay's compromise plan was to admit California as a free state, but also to pass stringent laws that would prohibit any Northerner from aiding runaway slaves in any way. Clay, from the border state of Kentucky, was an ideal compromiser. But for it to pass, Daniel Webster, champion of New England, had to lend his support.

Webster had already spoke out against the popular Northern view of slavery. Now he supported Clay's Omnibus Bill, including the notorious Fugitive Slave Act. For the sake of the Union, he sacrificed his political future—he would never be President now. All New England saw him as betraying their interests.

Meanwhile, John C. Calhoun, the Southern leader in Congress, died, and Zachary Taylor, elected only a few months before, died in office. Millard Fillmore was President, and Webster was named his Secretary of State. Fillmore signed into law the Fugitive Slave Act. And John Greenleaf Whittier, the abolitionist poet, excoriated Webster.

WHITTIER :

> So fallen so lost the light withdrawn
> > Which once he wore
> The glory from his gray hairs gone
> > For evermore
> Oh, dumb be passion's stormy rage,
> > When he who might
> Have lighted up and led his age
> > Falls back in night

●

NARRATOR : By the mid-1840s, Henry Ward Beecher had made himself into one of the leading revivalist preachers of the West, with techniques borrowed from the Apostles, and by taking advantage of his own talent for close observation and mimicry, in compensation for a poor memory.

Great outdoor revival meetings taught him most. There he found the liberty that his mind demanded—in the camp-meetings, where horns were blown, chants and hymns and shouts of ecstacy filled the air, and crowds rushed forward to be immersed in the river. It became his milieu, and the unbridled atmostphere unleashed his talents as nothing else had done before. He became a speaker of enormous power, learning here the wellsprings of those great religious emotions of hope and fear and despair and bliss. No seminary could have trained him for the work he was about to commence.

Yes when he tried to create a revival in town, in his own church, he failed. His freedom of thought met social pressures in Indianapolis, particularly on the subject of slavery. And he held back because he felt that he would be dismissed if he spoke out.

HENRY : At the time, the people of Indiana did not dare to say that their souls were their own, or that the Negro's soul was his own. It seemed to me that if I spoke out, my church would be shut up, and that I should be deprived of the means on which I depended for the support of my family.

On a certain day, while reflecting upon the unhappy state of my affairs, I read this passage "Let your conversation be without covetousness"—that is, Do not borrow trouble about where your salary is coming from—"and be content with such things as ye have." "Why yes," I thought, "I have not many things, but I will be content with them."

NARRATOR : Henry Beecher's anti-slavery stance began in the Amherst debating society—the proposition was whether or not recolonization of African-American slaves back to Africa was suitable.

HENRY : Fortunately, I was assigned the negative side of the question. In preparing to speak I prepared my whole life. I contended against colonization as a condition of emancipation—enforced colonization was little better than enforced slavery—and advocated immediate emancipation on the broad ground of human rights.

NARRATOR : But though Henry volunteered to protect Birney's abolitionist paper—with arms if necessary—when mob action threatened Cincinnati, he is not on record as speaking on slavery during his Lawrenceburgh years. In Indianapolis, a hundred miles from the nearest legal slavery, Henry still did not open the subject directly. On one occasion, he illustrated a point with the story of a captive of the Algerians—a white slave with non-white masters.

HENRY : They all thought I was going to apply it to slavery; but I did not. I applied it to my subject, and it passed off—and they all drew a long breath. It was not long before I had another illustration from that quarter. And so, before I had been there a year, I had gone all over the sore spots of slavery, in illustrating the subjects of Christian experience and doctrine. It broke the ice.

NARRATOR : Slavery had vociferous apologists in Congress calling for extension of slavery as a right in the territories. Of the vast Louisiana Purchase, only Louisiana and Missouri had been admitted to the Union—both as slave states. Some Southern visionaries saw slavery extended to Texas, the northern Mexican territories, and even to the Caribbean, Cuba and Central America. This Caribbean Basin slave empire idea motivated several filibuster, or freebooter, expeditions, including one to Cuba. East and West Florida had been wrested from the weak Spanish Empire before the politicians in Washington could say boo—why not statehood for Cuba?

Every Southern state was a different case—the border states of Virginia, Kentucky, Maryland, Delaware were pretty lukewarm about slavery, but the cotton belt states, led by South Carolina, were organized around slave labor for the cotton plantations. A lot of hand picking was needed to feed the efficient cotton gin and the textile mills of New England and Britain.

James Oglethorpe, the founder of Georgia, had been one of the first Americans to denounce slavery. The original settlement had been designed for freeholders, to form a buffer between South Carolina and the Spanish Floridas. At first, slavery was banned, but in 1749 it was made legal, and Virginia and Carolina planters moved down to settle the coast.

•

In the mid 1820s, Fanny Kemble, an English actress touring in America, met and married Pierce Mease Butler, a wealthy Philadelphia gentleman.

FANNY : When I married Mr. Butler, I knew nothing of these dreadful possessions of his. The family into which I have married are large slaveholders; our present and future fortune depend greatly upon extensive plantations in Georgia.

I am prejudiced against slavery, for I am an Englishwoman, in whom the absence of such a prejudice would be disgraceful.

NARRATOR : William Ellery Channing, the Unitarian leader, influenced her. Henry Carey was set to publish Fanny Kemble's journal in 1835, including a long diatribe against slavery. Her husband, however, persuaded her to delete the anti-slavery portion.

That same year, Channing published a little book called *Slavery*—it went through four editions quickly. Channing said that slavery must be discussed. The point, he said, was to plead the cause of the slave with his or her owner. The Christian way was to win the slaveowner to repentance. Although the slave was wronged, the slave owner was not necessarily depraved—unless he or she persisted.

There is no good in slavery, said Channing. It crushes the human spirit. It denies the dignity of labor. it extinguishes reason. It breeds cruelty and irresponsibility.

Therefore, emancipation is the answer—but emancipation by the slaveowner. This means educating the slaves, and bringing them to a moral life, as well as freeing them.

Fanny spoke at length with the overseer for Mr. Butler's estate.

FANNY : The fact is—and I have it not only from observation of my own, but from the distinct statement of some of the most intelligent Southern men that I have conversed with—the only obstacle to immediate abolition throughout the South is the immense value of the human property.

OVERSEER : I'll tell you why abolition is impossible: because every healthy Negro can fetch a thousand dollars in the Charleston market at this moment.

FANNY : Can many of the slaves here read?

OVERSEER : No; very few, I'm happy to say. Those few are just so many too many.

FANNY : Why, have you observed any insubordination in those who do read?

OVERSEER : No, I have no special complaint to bring against them. I speak by anticipation. Every step they take toward education makes them think too much of themselves. Their condition is not to be changed—so, they'd better not learn to read.

Oh, and the masters who take up with the preaching and the teaching and the moral instructions of the Yankees, they think they're being kind. They're being cowardly—they crumble up what they suppose may prove a little harmless religion and mix it with what the Bible says about masters and slaves, and then trust their slaves to swallow it all and not do them any harm. they want better Christians for slaves—and so, no doubt, they are. But it is a very dangerous experiment.

FANNY : I'll quite agree with you there.

OVERSEER : You know, hiring free labor would be more profitable even on these plantations. The work of slaves gives you the worst quality and the smallest quantity. And then there's having charge of them growing up and then growing old, and in the meantime you feed them and clothe them—which is a considerable cost. No,

187

I myself am in favor of free labor all around.

FANNY : I also listened with infinite interest to the opinions of Mr. King, a man of uncommon shrewdness and sagacity, who was born in the very bosom of slavery, and has passed his whole life among slaves. This was his verdict.

KING : I hate slavery with all my heart; I consider it an absolute curse wherever it exists. It will keep those states where it does exist fifty years behind the others in improvement and prosperity.

As for its being an irremediable evil—a thing not to be helped or got rid of—that's all nonsense; for, as soon as people become convinced that it is their interest to get rid of it, they will soon find the means to do so, depend on it.

•

NARRATOR : The New Testament was Henry's chief study, reading, re-reading, always to get at the living thought of the writer, to understand and put himself in possession of the writer's experience. One analysis that he published is like a lawyer's brief in its detail.

For his sermons, much preparation was done, suitable for his method.

HENRY : I have half a dozen or more topics lying loose in my mind through the week; I think of one or another, as occasion may serve, anywhere—at home, in the street, in the horse-car. I rarely know what theme I shall use until Sunday morning. Then, after breakfast, I go into my study, as a man goes into his orchard; I feel among these themes as he feels among the apples, to find the ripest and the best; the theme which seems most ripe I pluck; then I select my text, analyze my subject, prepare my sermon, and go into the pulpit to preach it while it is fresh.

NARRATOR : In fact, he would write out the first few pages, often still writing as he entered the church, adding notes as the choir was singing. Then, he would read from his notes, throw in an idea, come back to his notes, then drop them altogether as his theme developed from the weeks of rumination on this topic.

Lyman Abbott once wanted his opinion on a book on phrenology—he called at dinnertime.

HENRY : I never read a book through. A book is like a fish: you cut off the head, you cut off the tail, you cut off the fins, you take out the backbone, and there is a little piece of meat left.

ABBOTT : At the end of the first course, he left the table and sat down by the window, took the pages, and ran over them rapidly.

HENRY : Yes! No! that is not true. Ah! that is old. Yes, that is so. Well, I don't know about that.

ABBOTT : In 15 minutes he had gone through the volume and knew it better than I did after an hour or two of examination.

NARRATOR : On a revival trip to Madison, Julia Merrill heard Henry preach again. Eunice had said that she envied Julia's being there with him, and Henry replied.

HENRY : You have no reason to envy. Give my love to Elizabeth Bates and a good warm kiss, as the kiss for Julia is on hand.

•

NARRATOR : But in that short interval before his return to Indianapolis, Henry's relationship with Julia Merrill suddenly changed. Henry could no longer treat Julia fondly as a daughter; he did not encourage her. Julia, on her part, made no attempt to hide a deepening love for Henry.

By 1846, Henry's salary was getting even more difficult to collect, and when he resigned as Clerk of the Presbytery, it was clear that he was thinking of leaving Indianapolis. With his usual cautious boldness, Henry resolved to speak out on slavery. A church directive had instructed ministers to speak out, though few had done so. Then the Mexican War started in May; some feared that the new territories—Texas, the whole Southwest, and the coveted California—would simply extend slavery to the Pacific. He remembered Lyman Beecher's advice on controversy.

LYMAN : True wisdom consists in advocating a cause only so far as the community will sustain the reformer.

NARRATOR : Nevertheless, at the very end of his pastorate in Indianapolis, Henry Ward Beecher preached two sermons denouncing slavery. The first sermon dealt with Moses and the Hebrews in bondage to Pharaoh. With no untoward reaction to that, he scheduled a second sermon for a day that the U.S. District

Court would be sitting in Indianapolis, with Judge John McLean in attendance, and chances of violence would be less. This time, he spoke directly and bluntly against slavery in America, and about the duty of Christians. One newspaper reprinted the sermons. Justice McLean was asked what he thought of the sermon.

McLEAN : I think if every minister in the United States would be as faithful it would be a great advance in settling this question.

NARRATOR : On returning from a trip, Henry found a letter from the New York group that was planning to build a new church in Brooklyn, and wanted Henry Ward Beecher to be its first pastor. Their offer was attractive.

CUTLER : You can probably do as much or more for the West by living here, you could publish much to benefit the world. Your influence would be felt beyond the Atlantic as well as West of the Alleghenys. You would have a world of people here to listen to your preaching, you would have much to stimulate to study and action—other minds here to vie with, to see who should best sow Christ and build up his Kingdom. Suppose you were to come and stay five years, then return to the West you would be eminently better fitted to be a General in the Army opposed to Satan

NARRATOR : At first, Henry declined. They persisted. Lyman advised him against it, fearing that New York would be the downfall of his unsteady son. So, Henry Beecher went to New York during Anniversary Week to give sermons—in the evening 800 people crowded into the building to hear him speak. He spoke nervously, but the *New York Tribune* printed the whole sermon on its front page, and Beecher received another invitation to preach at Cranberry Street.

He also spoke in Boston to the Home Missionary Society, the Temperance Union, the Commissioners for Foreign Missions, plus sermons in Boston's churches. Suddenly the New Yorkers, fearful that Boston might snatch the prize, besieged him with letters and requests to accept their offer.

Another factor was Eunice's health—friends in the East who had not seen her in years were shocked by her weakness.

Henry C. Bowen, one of the New Yorkers, wrote to Lyman Beecher to overcome his opposition; he also urged Lyman's old friend Dr. Taylor to write the older Beecher. To no avail.

LYMAN : Henry is settled in Indianapolis at a point of great influence, where he could do great good, and it would be folly to remove him. In the vicinity of New York he would simply sink out of sight among the greater men, and have no especial influence, except in a very limited sphere.

NARRATOR : The prestigious Park Street Church in Boston, where Edward had been pastor, and Lyman and Henry had both given sermons, did extend Henry an invitation to become associate pastor.

Though Henry didn't write back to Indiana for the first few weeks, he did acknowledge a bank draft from Julia Merrill and Elizabeth Bates.

HENRY : Although out of means, and either obliged to borrow, or to receive payment for preaching each Sabbath, still the bank draft was not half so welcome as was the feeling that you thought of me and mine, and thought so much as to enter into our probable wants, and to make provision for them, when such provision was, as I very well know, not easy for you.

And now dear Julia, you may well imagine how much more I think and feel than I can write. So you must call upon your imagination to interpret an ampler meaning than these hasty lines can give.

NARRATOR : Then, 15-month-old George died, and Eunice and Henry both mourned, Eunice especially.

EUNICE : My heart is almost broken by this year's trials. I miss his small step by my chair. I miss him at the morning prayer. I miss him all day everywhere and I have the wildest longings to look into his grave and see if he is indeed there—or if this be not a horrible dream. I think you would have some trouble to recognize your sister in the thin-faced, grey-headed, toothless old woman you would find here.

•

NARRATOR : In June 1847, the Plymouth Church was formally organized, and Henry was unanimously called to be pastor. Henry again postponed his answer as he journeyed back West to make his decision.

Finally, Henry gave in to the persistent group of gentlemen

from Brooklyn who had no church building, no name, and only a handful of members—but who insisted on having Henry Ward Beecher as their pastor.

Eunice had suffered enough West to last her the rest of her life; her health required the move. She left Indianapolis ahead of him; he rode on the newly-opened train line to the East, seated on boards in a boxcar. When Eunice published her novel, it was an indictment in detail of the American West, a bitter attack on the mud and pigs, callous neighbors, do-nothings and misfits, and unflattering to her husband. Even friends of his—Samuel Merrill and John Ketcham—were not sorry to see him leave the Second Presbyterian Church in Indianapolis.

MERRILL : We have liked him as a preacher but many of the Church as I now learn complain much of him as a pastor.

KETCHAM : Henry Beecher was a great man in the pulpit—but woefully deficient in every other respect. Often he has failed to attend prayer meeting without any excuse. Never has been in Sabbath School more than thrice in his residence here of seven years. Visits almost none among his people. Makes appointments for meetings of Session, and half the time forgets them. Always funny and often frivolous.

Well, he always made a noise wherever he went and we were flattered by it and held on. The truth is, we, as a town, feel that we are losing a valuable citizen; but he has never endeared himself as a pastor to his church—he has not been a pastor at all—only a brilliant preacher—and brilliant he is.

NARRATOR : Julia Merrill was very upset when Henry resigned. She planned to go with him on a buggy ride from Greenwood to Indianapolis, but Julia's mother was very ill and insisted that she accompany her to Cincinnati immediately.

JULIA : Oh, Elizabeth, I had so hoped to see Mr. Beecher again—but—I could not. I rode silently along for miles, and thought over for the thousandth time all those happy days which are gone.

NARRATOR : She wrote to her sister Catherine to come take care of their mother.

JULIA : Oh Kate, what am I to do? You know how badly I want to get home to see Mr. Beecher before he goes—I must stay, as long as there is any necessity on Ma's part. I could stay very willingly, but if I am to be detained here for no earthly reason, why, I shall almost rebel. You know if I should miss seeing him altogether how many long years may elapse before I see him again.

NARRATOR : But Mrs. Merrill grew worse, and insisted on going back home to die. Catherine Merrill met Julia and their mother near Columbus, and together they journeyed slowly to the capital.

HENRY : Mrs. Merrill is very low and sinking fast. It would be miraculous if she lived many weeks.

NARRATOR : Two weeks later, she was dead. Meanwhile, Henry was winding up his affairs, taking advantage of the New Yorkers' offer to help him clear up all outstanding debts. Henry Bowen warned, however:

BOWEN : I owe you nothing. If you get into debt when you get here you must look out for yourself as I am afraid my agency or the agency of your friends will not be quite so promptly responded to a second time for the same thing.

NARRATOR : Eunice and the family went on ahead, and Henry stayed alone to pack up all his books and sell the furniture. In September he gave his farewell sermon; he could leave knowing his church was united, and had grown to 270 members. Three days later, the first run of the new Madison and Indianapolis Railroad came steaming into town at 12 miles per hour. Beecher boarded it as it left an hour and a half late. Only Julia Merrill went along to say goodbye.

His first letter back was to her.

HENRY : Julia, from me you have probably received more ideas, more influences going to form opinion and character than from all others.

As I sat upon the wharf-boat and looked upon the water I thought of the passage of life. Who knows the fate of that half wilted flower that is flowing past? At what point will it sink? Who that sees these passing objects can have one idea of their destiny, except that they will be wafted down, no one can tell when. And who can look down that darker strand on which WE lie, or tell its events—or presume our history. Those who best know themselves—how longingly do they desire shadows to depart, and the reality to come. The number is few; few sit waiting for hope of glory; yet there are some: some who awaken to sing at the approaching dawn as birds do in the twilight of morning. And when such find each other out, it seems hard that they should be parted. But of this too God knows best.

NARRATOR : Henry's new church in Brooklyn took the name Plymouth Church, and it would become the largest church in America.

THE TURNING POINT
1848–1850

At mid-century, gold has just been discovered in California, the harsh Fugitive Slave Law has caused an uproar in the North, Henry Ward Beecher is newly installed in his Plymouth Church in Brooklyn, Harriet Beecher Stowe is quietly gathering materials for a book, Edward and Charles Beecher are writing and debating, Catharine Beecher's travels are almost incessant in the cause of women's education. Catharine's *Treatise on Domestic Economy* had been so popular that Catharine and Harriet elaborated it, combined it with Catharine's cookbook, and reissued it as *The Housekeeper and Healthkeeper*; hardly a home in America was without it.

Catharine did a survey of health of American women, and found that 35% were habitual invalids, 42% delicate or diseased, and only 23% were strong. This finding drove her to write *Letters to the People on Health and Happiness*, and also *Physiology and Calesthenics*, with many modern ideas on health incorporated in them.

In her book *The True Remedy for the Wrongs of Women*, Catharine names the three branches of women's essential education: training children, nursing the sick, and running a household.

In 1845, Harriet applauded Catharine's book, *Duty of American Women*.

HARRIET : It is a stroke well aimed, well struck and must do good; well done Katy.

NARRATOR : Since George Beecher's death in 1843, Catharine Beecher developed her plans for women's education. She traveled, often using a man as a spokesperson. For three years, Calvin Stowe was persuaded to act as figurehead for her ambitions.

Sarah Beecher, George's widow, was independently wealthy—and at Catharine's urging offered to sponsor a seminary in

Putnam, Ohio, and to see to it that Catharine never would have to struggle for lack of funds. Thomas K. Beecher was pressed into service as a speech-giver also—and Catharine managed to avoid being tied down to any school; she much preferred fund-raising and organizing.

The titles of her speeches are revealing: "The Evils Suffered by American Women and American Children: The Causes and the Remedy," "The Duty of American Women to Their Country," and "An Address to the Protestant Clergy of the United States." Her vision of a country redeemed by women—women united regardless of class, for poor women were exploited labor and upperclass women were suppressed and restricted—both groups, as teachers, could change the growing bitterness and divisiveness in the country.

CATHARINE : Soon, in all parts of our country, in each neglected village, or new settlement, the Christian female teacher will quietly take her station, collecting the ignorant children around her, teaching them habits of neatness, order and thrift; opening the book of knowledge, inspiring the principles of morality, and awakening the hope of immortality. Soon her influence in the village will create a demand for new laborers, and then she will summon from among her friends at home, the nurse for the young and sick, the seamstress and the mantuamaker; and these will prove her auxiliaries in good moral influence, and in sabbath school training. And often as the result of these labors, the Church will arise, and the minister of Christ be summoned to fill up the complement of domestic, moral and religious blessing.

It is to be lamented that the principle of national patriotism has had very little nourishment in our country, and, instead, has given place to sectional or state partialities. What more promising method for remedying this defect than uniting American women of every state and every section in a common effort for our whole country.

NARRATOR : Catharine became an excellent publicist. She would first pitch a town's most prominent figure, then use the endorsement to form a substantial local committee. As she went through the country, she gained support from America's top educators—Horace Mann, Henry Barnard, and others. Even those of a different persuasion found such ploys hard to refuse.

In 1846, Catharine could fund a fulltime agent, and Calvin was released from his obligation to her. William Slade, the former governor of Vermont, undertook the task.

At first they traveled together, speaking in the East, through the end of 1846. Then Slade went to Cincinnati to find places for the missionary teachers, while Catharine stayed East to prepare them for their difficulties—seventy women made the journey, and most paid back the $100 given them when they started out. But though the movement was a success, and proved a mighty influence, two things were happening to change the complexion of Catharine's situation. On the one hand, she was dissatisfied to sit around idly now that funds were available and the organization could operate without her. And on the other, Slade was unable to find support in Cincinnati, so he moved his base to Cleveland and renamed the association. Catharine now had a rival. She decided to strike out on her own again.

Both Henry Ward and Lyman Beecher attended Charles Beecher's first sermon, *The Bible a Sufficient Creed*—his remarks were widely quoted throughout the country, but wrongly attributed to Henry Ward Beecher, who was currently the most famous Beecher.

•

At his new church in Brooklyn, Henry Ward Beecher gave his own declaration of principles in his first sermon. It foreshadowed a great career.

HENRY : If you come into this church, I want you to understand distinctly that I will wear no fetters; that I will be bound by no precedent; that I will preach the Gospel as I apprehend it, whether people will hear or whether they will forebear, and that I will apply it without stint, and sharply and strongly, to the overthrow of every evil and to the upbuilding of all that is good.

How hateful is that religion which says, "Business is business and politics is politics and religion is religion"; Religion is using everything for God; but many people dedicate business to the Devil and shove religion into the cracks and crevices of time and make it the hypocritical outcrawling of their leisure and their laziness.

In the first sermon that I preached on the Sunday night in the new Plymouth Church, when I had accepted the call and came there in the fall, I made a proclamation of my sentiments on the slavery matter, on temperance matters, on war and peace, on all those great themes in which I have had zeal in all my public life, in the most explicit manner. I declared to them that if they continued to attend, or any of them wished to attend, my church on the supposition that I was going to be silent, or prudentially dumb, I wished to remove that impression at once, for I intended to be positive, active, and energetic on all those subjects.

NARRATOR : For six months Henry Beecher's congregations were small—he was a backwoods preacher who dressed comfortably, not fashionably, he was ruffling feathers with his talks against slavery, against the liquor trade. All warnings to him to avoid controversy at the outset of his career in New York he ignored.

HENRY : I do not know what it is in me, whether it is my father or my mother or both of them—but the moment you tell me that a thing that should be done is unpopular, I am right there, every time.

NARRATOR : Then people started coming in increasing numbers—when the Plymouth Church burned down in 1849, its auditorium had proved hopelessly inadequate. The new church was well-lit, with no stained glass or gingerbread, and with large church parlors. The auditorium could seat two thousand—but within a few months, aisle sets were added so that it could seat twenty-five hundred—and three thousand could be crowded in—and for the next 37 years, the Plymouth Church was crowded. The saying went, "If you want to hear Henry Ward Beecher preach, take the ferry to Brooklyn and then follow the crowd." People of many different beliefs came from all over the city to hear him preach.

But though Henry Ward Beecher had succeeded in converting four hundred people in two years, he was convinced that conversions were not enough; to solve social problems, a minister must work directly to correct social injustices and any other conditions that made right living impossible. "Right living" was his definition of religion—he believed that reform was an essential part of his job—not only to save souls, but to make conditions such that they could stay saved. And number one on his agenda to change was slavery. The immorality of slavery affected not only the slave but also the master.

Henry Beecher decided to dramatize the situation. A slave had been sent to the slave market by her white master and father. The trader who bought her for $1,200 decided to give her the chance to buy her own freedom and put up $100 of it himself. He let her go to Washington, where she raised another $400. Someone asked Henry Ward Beecher if he would raise the rest—he would if she would come to Brooklyn.

And so, one Sunday in 1848, Henry Ward Beecher read the text, "Then said Jesus unto them, I will ask you one thing: Is it lawful on the Sabbath day to do good, or to do evil? to save life, or to destroy it?" Then he called down—

HENRY : Come up here, Sarah, and let us all see you.

NARRATOR : The black woman came up on the platform, embarrassed and trembling.

HENRY : And this is a marketable commodity. Such as she are put into one balance and silver into the other. I reverence woman. For the sake of the love I bore my mother I hold her sacred even in the lowest position and will use every means in my power for her uplifting. What will you do now? May she read her liberty in your eyes? Shall she go free?

NARRATOR : The collection plates were passed around, and sobbing could be heard in the auditorium. Soon the plates came back overflowing with money and jewelry. When Beecher announced that they had reached the necessary amount, the congregation burst into applause.

HENRY : When the old Jews went up to their solemn feasts they made the mountains round about Jerusalem ring with their shouts. I do not approve of an unholy clapping in the house of God, but when a good deed is well done it is not wrong to give an outward expression of our joy.

LYMAN BEECHER : *Letter of January 2, 1848:*

Henry, you are a good boy for writing me that long, comforting letter. It cheered us all. I thank you for your Thanksgiving sermon; and though I could not write as you do, it is a pleasure to think that perhaps you have breathed an atmosphere with me without which you might not have been able to do it. You cannot conceive how much joy your successful revival labors afford me, and that efficient influence you are beginning to exert on the public mind, somewhat in the way God has helped me to do; and that so near the close of my day I see the wisdom of God and the power of God in younger hands, to send on the glorious, growing work down through another generation. God preserve and bless you!

NARRATOR : Periodically, Catharine Beecher retreated to a water spa at Brattleboro, Vermont—Harriet had stayed there in 1845 for seven months—one of her lengthy stays away from Calvin. In Brattleboro, Catharine cultivated a friendship with Delia Bacon, an outstanding former student, who was a writer of historical fiction and a popular lecturer, sister of Leonard Bacon.

Delia was involved in a messy situation with Alexander MacWhorter, recently ordained—MacWhorter denied proposing to Delia, and he was supported by Nathaniel Taylor, Lyman Beecher's close friend, and a good support for Catharine at the time of her own crisis. Catharine stayed with Delia—and the decision of the New Haven West Association was to proceed with a trial against MacWhorter for calumny, falsehood and disgraceful conduct.

Catharine's talk with Taylor at this time surprised her—but it was now through Delia Bacon's case that Catharine could attack the tradition that had denied her a personal happiness and allowed her such a narrow platform for a life of self-sacrifice. For two weeks of eight-hour days, Catharine sat with Delia Bacon at the trial, she spoke frequently as a witness, and supported Delia throughout. The decision of "imprudence" but not guilt set Catharine reeling.

CATHARINE : This decision, adopted by men who from early life I had regarded as the central agency of a great and powerful system of influences, came like desolation. During the sleepless night that followed, the waking visions that haunted the hours of rest seemed like some of those troubled dreams of the sickbed, when the sun seems moving from its center, and all the heavenly bodies are rushing from their courses in confusion and dismay.

NARRATOR : In 1848, Catharine wrote a manuscript about Delia Bacon's trial, called *Truth Stranger than Fiction*, in which she attacks Nathaniel Taylor, Joel Hawes, Yale, and the Congregational

Church. Delia herself was not interested.

DELIA BACON : I am tired of being a victim! I do not wish to be a hero. I cannot purchase anything but heaven at this cost. So you see beforehand some of the fiery garlands and sacrificial ornaments of this new kind of martyrdom to which, without my own consent, you wish to dedicate me.

NARRATOR : Lyman Beecher was appalled by the idea of his daughter attacking his church and his friend, and he and the Beecher sons tried to secure the manuscript and destroy it.

CATHARINE : My various brothers were in full pursuit, some of them fancying an insane hospital my only proper residence. The blame and outcry of those who would still hush up this monstrous outrage will all be turned on me. Let it come. I cannot suffer in a better cause.

Delia, the Almighty hand which has erased this purpose from your mind, has written it, as with living fire, upon mine, and if all the human voices on this vast globe should come up in one roar of rebuke and defiance, it would not move me. A hand that I cannot relinquish has led me on, a voice that I will not disobey has bade me go forward.

NARRATOR : She and Delia Bacon shared a room at the Round Hill Water Cure in Northampton for a month. Finally, Catharine obtained Delia's consent, and in 1850, at her own expense, Catharine published *Truth Stranger than Ficiton*, and sent it to every Congregational association in New England, and to the journals.

In 1849, Edward Beecher's book *Baptism, with Reference to Its Import and Modes* shows the serious side of Edward Beecher the scholar, historian, and proponent. The book grew out of a debate in print with British Baptist leader Alexander Carson—Beecher's conclusion is that the interpretation of just one word—baptism— separates Baptists from other Protestants. Edward's attempt to reconcile the faiths failed—but he learned.

EDWARD : In practice words are things. Systems grow out of words, indeed the life of a whole denomination may depend on certain interpretations of words, which come to have an organic life of tremendous power.

No more can an architect of society work without the appropriate means. It is not self-denial, but self-sacrifice, to live in anguish from a view of what ought to be done and could be done, with a consciousness of the power to do it with appropriate means, and yet without the ability to secure these means.

NARRATOR : When Henry's church burned down in 1849, he had the seats in the new church curved around a central platform with no pulpit or podium down in front.

HENRY : It is perfect, because it is built on a principle—the principle of social and personal magnetism, which emanates reciprocally from a speaker and from a close throng of hearers. I want them to surround me, so that they will come up on every side, and behind me, so that I shall be in the center of the crowd, and have the people surge all about me!

Heretofore I have had to labor uphill, to carry everything, and do everything. Now I seem to have gone to the opposite extreme. Now it is a question how I shall come out of prosperity. I came East with a silken noose about my neck and did not know it.

NARRATOR : Walt Whitman was more than a little drawn to Henry Ward Beecher as an orator, and a model for the new poetry that he was searching for. When Whitman finally produced his first book of poems, *Leaves of Grass* in 1855, Beecher looked on favorably.

•

Charles Beecher wrote his first book, *Pictures of the Virgin and Her Son,* in Fort Wayne. When the Fugitive Slave Law was passed, Charles preached a sermon called "The Duty of Disobedience to Wicked Laws." For this, the city's ministerial association expelled him. But the sermon was printed as a pamphlet, and had a wide circulation in the North.

In 1851, he moved to Newark, New Jersey to reorganize a failing Presbyterian church into a thriving Congregational one. Here, he preached temperance and elaborated his anti-slavery position—like all the Beechers, he was not an abolitionist, but was opposed to slavery on moral and religious grounds.

Charles briefly served, at brother Edward's request, as professor of rhetoric at Knox College in Galesburg, Illinois, but then returned East to head the Congregational Church in Georgetown, Massachusetts, north of Boston. Georgetown would be his home for the next thirty years.

Henry Ward Beecher's salary at Plymouth Church quickly went to $3,300, and he was presented with a beautiful horse and carriage. Henry made the Grand Tour of Europe in 1850, alone. He saw his first ruined castle.

HENRY : I was entirely possessed and almost demented. I walked in a dream along the line of the westward wall. I had never before looked upon an old building! The cornices were not wood painted like stone, but stone curled, and carved. With us, stairs are such matters of mere convenience that I had no conception of the architectural effects to which they are susceptible. The fact is, we have no ceilings to paint, ours being low, circumscribed, and without grandeur. The number of pictures—the great number of pictures—not stuff to fill up—but noble, enchanting pieces, some of vast size, of wonderful brilliance, of novel subjects!

I am here. I am yours; do what you will with me; I am here to be intoxicated.

NARRATOR : Once home, Henry became a collector of books, rugs, precious stones, or "color-opiates," as he called them; he carried them loose in his pockets. If Eunice had resented their poverty before, she deplored their wealth even more. She held herself aloof from Henry's church; few came to know her.

Henry Ward Beecher came to believe that slavery and free labor were contradictory principles, one of which must wipe out the other. His study of the Constitution led him to believe that the founders knew this and fully expected slavery to die out naturally. The cotton gin changed things temporarily, making slavery profitable again.

HENRY : In 1850, when the controversy came up about Clay's Omnibus Bill, including the Fugitive Slave Laws, I was thoroughly roused, and in the pulpit and with my pen I attacked with the utmost earnestness the infamous Fugitive Slave Bill. It was then that I wrote that article, "Shall We Compromise?" If anyone will compare that article with Mr. Seward's subsequent speech he will find that it was reducing to a mere minimum the article on "Shall We Compromise?"

NARRATOR : Henry Clay's bill admitted California into the Union as a free state, but also passed the tough Fugitive Slave Laws, forbidding Northerners to aid or shelter runaway slaves. Harriet Beecher Stowe describes Henry's reaction.

HARRIET : I was then in Maine and I well remember one snowy night Henry's riding till midnight to see me, and then our talking till near morning what we could do to make headway against the horrid cruelties against the defenseless blacks. Henry told me then that he meant to fight that battle in New York; that he would have a church that would stand by him to resist the tyrannic dictation of Southern slaveholders. I said: "I, too, have begun to do something; I have begun a story, trying to set forth the sufferings and wrongs of the slaves." "That's right, Hattie," he said; "finish it and I will scatter it thick as the leaves of Vallambrosa." And so came *Uncle Tom* and Plymouth Church became a stronghold where the slave always found refuge and a strong helper.

NARRATOR : Henry Ward Beecher's "Star Papers" in *The Independent* hit home, especially "Shall We Compromise?"

HENRY : These oppugnant elements, slavery and liberty, inherent in our political system, animating our Constitution, checkering our public policy, breeding in our members of state opposite principles of government and making our whole wisdom of public legislation on many of the greatest questions cross-eyed and contradictory—these elements are seeking each other's life. One or the other must die. The very value of our Union is to be found in those principles of justice, liberty and humanity which inspire it. If these principles must be yielded up to preserve the Union, then a corpse will be left in our arms, deflowered, lifeless, worthless. Religion and humanity are a price too dear to pay even for the Union.

NARRATOR : This piece was read to the dying Southern leader John C. Calhoun. He said about it—

CALHOUN : That man understands the thing; he has gone to the bottom of it; he will be heard from again.

NARRATOR : Henry Ward Beecher's "Star Papers" and his dramatic freedom auctions made him into a nationally recognized leader of the anti-slavery movement, even though he was not an abolitionist.

Catharine Beecher, though always independent, had begun to alienate her own family. Even Lyman Beecher felt her increasing isolation. When George's widow Sarah offered Catharine a permanent home, Lyman encouraged her.

LYMAN : I spoke to her of my sympathy for Catharine more than for all the rest of my children, when I should be called away—and herself without support of her own and without health in the decline of life. When in health and prosperity, Catharine had cast her bread upon the waters. None of her age and with her means have been more public-spirited and liberal than she. May they all remember this.

NARRATOR : It was through Harriet that Catharine approached the family again. For one year, while Harriet was preparing her book, Catharine took time out from her education associations to handle Harriet's household, including seven children and Calvin Stowe.

In 1852, Catharine Beecher founded the American Women's Educational Association, finally an organization entirely run by women. In retrospect, she said of it:

CATHARINE : Since the formation of this Association, more than twenty colleges and professional schools have been opened to women, so that all women of the higher grades of intellect, who wish to enter men's professions, are amply provided with all needed advantages. In consequence of this, the Association has changed its plans and is now aiming to secure the proper training of the women of the lower classes.

THE BOOK: 1
1850–1852

Lyman Beecher had early recognized Harriet's gifts. She and George were the readers of the family, but Harriet would sometimes fall into deep revery, and have to be shaken awake. When Harriet was seven, Lyman said—

LYMAN : Hattie is a genius. I would give a hundred dollars if she was a boy. She is as odd as she is intelligent and studious.

HARRIET : Mr. Brace, Sarah Pierce's nephew, exceeded all teachers I ever knew in the faculty of teaching composition. The constant excitement in which he kept the minds of his pupils—the wide and varied regions of thought into which he led them—formed a preparation for teaching composition, the main requisite for which, whatever people may think, is to have something which one feels interested to say.

NARRATOR : At twelve, she wrote an essay, "Can the Immortality of the Soul Be Proved by the Light of Nature?"

HARRIET : It was condensed and logical, fearfully vigorous in conception and expression, and altogether a very melancholy piece of literature to have been conceived and written by a girl of that age. Father, who was sitting on high by Mr. Brace, brightened and looked interested and at the close I heard him ask, "Who wrote that composition?" "Your daughter, sir!" was the answer. It was the proudest moment of my life. There was no mistaking father's face when he was pleased and to have interested him was past all juvenile triumphs.

NARRATOR : When Lyman moved to Cincinnati, Harriet went along, in part to help Catharine establish a new school there, and to work as her main assistant.

Charles had already given his sister glimpses of slavery in New Orleans, center for the slave market for the plantations of the Deep South. She had seen and heard other stories, of the Underground Railway, of escapes over ice floes on the Ohio River.

At Edward and Katy Beecher's home in Jacksonville, Illinois, she had met the Rev. Josiah Henson, a Christian freedman, who gave her the model for Uncle Tom. The river trade and her own excursions with her father into Kentucky supplied other details, all of which would be of use later.

On a visit to brother William in Putnam, Ohio, Harriet reports:

HARRIET : The good people here, you know, are about half abolitionists. I should think them about as ultra as to measures as anything that has been attempted, though I am glad to see a better spirit than marks such proceedings generally.

NARRATOR : In Cincinnati, Catharine commented on the fact that while she earned $30 from her stories, Harriet earned $300. Both she and Lyman encouraged Harriet's ambitions to be a writer. So did Calvin Stowe.

CALVIN : My dear, you must be a literary woman. It is so written in the book of fate. Make all your calculations accordingly. Get a good stock of health and brush up your mind. Drop the E. out of your name. It only encumbers it and interferes with the flow and euphony. Write yourself fully and always Harriet Beecher Stowe, which is a name euphonious, flowing, and full of meaning.

I want you to come home as quick as you can. The fact is I cannot live without you, and if we were not so prodigious poor I would come for you at once. There is no woman like you in this wide world. Who else has so much talent with so little self-conceit; so much reputation with so little affectation; so much literature with so little nonsense; so much enterprise with so little extravagance; so much tongue with so little scold; so much sweetness with so little softness; so much of so many things and so little of so many other things?

HARRIET : On the whole, my dear, if I choose to be a literary person, I have, I thing, as good a chance of making profit by it as anyone I know of. But with all this, I have my doubts whether I shall be able to do so.

Our children are just coming to the age when everything depends on my efforts. They are delicate in health, and nervous and excitable, and need a mother's whole attention. Can I lawfully divide my attention by literary efforts?

There is one thing I must suggest. If I am to write, I must have a room to myself, which shall be my room. All last winter I felt the need of some place where I could go and be quiet and satisfied.

I can earn $400 a year by writing, but I don't want to feel that I must, and when weary with teaching the children, and tending the baby, and buying provisions, and mending dresses, and darning stockings, sit down and write a piece for some paper.

NARRATOR : Meanwhile, Cincinnati suffered a cholera epidemic again, and this time it claimed Samuel Charles Stowe, Harriet and Calvin's baby. When Calvin received an offer from Bowdoin College in Brunswick, Maine, they moved back East.

On the way, Harriet came to Boston with her children, to visit her brother Edward Beecher, the friend of the murdered abolitionist Elijah Lovejoy. Edward was revolted by the Fugitive Slave Law, and they talked of little else.

Even after Harriet and Calvin arrived in Brunswick, Katy, Edward's wife, sent Harriet letters describing scenes of captured slaves, in the hope that Harriet would use her powers as a writer against slavery.

KATY : I remember distinctly saying, "Now, Hattie, if I could use a pen as you can, I would write something that would make this whole nation feel what an accursed thing slavery is."

HARRIET : Tell sister Katy I thank her for her letter and will answer it. As long as the baby sleeps with me nights I can't do much at anything, but I will do it at last. I will write that thing if I live.

To me it is incredible, amazing, mournful! I feel as if I should be willing to sink with it, were all this sin and misery to sink in the sea. I wish father would come on to Boston, and preach on the Fugitive Slave Law as he once preached on the slave-trade, when I was a little girl in Litchfield. I sobbed aloud in one pew and Mrs. Judge Reeves in another. I wish some Martin Luther would arise to set this community right.

•

NARRATOR : When Lyman Beecher retitred as the age of 75, Catharine urged him to return East to stay with various of his children, and to edit his papers.

CATHARINE : As for father, he is beating about to find places to preach so as to save souls. I think I never heard him preach better, and it grieves me to see how little he is appreciated and that half of his energies are out of employ. There are small minds at helm now in these parts and the sooner father is put where he can have full scope and fair appreciation the better for him and the cause he is serving. It will add years to his life to put him in the right place and that now is not at the West.

NARRATOR : But when he did move back to Boston to be by Edward, his spirits did not improve. He was no longer the patriarch, but the dependent. He gathered his papers, and published his sermons, but writing his autobiography was too much for him. As Charles reports, Lyman Beecher was declining.

CHARLES : His mind was gradually retreating and hiding itself as in some deep mysterious cave. When it was clear that he could no longer write, I then took responsibility for completing the autobiography.

•

NARRATOR : Catharine's relationship with Harriet had suffered some ravages over money, especially during the failure of her Cincinnati school. But differences were patched up, and Catharine agreed to help Harriet for one year, running the Stowe household of seven children.

It was an opportune time. Harriet Beecher Stowe was writing a serial, intended for the *National Era,* a small-circulation abolitionist paper out of Washington, D.C., edited by Gamaliel Bailey. Catharine's volunteer effort to help Harriet gave her enough time to write some of the early chapters of *Uncle Tom's Cabin.* Catharine also organized a boarding school of Beecher nieces and nephews, and thereby was able to purchase a new furnace, furniture, carpets, wood, and coal.

CATHARINE : The only way I could make Calvin comfortable about this arrangement was by taking all the task myself and agreeing to foot all the bills that were not covered by the salary and income from the pupils.

HARRIET : Catharine's affairs have now become in a measure interwoven with mine. She has agreed to give me a year of her time to act conjointly with me and my own children. Her help is essential here—though she has had to leave her work on behalf of women teachers.

CATHARINE : At eight o'clock we are through with breakfast and prayers and then we send off Mr. Stowe and Harriet both to his room in the college. There was no other way to keep her out of family cares and quietly at work and since this plan is adopted she goes ahead forthwith. I look forward with the greatest interest to our winter's work.

NARRATOR : During this period, Lyman Beecher visited the Stowes—Calvin, after all, had been his star professor at Lane Seminary. Calvin would take over the kitchen table with his piles of papers, rearranging them into other piles of papers, not noticing that he had displaced Harriet, who sat on the back porch steps with a portfolio on her lap, writing chapters of her serial. She wrote other chapters while visiting Edward and Katy Beecher— the same Katy who had encouraged her to persevere.

The 1840s also saw the emergence of a remarkable man, an escaped slave named Frederick Douglass, speaking on behalf of the abolitionist movement. William Lloyd Garrison welcomed him to their ranks.

GARRISON : The experience of Frederick Douglass, as a slave, was not a peculiar one; his lot was not especially a hard one; his case may be regarded as a very fair specimen of the treatment of slaves in Maryland, in which State it is conceded that they are better fed and less cruelly treated than in Georgia, Alabama, or Louisiana. yet how deplorable was his situation! what terrible chastisements were inflicted upon his person! what still more shocking outrages were perpetrated on his mind! how like a brute he was treated.

NARRATOR : On speaking tours, Frederick Douglass told his own story.

DOUGLASS : I have had two masters. My first master's name was Anthony. I do not remember his first name. He was not considered a rich slaveholder. He owned two or three farms, and about thirty slaves. The overseer's name was Plummer. Mr. Plummer was a miserable drunkard, a profane swearer, and a savage monster. He always went armed with a cowskin and a heavy cudgel. I have known him to cut and slash the women's heads so horribly that even master would be enraged at his cruelty.

He would at times seem to take great pleasure in whipping a slave. I have often been awakened at the dawn of day by the most heart-rending shrieks of an old aunt of mine, whom he used to tie up to a joist, and whip upon her naked back till she was literally covered with blood. No words, no tears, no prayers, from his gory victim, seemed to move his iron heart from its bloody purpose. The louder she screamed, the harder he whipped. Not until overcome by fatigue would he cease to swing the blood-clotted cowskin.

I remember the first time I ever witnessed this horrible exhibition. I was quite a child, but I well remember it. I never shall forget it whilst I remember anything. It was the blood-stained gate, the entrance to the hell of slavery, through which I was about to pass.

HARRIET BEECHER STOWE, *Brunswick, July 9, 1851*

To Frederick Douglass, Esq.:

Sir,

You may perhaps have noticed in your editorial readings a series of articles that I am furnishing for the *Era* under the title of *Uncle Tom's Cabin, or Life Among the Lowly.*

In the course of my story, the scene will fall upon a cotton plantation. I am very desirous, therefore, to gain information from one who has been an actual laborer on one, and it occurred to me that in the circle of your acquaintance there might be one who would be able to communicate to me some such information as I desire. I have before me an able paper written by a Southern planter, in which the details and modus operandi are given from his point of sight. I am anxious to have something more from another standpoint. I wish to be able to make a picture that shall be graphic and true to nature in its details.

For some weeks past I have received your paper through the mail, and have read it with great interest, and desire to return my acknowledgments for it. It will be a pleasure to me at some time when less occupied to contribute something to its columns.

DOUGLASS : Sunday was my only leisure time. I spent this in a sort of beast-like stupor, between sleep and wake, under some large tree. At times I would rise up, a flash of energetic freedom would dart through my soul, accompanied with a faint beam of hope, that flickered for a moment, and then vanished. I sank down again, mourning over my wretched condition. I was sometimes prompted to take my life, and that of the overseer, but was prevented by a combination of hope and fear. My sufferings on this plantation seem now like a dream rather than a stern reality.

Our house stood within a few rods of the Chesapeake Bay, whose broad bosom was ever white with sails from every quarter of the habitable globe. Those beautiful vessels, robed in purest white, so delightful to the eye of freemen, were to me so many shrouded ghosts, to terrify and torment me with thoughts of my wretched condition. I have often, in the deep stillness of a summer's Sabbath, stood all alone upon the lofty banks of that noble bay, and traced, with saddened heart and tearful eye, the countless number of sails moving off to the mighty ocean. The sight of these always affected me powerfully. I would pour out my soul's complaint, in my rude way, with an apostrophe to the moving multitude of ships—

"You are loosed from your moorings, and are free; I am fast in my chains, and am a slave! You move merrily before the gentle gale, and I sadly before the bloody whip! You are freedom's swift-winged angels, that fly around the world! I am confined in bands of iron! Oh, that I were free! Oh, that I were on one of your gallant decks, and under your protecting wing! Go on, go on. Oh, that I could also go! Could I but swim! If I could fly! Oh, why was I born a man, of whom to make a brute!"

HARRIET : I have noticed with regret your sentiments on the church. I am a minister's daughter, and a minister's wife, and I have had six brothers in the ministry; I certainly ought to know something of the feelings of ministers on this subject. I was a child in 1820 when the Missouri question was agitated, and one of the strongest and deepest impressions on my mind was that made by my father's sermons and prayers, and the anguish of his soul for the poor slave at that time.

Every brother I have has been in his sphere a leading anti-slavery man. One of them was to the last the bosom friend and counselor of Lovejoy. As for myself and my husband, we have for the last seventeen years lived on the border of a slave State, and we have never shrunk from the fugitives, and we have helped them with all we had to give. I have received the children of liberated slaves into a family school, and taught them with my own children.

Everything is against you, but Jesus Christ is for you, and he has not forgotten his church, misguided and erring though it be. I have looked all the field over with despairing eyes; I see no hope but in him. This movement must and will become a purely religious one. The light will spread in churches, the tone of feeling will rise, Christians North and South will give up all connection with, and take up their testimony against, slavery, and thus the work will be done.

•

NARRATOR : The original commitment from the *National Era* was for three installments of a serial called *Uncle Tom's Cabin, or Life Among the Lowly,* starting in June 1851. It actually ran until April 1852. The abolitionist audience was not altogether pleased, for the story played up the picturesque and patriarchal side of the slavery system, showing some masters as fond of their slaves as if they were their own children (which was often the case). Uncle Tom's first two owners were kindly Southerners, and the third, Legree, was a Yankee.

Altogether, Harriet Beecher Stowe received $300 for the serial publication of *Uncle Tom's Cabin* from Gamaliel Bradley of the *National Era.*

BRADLEY : Mrs. Stowe has at last brought her great work to a close. We do not recollect any production of an American writer that has excited more general and profound interest.

NARRATOR : Catharine's own *Essay on Slavery and Abolitionism,* written to oppose the thorough-going abolitionism of the Grimke sisters, Angelina and Sarah, may have helped Harriet frame her appeal.

CATHARINE : Women should appeal to the kindly, generous, peaceful and benevolent principles of those they oppose; the woman's influence is best pursued through the domestic and social circle.

NARRATOR : John P. Jewett, a Boston publisher, offered the Stowes a half share in profits for book publication of the work. Calvin Stowe protested that he was too poor to speculate; Mrs. Stowe should receive a ten percent royalty on all sales.

HARRIET : I did not know until a week afterward precisely what terms Mr. Stowe had made, and I did not care. I had the most perfect indifference to the bargain.

NARRATOR : While awaiting the first copy of the book, Mrs. Stowe read Horace Mann's speeches, from the same publisher.

HARRIET : After sending the proof-sheet to the office I sat alone reading Horace Mann's eloquent plea for these young men and women, then about to be consigned to the slave warehouse of Bruin & Hill in Alexandria, Virginia—a plea impassioned, eloquent, but vain, as all other pleas on that side had ever proved in all courts hitherto. It seemed that there was no hope, that nobody would hear, nobody would read, nobody pity; that this frightful system, that had already pursued its victims into the free states, might at last even threaten them in Canada.

NARRATOR : And then, to this housewife who had one book to her name, who had never lived in the South, who had no reputation except as a writer of sentimental Christmas stories, the letters started coming in. Henry Wadsworth Longfellow:

LONGFELLOW : I congratulate you most cordially upon the immense success and influence of *Uncle Tom's Cabin*. It is one of the greatest triumphs recorded in literary history, to say nothing of the higher triumph of its moral effect.

NARRATOR : John Greenleaf Whittier, the abolitionist poet.

WHITTIER : What a glorious work you have wrought. Thanks for the Fugitive Slave Law! Better would it be for slavery if that law had never been enacted; for it gave occasion for *Uncle Tom's Cabin*.

My young friend Mary Irving writes me that she has been reading it to some twenty young ladies, daughters of Louisiana slaveholders, near New Orleans, and amid the scenes described in it, and that they, with one accord, pronounce it true.

NARRATOR : William Lloyd Garrison.

GARRISON : I estimate the value of anti-slavery writing by the abuse it brings. Now, all the defenders of slavery have let me alone and are abusing you.

HARRIET : Calvin, I have been in such a whirl ever since I have been here in Boston. I found business prosperous, Jewett animated. He has been to Washington and conversed with all the leading senators, Northern and Southern. Seward told him it was the greatest book of the times, or something of that sort, and he and Sumner went around with him to recommend it to Southern men and get them to read it.

NARRATOR : Other letters threatened and damned the book.

HARRIET : They were so curiously compounded of blasphemy, cruelty, and obscenity, that their like could only be expressed by John Bunyan's account of the speech of Apollyon: "He spake as a dragon."

NARRATOR : While Harriet was away in New York, Calvin Stowe received an invitation to the professorship of Sacred Literature at Andover, Massachusetts. The Stowes moved into an old stone workshop, briefly used as the seminary's gymnasium—but now it was to become the Stone Cabin, where the Stowes were to receive famous guests, and where numerous philanthropic enterprises would be begun.

Meanwhile, hundreds of thousands of copies came rolling off the newly available automatic steam-driven printing presses. Dramatizations of *Uncle Tom's Cabin* began appearing spontaneously—these rights had not been secured with the copyright. Plays of *Uncle Tom* began in New York, Boston, at two theaters in London. Calvin comments.

CALVIN : The drama of *Uncle Tom* has been going on in the National Theatre of New York all summer with most unparalleled success. Everybody goes night after night, and nothing can stop it. The enthusiasm beats that of the run in the Boston Museum out and out. The *Tribune* is full of it. The *Observer*, the *Journal of Commerce*, and all that sort of fellows, are astonished and nonplussed. They do not know what to say or do about it.

NARRATOR : Unauthorized English editions poured forth— there being no international copyright protection at the time— just as the Americans had pirated Dickens and Scott for years.

Madame Belloc issued an authorized French translation, for which Mrs. Stowe wrote in her introduction.

> It has been said that the representations of this book are exaggerations! and oh, would that this were true! Would that this book were indeed a fiction, and not a close mosaic of facts! But that it is not a fiction the proofs lie bleeding in thousands of hearts; they have been attested by surrounding voices from almost every slave state, and from slave-owners themselves. Since so it must be, thanks be to God that this mighty cry, this wail of an unutterable anguish, has at last been heard!

> In its commencement slavery overspread every State in the Union; the progress of society has now emancipated the North from its yoke. In Kentucky, Tennessee, Virginia, and Maryland, at different times, strong movements have been made for emancipation—movements enforced by a comparison of the progressive march of the adjoining free states with the poverty and sterility and ignorance produced by a system which in a few years wastes and exhausts all the resources of the soil without the power of renewal.

> The time cannot be distant when these States will emancipate for self-preservation; and if no new slave territory be added, the increase of slave population in the remainder will enforce measures of emancipation.

> Here, then, is the point of the battle. Unless more slave territory is gained, slavery dies; if it is gained, it lives. Around this point political parties fight and maneuver, and every year the battle wages hotter.

NARRATOR : Fanny Kemble wrote a letter to the editor of the *London Times* in defense of the accuracy of Harriet Beecher Stowe's portrayal of slavery in *Uncle Tom's Cabin*.

KEMBLE : In treating Mrs. Harriet Beecher Stowe's work as an exaggerated picture of the evils of slavery, I beg to assure you that you do her serious injustice. Of its truth and moderation as a representation of the slave system in the United States, I can testify with the experience of an eyewitness, having been a resident in the Southern states. With the exception of the horrible catastrophe, the flogging to death of poor Tom, she has portrayed none of the most revolting instances of crime produced by the slave system.

The South Carolina gentry have been fond of styling them-selves the chivalry of the South, and perhaps might not badly represent, in their relations with their dependents, the nobility of France before the purifying hurricane of the Revolution. The planters of the interior of the Southern and Southwestern states, with their furious feuds and slaughterous combats, their stabbings and pistolings, their gross sensuality, brutal ignorance, and des-potic cruelty, resemble the chivalry of France before the horrors of the Jacquerie admonished them that there was a limit even to the endurance of slaves.

In Maryland, Kentucky, and Virginia, the outward aspect of slavery has ceased to wear its most deplorable features. Their soil and climate are alike favorable to the labors of a white peasantry; the slave cultivation has had time to prove itself destructive there.

I do not believe the planters have any disposition to put an end to slavery, nor is it perhaps much to be wondered at that they have not. How far they are right in anticipating ruin from the manu-mission of their slaves I think questionable, but that they do so is certain. The question is not alone one of foregoing great wealth or subsistence; it is not alone the consenting to social equality.

Freedom in America is not merely a personal right; it involves a political privilege. Freemen there are legislators. The rulers of the land are the majority of the people, and in many parts of the Southern states the black free citizens would become, if not at once, yet in process of time, inevitably voters, landholders, del-egates to state legislatures, members of assembly—who knows?—senators, judges, aspirants to the presidency of the United States.

NARRATOR : George Sand said this in her review:

GEORGE SAND: Mrs. Stowe is all instinct; it is the very reason she appears to some not to have talent. Has she not talent? What is talent? Nothing, perhaps, compared to genius; but has she genius? She has genius as humanity feels the need of genius—the genius of goodness, not that of the man of letters, but that of the saint.

NARRATOR : Harriet's book was the first best-seller. Even the new automatic book presses had a hard time keeping up with demand. Three hundred thousand copies were sold in the first year, and one and a half million overseas in twenty languages. Even in the South it was popular at first—it was the first time anyone on the anti-slavery side had even attempted to present the situation fairly.

To one of her children, Harriet wrote these words:

HARRIET : I well remember the winter you were a baby and I was writing *Uncle Tom's Cabin*. My heart was bursting with the anguish excited by the cruelty and injustice our nation was showing to the slave, and praying God to let me do a little and to cause my cry for them to be heard. I remember many a night weeping over you as you lay sleeping beside me, and I thought of the slave mothers whose babes were torn from them.

FAME
1852–1853

The publication of *Uncle Tom's Cabin* was a phenomenon in publishing. This enormously successful book told simple stories of slavery in sentimental fashion. Even though the author intruded her own opinions freely, the tale was remarkably free from the acrimonious debate going on between abolitionists and states-righters. The surprise was that this little book sold out edition after edition, was quickly translated into twenty languages, the London stage held as many as three dramatized versions of it at once—and Harriet Beecher Stowe, who the year before had been an unknown housewife with seven children was this year's toast of Europe and America.

Overnight, Harriet's fame overshadowed those of her brothers and sister, even that of her father. At 78, Lyman Beecher had almost outlived his audience, though he was just beginning to prepare his sermons, and the long awaited *Autobiography of Lyman Beecher*. Unfortunately, he was no longer organized enough to accomplish much without help. The family decided that Charles Beecher should help him put his papers in order.

Meanwhile, Edward Beecher, the brilliant scholar and the theologian of the family, had just brought out his startling new doctrine in which he reconciles free will and original sin, an argument that he first broached privately to his brother Charles thirty years before. The book, *The Conflict of Ages*, marks the high point of his career.

Edward Beecher had been at the Salem Street Church in Boston since 1844, and since 1849 had been editor of *The Congregationalist. The Conflict of Ages* was published in 1853, just one year after Harriet's book.

Nearly a hundred pages are devoted to historical analysis, in which Edward Beecher shows the dialectic of theological ideas of different ages, culminating in his own doctrine of the pre-existence of souls. This idea had been suggested at various times in the past, perhaps most clearly by Origen. Edward describes a series of religious experiences, beginning with the description in Jonathan Edwards' *Personal Narrative* of the experience of human depravity before God.

EDWARDS : The very thought of any joy arising in me, on any consideration of my own amiableness, performances, or experiences, or any goodness of heart or life, is nauseous and detestable to me.

NARRATOR : But Edwards did not satisfy the new ideas of honor and right. The Unitarianism of John Adams, and especially of William Ellery Channing, came into being as a response to those ideas.

A third experience arose in Universalists, who reconciled depravity and justice by rejecting the idea of eternal punishment; thus God was made to be honorable.

A fourth experience was the New School of Calvinism, a theology of revivals. Samuel Hopkins represented this view; Hopkinsian theory rejected the idea that Adam's sin cast a shadow on the human race, and also rejected innate sinfulness before knowledge and voluntary action was possible—in other words, infant depravity was denied.

Would there be no end of reactions and counter-reactions? That fear, says Edward Beecher, is the fifth experience. Its defining quality was the eclipse of the glory of God, by accepting both total depravity and also honor and right.

EDWARD : For a time, the system of this world rose before my mind, in the same manner, as far as I can judge, as it did before the minds of Channing and Foster. I can, therefore, more fully appreciate their expression of their trials and emotions. But I was entirely unable to find relief as they did. The depravity of man neither Christian experience, the Bible, nor history, would permit me to deny. Hence, for a time, all was dark as night.

The transition in my own case was as if, when I had been groping in some vast cathedral, in the gloom of midnight, vainly striving to comprehend its parts and relations, suddenly before the vast arched window of the nave a glorious sun had suddenly burst forth, filling the whole structure with its radiance, and showing in perfect harmony the proportions and beauties of its parts.

NARRATOR : This was the sixth experience, that Edward hoped would reunite Christians everywhere—the acknowledgment of the pre-existence of souls. Orthodoxy could be preserved, and God could also be just. Critics were quick to point out that the idea was not new—it came from Indian philosophy, Origen, Julius Muller, Pythagoras, Empedocles, Fludd. Edward Beecher didn't claim originality, he merely aimed to reconcile orthodoxy and radical politics, just as earlier in his career, he had tried to reconcile the Baptists and other Protestants with a clarification of semantics.

The Conflict of Ages made quite a stir in religious circles—the book went through five printings and seven editions in two years. It raised a great debate.

•

When Charles Beecher took over the writing of Lyman Beecher's autobiography, he sensed a common Beecher problem that they all would have to answer—how could they maintain the vitality that had motivated Lyman Beecher when their father was gone? He had believed without question in an eternal afterlife. Every other Beecher had rebelled in one way or another.

CHARLES : The work on his autobiography is deeply affecting. It is really one of the most solemn things I have attended to.

Is eternal punishment a reality? Father thought so. He never doubted. Strike that idea out of his mind, and his whole career would be changed, his whole influence on us modified. Yet Isabella and Mary, I fear, reject father's belief on this point, and Hatty's mind is I fear shaken—do you believe in it? Do you really believe that the wicked will exist forever, and continue forever in sin? Do you believe this? How can we affect our children as Father did us, if we have not the same concern for them, the same sense of their awful danger? I confess that I have no real communion with God, nor do I have life to struggle for any. Though my soul is cold as death, I feel a kind of settled resolution not to waste my life.

I know that there is no way of recapturing the early unity of the family. I have been deeply touched for Catharine in reading over her early letters. I wish you could read them. All before and after her engagement with Fisher, and his death. All her deep and painful struggles in religious matters for years. How she has suffered! How she has been tried! And yet the character she shows is a very interesting one—I mean in her letters.

Now I know she has peculiarities that repel some from her. And yet it seems sad to me to see her cast out as it were from the family circle by Mary and Hatty and you—not that she is really cast out—but something virtually pretty near it. Yet she is sincere and kind, and benevolent. That is, she seems to have been so, both by natural impulse and on principle. Cannot she be made to feel more of the warm sympathy of fraternal affection in her loneliness?

NARRATOR : With Lyman Beecher's increasing confusion, Catharine felt the lack of his intellectual prodding—but she still had much to do to round out her vision of women's culture based on domesticity, and to re-establish morality without the religious dogmas of Calvinism. Harriet was instrumental in bringing her back into the family.

HARRIET : Please read Catharine's *True Remedy for the Wrongs of Women*. I beg you will not let another day pass without reading it as an act of justice to yourselves and to the public. Until I read it, I had no proper appreciation of her character and motives of action for this eight or ten years past. I considered her strange, nervous, visionary and to a certain extent unstable. I see now that she has been busy for eight years about one thing: a thing first conceived upon a sickbed when she was so sick and frail that most women would have felt that all they could hope for was to lie still and be nursed for the rest of their lives, then she conceived this plan of educating our country by means of its women and this she has steadily pursued in weariness and painfulness, in journeying in peril of life and health, in watching and prayer.

Her work has been so spread out from Maine to Georgia and from Massachusetts to Iowa that we could not see that it formed a great whole, and have supposed that she was constantly attempting and constantly failing. She has earned and spent nearly $5,000 in the last few years, and she has worked as yet almost against even her own family, for hitherto you know that we have not had full confidence in her plans, but the time has come when in my judgment there is ground and full ground for such confidence and when to neglect them any longer would be unwise and inexcusable. Not everything she has done has succeeded, yet the movement as a whole is a sublime specimen of that force of character which God gives to an individual now and then when he has a purpose to carry by them and which may almost be regarded as an inspiration.

Furthermore, this thing has got to go, and it will go either in your hands and under your influence or it will go by the aid of such men as Horace Mann, Horace Greeley and all that modern reform party who all stand waiting for the moment when Catharine will come on their side. While you, Henry, and you, father, have been lukewarm and full of other things, the reformers meet with Catharine with the warmest of zeal with offers of time, money, influence, everything. They are noble men, noble minded, noble hearted, energetic, and yet I would rather they came into the movement as accessories than as leaders.

CATHARINE : I have been mortified and astonished to see men of piety and men I thought clear-headed as befogged as I found them all over the country. When worldly men such as Horace Greeley take such high Gospel ground and our leading ministers take such low worldly ground, how will the problem work out? Although I will say that Henry's pieces on that Fugitive Slave Law, which I hope is yet to be whipped off to the ends of the Universe, suit me exactly.

NARRATOR : Harriet shared this view of Catharine's about the American clergy. In *Uncle Tom's Cabin*, she singled out the Reverend Joel Parker as justifying slavery because it had, in his words, "no evils but such as are inseparable from any other relations in social and domestic life."

Ever since 1837, when a mob killed Elijah Lovejoy, Edward Beecher had blamed Parker, leader of the Colonization Society, for the fatal rabble-rousing, and had named Parker in his book, *Narrative of the Riot at Alton*. Harriet also had named him in early editions of *Uncle Tom's Cabin*, and Edward helped gather materials to refute Parker's disavowals.

HARRIET : Edward is exhuming all sorts of Parker's inconvenient declarations and arranging them in most uncomfortable proximities, and is up to his chin in documents which he reads and makes more of with that grave thoughtful smile peculiar to him.

NARRATOR : When Parker threatened a lawsuit, Harriet stood her ground.

HARRIET : I grant I am a woman, but withal a woman well reputed.

NARRATOR : Henry Ward Beecher and Calvin Stowe negotiated a settlement, and Harriet withdrew the quotation from later editions. But her indictment of the American clergy is clear in *Uncle Tom*, and she was not hesitant to state publicly that the clergy was not worthy of being the nation's moral arbiters, and that they violated rather than upheld natural human virtues, in particular toward women and blacks.

NARRATOR : Edward's book, *The Conflict of Ages*, was a shock to some because he had always been known as the conservative Beecher, the orthodox one. Yet the book proved Edward right in thinking that his was the characteristic religious experience of his time. By telling his personal truth, he touched depths in a lot of people. Nevertheless, hardly anyone went along with his solution.

Other Beechers were publishing notable books about the same time that Harriet and Edward were—Catharine's *The True Remedy for the Wrongs of Women* had just come out in 1851, as well as Charles Beecher's *The Duty of Disobedience to Wicked Laws*—a diatribe against the Fugitive Slave Laws, that lost Charles his position. And Henry Ward Beecher was now well established as the most popular preacher of the day.

Reaction to Edward's theological bombshell *The Conflict of Ages* came from every side. Oliver Wendell Holmes, Emerson and others remarked on it.

E.A. Park and Leonard Bacon complained that Edward Beecher attacked his friends and praised his enemies. The Old School reviewer, Charles Hodge, greeted the book as if from an ally, while David Lord, another Old School Calvinist, scoffed at it entirely. H.B. Smith predicted that, rather than heal divisions, it would create them.

On the other side, the Universalist Hosea Ballou felt that Edward Beecher had indeed laid bare the conflict that had given rise to Universalism. Jacob Blain, a "destructionist," felt that Edward had torn down the old house and had not provided a new one—which he felt was the right thing to do.

The Unitarians, too, in general approved. George Ellis, editor of the *Christian Examiner*, declared that, despite some deficiencies, it was "the most important contribution which has been made for years to our religious literature." Hiram Parker wrote a counter-book, *The Harmony of Ages*, but it was an amateur job compared to Edward Beecher's book. Another counter-book, *The Conflict of Ages Ended*, by Henry Weller, was sent to Beecher as it appeared in installments in the Swedenborgian journal *The Crisis;* actually, this book was written to extend Edward's ideas, not to refute them. It provoked another Swedenborgian critique from the elder Henry James, called *The Nature of Evil*, a major work in its own right.

Catharine Beecher had a more personal reaction to Edward's book. He had been very close to her through her spiritual crisis, and had tutored her while she developed her *Mental and Moral Philosophy*. She first published her religious views in 1836, in *Letters on the Difficulties of Religion*—a popular book, in which she says—

> I am sure God does not require anything of us but what we have full ability to perform.

NARRATOR : It is said that she was only the third person—after her mother, Roxana Foote, and Lyman Beecher's second wife Harriet Porter—that moved Lyman Beecher's faith toward toleration.

She saw that, whereas she had softened and secularized Calvinism, Edward Beecher's *The Conflict of Ages* would undermine the doctrines of Calvinism itself. He posited a pre-existent state of sin that the Creator wasn't responsible for. But Catharine wasn't satisfied with this formulation.

CATHARINE : I reply How do you get this? If you say by a Revelation from God, I say before I can confide in His teachings I must have proof that all this horrible misery and wrong resulting from the wrong construction or nature of mind is not attributable to the Creator of All Things. His mere word is nothing from the Author of a system which is all ruined and worse than good for nothing. He must clear his/her character before He can offer me a Revelation!

NARRATOR : When she published her *Religious Training of Children*, Catharine denied the doctrine of original sin altogether.

CATHARINE : The infant mind is the creation of God and we impeach His wisdom of goodness when we deny that it is rightly constructed. Sin arises not from depraved nature but from depraved action, and there is no sin previous to voluntary transgression.

NARRATOR : These ideas of Catharine's would find their way into Harriet's novels—*The Minister's Wooing*, and *Old Town Folks*. There is no doubt that Catharine's ideas influenced her brothers as well, for they were in doctrine closer to her than to the more rigid Calvinism of their father, Lyman Beecher.

As Harriet suddenly became famous, Catharine undertook to renegotiate Harriet's royalties with John P. Jewett, publisher of *Uncle Tom's Cabin*, from ten percent royalties to fifty percent of profits, as originally proposed—and then rejected by the cautious Calvin Stowe. Though other Beechers looked on in dismay, Harriet appreciated the efforts. The two sisters shared the unique problem of being a Beecher without having a minister's platform to speak from.

Harriet had several times worked with Catharine in her schools. Catharine edited and arranged with Harper and Brothers for publication of Harriet's first book, *The Mayflower, Sketches of the Descendants of the Pilgrims*. In an introduction to those stories, Catharine wrote:

> Mrs. Stowe's fiction has the ability to improve the manners by an acquaintance with the refinements of polished society, to increase a knowledge of the world by vivid pictures of people and things, to cultivate the taste by exhibitions of the beautiful, correct, and pure, to elevate the sentiments, to expand the generous and benevolent sympathies, and to cherish religious principles and pious aspirations.

NARRATOR : Now that Harriet Beecher Stowe was in the forefront of the anti-slavery movement, she found herself in odd company. William Lloyd Garrison had been outspoken and dogmatic, yet his paper *The Liberator* had great circulation. Harriet wrote a letter to the editor.

HARRIET : In regard to you, your paper, and in some measure your party, I am in an honest embarrassment. I sympathize with you fully in many of your positions. Others I consider erroneous, hurtful to liberty and the progress of humanity. Nevertheless, I believe you and those who support them to be honest and conscientious in your course and opinions. What I fear is that your paper will take from poor Uncle Tom his Bible, and give him nothing in its place.

GARRISON : I do not understand why the imputation is thrown upon *The Liberator* as tending to rob Uncle Tom of his Bible. All Christendom professes to believe in the inspiration of the volume, and at the same time all Christendom is by the ears as to its real teachings. Surely you would not have me disloyal to my conscience.

HARRIET : My objection is to the mode in which these things are handled in *The Liberator* in general tone and spirit. If your paper circulated only among those of disciplined and cultivated minds, skilled to separate truth from falsehood, I should feel less regret. But your name and benevolent labors have given your paper a circulation among the poor and lowly.

•

NARRATOR : In 1854, Stephen A. Douglas's idea of squatter's sovereignty displaced the Missouri Compromise—and Bleeding Kansas resulted, with pro-slavery bands of armed men from Missouri who went across the border, seized the legislature, and put in their own men by terrorism, thus officially carrying Kansas for slavery. Henry Ward Beecher and Edward Everett Hale, the son-in-law of Henry's sister Mary, were among those gathering support for the stream of anti-slavery colonists from the North. When someone suggested that they send Bibles, Henry Beecher said:

HENRY : Sharpe's rifles are a greater moral agency than the Bible there.

NARRATOR : Many of the rifles arrived in Kansas in crates marked "Bibles." After that, all the rifles sent to Kansas became known as Beecher's Bibles.

When the Hungarian patriot Louis Kossuth came to America amid great fervor, he spoke at Henry Ward Beecher's Plymouth Church. And on the publication of Walt Whitman's *Leaves of Grass*, fellow phrenologist Henry Ward Beecher called on Whitman. Both of them were city walkers, conversant with the shops, galleries, museums, piers. Whitman had originally intended his book to be accompanied with lectures, as "two co-expressions." But unlike Beecher, Whitman had no crowds around him, except in the pages of his book.

William Beecher, by one year the eldest Beecher son, obtained a post in Toledo, Ohio, then a town of 1,800 people, in 1844, but he and a deacon battled each other at every turn. William was forced to sue for his salary—he won, but of course, being a Beecher, he had to resign.

His next post was to build a church out of nothing in Euclid, Ohio, at a tiny salary. After three years, he gave up. His last church was in North Brookfield, Massachusetts, where he was also post-master.

•

After his book publication, Edward Beecher resigned from *The Congregationalist* in 1853, and then from his pastorate at the Salem Street Church.

Two years later, he published a very narrow book, *The Papal Conspiracy Exposed*, and went to Galesburg, Illinois, where he founded a new church. He also taught as a lecturer at Knox College. The Beecher house became a station on the Underground Railway, helped by a railroad conductor who lived just over his back fence. Edward also was enlisted into the women's movement, accepting the presidency of a women's suffrage convention in Springfield.

Harriet had written several chapters of *Uncle Tom's Cabin* in Edward's study while visiting him and Katy. She also used the Alton Riot as the model for her second anti-slavery novel, *Dred*. Clayton is Edward Beecher, Father Dickinson is Elijah Lovejoy.

Critic James Russell Lowell commented on Mrs. Stowe's anti-slavery novels.

LOWELL : It has always seemed to us that the anti-slavery element in the two former novels by Mrs. Stowe stood in the way of a full appreciation of her remarkable genius, at least in her own country. It was so easy to account for the unexampled popularity of *Uncle Tom* by attributing it to a cheap sympathy with sentimental philanthropy! As people began to recover from the first enchantment, they began also to resent it and to complain that a dose of that insane Garrison-root which takes the reason prisoner had been palmed upon them without their knowing it, and that their ordinary water-gruel of fiction, thinned with sentiment and thickened with moral, had been hocussed with the bewildering hasheesh of Abolition.

The secret of Mrs. Stowe's power lay in that same genius by which the great successes in creative literature have always been achieved—the genius that instinctively goes right to the organic elements of human nature, whether under a white skin or a black, and which disregards as trivial the conventional and factitious notions which make so large a part both of our thinking and feeling. The creative faculty of Mrs. Stowe, like that of Cervantes and of Fielding, overpowered the narrow specialty of her design, and expanded a local and temporary theme with the cosmopolitanism of genius.

NARRATOR : And in a personal letter, he writes:

LOWELL : My dear Mrs. Stowe, I certainly did mean to write you about your story, but only to cry bravissima! with the rest of the world. You are one of the few persons lucky enough to be born with eyes in your head, that is, with something behind the eyes which makes them of value.

May I, a critic by profession, say the whole truth to a woman of genius? Yes?

In the first place, pay no regard to the advice of anybody. In the second place, pay a great deal to mine! My advice is to follow your own instincts—to stick to nature, and to avoid what people commonly call the Ideal. Don't I feel it every day in this weary editorial mill of mine, that there are ten thousand people who can write Ideal things for one who can see, and feel, and reproduce nature and character? Let your moral take care of itself, and remember that an author's writing-desk is something infinitely higher than a pulpit.

THE BOOK: 2
1853–1856

The explosive success of *Uncle Tom's Cabin* was unprecedented. Tribute came from every direction. Suddenly Harriet Beecher Stowe was a household word, a focus for many people's frustrated energies, especially since she was the sister of the reformist preacher Henry Ward Beecher.

Henry describes how he managed the daily life of the most famous preacher in America.

HENRY : There are but three rules. Eat well, sleep well, and laugh well.

Let me give you an example. It is six o'clock in the morning. The day is begun. The family is emerging. Breakfast will be ready in half an hour. You look for *The Tribune*. The bell rings. A man has called thus early for fear you might be out. You dispatch his business.

Sitting down to breakfast the bell rings and the servant says the man will wait. But what pleasure can one have at meal with a man upstairs waiting for him? You run up. Can you marry a couple at so-and-so? That is settled. Prayers are had with the family. The bell rings once, twice, three times.

When you rise there are five persons waiting for you in the front parlor. A young man from the country wishes your name on his circular for a school. A young woman in failing health by confinement to sewing does not know what to do; behind in rent; cannot get away to the country; does not wish charity, only wishes someone to enable her to break away from a state of things that will in six months kill her. Another calls to inquire after a friend of whom he has lost sight. While you are attending to these the bell is active and other persons take the place of those who go.

A kind woman calls in behalf of a boarder who is out of place, desponding, will throw himself away if he cannot get some means of livelihood. Another calls to know if I will not visit a poor family in great distress in Morton Street. A good and honest-looking man comes next; is out of work, has "heard that your riverince is a kind man" etc. Another man wants to get his family out of Ireland; can pay half, if someone will intercede with ship-owners to trust him the balance. A stranger has died and a sexton desires a clergyman's services. Several persons desire religious conversion.

It is after ten o'clock. A moment's lull. You catch your hat and run out. Perhaps you have forgotten some appointment. You betake yourself to your study, not a little flurried by the contrariety of things which you have been considering.

You return to dine. There are five or six persons waiting for you. At tea you find others also with their diverse necessities.

This is not overdrawn and for many months of the year it is far underdrawn. There is no taxation compared to incessant various conversation with people for whom you must think, devise and for whose help you feel yourself often utterly incompetent.

NARRATOR : To escape this pressure, Henry went to his summer home in Peekskill on the Hudson. During hay fever season, he and Eunice went to the White Mountains.

While visiting Henry in Brooklyn, Harriet learned of the case of the Edmondsons. Three years before, Henry Ward Beecher had raised $2,250 from his congregation to purchase the freedom of two daughters of a free black and his slave wife. Harriet took on the financial responsibility for their education; Mrs. Edmondson now sought $1,200 for the release of her two remaining children, and Harriet Beecher Stowe made an appeal for funds. Before she left New York, she wrote out a check for the whole amount.

HARRIET : Had a very kind note from A. Lawrence enclosing a $20 gold piece for the Edmondsons. Isabella's ladies gave me $25, so you see our check is more than paid already.

NARRATOR : One indirect encounter that Harriet had while she was in New York, was with Jenny Lind, the "Swedish Nightingale."

HARRIET : Well, we have heard Jenny Lind, and the affair was a bewildering dream of sweetness and beauty. Her face and movements are full of poetry and feeling. She has the artless grace of a little child, the poetic effect of a wood nymph, is airy, light, and graceful.

Today I sent a note of acknowledgment with a copy of my book. I am most happy to have seen her, for she is a noble creature.

NARRATOR : Jenny Lind sent back this note.

JENNY LIND : My dear Madam—Allow me to express my sincere thanks. You must feel and know what a deep impression *Uncle Tom's Cabin* has made upon every heart that can feel for the dignity of human existence: so I with my miserable English would not even try to say a word about the great excellency of that most beautiful book, but I must thank you for the great joy I have felt over that book.

I have the feeling about *Uncle Tom's Cabin* that great changes will take place by and by, from the impression people receive out of it, and that the writer of that book can fall asleep today or tomorrow with the bright, sweet conscience of having been a strong means in the Creator's hand of operating essential good in one of the most important questions for the welfare of our black brethren. God bless and protect you and yours, dear madam.

NARRATOR : Senator Charles Sumner of Massachusetts wrote to Calvin Stowe:

SUMNER : All that I hear and read bears testimony to the good Mrs. Stowe has done. The article of George Sand is a most remarkable tribute, such as was hardly ever offered by such a genius to any living mortal. Should Mrs. Stowe conclude to visit Europe, she will have a triumph.

NARRATOR : And Charles Kingsley in England wrote her.

KINGSLEY : As for your progress and ovation here in England, I have no fear for you. You will be flattered and worshipped. You deserve it and you must bear it. I am sure that you have seen and suffered too much and too long to be injured by the foolish yet honest and heartfelt lionizing which you must go through.

I have many a story to tell you when we meet about the effects of the great book upon the most unexpected people.

NARRATOR : Prince Albert persuaded Queen Victoria to read it; Lord Carlisle wrote a preface for an English edition, Lord Macaulay reviewed it in England, George Sand in France, Heinrich Heine in Germany, George Sand said:

GEORGE SAND : The book has faults. We need not pass them in silence, we need not evade the discussion of them—but you need not be disturbed about them, you who are rallied on the tears you have shed over the fortunes of the poor victims in a narrative so simple and true. These defects exist only in relation to the conventional rules of art which never have been and never will be absolute. If its judges, possessed with the love of what they call artistic work, find unskilled treatment in the book, look well at them to see if their eyes are dry when they are reading this or that chapter.

•

NARRATOR : Meanwhile, the abolitionist movement, unsure of this unexpected ally, carried on its activities. Wendell Phillips had joined the abolitionist camp at the time of the Alton riots. Frederick Douglass, an escaped slave, added great moral force to the movement.

PHILLIPS : Frederick Douglass, some years ago, when you were beginning to tell me your real name and birthplace, you may remember I stopped you, and preferred to remain ignorant of all. I reflected that it was still dangerous, in Massachusetts, for honest men to tell their names! You publish your declaration of freedom with danger compassing you around. In all the broad lands which the Constitution of the United States overshadows, there is no single spot—however narrow or desolate—where a fugitive slave can plant himself and say, "I am safe." I am free to say that, in your place, I should throw the manuscript into the fire.

NARRATOR : At a certain point in his life as a slave, something happened to Douglass. It changed his life. Mr. Covey, his second master, was about to tie him up for a whipping, calling for help from one of his hands.

DOUGLASS : Hughes came, and, while Covey held me, attempted to tie my right hand. While he was in the act of doing so, I watched my chance, and gave him a heavy kick close under the ribs. This kick fairly sickened Hughes, so that he left me in the hands of Mr. Covey. This kick had the effect of not only weakening Hughes, but Covey also. When he saw Hughes bending over with pain, his courage quailed. He asked me if I meant to persist in my resistance. I told him I did, come what might; that he had used me like a brute for six months, and that I was determined to be used so no longer.

With that, he strove to drag me to a stick that was lying just out of the stable door. He meant to knock me down. But just as he was leaning over to get the stick, I seized him with both hands by his collar, and brought him by a sudden snatch to the ground.

By this time, Bill came. Covey called upon him for assistance. Bill wanted to know what he could do. Covey said, "Take hold of him, take hold of him!" Bill said his master hired him out to work, and not to help whip me; so he left Covey and myself to fight our own battle out. We were at it for nearly two hours. Covey at length let me go, puffing and blowing at a great rate, saying that if I had not resisted, he would not have whipped me at all. The whole six months afterwards, that I spent with Mr. Covey, he never laid the weight of his finger upon me in anger.

This battle with Mr. Covey was the turning-point in my career as a slave. It rekindkled the few expiring embers of freedom, and revived within me a sense of my own manhood. From this time I was never again what might be called fairly whipped, though I remained a slave four years afterwards. I had several fights, but was never whipped.

The only explanation I can now think of is that Mr. Covey enjoyed the most unbounded reputation for being a first-rate overseer and negro-breaker. That reputation was at stake, and had he sent me—a boy about sixteen years old—to the public whipping post, his reputation would have been lost.

NARRATOR : Once the criticism of *Uncle Tom's Cabin* started in earnest, Harriet set her face to the task of refuting it with a massive compilation of facts culled from laws, newspapers, court records, and private papers, called *A Key to Uncle Tom's Cabin*.

When Harriet and Calvin Stowe were given the opportunity of a free transatlantic trip for the anti-slavery movement, the Stowes plunged ahead. Charles Beecher went along as Harriet's secretary. They were in for quite a reception.

HARRIET : Much to my astonishment, I found quite a crowd on the wharf, and we walked to our carriage through a long lane of people, bowing and looking very glad to see us. Everywhere there was a warm welcome. What pleased me was that it was not mainly from the literary, nor the rich, nor the great but the plain, common people. The butcher came out of his stall and the baker from his shop, the miller dusty with flour, the blooming comely young mother, with that hearty, intelligent, friendly look as if they knew we should be glad to see them.

ELIZABETH BARRETT BROWNING : Never did lioness roar so softly.

NARRATOR : Those were the words of Elizabeth Barrett Browning, as the Stowe entourage departed for a tour of Scotland.

HARRIET : We found similar welcomes in many succeeding stopping-places; and though I did wave a towel out of the window, instead of a pocket handkerchief, and commit other awkwardnesses, from not knowing how to play my part, yet I fancied, after all, that Scotland and we were coming on well together.

•

At Glasgow, friends were waiting in the stationhouse. Earnest, eager, friendly faces, ever so many. Warm greetings, kindly words. A crowd parting in the middle, through which we were conducted into a carriage, and loud cheers of welcome, sent a throb, as the voice of living Scotland.

All this day is a confused dream to me of a dizzy and overwhelming kind. So many letters that it took brother Charles from nine in the morning till two in the afternoon to read and answer them in the shortest manner; letters from all classes of people, high and low, rich and poor, in all shades and styles of composition, poetry and prose; some mere outbursts of feeling; some invitations; some advice and suggestions; some requests and inquiries; some presenting books, or flowers, or fruit.

NARRATOR : The high point of the trip may have been back in London, a Lord Mayor's luncheon at Stafford House.

HARRIET : At about eleven o'clock we drove under the arched carriage-way of a mansion externally not very showy in appearance.

When the duchess appeared, I thought she looked handsomer by daylight than in the evening. She received us with the same warm and simple kindness which she had shown before. We were presented to the Duke of Sutherland. He is a tall, slender man, with rather a thin face, light-brown hair, and a mild blue eye, with an air of gentleness and dignity.

Among the first that entered were members of the family, the Duke and Duchess of Argyll, Lord and Lady Blantyre, the Marquis and Marchioness of Stafford, and Lady Emma Campbell. Then followed Lord Shaftesbury with his beautiful lady, and her father and mother, Lord and Lady Palmerston. Lord Palmerston is of middle height, with a keen dark eye and black hair streaked with gray. There is something peculiarly alert and vivacious about all his movements; in short, his appearance perfectly answers to what we know of him from his public life.

One has a strange, mythological feeling about the existence of people of whom one hears for many years without ever seeing them. While talking with Lord Palmerston I could but remember how often I had heard Father and Mr. Stowe exulting over his foreign dispatches by our own fireside. There were present, also, Lord John Russell, Mr. Gladstone, and Lord Granville. The latter we all thought very strikingly resembled in his appearance the poet Longfellow.

After lunch the whole party ascended to the picture gallery, passing on our way the grand staircase and hall, said to be the most magnificent in Europe. The company now began to assemble and throng the gallery, and very soon the vast room was crowded. Among the throng I remember many presentations, but of course must have forgotten many more. Archbishop Whateley was there, with Mrs. and Miss Whateley; Macaulay, with two of his sisters; Milman, the poet and historian; the Bishop of Oxford, Chevalier Bunsen and lady, and many more.

When all the company were together, Lord Shaftesbury read a very short, kind, and considerate address in behalf of the ladies of England, expressive of their cordial welcome.

This Stafford House meeting, in any view of it, is a most remarkable fact. Kind and gratifying as its arrangements have been to me, I am far from appropriating to myself individually as a personal honor. I rather regard it as the most public expression possible of the feelings of the women of England on one of the most important questions of our day, that of individual liberty considered in its religious bearings.

NARRATOR : It was on this occasion that the Duchess of Sutherland presented a gold chain and shackle to Mrs. Stowe.

She was also presented with five hundred thousand signatures of the women of England, from every economic class, bound in 26 volumes, as a petition to the United States against slavery.

Cassius Clay commented:

CLAY : It will help our cause by rendering it fashionable.

NARRATOR : Another day she had lunch with Lady Byron.

HARRIET : We had a few moments of deeply interesting conversation. She is of slight figure, formed with exceeding delicacy and her whole form, face, dress and air unite to make an impression of a character singularly dignified, gentle, pure, and yet strong.

NARRATOR : Then they were off to Paris, where Hilaire Belloc, husband of Mrs. Stowe's French translator, painted her portrait. On the way to Geneva, Charles noted:

CHARLES : The people of the neighborhood, having discovered who Harriet was—it was Scotland over again. We have had to be unflinching to prevent her being overwhelmed. It was touching to listen to the talk of these secluded mountaineers. All had read Uncle Tom, and it had apparently been an era in their life's monotony, for they said, "Oh, madam, do write another! Remember our winter nights here are very long!"

NARRATOR : After her return to the United States, Harriet Beecher Stowe threw herself fulltime into anti-slavery work. She had been entrusted with a lot of English money to be used in the anti-slavery campaign—some was used in freeing slaves, and supporting them, some for anti-slavery lectures, publications, schools, public meetings—for many of which she herself wrote speeches. Her correspondence with people all over the world was voluminous. In the midst of all this, she continued to be a mother, and to write. *Sunny Memories*, a journal of the English trip, drawing extensively on Charles's journal of their travels, was soon published, as well as a revision of her earlier book, *The Mayflower*.

Back in America, Mrs. Stowe found her brother Henry Ward, and her nephew Edward Everett Hale, absorbed in the Kansas-Nebraska problem. The South wanted to bring in Kansas as a slave state; Stephen Douglas developed his own attempt at compromise, the doctrine of squatter's sovereignty, or the right of each new territory to decide for itself whether or not slavery would be allowed. Missouri raiders immediately began interfering in Kansas territory politics with threats and violence. Harriet followed the debate and at last issued her own appeal addressed to the women of America.

HARRIET : A question is now pending in our National Legislature which is most vitally to affect the temporal and eternal interests, not only of ourselves, but of our children and our children's children for ages yet unborn. Through our nation it is to affect the interests of liberty and Christianity throughout the world.

There is but one feeling and one opinion upon this subject among us all. I do not think there is a mother who clasps her child to her breast who would ever be made to feel it right that that child should be a slave, not a mother among us who would not rather lay that child in its grave.

All this is inherent in slavery. It is not the abuse of slavery, but its legal nature. And there is not a woman in the United States, where the question is fairly put to her, who thinks these things are right.

But though our hearts have bled over this wrong, there have been many things tending to fetter our hands, to perplex our efforts, and to silence our voice. We have been told that to speak of it was an invasion of the rights of states.

But a time has now come when the subject is arising under quite a different aspect.

The question is not now, Shall the wrongs of slavery exist as they have within their own territories, but shall we permit them to be extended all over the free territories of the United States?—a region nearly equal in extent to the whole of the free states?

Nor is this all! By a decision of the Supreme Court in the Lemmon case, it may be declared lawful for slave property to be held in the Northern States.

And now you ask, What can the women of a country do?

The women of England refused to receive into their houses the sugar raised by slaves. Women were unwearied in going from house to house distributing books and tracts upon the subject.

238

They were associated in corresponding circles for prayer and labor. Petitions to the government were prepared and signed by women of every station in all parts of the kingdom.

When I was in England, although I distinctly stated that the raising of money was no part of my object there, it was actually forced upon me by those who could not resist the impulse to do something for this great cause. Nor did it come from the well-to-do alone; but hundreds of most affecting letters were received from poor working men and women, who enclosed small sums in postage-stamps to be devoted to freeing the slaves.

Nor is this deep feeling confined to England alone. I found it in France, Switzerland, and Germany. There has been a universal expectation that the next step taken by America would surely be one that should have a tendency to right this great wrong. Those who are struggling for civil and religious liberty in Europe speak this word slavery in sad whispers, as one names the fault of a revered friend. They can scarce believe the advertisements in American papers of slave sales of men, women, and children, traded like cattle. The advocates of despotism hold these things up to them and say: "See what comes of republican liberty!"

•

NARRATOR : Harriet spent an extra day, on returning from Italy, with Lady Byron, and as soon as she got home, wrote her.

HARRIET : Dear Friend—I left you with a strange sort of yearning throbbing feeling—you make me feel quite as I did years ago, a sort of girlishness quite odd for me. I often think how strange it is that I should know you—you who were a sort of legend of my early days—that I should love you is only a natural result.

NARRATOR : Among the intimacies that Harriet and Lady Byron shared was a common interest in spiritualism. Harriet hoped to communicate with her drowned son Henry, and daughter Eliza. Her ideas of the spirit-world, influenced by Calvin's experiences, also affected her religious conceptions.

HARRIET : My dear Friend—I did long to hear from you at a time when few knew how to speak, because I knew that you did know everything that sorrow can teach—you whose whole life has been a crucifixion, a long ordeal.

I think very much on the subject on which you conversed with me once—the future state of retribution. It is evident to me that the spirit of Christianity has produced in the human spirit a tenderness of love which completely revolts from the old doctrine on the subject.

I have become acquainted with a friend through whom I receive consoling impressions of these things—a Mrs. E., of Boston, a very pious, accomplished, and interesting woman, who has had a history much like yours in relation to spiritual manifestations. Without doubt she is what the spiritualists would regard as a very powerful medium. I have found that when I am with her I receive very strong impressions from the spiritual world, so that I feel often sustained and comforted, as if I had been near to my Henry and other departed friends.

I cannot, however, think that Henry strikes the guitar—that must be Eliza. Her spirit has ever seemed to cling to that mode of manifestation, and if you would keep it in your sleeping room, no doubt you would hear from it oftener.

One thing I am convinced of—that spiritualism is a reaction from the intense materialism of the present age. Luther, when he recognized a personal devil, was much nearer right. We ought to enter fully, at least, into the spiritualism of the Bible. Circles and spiritual jugglery I regard as the lying signs and wonders with all deceivableness of unrighteousness, but there is a real scriptural spiritualism which has fallen into disuse, and must be revived. There are, doubtless, people who, from some constitutional formation, can more readily receive the impressions of the surrounding spiritual world. Such were apostles, prophets, and workers of miracles.

NARRATOR : George Eliot and Harriet corresponded on the same subject.

ELIOT : Apart from personal contact with people who get money by public exhibitions as mediums or with semi-idiots such as those who make a court for Mrs. X, or other feminine personages of that kind, I would not willingly place any barriers between my mind and any possible channel of truth affecting the human lot.

•

NARRATOR : While in Rome after the death of the Stowes'

son Henry, Harriet saw a great deal of the Brownings—Robert and Elizabeth—and found they shared an interest in the occult. Elizabeth Barrett Browning wrote her:

ELIZABETH : I don't know how people can keep up their prejudices against spiritualism with tears in their eyes—how they are not, at least, thrown on the "wish that it might be true," and the investigation of the phenomena, by that abrupt shutting in their faces of the door of death which shuts them out from the sight of their beloved. My tendency is to beat up against it like a crying child. Not that this emotional impulse is the best for turning the key and obtaining safe conclusions—no. I did not write before because I always do shrink from touching my own griefs, one feels at first so sore that nothing but stillness can be borne.

I should congratulate you, my dear friend, on the great crisis you are passing through in America. If the North is found noble enough to stand fast on the moral question, whatever the loss or diminution of territory, God and just men and women will see you greater and more glorious as a nation.

I had much anxiety for you after the Seward and Adams speeches, but the danger seems averted. How you must feel, you who have done so much to set this accursed slavery in the glare of the world, convicting it of hideousness! They should raise a statue to you in America and elsewhere.

NARRATOR : Harriet's second novel on slavery, *Dred*, exposed the demoralizing effect that slavery had on the masters, and on white people generally. The English edition sold 100,000 copies in the first month—some, including the Queen, liked it better than *Uncle Tom's Cabin*.

So it was that in 1856, the Stowes were in England again, invited by Harriet Martineau and others. This time, they would have an unexpected encounter. Calvin Stowe describes the scene.

CALVIN : Yesterday we had just the very pleasantest little interview with the Queen that ever was. None of the formal, drawing-room, breathless receptions, but just an accidental, done-on-purpose meeting at a railway station while on our way to Scotland. The Queen seemed really delighted to see my wife and remarkably glad to see me for her sake. She pointed us out to Prince Albert who made two most gracious bows to my wife and two to me while the four royal children stared their big blue eyes almost out looking at the little author of *Uncle Tom's Cabin*.

THE SECOND REUNION
1855

The second Beecher family reunion took place in 1855, when Lyman Beecher was eighty years old. Nine brothers and sisters met at Henry Ward Beecher's home in Brooklyn. Two were missing—George had committed suicide twelve years before, and James, the youngest, was in Hong Kong, a missionary preacher.

Though Lyman Beecher, the patriarch, had retired only four years before, and had tried to write his autobiography, he was fast losing ground. His deterioration affected all his children. Prompted by Catharine or Harriet, their father remembered scenes long past, sometimes before they were born. It would be the last time, probably, that most of them would see the old preacher.

LYMAN : My father, David Beecher, the son of Nathaniel, was short, like his mother, and could lift a barrel of cider and carry it into the cellar. He was a blacksmith, and worked on the same anvil his father had before him, on the old oak stump. He lived well, according to the times, and laid up four or five thousand dollars. He was one of the best-read men in New England, well versed in Astronomy, Geography, and History, and fond of politics.

He always kept a number of college students and of representatives to the legislature as boarders, being fond of their conversation. He often kept pace with his student-boarders in their studies, frequently spending his evenings in their rooms. He had a tenacious memory for what he read, but was entirely careless and forgetful as to his dress, hat, etc. Your Aunt Esther says she has known him at least twelve times come in from the barn and sit down on a coat-pocket full of eggs, jump up, and say, "Oh, wife!"

"Why, my dear," she would reply, "I do wonder you can put eggs in your pocket after you have broken them so once."

"Well," he would say, "I thought I should remember this time." He was, on the whole, a good deal like me. He was just of my height—five feet seven and a half inches—with the same colored hair, eyes, and complexion, though I am a little heavier. If father had received a regular education he would have been equal to anybody.

From keeping boarders, it came about that his table was rather better than farmers' tables, and his cooking and seasoning rather too rich, and so he suffered severely from dyspepsia, and this produced hypochondria. He would pass from a state of cheerfulness to one of acute distress, apparently without cause. I knew all about them; have had just such feelings myself.

NARRATOR : By this time, Henry Ward Beecher had replaced Edward as the family mainstay. Not only was he the most famous clergyman in America, and a rich one at that, he had sheltered Charles and Thomas, and had kept in close touch with Harriet and Lyman and the others. Though his own marriage was not ideal—Eunice was a bitter, withdrawn woman—family was important to Henry.

As in Indianapolis, he was careless about other pastoral duties, but he was highly successful as a preacher. His church seated 2,500, and it was usually overflowing. But even large audiences were not enough for Henry. Each sermon must not be simply well received, it must accomplish its purpose.

HENRY : I never shoot an arrow at a venture; I always aim at a mark, though I may not hit the mark I aim at.

Others had learned this. It was the secret of success in everyone who ever was eminent for usefulness in preaching. But no one can inherit experience; it must be born in each for himself.

NARRATOR : Henry kept up an interest in phrenology, not to know the bumps in the skull, but because it gave him a method of studying men and women. Later, in sermons, he was often able to characterize people with great detail, imitating the posture, gestures, and intonations of a blacksmith, farmer, or shopkeeper.

At Plymouth Church, there was always a great amount of talking—in the informal meetings, and before and after services. Conversation did not stop when the organ began, but instantly, when Beecher began, there was a hush. The congregation knew that when Henry Ward Beecher began, he always spoke in low tones. After benediction, he stayed around to shake hands, and somehow the large church was run like a rural New England meetinghouse, friends meeting friends and exchanging social gossip, and strangers were greeted.

John Zundel, the church organist, was self-trained musically, but spiritual in his music.

ZUNDEL : I cannot pray with my lips, I pray with my fingers.

NARRATOR : Zundel's emphatic pedal-stomping style fit well with Henry Ward Beecher's insistence on music to be sung, not listened to. The result of two or three thousand untrained people singing melody was not often graceful, but every Sunday that swelling outpouring of emotion was intense. At the time, congregational singing was not the common practice—there was no hymnbook written for communal singing.

With help from brother Charles, Plymouth Church's *Temple Melodies* was created to fill that need, but it only gave Henry the ambition of a larger undertaking, to be called the *Plymouth Collection*. He would include Calvinist writers and Arminians, Roman Catholic authors and Unitarians and non-religious poets such as Mrs. Browning, William Cullen Bryant, John Greenleaf Whittier, and James Russell Lowell. The *Plymouth Collection* was almost unique, yet because it now defined a new field, many hymn-writers turned to this new genre. By now, the *Plymouth Collection* is hopelessly out of date, but it did as much to change church music in America as any other single book.

LYMAN : My mother was tall, well-proportioned, dignified in her movements, fair to look upon, intelligent in conversation, and in character lovely. I was her only child. She died of consumption two days after I was born. I was a seven-months' child; and when the woman that attended on her saw what a puny thing I was, and that the mother could not live, she thought it useless to attempt to keep me alive. I was actually wrapped and laid aside.

But, after a while, one of the women thought she would look and see if I was living and, finding I was, concluded to wash and dress me, saying, "It's a pity he hadn't died with his mother." So you see it was but by a hair's-breadth I got a foothold in this world.

HARRIET : With all that was truly great among humans, Father felt a kindred sympathy. Genius and heroism would move him even to tears. I recollect hearing him read aloud Milton's account of Satan's marshaling his forces of fallen angels after his expulsion from heaven. The description of Satan's courage and fortitude was read with such evident sympathy as quite enlisted me in his favor, and in the passage.

> Millions of spirits, for his fault amerced
> of heaven, and from eternal splendors flung
> for his revolt, yet faithful how they stood,
> their glory withered; as when heaven's fire
> hath scathed the forest oaks, or mountain pines,
> with singed top, their stately growth, though bare,
> stands on the blasted heath. He now prepared
> to speak; whereat their doubled ranks they bend
> from wing to wing, and half enclose him round
> with all his peers; attention held them mute.
> Thrice he essayed, and thrice, in spite of scorn,
> tears, such as angels weep, burst forth.

On reaching this point, Father burst into tears himself, and the reading ended.

NARRATOR : Henry Ward Beecher's *Star Papers*, so named because on their first publication in *The Independent*, he signed them with an asterisk only, were published in 1855. By this time, Henry had begun his series of familiar essays on many topics in *The Independent*; often these simply celebrated the life of the senses.

HENRY : Today is goblet day. The whole heavens have been mingled with exquisite skill to a delicious flavor, and the crystal cup held out to every lip. It is a luxury simply to exist.

NARRATOR : He also established a farm at Lenox, and when that proved too far, another, called Boscobel, at Peekskill. Henry Ward Beecher was becoming a popular naturalist, an apologist for beauty and art. In earlier days, Lyman Beecher had not been kind to such an attitude.

LYMAN : It's all moonshine with no doctrine, nor edification, nor sanctity in it, and I despise it.

NARRATOR : But out of Henry's celebration of life came his mature philosophy of love.

HENRY : Let there be a perpetual tropical luxuriance of blessed love. I never knew how to worship until I knew how to love; and to love, I must have something that, touching my heart, shall not leave the chill of ice but the warmth of summer.

We are standing on the eve of a great day—a day multitudinous with truths and struggles. The life of the common people is the best part of the world's life. The life of the common people is the life of God.

LYMAN : I remember in those days how the selectmen visited the farmhouses, and took an inventory and gave receipts. We paid in beef. The kitchen was full, and they came in with carts and carried it to the army.

HARRIET : Was there no complaining?

LYMAN : No complaint; not a word.

HARRIET : We were independent already, and only determined we would remain so.

LYMAN : Yes. If we had been slaveholders, we should have gone to the dogs.

HARRIET : Were there not some that held slaves, then?

LYMAN : Yes, a few. Darb, the fiddler, was a slave; belonged to old Mr. Ben Rossiter. Darb came in one evening and played dancing tunes after I was abed. There were about a dozen slaves in North Guilford, but the slavery was very lenient. Old Priest Fowler's Moses was quite the man of business; sent Johnny Fowler to college, and paid the bills, managed the farm, rung the church bell, and was factotum. He lived a slave because he was a king.

•

NARRATOR : Henry Ward Beecher's oratory was a marvel. Here is one eyewitness report: "It was a lesson in elocution to hear Mr. Beecher read a Scripture lesson. You might not agree with his interpretation, but you could not misunderstand it. I recall once hearing him, in a sermon on the gentleness of Christ, pause and say:

HENRY : But did not Christ denounce the Pharisees with bitterest invective? That depends upon the spirit with which he uttered and with which we read his words.

NARRATOR : "Then he took up the New Testament, turned to the twenty-third chapter of Matthew and read three or four verses—'Woe unto you, scribes and Pharisees, hypocrites'—with thunder in the tones, frown upon the brow, wrath in the voice; then, without note or comment, he read them again as a lamentation, with infinite pathos, with suppressed tears in the tones of his voice. Then he closed the New Testament and went on with his sermon."

NARRATOR : The head of Yale when Lyman Beecher went there had been Timothy Dwight, leading the student body back to an earlier Calvinism that had almost disappeared.

DWIGHT : The numbers of the Poet, the delightful melody of the Song, the fascination of the Chisel, the spell of the Pencil, have all been volunteered in the service of Satan, for the moral destruction of unhappy humanity.

NARRATOR : Lyman Beecher's religious experience occurred at Yale under Timothy Dwight's hellfire regime. Lyman was spending a weekend at home, when his stepmother remarked that a drunk passing by had once been religious—she hoped that he might escape hell.

LYMAN : I rose to pray and had not spoken five words before I was under as deep a conviction as ever I was in my life. The sinking of the shaft was instantaneous. I understood the law and my heart as well as I do now or shall in the Day of Judgment, I believe. The commandment came, sin revived, and I died, quick as a flash of lightning.

The first time I went afishing, Uncle Benton took me down to Beaver Head, tied a brown thread on a stick, put a crooked pin on it and a worm, and said, "There, Lyman, throw it in." I threw it in, and out came a shiner! The first time I caught a perch was at Quinnepaug Outlet. He got off my hook and fell in the shallows, and began to flapper off, and away I went after him down the shallows on all fours, quicker than a flash.

Another time I found a school of perch in a hole under the roots of a tree, and took them all out with my hand.

I always liked "training-day," because then I could go a-fishing. Fished all day till dark, and felt sorry when night came. That was my passion. Couldn't leave off till the bullheads had done biting. Once, at the saw-mill, I hooked a pickerel without bait; how I whopped him out!

Used to follow the trout brook round to the mill-dam. Once, below the dam, in a deep hole, I saw six salmon trout. Dropped my hook with a grasshopper; none of 'em bit. Tried a worm, squirmed lively; one of 'em struck it; took him out. Cut a stick, strung him; baited my hook, threw in; another of 'em struck it; pulled him out, strung him; another, and another, till I had the whole six.

HENRY : I seldom succeed when I try. The best things are unexpected insofar as my work is concerned. I always have floating in my head half-formed thoughts I would like to utter. Saturday is my day of rest. I am apt to spend it on my farm at Peekskill under the trees. I sleep soundly Saturday night; I sleep vicariously for my congregation. After breakfast I go into my study, feel of my different themes, the one that is ripe I pluck, select my text, organize my thought, and go into the pulpit with my theme fresh, my mind and heart full of it.

LYMAN : Annis was a noble girl, and had a great influence over my character. She was about thirteen, intelligent and well-favored. She was nurse, mother, sister, and all. She and Aunt Benton fill up the memory of my early days.

She was pious, and, though little was said to children then, talked with me about my soul. I remember one night, when the northern lights were very bright, a blood-red arch from horizon to zenith, and light enough to read out of doors. Everybody was out looking at it, and Uncle Stephen Benton said, "Ah! we don't know at what time the day of judgment will come—at midnight or at cock-crowing."

The thought flashed through my mind, "It has come now," and I felt all the dismay of the reality. I began to cry. Annis quieted me, and, after I went to bed—I always slept with her—she talked with me about my soul.

I remember near the close of the War, when New Haven was attacked by the British, Aaron Burr happened to be there, and took command of a party of militia. Father took his old firelock and went out with them. But the British were too strong for them, and the word came each one to look out for himself. Father was down in the "second quarter," so called, and happened to see a scout; he raised his gun, and stood deliberating whether he could kill a fellow-being. The click of a trigger nearby turned his head toward a British marksman, who had no such scruples, but was aiming straight at his head. He popped down into a ravine, losing his gun and hat, and wandered about all that hot July day bareheaded, and got a sunstroke, from which he never wholly recovered.

NARRATOR : Henry Beecher's great powers of sympathy allowed him to vividly portray scenes and characters, to make his congregation feel the presence of a living god there on the platform with him. His rather ordinary face had as much flexibility as his voice, and took on the character of the person he was describing. But all these skills were held to a moral purpose, and thus he never repeated a performance or a sermon.

•

Edward Beecher's *The Conflict of Ages* introduced the idea of the pre-existence of souls into Calvinism. Lyman Beecher, among others, didn't immediately respond to this theological argument.

LYMAN : Edward, you've destroyed the Calvinist barns, but I hope you don't delude yourself that the animals are going into your little theological hencoop!

NARRATOR : Colonel Robert G. Ingersoll, the great atheist, had nothing good to say about Calvinism.

INGERSOLL : Henry Ward Beecher was born in a Puritan penitentiary, of which his father was one of the wardens—a prison with very narrow and closely grated windows. Under its walls were the rayless, hopeless and measureless dungeons of the damned, and on its roof fell the shadow of God's eternal frown. In this prison the creed and catechism were primers for children, and from a pure sense of duty their loving hearts were stained and scarred with the religion of John Calvin.

NARRATOR : Catharine Beecher was more specific in her complaint, but every Beecher could vouch for its accuracy.

CATHARINE : What a record of vain attempts for twenty years, not in a single case rewarded with success! What anxiety, perplexity, disappointment, and agonizing fear are there recorded on the part of the father, and what suffering and vain efforts on the part of the children!

REV. THOMAS DAVIES (editor of *Christian Spectator*—1819) : In his study Dr. Beecher spoke of the methods of mental culture. He said that it was not until he had been three years a preacher that he acquired the power of properly examining, discussing, and presenting important subjects in a sermon; and showed me, in folio form, a volume in which he wrote plans, arguments, and illustrations of discourses which he had preached, and said that, if the sermons should be burned or lost, that from the notes these contained he could reproduce them.

LYMAN : A new day was dawning as I came on the stage, and I was baptized into the revival spirit. It was the age of French Infidelity. There was a leaven of skepticism all over the world. The question was, Revival or Infidelity. I did not attack infidelity directly. Not at all. That would have been cracking a whip behind a runaway team—made them run the faster. I always preached right to the conscience. Every sermon with my eye on the gun to hit somebody.

After spending about two years in fitting for college, I went home to Father's in New Haven, and spent a month before Commencement. I was eighteen. Farmer's life and farmer's fare had made me strong and hearty beyond anything I should have reached if I had grown up in Father's family, though that was far more intellectual. I built up the physical first, the intellectual afterward.

Father was now living with his fifth wife, and Esther, her daughter, was about thirteen, and forever reading. Then there were Polly, Lydia, and David, so that there was a pretty good family of us. Besides, there were several boarders, and, at Commencement, the house was always filled to overflowing with company.

•

NARRATOR : Oratory was in full flower, as Henry Ward Beecher, Theodore Parker, Wendell Phillips, Emerson, Greeley, John B. Gough and others ranged the countryside speaking on everything of public concern. But Henry Ward Beecher was extraordinarily sensitive to his audience's moods, and free to express emotions, to cry, to shout, to move, to speak candidly and to wax rhetorical— and speaking before such large crowds seemed to give him energy rather than to sap him. He captured audiences in New York, New England, and the West. As Theodore Parker said:

PARKER : The Rocky Mountains are his sounding board. He is eternally young and positively wears me out with his redundant, superabundant, ever-recovering, and ever-renewing energy. Mr. Beecher has great strength of instinct, of spontaneous human feeling. He has a genius to be loved. He captivates people without an effort. People look upon him as a national institution, a part of the public property.

HENRY : The voice is the bell of the soul, or the iron and crashing of the anvil. It is a magician's wand, full of incantation and witchery; or it is a scepter in a king's hand, and sways people with imperial authority. At times, there are no gestures comparable to the simple stature of the person him/herself.

I think of everything that makes my soul a terrible house of imagery. No one can go down into the dungeon of his own experience and not come up with a shudder and a chill.

NARRATOR : There seemed to be nothing special about Henry Ward Beecher—his face was plain and a bit puffy, his voice was not unusual. He would begin on a conversational level, then explosively he would be gay, sad, fulsome, or warmly falling. He was a superb mimic of the gestures of a blacksmith, a fisherman, a drunkard, a sailor. Some complained that his transitions were too quick, that he made religion an entertainment—but to every audience large or small, he bathed them in his warmth, and gave them all his gospel of love.

Henry David Thoreau called him a magnificent pagan. And Bronson Alcott said:

ALCOTT : It was a spectacle. I pronounced it good, very good—the best that I had witnessed for many a day.

LYMAN : Thought I could preach till I heard Henry.

HARRIET : Did Uncle Lot pay your bills through college?

LYMAN : In great part, and what he did not pay father paid himself. Father used to have the "hypo" dreadfully about supporting me. Esther heard him telling her mother he could not stand it; he should certainly have to take me out of college, or they should all go to ruin. She answered—she was my stepmother—that she couldn't have it so; and said that her property might go to pay my bills. There was some property of hers, and he had the use of it.

HARRIET : Did you know how he felt?

LYMAN : Yes, I knew that he was bankrupt, as he supposed. I recollect saying, "Father, you needn't be concerned; you have enough to live on at present; and when I get through and have a home, I'll take care of you."

"Pooh! poor fellow!" said he, "you'll scratch a poor man's head all your lifetime."

I did help myself a little, though. Staples, the butler, left college six weeks before the end of the year, and I took the buttery, and bought out his stock for about $300, which I borrowed. I went into it hot and heavy. One day I bought a lot of watermelons and canteloupes, and trundled them across the green on a wheelbarrow, in the face of the whole college. I sent to New York by an English parson—a judge of the article—and bought a hogshead of porter. It's odd; but I can remember selling things to Moses Stuart—two classes below me.

That buttery was a regular thing in those days; it has wholly disappeared since, and is almost forgotten. The old Latin laws are a curiosity.

HARRIET : Did it pay well?

LYMAN : Well, I paid my note, and besides $100 in bad debts, cleared my Commencement expenses, bought a suit of clothes, and had $100 in cash. I worked hard. If I had gone into busienss then I should have made money.

NARRATOR : In the house of General Andrew Ward, Lyman Beecher found the girl Roxana that he would marry, who would bear his first eight children. But he had gone there one day determined to see if her faith could follow his vision, or else he would break off the engagement.

LYMAN : I explained my views, and laid before her the great plan of redemption. As I went on, her bosom heaved, her heart melted, and mine melted too; and I never told her to her dying day what I came for.

NARRATOR : Lyman Beecher was always the dominant force in the Beecher family, even after his sons and daughters left home. But he never squelched their initiative or suppressed their individuality or kept them back. Henry Ward Beecher said of him:

HENRY : He thought he was great by his theology; everybody else knew he was great by his religion.

NARRATOR : His theology had led him to preach his first sermon in Litchfield against morality—the notion that mere goodness could get one into heaven. But despite his theology, Lyman Beecher spoke against slavery, dueling, intemperance, and other social evils. And that, finally, was the lesson his children learned from him—that people couldn't live right if social ills such as slavery were allowed to exist.

So it was that they all became reformers in one way or another, working to make this world better—Catharine in women's education, Henry and Harriet against slavery, most of them, especially Edward, Charles, and Henry, in theology, Charles in music, Thomas in the institutional church, Isabella in women's suffrage, James in tolerance.

LYMAN : One morning I went out for a duck hunt. 'Twas a great deal earlier than I had supposed; but I kept on, and came down the east shore, where the surf is always foaming up on the beach—wave after wave, rolling and roaring, as high as your head; but now, for once it was still; you couldn't hear a sound except a little softly murmuring noise as the ripples came creeping up the beach; 'twas as still as stillness itself. I laid down my gun and sat down to hear such a silence as I never did before. I forgot the ducks.

THE POT BOILS OVER
1854–1860

During the Fillmore and Buchanan years, sectional division was destroying the Whig Party and had weakened the Democrats. President Fillmore had been war hero Zachary Taylor's running mate, a product of the Albany Regency political machine under Thurlow Weed. When Taylor died in office, Fillmore carried on. He was an able politician, but he had no program.

Henry Ward Beecher became nationally known overnight as an anti-slavery leader at a fund-raising event at the Broadway Tabernacle. Two black girls had fled Washington, had been caught, and were about to be shipped to New Orleans. When Beecher took the platform, he dramatized a slave auction to drive home the reality of the situation. He called for bids like an auctioneer, and before the meeting ended, the money had been raised. This auction for freedom was repeated in other cases, over the next ten years.

But though he dramatized the individual plight, and though he believed slavery to be a national sin, Beecher did not call for its immediate abolition. Many people shared Henry Ward Beecher's opinion that slavery would die of its own accord, if it were simply contained.

HENRY : Let slavery alone. Let it go to seed. Hold it to its own natural fruit. Cut off every branch that hangs beyond the wall, every root that spreads. Shut it up to itself and let it alone. We do not ask to interfere with the internal policy of a single state by congressional enactments. We only ask that a line be drawn about it.

When slavery begins, under such treatment, to flag, we demand that she be denied political favoritism to regain her loss; we demand that no laws be enacted to give health to her paralysis and strength to her relaxing grasp. She boldly and honestly demanded a right to equality with the North, and prophetically spoke by Calhoun that the North would preponderate and crush her. It is true. Time is her enemy.

NARRATOR : The South also believed that the extension of slavery was necessary for its continued existence. Robert Toombs of Georgia wanted to annex South American countries as slave states. Pierre Soule of Louisiana, among others, spoke of annexing Cuba to expand the slave power.

The giants of the Congress from Jackson's day had put their best efforts into the Compromise of 1850—and within a little more than a year of each other Henry Clay, Daniel Webster and John C. Calhoun all died. New leaders stepped forward—Stephen Douglas of Illinois, William H. Seward, Salmon P. Chase, Horace Greeley, Abraham Lincoln.

When the Compromise of 1850 was passed, the Fugitive Slave Law provision, though nominally harsh, was in fact little enforced. One Boston marshal would seek runaway slaves by going to see William Lloyd Garrison first. The fugitive he was sent after would soon be in Canada.

The main effect of the 1850 Compromise was the politicians' relief from anti-slavery agitation. It appeared that the question of the future of slavery was settled. President Fillmore thought so.

FILLMORE : The agitation, which for a time threatened to disturb the fraternal relations which make us one people is fast subsiding. I congratulate the nation upon the general acquiescence in these measures of peace which has been accepted in all parts of the Republic.

•

NARRATOR : When statehood for Kansas came up, Southerners wanted to see Kansas brought in as a new slave state; Northerners opposed them. Stephen A. Douglas, the Little Giant from Illinois, sponsored a new idea: the notion of squatters' sovereignty—in other words, the party to decide whether or not there would be slavery in Kansas should not be the government, but the new settlers. The whole delicate balance built over years of compromise in Congress would be thrown out the window under Douglas's plan.

Two weeks after Douglas's Kansas-Nebraska Bill came up, Henry Ward Beecher knew his mind.

HENRY : The Nebraska bill is the death-struggle of slavery for expansion, seeing that she must have more room to breathe or suffocate. All question as to whether slavery shall be agitated is now at an end. The South says it shall be agitated, and she cannot help it. The mask is off, and all disguises are thrown to the winds, and the slave power stands out in its true character, making its last and most infamous demands upon the North. All we have to do is to say No.

NARRATOR : Within four months the Kansas-Nebraska Bill was passed, incorporating the principle Douglas called squatter sovereignty—that each new state was to declare itself free or slave. Marauders from slave-state Missouri made forays into the new state of Kansas, killing and harassing settlers. The first legislature was invaded and overthrown by force of arms, and a pro-slavery constitution was written and sent to Washington. This Lecompte constitution was disputed by many, but President Fillmore favored accepting it.

When someone said they should send Bibles to the helpless settlers in Kansas, Henry Ward Beecher declared that Sharpes rifles would be a stronger moral influence than Bibles. These rifles came to be called "Beecher's Bibles."

•

Meanwhile, it became clear to politicians that neither the Whig nor the Democratic Party would be willing to take an anti-slavery stand. Millard Fillmore the Whig, and Franklin Pierce the Democrat had both upheld the demands of the slave states. Could there be a third party? The Liberty Party, under James G. Birney, had been large enough to throw the 1844 election to James K. Polk, defeating Henry Clay's last bid for the presidency. Yet the Liberty Party did not seek broad support.

Salmon P. Chase, Charles Sumner, and Wade thought the time had come to organize the many opponents of slavery into a national party. William H. Seward and Thurlow Weed at first stayed away. Cassius Clay of Kentucky was eager to join a new party.

Once the groups met together, settling on the candidacy of John C. Fremont, the Western adventurer and son-in-law of Thomas Hart Benton, Henry Beecher at once began to work for his election, taking a leave of absence from his church to campaign for Fremont. He gave three-hour speeches several times a week in the open air, to as many as ten thousand people until attacks of dizziness slowed him down. The Republicans lost that year, but made remarkably good showings throughout the North and East. In most Southern states, Republicans didn't even have conventions.

The victor in the 1856 presidential campaign, James Buchanan, was an outstanding diplomat, but he knew no solution except compromise on the slavery issue. In his inaugural address he said that states had no right to secede—but on the other hand, the federal government had no right to stop them. He also tried to balance North and South in his Cabinet appointments—later on, that mistake would be costly to the Union. So much for diplomacy.

·

Isabella Beecher Hooker felt herself very much in the shadow of her more famous sisters and brothers. Edward was regarded as a leading theologian, Catharine as perhaps the foremost leader in women's education, Harriet had skyrocketed to fame with her book, Henry had a national reputation as an orator. Even Charles received national attention with his bold anti-authoritarian pronouncements.

The furthest Isabella had gone by this time was to be one of the first women to wear Amelia Bloomer's Turkish-style pantaloons with knee-length overskirt. In what field could she make her mark? She studied political economy, she considered a career as a water-cure gynecologist. And she read law with her husband John—an exercise that would come in handy later.

Charles Beecher had reorganized a failing church in Newark, New Jersey into a thriving one. He preached temperance and anti-slavery in his outspoken manner. When the Fugitive Slave Law was passed, Charles was expelled for his sermon, *The Duty of Disobedience to Wicked Laws,* by the ministerial association of Newark. But the sermon was printed as a pamphlet, and it had a wide circulation in the North.

When his sister Harriet's novel, *Uncle Tom's Cabin,* became a runaway bestseller, she chose Charles to accompany her to Europe as her secretary and companion. Her book of travel notes from that trip drew heavily on Charles's diary as well as her own.

·

In 1855, it was Catharine who organized the last family reunion, soon after Lyman Beecher's eightieth birthday. By now, the old patriarch had lost much of his intellectual acuity. He would remember scenes of long ago as if it were yesterday, but might not respond if addressed directly. Catharine was heard to remark that she felt closer to her father's experience than to that of her brothers and sisters.

CATHARINE : The last two or three years I have felt more and more of that peace that passeth all understanding. As every year brings me nearer to departed friends, the veil that separates us seems to grow thinner so that I feel almost as near and present with those who are with the Lord as with those who are still prisoned in these earthly tabernacles.

NARRATOR : Catharine Beecher suffered nervous complaints throughout her life, and like her sisters Isabella and Harriet, often retreated to water cure spas. The water cure itself became the subject of another of Catharine's books, *Letters to the People on Health and Happiness.* She praised its powers of restoring health.

Over two hundred water cure centers had sprung up, catering mainly to women. They provided a freedom of sensuality for women not available elsewhere—including massage, exercise, bathing and other attentions to the body. Bodily conditions could be discussed openly.

CATHARINE : The experience of each individual gradually becomes known to most of his or her fellow patients, thus providing assurances that certain problems are shared by others.

NARRATOR : Even abortions were available in some water cure spas. Abortion had been made illegal by state laws, yet every newspaper advertised abortive pills, in the form of pills to "begin the monthly cycle." Russell Trall's *Hydropathic Encyclopedia* of 1853 talked of the "safe period" and other methods of contraception. Trall held that a woman had an absolute right to determine when she should and when she should not conceive. Hydropathy, the water cure, took a holistic approach.

On the other hand, orthodox medicine denied women this right. One leading specialist in uterine diseases still taught students to insert leeches into the womb, even though he admitted that it could "induce a paroxysm of almost intolerable suffering."

Dr. Hugh Hodge also did not believe that women should make such decisions.

HODGE : The dread of suffering, fears respecting their own health and strength, the trouble and expense of large families, and, professedly, also, the responsibility incurred in the education of children, these and other reasons equally futile and trifling induce women to destroy the product of that conjugal union for which marriage was instituted.

NARRATOR : Besides the water cure, however, Catharine Beecher also taught the importance of knowledge of the human body, exercise, proper diet and clothing, cleanliness and fresh air. Corsets were condemned.

·

In 1857, Harriet's eldest son, Henry, drowned in the Connecticut River by Dartmouth, where he had just entered as a freshman. Catharine had recently come out with her book *Common Sense Applied to Religion, or the Bible and the People*— which developed her ideas of morality, including the idea that God saved those who seemed to want to be saved, not just those who had been converted. Harriet's great loss led her to the same conclusion.

HARRIET : If ever I was conscious of an attack of the Devil trying to separate me from the love of Christ, it was for some weeks after the terrible news came. I was in a state of great physical weakness, most agonizing, and unable to control my thoughts. Distressing doubts as to Henry's spiritual state were rudely thrust upon my soul. It was as if a voice had said to me: "You had perfect confidence that He would never take your child till the work of grace was mature Now He has hurried him into eternity without a moment's warning, without preparation, and where is he? No, it is our duty to assume that a thing which would be in its very nature unkind, ungenerous, and unfair has not been done; Henry surely must be in heaven.

NARRATOR : She also wrote more philosophically to the Duchess of Sutherland:

HARRIET : While I was visiting in Hanover, where Henry died, a poor, deaf, old slave woman, who has still five children in bondage, came to comfort me. "Bear up, dear soul," she said, "you must bear it, for the Lord loves ye." She said further, "Sunday is a heavy day to me, 'cause I can't work and can't hear preaching and can't read so I can't keep my mind off my poor children. Some of 'em the blessed Master's god and they's safe; but oh, there are five that I don't know where they are." What are our mother sorrows to this! I shall try to search out and redeem these children.

NARRATOR : But this was not enough for Harriet—she had but recently read Catharine's letters of 1822 and in the unfinished autobiography that her father was trying to write, she saw the whole sweep of Lyman Beecher's career in New England Calvinism. These ingredients, along with her personal sorrow, went into *The Minister's Wooing,* a novel of eighteenth century New England. Especially revealing is her portrayal of Catharine as Mary Scudder, paying tribute to her strength of character and intellectual independence.

HARRIET : Mary was only a recast in feminine form of her father's nature. The elixir of the spirit that sparkled within her was of that quality of which the souls of poets and artists are made; but the keen New England air crystallizes into ideas, and restricts many a poetic soul to the necessity of expressing itself only in practical living.

It was easy enough for Mary to believe in self-renunciation, for she was one with a born vocation for martyrdom; and so, when the idea was put to her of suffering eternal pains for the glory of God and the good of being in general, she responded to it with a sort of sublime thrill, such as it is given to some natures to feel in view of uttermost sacrifice.

NARRATOR : Another aspect of Catharine was seen in the mother of the drowned suitor, Mrs. Marvyn.

MRS. MARVYN : I have thought, in desperate moments, of giving up the Bible itself, but what do I gain? Do I not see the same difficulty in nature? I see everywhere a Being whose main ends seem to be beneficent, but whose good purposes are worked out at terrible expense of suffering, and apparently by the total sacrifice of myriads of sensitive creatures. I see unflinching order, general goodwill, but no sympathy, no mercy. Storms, earthquakes, volcanoes, sickness, death, go on without regarding us. Everywhere I see the most hopeless, unrelieved suffering—and for aught I see, it may be eternal. We see a Being who gives Himself for us—and more than that, harder than that, a Being who consents to the suffering of a dearer than self.

HARRIET : Mrs. Marvyn's mind is enchained by glacial reasonings, in regions where spiritual intuitions are as necessary as wings to birds. She could not transcend the logical system that entrapped her.

•

NARRATOR : Catharine Beecher in her life managed to rearrange the elements of the Calvinist culture she grew up in, and to redirect her energies with a missionary zeal—yet she, like Mrs. Marvyn, up to now had not questioned its structure. Harriet, in this novel, was able to handle human nature in its social setting, that is, human beings as they really are, rather than as religion or morality would have them be.

Catharine's common sense applied, and the next book, *An Appeal to the People on Behalf of Their Rights as Authorized Interpreters of the Bible* marked a change—Catharine at last could deal with the social dynamics of Calvinism. Though written as an attack, these two books did much to rescue Calvinist morality from oblivion.

CATHARINE : As to this theological question, it is to me now not a theory alone, it is practical. The whole educational operation I have been carrying on the last seven years is stopping to have this question settled. After you have read my book you will understand this better.

•

NARRATOR : Thomas K. Beecher, in Elmira, New York, outlined his own independent conclusions about theology, as Isabella Beecher Hooker reports. When Thomas made up his mind, he was not shy about speaking out.

ISABELLA : Thomas proclaimed it to his congregation. Henry, it was a capital sermon—and the first I have ever heard on the state of the soul between death and judgment. He announced Hades explicitly and the gospel preached there to those who have never really heard it in this life—the argument was clear and logical—illustrations admirable—application so serious and discriminating as to make all abuse of the new doctrine improbable if not impossible.

It was one of a series of sermons—he has long been concocting—and the way has been admirably prepared by previous discourses—on physiology—law of physical death, etc., etc.

NARRATOR : Henry Ward Beecher once described himself as "a cordial Christian evolutionist"—what need did he have for intricate theories? He preached that "Christ is only God made easy." Henry's gentle liberalism, his earnestness about social reform proved durable in the long run. Thomas Beecher had independently arrived at similar conclusions.

Charles Beecher briefly served, at brother Edward's request, as professor of rhetoric at Knox College in Galesburg, Illinois. But he soon returned East to head the Congregational Church in Georgetown, Massachusetts, north of Boston. He would stay there thirty years.

When President Buchanan ordered a day of fasting for the sin of opposing slavery and provoking Southern rebellion, Charles wrote a resolution against Buchanan, signed by a majority of his congregation.

CHARLES : This is an act of treasonous conspiracy, and an act of hypocrisy in the highest degree insulting and detestable.

•

NARRATOR : Edward Beecher was disappointed that his book *The Conflict of Ages* had not started a great unification of Christian sects. As lecturer at Knox College, he volunteered his house as a station on the Underground Railway. He was also active in the women's movement.

Finally, he brought together all the reviews and all the critiques, including the counter-books, that *The Conflict of Ages* had provoked, with the intention of rebutting them.

EDWARD : To answer them would require a wearisome amount of controversial detail. But, on reflection, I saw that almost all the objections to my views had their roots in false conceptions of God, and erroneous views of his system growing out of them. I determined, therefore, entirely to avoid controversial detail, and to concentrate my energies on the great organic law of the universe, as growing out of a true conception of God, and to apply it to that perfect organization of earthly society and of the universe which lie in the future.

NARRATOR : This consideration allowed Edward to produce his next work, a sequel to the last one, called *The Concord of Ages,* published in 1860. He tried to answer all criticisms, and to reaffirm a sympathetic god unable to prevent human compulsions to sin. Political events and impending war crowded in, overshadowing theology, and Edward's book had no significant impact.

Meanwhile, William Beecher continued to serve quietly at a church in North Brookfield, Massachusetts, where he was also postmaster, with no salary disputes, and a small congregation.

·

It was 1860, however, when Abraham Lincoln gave his Cooper Union speech that would lead him on to the Republican Party nomination, that the anti-slavery movement had a real shot at the presidency. Lincoln took the opportunity while he was in New York to make the trip thousands had before him—across the Brooklyn Ferry to visit Henry Ward Beecher's Plymouth Church on the Sunday after he spoke. He sat in the fifth row back from the platform.

Lincoln's Cooper Union speech became the Republican platform for 1860.

LINCOLN : Let us have faith that right makes might; and in that faith let us, to the end, dare to do our duty as we understand it.

NARRATOR : In the four months between Lincoln's election and his inauguration, the nation was leaderless. James Buchanan had no backbone, and Abraham Lincoln had no authority until March 4, 1861. States' rights were being tested as the Deep South states, led by South Carolina, voted money for war, declared secession, and met to form the Confederate States of America. Buchanan had no ground to stand on. Diplomatically, he had boxed himself into a corner. He denied the rights of states to secede, yet he denied any federal power of coercion if they did secede.

While Buchanan was still in office, seven states held conventions and proclaimed their withdrawal from the Union. The

Secretary of War, a Southerner, used his power to equip seceding states. The U.S. brigadier general commanding the Department of Texas turned over his whole army to the Confederates. Before Mr. Lincoln was in the White House, the South possessed every Southern fort except for three: Fort Sumter, Key West, and Fort Pickens.

Southerners were not unanimous in the decision to secede—if there had been popular referendums, perhaps only South Carolina would have seceded. But once the fact was accomplished, loyalty for the Southern way of life became the central organizing fact of life in the Confederacy.

The North was just as divided. The Radical Abolitionists favored getting rid of the Southern states. Many simply feared the destruction that would follow a civil war. Even Horace Greeley in his *New York Tribune*, the most influential Republican journal, wrote:

GREELEY : If the cotton states decide that they can do better out of the Union than in it, we insist on letting them go in peace. We hope never to live in a republic whereof one section is pinned to the residue by bayonets.

NARRATOR : Abraham Lincoln recognized the danger in this opinion—it had been years before he himself arrived at the position that the Union came first.

LINCOLN : Prevent as far as possible any of our friends from demoralizing themselves and their cause by entertaining propositions for compromise of any sort on slavery extension. There is no possible compromise upon it but what puts us under again, and all our work to do over again.

NARRATOR : Even after the election of Lincoln, Henry Ward Beecher did not believe the Union was doomed.

HENRY : It is absurd to suppose that the South with all her interest in the Union will leave it, and therefore I say the South will never leave the Union. There is a man now at the helm of the ship of state who will guide her safely through the perils which encompass her, a man who knows not what it is to be scared.

NARRATOR : But the visionaries among the Confederate leaders were intent on establishing a semi-tropical republic based on slavery, including Mexico, Central Ameria, and the West Indies. Secession was only the first step.

As events got worse, Beecher gave a sermon against compromise.

HENRY : The North loves liberty, and will have it. We will not aggress on you. Keep your institutions within your own bounds; we will not hinder you. You shall have the Constitution intact, and its full benefit.

But if you ask us to augment the area of slavery; to cooperate with you in cursing new territory; if you ask us to make the air of the North favorable for a slave's breath, we will not do it! We love liberty as much as you love slavery, and we shall stand by our rights with all the vigor with which we mean to stand by justice toward you.

NARRATOR : Events were to overwhelm such sentiments. The choices that people had to make were much tougher—sometimes breaking families apart. In the border states, people had to vote with their feet, and in just a few weeks, they would vote with their guns.

THE LAST GATHERING
1863

As the 1840s had worn on, Lyman Beecher's life in Cincinnati grew more and more lonesome, as the youngest of his children made their way into the world. James went to sea without his father's blessing, Isabella married in Hartford, Charles at last was ordained, and only Thomas was left.

Thomas K. Beecher in any other family would have been considered eccentric, but among Beechers he was simply another independent individual who made his own mind up, and acted on his convictions.

In 1842, he was already a young skeptic, not only about religion, but also about school. He had to be convinced by his brother Henry to return and graduate from Illinois College, where his elder brother Edward Beecher was president. Though he loved Edward as a brother, Thomas found little in common with him.

THOMAS : Edward is twenty years older and preoccupied with theology and farfetched theories.

NARRATOR : On graduation, Thomas returned to the family home at Walnut Hills outside Cincinnati, only to argue with his father, Lyman Beecher, telling him that church doctrine was "shadowy nothings." Still, he had good memories of those days.

THOMAS : How unlike a student's Father's room always was, and what singular ways of studying! Do you remember the gun he used to keep loaded by the door ready for the passenger pigeons that in the 1830s came over by millions. Father would sit in his study-chair, deeply occupied and set me by the cocked gun to watch for game.

But he would hear the roar of wings as soon as I; and with remarkable jumps for a divinity doctor would get out the door, have his shot at the birds and then go back to his pen. His spectacles used to delay him, and I well remember his delight with a new pair which he brought home, each glass composed of a plane half and a convex half. Looking through the convex lower section he wrote metaphysics; through the upper he shot pigeons.

NARRATOR : At his own suggestion, Thomas went up to Indianapolis, to spend some time with Henry. Lyman Beecher consented, but—

THOMAS : He wrote long letters to Henry as one physician to another when he transfers a patient.

LYMAN : Henry, Thomas's bent of mind is so strong for the natural sciences and his originality and power of mind and mechanical execution and his attained qualifications are so distinguished for a professor of chemistry and natural philosophy that my heart had let go of its favorite purpose that he should preach; and yet I feel reproved almost in giving it up, as if my faith had failed, though, as in the case of Charles, I do not give it up, and only yield to an irresistible Providence, still hoping and desire he may be a minister.

NARRATOR : Thomas worked for a year making astronomical instruments, and the next year he was assistant to a professor of chemistry and pharmacy at Ohio Medical College.

It was hard for him to finally leave Lyman Beecher, since he was the last to go. In sympathy with his plight, Harriet wrote Thomas describing her own spiritual struggles, even though she had never been under pressure from Lyman to join the ministry.

Lyman Beecher gives some evidence of an openness to new ideas, such as pre-existence, even though the same idea expressed later in Edward's theology makes him uneasy.

LYMAN BEECHER, *July 3, 1847, to Charles Beecher*:

Charles, your account of your two children, in their developments, seems as if you had got some of my old letters to Grandmother Foote, from 1808 to 1817, when a succession of young people began to give premonition of an order of mind such as Roxana and I had not seen. Their elements of language are doubtless innate knowledge, or else the dim reminiscences of their pre-existent state, fast vanishing away by the diversions and exigencies of this world.

God speed them to good scholarship, and a copious assortment of good thoughts and burning words, till they shall pass from the dialect of earth to that of heaven—the old forgotten language, I suppose. Don't you think, if we could anyhow get a peep at the libraries above, we could make some splendid discoveries, which exist, in spite of our telescopic minds, very much not "in," but "ultra nubibus"?

NARRATOR : At last, Thomas Beecher gave in to paternal pressure; he began his study for the ministry with one year at Yale. But he was soon enlisted in one of Catharine's speaking tours for women's education, giving speeches that Catharine wrote, because at the time women were not considered respectable speakers.

Then he was given charge of the Northeast Grammar School in Philadelphia. The experience was not altogether edifying. Later he was offered the post of principal of the new public high school in Hartford, where he worked two years.

In Hartford, Thomas heard Horace Bushnell preach. Bushnell believed that religion was a personal experience, but also that participation in community problems was within the province of religion. Here at last was a role model that would satisfy both Thomas's teaching and his preaching inclinations. He returned to Cincinnati for one more year with his father, before he too left the nest, eventually to settle in Elmira, New York.

•

At the end of his public career in Cincinnati, Lyman Beecher came East, and stayed at various times near Edward in Boston, Harriet in Andover, and in Brooklyn to live near Henry Ward Beecher, where he kept his own house on Willow Street. Off and on, he tried to write an autobiography, since he spent much of his time now remembering.

LYMAN : Our dangers in the War of 1812 were very great. People had long been divided on questions of national policy. When war was declared, a state of feeling existed most alarming. Had popular feeling once burst through restraint, no tongue can utter the woes we should have suffered.

Another danger was the loss of the liberty of speech and of the press. In the Revolutionary War the people were nearly unanimous. But now a powerful minority in Congress were opposed to the war, and nearly half the people of the nation. Yet a disposition was manifested to cut short all opposition by summary process.

In many cases the thing was done; in every part of the land it was threatened; and if it had been accomplished we should have been slaves. The danger at one moment was pre-eminent.

Another peril was that of a military despotism. The militia was our only safeguard.

At the same time, we were in jeopardy of national dismemberment. Party feeling inflamed by war, and made violent by calamity, had prepared the masses for desperate measures. A state of feeling was awake, and a course of things was rolling on, which threatened to burst the ties that made us a nation. Thick clouds begirt the horizon; the storm roared louder and louder; it was dark as midnight; every pilot trembled, and from most all hope that we should be saved was taken away. And when from impenetrable darkness the sun burst suddenly upon us, and peace came, we said, "Our soul is escaped as a bird out of the snare of the fowler. The snare is broken, and we are escaped."

NARRATOR : When the Civil War finally came, Lyman Beecher was barely aware of it. Harriet came to stay with him at the end. He was eighty-eight years old.

LYMAN : If God should tell me that I might choose (hesitates) —that is, if God said that it was His will that I should choose whether to die and go to heaven, or to begin my life over again and work once more, I would enlist again in a minute

HARRIET : Father, I always had a feeling that your prayers prevailed.

LYMAN: Did you? I am glad of it; but if they did, they met with heavy clouds between sometimes. I have been in the pulpit sometimes when all power even to pray has been taken away. Oh, I remember such times! and I remember, too, when the light broke in again.

Henry, Catharine, do you recall the cholera epidemic, not the first one? How little of the history of the heart can ever be written, and, if it were, could ever be reached by language; and, if it could, the world itself could not contain the books which should be written, and one generation would have no more than time to read the history of another.

Now what a scene was that sickness, and all but sudden death of Harriet! It was a violent attack of cholera, running for three hours without medical aid into a regular collapse, with spasms, burning, and cramps, and the stamp of death on her face. When the doctor came he was thunderstruck, and made prescriptions without any hope she would live. I did not get back till he was gone, and came into her room, and, coming to the bedside, realized her state. She was sinking. The universal languor and distress of death was upon her. I immediately took her hands in mine and began to rub them with perseverance and vigor, while the most powerful remedies were applied for an hour without any perceptible effect.

The first indication of the reversed and healthful action of the system was the excitement produced by the stimulation of the brandy, which at first I mistook for delirium. It was terrible for a moment. Dying, as I feared, she began to sing, and called on Mary, in a wandering way, to sing. But it was soon apparent that the ebbing tide was rising, and then my heart sang also and gave thanks; yet through the night she was so low that if a relapse should take place she would not live an hour.

Mary stood by her all the while with a mother's solicitude and care. I could not leave her, and slept on the settee in the dining room, hot as an oven and thronged with mosquitoes, sleepless from their annoyance, and conscious of every noise and movement. The night of suspense passed safely, and she was better in the morning.

HARRIET : Twice before his departure, his spirit seemed for a moment to throw off the torpor that was upon it with premonitions of approaching triumph. The first was when he quoted those words of Paul, "I have fought a good fight, I have finished my course, I have kept the faith; henceforth there is laid up for me a crown, which God, the righteous judge, will give me in that day"; and added, "That is my testimony; write it down; that is my testimony."

The other was still more impressive, when the veil was rent for a few hours, and a vision of transfiguration was vouchsafed. He called to his daughter, thinking it was his wife:

LYMAN : Mother, mother, come sit beside me; I have had a glorious vision of heaven.

HARRIET : His countenance was luminous, his utterance full and strong, as in his best days. He continued:

LYMAN : I think I have begun to go. Oh, such scenes as I have been permitted to behold! I have seen the King of Glory himself. Blessed God for revealing thyself! I did not think I could behold such glory while in the flesh.

HARRIET : He prayed in an inspired manner for some time, and then soliloquized.

LYMAN : Until this evening my hope was a conditional one; now it is full, free, entire. Oh, glory to God!

HARRIET : Had you any fear?

LYMAN : No, none at all, and what is wonderful, I have no pain either.

HARRIET : I then repeated the words, "I shall be satisfied when I awake in thy likeness."

LYMAN : How wonderful that a creature can approach the Creator so as to awake in His likeness! Oh glorious, glorious God!

HARRIET : I rejoice with you, father.

LYMAN : I know you rejoice as a pious woman, but you cannot enter into my experience now.

HARRIET : Father, did you see Jesus?

LYMAN : All was swallowed up in God himself.

HARRIET : For an hour he was in this state, talking and praying. The next day he remarked that he had an indistinct remembrance of some great joy. The last indication, on the day of his death, was a mute response to his wife, repeating,

> Jesus, lover of my soul,
> Let me to thy bosom fly.

The last hours of his earthly sleep his face was illuminated with a solemn and divine radiance, and softly and tenderly, without even a sigh, he passed to the everlasting rest.

•

NARRATOR : For one last time, at Lyman Beecher's funral, the family came together. The year is 1863, the middle of the War Between the States. Everyone's life was in ferment. Thomas served briefly as a chaplain in the war, until he uncovered a copperhead, or Southern sympathizer, plot to kill Lincoln and other Republican leaders, thereby hoping to destroy the government. James was among the first to volunteer for military duty, and he was placed in charge of training and commanding a black regiment. Thomas writes about the gathering.

THOMAS : We are having a blessed time. All are here except Edward and James. Last evening, and this morning at breakfast, the reminiscences and tone of feeling were inexpressibly rich; lively and not light, brilliant and diversified, and yet full of feeling. This morning at table, and afterward at family prayer, which was family praise, singing being our chief occupation, there was an unpremeditated outburst of memories of the most beautiful and touching character.

We feel that our dear father is not taken from us, but given back to us again. The feeling in all our hearts is more of desire for consecration to Christ's work than I ever knew it to be—more as of old when Father was himself among us in the fullness of spirit.

May the Holy Spirit enable us to carry away the new fire in our souls, and kindle others.

Charles?

•

CHARLES : Let me share with all of you this memory of Father. My case was prolonged by doubts, but it brought me close to the good work that Father had done for so many years in every circumstance.

In my senior year in college I read Jonathan Edwards's *Inquiry Respecting the Freedom of the Will*, in the first part of which the author apparently annihilates free agency, while in the second part he proves from scripture that nevertheless men are subjects of moral obligation.

Deistical and atheistical writers, availing themselves eagerly of the abstract portions of the *Inquiry*, and contemning its biblical conclusions, carried on the unfinished reasoning in their own manner. This describes precisely my own course. I was neither a patient nor a thorough student of Edwards at that time.

It was by just such reasonings, consistently carried out, that I made shipwreck of the faith, and became, for a season, a confirmed fatalist. My father did all that could be done under the circumstances, to no avail. I can never forget the impression of those encounters, in which all a father's influences were thrown back like waves from a rock. Never will memory cease to recall the look, the tone, the attitude with which he bade me farewell on my departure to New Orleans.

"My son," he said, with quivering lip, "eternity is long!" and, with a glance of anguish and a grasp of the hand, he turned away.

It was in New Orleans that I expressed my feelings in a poem published there:

> Oh, must I live a lonely one,
>   unloved upon the thronged earth,
> without a home beneath the sun,
>   far from the land that gave me birth?
>
> Alone—alone I wander on,
>   an exile in a dreary land;
> the friends that knew me once are gone;
>   not one is left of all their band.
>
> I look upon the boiling tide
>   of traffic fierce, that ebbs and flows,
> with chill disgust and shrinking pride,
>   that heartfelt misery only knows.

And so on for several stanzas more. Dr. Beecher did not give up on me for six years, busy years for him as he went through his heresy trial and the breakup of much of the family.

I eventually found my way back to the fold in preparation for the ministry, albeit with grave questions of the Confession. At that time I said, "I can accept it, yet so that my liberty of differing therein, in all cases where there is question of agreement with scripture, be not diminished, but rather established."

This question and others, Dr. Beecher answered completely.

Brother Henry, do you wish to add something?

HENRY : Yes, this one's for you, Thomas. I want to read this letter that Father wrote when he was in Cincinnati—you may not have known how much he cared.

> Henry, since your letter to Thomas, speaking of your preaching and the prospect of a revival, he began to speak about going to Indianapolis. Harriet thinks, and the same occurred to me, that he was moved to do so with the hope of becoming a true Christian; and, though I could employ him just now in assisting me, I have preferred that he should be with you. He said, when he first read your letter, "Well, I think I had better go and help Henry."
>
> He has earned a high reputation in his year's labor and study with Dr. Lock, of the Medical College of Ohio.

•

THOMAS : I remember an earnestness which used to betray Father into a curious repetition whenever he would bend his energy to a profitable exhortation about my waywardness: "This is the most important year of your life, my son; you have come to the turning point of your history." The first time he told me so I was a lad just turned eleven years; and by many letters and words I was certified four times a year or oftener that I was at an "important," "critical," "decisive" turning point in my career, until I became a teacher at Philadelphia.

In 1846 Father was sorely exercised by the severity of my work in Philadelphia. He feared a sudden breakdown. His urgency could not abide the slowness of the mail; he must save me by telegraph—I suspect his very first telegram. Aided by Isabella, he undertook his costly ten words to save a son thus:

LYMAN : My very dear son, I have worked more—

ISABELLA : Father, father, you can't write so much; don't say "My very dear son."

LYMAN : Dear son, Trust a father's experience, and let me tell you—

ISABELLA : No, no, father, skip all that. You can't make love by telegraph. Tom knows your love.

THOMAS : An hour was spent learning how to suppress his exuberant affection, till at last the message came into shape thus:

LYMAN : Ease up. Rest—sleep—exercise. Cold water—rub. No tobacco.—Father.

THOMAS : Some books of health contain less than this telegram.

HARRIET : There was an example—Charles, help me find that letter to Nathaniel Taylor, Father's old colleague—it would never do in a telegram. Yes, here we go.

LYMAN : Dear Taylor, I wish I had a son going to New Haven every month, and then I should write to you as often, and possibly get half as many letters from you, and make a beginning of talking things old and new.

You and I are the same as when we projected the *Christian Spectator,* and battled about the means of grace and episcopacy, and Hartford College, and Nettleton, and Tyler, and Woods, and Harvey, if you remember such a one. But now, like Bonaparte's battles and marshals, have all these gone through the little end of Time's telescope into the dim but not uninteresting distance; and how has our generation fallen off, and another and another pushed up behind us, and what things have come to pass which, had we lived in Connecticut, we should have written letters about, and held consultations and talked over so much, but have not talked about at all, and never shall till we have more time in another world.

Well, our personal identity remains, and our friendships and our children, one of whom, my son Thomas, will hand you this, whom, I doubt not, you will receive gladly for my sake and his own. He is a graduate of Illinois College, and raised under the ministration of Edward. He possesses, I think, a mind not inferior to any of my sons, and quickness, depth, and comprehension of discrimination surpassing almost any mind I have come in contact with.

Think that I am vain; I only give you the outline, to say that he would like to spend a little time in New Haven, and see and hold communion with your literati as one who will appreciate the society of literary folk, and all your literary treasure accumulated there since the time I entered Yale in 1792, when there was one rusty telescope, one air-pump, a prism, and one band and wheel to make the figure of the oblate spheroid, or the earth flattened at the poles.

THOMAS : At the end, the rest of you, even James, had left. Let me tell you how it was to be the last Beecher child.

Visiting home during one of my school vacations (1847), I found Father at last without a child to love or govern, and it seemed to me that his long-trained faculty was keeping itself fresh in training a very stubborn and active terrier called Trip. Trip had taken my place in the study and by the table.

At every interval of rest from writing, Father would talk a word or two to Trip. On the mantlepiece lay a short switch, and Trip knew where it lay. Ordinarily Trip would receive rebuke and exhortation with becoming quietness, but it was quite impossible to follow up the counsel with chastisement, for Trip had an eye ever to the mantelpiece.

If Father's hand tended thither, Trip tended toward the door or table, and no soothing blandishment would restore his filial confidence until Father, showing both palms, would say, "There, Trip-pee, Trip-pee, I forgive you this time, but you mustn't do so any more." For myself, I protest that Trip, if he lives, has memories of escape and forgiveness more gratifying than I.

Do you remember, Charles, how Father in those days used to carry a comb in his pocket for Trip, much to mother's annoyance? and those frequent excursions down to the bridge in the woods which Father and Trip would make, Father talking to the little dog, and promising cleanliness and relief in soothing tones such as New England boys used to hear o' Saturday nights? Trip was always grateful.

In all soberness, I declare that Father, in those days, found comfort in venting upon Trip those tender emotions which he could not suppress nor his own children longer receive.

This "staying with him" was, in the time of it, trying to me, yet it enriched me with my only deep knowledge of Father's loving heart.

I was a man—graduated, and competent to work and support him; yet he insisted on my staying with him to be supported. He felt that I was unsettled in religion, and was set in his determination to keep me near him and lead me to safety. Of course, irritated by frequent reproaches from the thoughtless for "living on my father," I was impatient to be gone, and many a passionate discussion came up between us on the matter.

I never gave up entirely until one morning, as I stood impatient on the south step of the study, in the sun. He came out suddenly, not knowing I was there. He sniffed the air, looked up into the maples, down upon me, put both hands upon my shoulders, looked me full in the face, and said, with broken utterance.

LYMAN : Tom, I love you; you mustn't go 'way and leave me. They're all gone—Jim's at college. I want one chicken under my wing.

THOMAS : Of course I stayed by until I left with a blessing.

•

NARRATOR : And in a private letter to his sister Isabella, Thomas confided his private feelings about the family.

THOMAS : I think I like Henry the best. He is the most like Father of all his sons, and as a speaker and writer far surpasses any divine I have ever heard, that is, in my opinion. Then for versatility of talent—one moment a farmer—next a nursery man—then a horticulturist—lawyer—doctor—minister—etc. he is certainly without equal among my friends. And then for warmth of affection, and adaptation for domestic usefulness—and happiness—he is hardly second to our dear Father who on these points I feel by daily experience that he is peerless.

My dear sister, I will not disguise from you that I feel terribly unsettled in my religious constitution. 'Tis what I have long feared—and I know not, nor can anyone predict save the Omniscient, where my resting place will be. I am in darkness on the philosophy of religion—the reality of it and the practice of it. Two points stick—the authenticity of the Bible, and, I must say it, the existence of God.

Again, supposing both these points proved, I see so much in the church, and among our own family even, to give me a disrespect to religion, that I feel doubts arising as it regards embracing a system whose lights and glory appear to me so slim and faulty.

Charles's newly recovered and painfully gained religion is rooted in self-deception. And Edward—I once almost worshipped Edward—as some of my letters to you indicate—but I am undeceived now. Either Edward is insane on some points—or else he is not a Christian, of the same kind as our father or brother Henry.

And I say without fear or hesitation that if religion were to make me another Edward—I say God deliver me from being pious. But if I could be a second Father, or Henry, untold wealth would not swerve my choice.

At War
1861–1863

The Beechers were all active during the War Between the States, or as it was later called, the Civil War. James Beecher, youngest of the brood, had run off on a clipper ship to China at a young age. When he'd returned, a ship's officer, he said—

JAMES : Oh, I shall be a minister. That's my fate. Father will pray me into it!

NARRATOR : He did serve at the Seamen's Bethel in Hong Kong, and had once been held for ransom by Chinese pirates. But when war broke out in the United States, James immediately returned from the Far East to enlist as chaplain of the First Long Island Regiment, called the Brooklyn Phalanx. He soon got himself transferred to military duty, and quickly was named senior captain of the regiment, then lieutenant-colonel of the 141st New York Volunteers.

Frederick Stowe, Harriet's eldest son, was a student at Harvard Medical School when the war brok out. The Stowes tried to dissuade him from enlisting, and so did their family friend, Dr. Oliver Wendell Holmes.

FREDERICK : I should be ashamed to look my fellows in the face if I did not enlist. People shall never say, "Harriet Beecher Stowe's son is a coward."

NARRATOR : Henry Ward Beecher had campaigned for Lincoln on the Republican ticket as tirelessly as he had for Fremont. When the war broke out, his eldest son Henry asked him if he might enlist.

HENRY : If you don't, I'll disown you.

NARRATOR : Meanwhile, the new Vice President of the Con-federate States of America, Alexander Stephens, declared the purpose of the new nation.

STEPHENS : The new Constitution has put at rest forever all the agitating questions relating to our peculiar institution—African slavery as it exists among us, the proper status of the negro in our form of civilization. This was the immediate cause of the late rupture and present revolution. Jefferson, in his forecast, had anticipated this as the "rock upon which the old Union would split." He was right. What was a conjecture with him is now a realized fact. But whether he fully comprehended the great truth upon which that rock stood and stands may be doubted.

NARRATOR : As preacher, editor of *The Independent*, lecturer, Henry Ward Beecher supported the war effort wholeheartedly. He took charge of equipping the 14th Long Island Regiment, using his house as a storehouse for military goods.

At 38, in 1862, Thomas K. Beecher joined the Army of the Potomac, as chaplain of the 141st New York Volunteers—at the same time that his younger brother James served in that outfit. Four months into his service, Thomas learned of a copperhead conspiracy to seize Lincoln and his Cabinet and install General George McClellan as dictator. Using his acquaintance with Lincoln from Illinois as an excuse to see him, Thomas Beecher presented his evidence. The plot was quicly uncovered and squelched. Thomas insisted, though, that the affair be kept private in order not to embarrass the officers in question. The incident ended Thomas's military career, however.

Despite his respect for Lincoln, Henry also criticized the President for being dilatory in declaring emancipation.

HENRY : The President seems to be a man without any sense of the value of time. We have been made irresolute, indecisive and weak by the President's attempt to unite impossibilities; to make war and keep the peace; to strike hard and not hurt; to invade sovereign States and not meddle with their sovereignty; to put down rebellion without touching its cause.

NARRATOR : One stormy night in 1862, a tall stranger came calling on Henry Ward Beecher, on a matter of great import. After four hours of earnest conversation that ended with a prayer, the man left. Eunice Beecher asked who it was, and Henry only smiled. After the assassination, he told her, it had been Lincoln himself.

As the war went on, Harriet wrote to Annie Fields, the publisher's wife.

HARRIET : I am going to Washington to see the heads of departments myself and to satisfy myself that I may refer to the Emancipation as a reality and a substance, not a fizzle-out at the little end of the horn, as I should be sorry to call the attention of my sisters in Europe to any such impotent conclusion—I mean to have a talk with "Father Abraham" himself.

NARRATOR : Frederick Stowe, Harriet's eldest son, was among the first to volunteer. While Harriet was visiting brother Henry in Brooklyn, news came that the 1st Massachusetts Regiment had just sailed by.

HARRIET : Immediately I was of course eager to get to Jersey City to see Fred. Sister Eunice said she would go with me, and in a few minutes she, Hatty, Sam Scoville, and I were in a carriage, driving towards the Fulton Ferry. Upon reaching Jersey City we found that the boys were dining in the depot, an immense building with many tracks and platforms. There was a crowd of people pressing against the grated doors, which were locked, but through which we could see the soldiers. It was with great difficulty that we were at last permitted to go inside.

When we were in, a vast area of gray caps and blue overcoats was presented. The boys were eating, drinking, smoking, talking, singing, and laughing. At last we spied Fred in the distance, and I went leaping across the tracks toward him. Immediately afterwards a blue-overcoated figure bristling with knapsack and haversack, and looking like an assortment of packages, came rushing towards us.

Fred was in high spirits, in spite of the weight, that he would formerly have declared intolerable for half an hour. I gave him my handkerchief, and we filled his haversack with oranges.

We stayed with Fred about two hours, during which time the gallery was filled with people, cheering and waving their handkerchiefs. Every now and then the band played inspiriting airs, in which the soldiers joined with hearty voices. While some of the companies sang, others were drilled, and all seemed to be having a general jollification.

NARRATOR : In 1862, Isabella Beecher Hooker travelled with her sister Harriet Beecher Stowe to Washington to see President Lincoln. They dined lavishly with Thomas in a tent encampment; the next day they saw James march by at the head of his regiment. When they visited a thousand freed slaves, they all hailed Harriet.

HARRIET : They sang a slow, solemn and plaintive music as wild as the free winds.

When we were introduced to Mr. Lincoln, we met a rough, scrubby, black-brown, withered, dull-eyed object. He was definitely a sincere man of feelings, but with indifferent speech and rustic manners.

NARRATOR : Congressman Henry Wilson brought her and Isabella in one day to see Abraham Lincoln. He strode across the room to greet Harriet.

LINCOLN : So this is the little woman who wrote the book that made this big war!

NARRATOR : He explained his go-slow border-state policy, and declared that yes, the Emancipation Proclamation would take effect the following month, January 1863.

•

She returned to her hotel to write her *Letter to the Women of England*. It was ten years after her visit to England, where she had been presented with twenty-six volumes of women's signatures to a petition against slavery. Harriet's reply, published in the *Atlantic Monthly*, describes the progress of the anti-slavery cause in the United States, ending with a plea for them to help change England's pro-Southern attitude. A few months later, Henry Ward Beecher would be in England delivering the same message in person.

HARRIET : During the past year the Republican administration has proceeded to demonstrate the feasibility of overthrowing slavery by purely constitutional measures. To this end they have instituted a series of movements which have made this year more fruitful in anti-slavery triumphs than any other since the emancipation of the British West Indies.

By another act, equally grand in principle, and far more important in its results, slavery is forever excluded from the Territories of the United States.

Lastly, and more significant still, the United States government has in its highest official capacity taken distinct anti-slavery ground. By this power it has been this year decreed that every slave of a rebel who reaches the lines of our army becomes a free person; that all slaves found deserted by their masters become free persons; that every slave employed in any service for the United States thereby obtains his liberty.

By this act the Fugitive Slave Law is for all present purposes practically repealed. Wherever our armies march they carry liberty with them.

Lastly, the great decisive measure of the war has appeared— the President's Proclamation of Emancipation.

Will our sisters in England feel no heartbeat at that event?

And now, sisters of England, let us speak to you of one thing which fills our hearts with pain and solicitude. It is an unaccountable fact, and one which we entreat you seriously to ponder, that the party which has brought the cause of freedom thus far on its way, during the past eventful year, has found little or no support in England. Sadder than this, the party which makes slavery the chief cornerstone of its edifice finds in England its strongest defenders.

A year and a half have passed; step after step has been taken for liberty; chain after chain has fallen, till the march of our armies is choked and clogged by the glad flocking of emancipated slaves; the day of final emancipation is set; the border States begin to move in voluntary consent; universal freedom for all dawns like the sun in the distant horizon, and still no voice from England. No voice? Yes, we have heard on the high seas the voice of a war-steamer, built for a man-stealing Confederacy, with English gold, in an English dockyard, going out of an English harbor, sailed by English sailors, with the full knowledge of English government officers, in defiance of the Queen's proclamation of neutrality!

Our sisters, we wish you could have witnessed this thanksgiving. We wish you could have heard the prayer of a blind old negro, called among his fellows John the Baptist, when in touching broken English he poured forth his thanksgivings. We wish you could have heard the sound of that strange rhythmical chant which is now forbidden to be sung on Southern plantations—the psalm of this modern exodus—which combines the barbaric fire of the Marseillaise with the religious fervor of the old Hebrew prophet:

> Oh, go down Moses,
> way down into Egypt's land!
> Tell King Pharaoh
> to let my people go!
> Stand away dere,
> stand away dere,
> and let my people go!

And now, sisters of England, we say to you, you have spoken well; we have heard you; we have heeded; we have striven in the cause, even unto death. We have sealed our devotion by desolate hearth and darkened homestead—by the blood of sons, husbands, and brothers. In many of our dwellings the very light of our lives has gone out; and yet we accept the lifelong darkness as our own part in this great and awful expiation. Sisters, what have you done, and what do you mean to do?

> In behalf of many thousands of American women,
> Harriet Beecher Stowe
> Washington, November 27, 1862

NARRATOR : Nathaniel Hawthorne congratulated her on the letter.

HAWTHORNE : I read with great pleasure your article in the last *Atlantic*. If anything could make John Bull blush, I should think it might be that; but he is a hardened and villainous hypocrite. I always felt that he cared nothing for or against slavery, except as it gave him a vantage-ground on which to parade his own virtue and sneer at our iniquity.

•

NARRATOR : In early 1863, Henry's dizzy spells came back, and he was persuaded to take a vacation trip to Europe. He found many friends in England urging him to speak out, to reverse public sentiment for the cotton-growing Confederate States. England's textile industry depended on the South's cotton, and the working class felt the pinch directly because their factories could not get enough cotton. Beecher refused, and continued on to the Continent. He felt that the British feared most a strong United States.

HENRY : I do not mean fear of a narrow and technical kind but the shadow that the future of our nation already casts is so vast that they foresee they are falling into the second rank—that the will of the Republic is to be the law of the world. There is no disguising of this among the English.

NARRATOR : On the Continent Henry met King Leopold of the Belgians at Brussels. A statesman among the European monarchs, his opinion was widely respected.

HENRY : After some conversation in which the King plainly intimated to me that he would rejoice in bringing us to terms and peace again, all the while intimating that the South could not be overcome, and that it would be very wise for us to make a compromise, and that he would be entirely willing to render service in that direction, I said to him: "Your Majesty"—I got it out once or twice right—"if there were any ruling sovereign in Europe to whom more than to another we should be glad to refer this question it would be to the King of Belgium, a judge among nations and adviser among kings; BUT we do not propose to refer it to anyone. We are going to fight it out ourselves; the strongest will win in our conflict and so it must be settled."

Turning from that, he asked me what I thought of sending Maximilian to Mexico—for at that time he had not been sent to be the emperor of this new nation the Latins had established there; and, without suitable diplomacy, I said to him: "Your Majesty, any man that wants to sit upon a throne in Mexico I would advise to try Vesuvius first; if he can sit there for a while, then he might go and try it in Mexico." This very soon brought our conversation to a close.

•

NARRATOR : Returning to England before his departure for home, Henry's friends made it clear that Parliament was soon to consider, and perhaps pass, a bill recognizing the Confederate States of America. The pro-Southern aristocracy was planning meetings in all the major industrial centers to win over the workers, who were angry at the lack of cotton to supply the mills.

Finally, Henry Ward Beecher assented—he would give five

speeches in the very heart of the industrial district: Liverpool, Manchester, London, Glasgow, Edinburgh.

In Manchester, his first stop, newspapers printed lies about him and anti-Beecher posters in red immediately appeared, charging him with slurs on England, opinions ranging from extermination of all Southerners to "the best blood of England must flow." These charges only made Henry all the more eager to speak, yet at the same time he was almost overwhelmed. A quarter of the hall was filled with hecklers and toughs sent in to break up the meeting. A friend describes his speech at Manchester:

MABIE : He felt as if he were surrounded by an almost impenetrable wall of prejudice and antagonism the moment he arrived in England. On the day on which he was to make his first speech, he was in an agony of depression all the morning, feeling quite unable to bear up under the awful burden of the concentrated animosity of a nation. He spent most of the morning on his knees, without any help; but finally arrived at a point where his prayer took the form of an offer to surrender everything and even to fail if that was God's will. Gradually the depression wore off, and was succeeded by a great sense of repose. When he finally drove to the hall his peace was like that of a mountain lake.

When he entered the hall, he found it packed with an audience collected for the express purpose of silencing him. Every time he opened his mouth his voice was drowned by the clamor of the hostile crowd. This went on so long that he began to fear that he should not get a chance to say anything. In the meantime he had studied his audience carefully, and it had photographed itself on his mind.

The green baize doors were fastened together. Seats had been brought in and placed around the side walls, and in some cases against these doors. In one of these seats a large, burly, red-haired, red-whiskered man was sitting, who was particularly vociferous, shouting, clapping his hands, pounding his feet, and throwing himself back in this chair. After about twenty minutes of attempted talk, in one of these paroxysms of racket, Mr. Beecher happened to be looking at this man, when he threw himself back with great violence, broke the fastenings of the door, and went head over heels in his chair down the stairs on the outside.

The whole thing was so instantaneous and so funny that Mr.

Beecher burst into a roar of laughter. The audience were astonished; turned around, following his glance, took in what had happened and began to laugh themselves.

That moment of relaxation he caught, made a witty remark which made them laugh still more, then told them a story which caught their attention, and from that moment held them without a break, as long as he chose to speak.

NARRATOR : Henry's own account is a little different.

HENRY : As soon as I began to speak the great audience began to show its teeth, and I had not gone on fifteen minutes before an unparalleled scene of confusion and interruption occurred. No American that has not seen an English mob can form any conception of one. I have seen all sorts of camp-meetings and experienced all kinds of public speaking on the stump; I have seen the most disturbed meetings in New York City, and they were all of them as twilight to midnight compared with an English hostile audience. For in England the meeting does not belong to the parties that call it, but to whoever chooses to go, and if they can take it out of your hands it is considered fair play.

This meeting had a very large multitude of people in it who came there for the purpose of destroying the meeting and carrying it the other way when it came to the vote. I took the measure of the audience, and said to myself, "About one-fourth of this audience are opposed to me, and about one-fourth will be rather in sympathy, and my business now is not to appeal to that portion that is opposed to me, nor to those that are already on my side, but to bring over the middle section."

How to do this was a problem. The question was, who could hold out longest. There were five or six storm centers, boiling and whirling at the same time; here someone pounding on a group with his umbrella and shouting, "Sit down there"; over yonder a row between two or three combatants; somewhere else a group all yelling together at the top of their voices. It was like talking to a storm at sea. But there were newspaper reporters just in front, and I said to them, "Now, gentlemen, be kind enough to take down what I say. It will be in sections, but I will have it connected by-and-by."

I threw my notes away, and entered on a discussion of the

value of freedom as opposed to slavery in the manufacturing interest, arguing that freedom everywhere increases a person's necessities, and what he needs he buys, and that it was, therefore, to the interest of the manufacturing community to stand by the side of labor through the country. I never was more self-possessed and never in more perfect good temper; and I never was more determined that my hearers should feel the curb before I got through with them.

NARRATOR : Finally, Henry Ward Beecher spoke without interruption for an hour, giving the history of slavery in America, and his own theory that the war was merely a violent phase of the inevitable struggle between irreconcilable principles—free labor and slavery. When he finished, the applause was tremendous, and hundreds came forward to shake his hand.

Liverpool was the next stop.

•

HENRY : Liverpool was worse than all the rest put together. My life was threatened, and I had communications to the effect that I had better not venture there. The streets were placarded with the most scurrilous and abusive cards.

NARRATOR : Because of the danger, some of Beecher's supporters went to the meeting armed. It took him an hour and a half to get the chance to speak at all.

HENRY : I sometimes felt like a shipmaster attempting to preach on board of a ship through a speaking-trumpet, with a tornado on the sea and a mutiny among the crew.

NARRATOR : Beecher's wit and repartee were needed at every juncture. Here is how a newspaperman reported part of the speech.

HENRY : Great Britain has thrown her arms of love around the Southerners, and turns from the Northerners. ("No.) She don't? I have only to say that she has been caught in very suspicious circumstances. (Laughter.)

If the South should be rendered independent— (At this juncture mingled cheering and hissing became immense; half the audience rose to their feet, waving hats and handkerchiefs, and in every part of the hall there was the greatest commotion and uproar.) You have had your turn now; let me have mine again. (Loud applause and laughter.) If this present struggle shall eventuate in the separation of America, and making the South— (Loud applause, hisses, hooting, and cries of "Bravo!") —a slave territory exclusively— (Cries of "No! No!" and laughter.)

(Interruption and uproar.) My friends, I saw a man once who was a little late at a railway station chase an express train. He didn't catch it. (Laughter.) If you are going to stop this meeting you have got to stop it before I speak; for after I have got the things out you may chase as long as you please, you will not catch them. (Laughter and interruption.)

NARRATOR : Even without all the give and take of these remarkable meetings, a careful reading reveals a detailed knowledge of the economic and industrial aspects of slavery, and comprehension of the constitutional issues involved—and the ability to describe clearly complex American affairs to an English audience.

HENRY : When I am asked, "Why not let the South go?" I return for an answer a question. Be pleased to tell me what part of the British Islands you are willing to let go from under the crown when its inhabitants secede and set up for independence?

NARRATOR : At Edinburgh, there were so many people to hear him that he had to be handed along over people's heads to get through the doors. He showed how the South had gotten their way in national policies until Lincoln was elected, at which point they rebelled.

HENRY : The day is coming when the foundations of the earth will be lifted out of their places; and there are two nations that ought to be found shoulder to shoulder and hand in hand for the sake of Christianity and universal liberty, and these nations are Great Britain and America.

NARRATOR : At Liverpool, Beecher received even more death threats—heavily armed disturbers sat in the galleries, but a large number of Beecher supporters also came armed, and announced—

MABIE : The first man that fires will rue it.

NARRATOR : The crowd didn't quiet down for an hour and a half.

HENRY : This attempt to cover the fairest portion of the earth with a slave population which buys nothing and a degraded white population that buys next to nothing, should array against it the sympathy of every true political economist and every thoughtful and farseeing manufacturer as tending to strike at the vital want of commerce—not the want of cotton, but the want of customers.

·

NARRATOR : By the time he reached Exeter Hall in London for his last speech, the battle had been won. He summed up his arguments—that the only cause for the war was slavery, that the North was fighting for free labor and free people everywhere. Grant had just won at Vicksburg, and Lee had just retreated from Gettysburg.

The British Parliament did not recognize the Confederate States of America, and pro-Southern sentiment subsided in England. It was England, after all, that had been first in Europe to abolish the slave trade more than fifty years before.

Henry Ward Beecher's five speeches made him the Union's unofficial spokesperson abroad. He now had an international reputation. Oliver Wendell Holmes commented:

HOLMES : They were, one might say, a single speech delivered piecemeal in different places. Henry Ward Beecher has performed a more remarkable embassy than any envoy who has represented us in Europe since Franklin pleaded the cause of the young Republic at the Court of Versailles.

NARRATOR : From this point on, Henry was kept apprised of all developments by Lincoln's government—and when he had questions, they were answered.

WAR AND PEACE
1863–1869

The Beechers and the rest of America survived through the end of the war and into a new era with new concerns and political realignments. Frederick Douglass had supported the women's movement as early as July 1848. In Seneca Falls, New York, the Woman's Rights Convention brought him together with Lucretia Mott and Elizabeth Cady Stanton, and their platform called for women's equality in the right to vote, to own property, to have a legal identity separate from a husband, and unrestricted opportunities for education and employment. It was a brave beginning for a long hard fight.

In New York State, the feminists launched a campaign to soften the divorce law—and were labelled free love advocates. Horace Greeley fought them, debating in the *Tribune* with Robert Dale Owen—and, by a few votes, the feminists lost. Then the war came, and the women's movement put its own concerns on hold and supported the abolitionists and the rights of blacks. Wendell Phillips promised: "After the slave, then the woman."

Though Isabella Beecher Hooker had early found Blackstone utterly opposed even to recognition of the separate identity of a wife from her husband, she had done no more than to begin a private correspondence with John Stuart Mill and his wife Harriet Mill, and to wear Amelia Bloomer's costume, a daring fashion in the 1850s.

Then in 1859, Isabella wrote a piece called "Shall Women Vote? A Matrimonial Dialogue," answering objections to women's suffrage, but with digressions and a weak conclusion—the wife would wait until public opinion demanded women's suffrage. She sent it to Thomas Wentworth Higginson, the essayist, who praised the idea but told her that deficiencies in style would have to be corrected—especially in a piece espousing radical views. The piece was never published.

About the same time, Charles Beecher in Newark published a report to the Congregational Association of New York and

Brooklyn called *A Review of the Spiritual Manifestations*. In it, he connected the activities of spiritualists, clairvoyants, and mediums with drugs and demon possession. But, he said, the Bible does not recognize such manifestations, and the mediums were usurping the Christ role of mediator between God and human. Nevertheless, these were honest errors, out of which may come good. Charles continued his research into spiritualism, and over the years he appears to have given them more credence.

Though Charles stayed a short time in Galesburg with Edward, and then at Andover with the Stowes, he came to Georgetown to stay. The family decided that Charles should be the one to organize Lyman Beecher's autobiography, including their own reminiscences, making it a family chronicle.

•

Then, in the year of Henry Beecher's greatest triumph, the famous speeches in Britain, his brother Charles suffered defeat. While sorrowing for his son, who had been wounded at Gettysburg, he faced the ordeal that confronted his father thirty years before—a heresy trial. The chief charge against Charles was his brother Edward Beecher's doctrine of the pre-existence of souls. Curiously, Edward himself had never once been accused of heresy, though he had published his doctrine ten years before in *The Conflict of Ages*.

The Essex North Conference officially declared Charles Beecher a heretic in 1863. And Charles protested.

CHARLES : I need hardly say that I regard the result of Council as not only slanderous, but mean beyond measure and as inevitably involving disgrace to all who accept it.

NARRATOR : About the time of Charles's trial, James Beecher was given the colonelcy of an experimental group, the 1st North Carolina Colored Volunteers—which he raised, organized, armed, and led for three years.

JAMES : I am amazed at the promptitude of these men to learn military drill. I wish doubtful people at home could see my three-weeks' regiment. I think we shall make creditable showing in three weeks more and the Government will not grumble at a regiment enlisted, organized, uniformed, armed, equipped, and handsomely encamped in six weeks.

NARRATOR : While on a trip North to secure arms, James Beecher's regiment was ordered into combat as a last resort at the Battle of Olustee in Florida. An officer describes the scene.

OFFICER : Our men were brave beyond description, and as their comrades fell around them, they stood up nobly without once shrinking. When the right arm of our color sergeant was broken, he knelt down and held up the dear old flag with his left until relieved.

NARRATOR : Even through his heresy trial, Charles's congregation stood by him, by and large. His townspeople elected him to the Massachusetts legislature in 1864. And he continued to work, publishing *Redeemer and Redeemed,* a book of his own blend of theology, including the pre-existence of souls.

And together with Edward, he wrote a reply to the panel which had defamed him, *The Result Tested*—they charged that the trial was simply revenge against Lyman Beecher's New School Calvinism and Charles's undiplomatic sermon-pamphlets blasting President Buchanan and the Fugitive Slave Law.

•

In the course of the War, in 1864, when Henry Ward Beecher learned that Lincoln had sent a delegation to the Confederate Vice President, he called on the President.

HENRY : We were alone in his receiving room. His hair was "every way for Sunday." It looked as though it was an abandoned stubble-field. He had on slippers and his vest was what was called "going free." He looked wearied and when he sat down in a chair looked as though every limb wanted to drop off his body. And I said to him, "Mr. Lincoln, I come to you to know whether the public interest will permit you to explain to me what this Southern commission means." Well, he listened very patiently and looked up to the ceiling for a few moments and said, "Well, I am almost of a mind to show you all the documents."

"Well, Mr. Lincoln, I should like to see them if it is proper." He went to his little secretary desk, and came and handed me a little card as long as my finger and an inch wide and on that was written—

"You will pass the bearer through the lines" or something to that effect.

"There," he said, "is all there is of it. Now Blair thinks something can be done, but I don't—but I have no objection to have him try his hand. He has no authority whatever but to go and see what he can do."

"Well," said I, "you have lifted a great burden off my mind."

NARRATOR : Lincoln instructed his Secretary of War Edwin Stanton to keep Henry Beecher informed of developments through the end of the war.

When Anna Dickinson came to Hartford, she was an eloquent speaker even at nineteen. Isabella took her home that night to talk—they discussed Harriet Mill's article in the *Westminster Review* on "The Enfranchisement of Women," and Anna allayed Isabella's fears of Elizabeth Cady Stanton and Susan B. Anthony.

During the war, the women's movement languished; factions were beginning to rise. While visiting her son-in-law Eugene in South Carolina, Isabella called on Caroline Severance, who enlisted her in the conservative faction. On the other side, Stanton and Anthony had opposed abandoning the women's movement even during wartime—although they did gather 400,000 signatures in favor of the Thirteenth Amendment, to abolish slavery.

The suffragists expected that after the war, the abolitionists would support their cause in turn. However, Reconstruction and the bitter struggles in the South took up most political energies—the feminist call for a constitutional amendment that gave the vote to both blacks and women was drowned out. When the Fourteenth Amendment was passed, it gave the vote to all male citizens. It was a serious setback for the women's movement.

With William Lloyd Garrison and others, Isabella helped found the New England Woman Suffrage Association. Isabella met the conservative suffragists—Julia Ward Howe, author of the "Battle Hymn of the Republic," Paulina Wright Davis, as well as Frederick Douglass and William Lloyd Garrison. Davis invited her to Providence to meet Elizabeth Cady Stanton and Susan B. Anthony. Isabella was won over by their arguments.

ISABELLA : While I have been mourning in secret over the

degradation of woman, you have been working through opposition and obloquy to raise her to self-respect and self-protection
through enfranchisement, knowing that with political rights come
equal social and industrial opportunities. Henceforth, I will at
least share your work and obloquy.

•

NARRATOR : Late in the war, James Beecher was leading a
charge at Honey Hill on the Charleston and Savannah Railroad
when he was shot and his horse was killed. The wound was serious, but not fatal.

James Beecher soon returned to active duty, and his troops
occupied half of Charleston, South Carolina. The first Sunday in
the liberated city, James Beecher spoke to his men as chaplain as
well as colonel. Dr. Marcy reports.

MARCY : He entered the pulpit through a crowd that filled every
standing place, in full uniform followed by members of his staff.
He unbuckled his sword, laying it tenderly on the desk, and took
for his text, "The liberty wherewith Christ hath made us free."
His impassioned oratory at times swayed the vast audience as a
mighty wind the treetops—again, recounting God's care for His
children, it fell as the soft dew from heaven, and there was not a
dry eye in the house, and when at the close all bent in prayer, broken sobs and utterances of "Thanks to God, we's free," attested
his power.

NARRATOR : After hostilities ceased, James Beecher's regiment
was the occupying force for ninety square miles, including two
towns and six hundred plantations. When he resigned his commission, James had achieved the brevet rank of brigadier general of
United States Volunteers.

When the fighting was over, Henry Ward Beecher was invited
to give an address marking the fourth anniversary of the fall of
Fort Sumter.

HENRY : But for the people misled, for the multitudes drafted
and driven into this civil war, let not a trace of animosity remain.
The moment their willing hand drops the musket and they return
to their allegiance, then stretch out your own honest right hand to
greet them. Recall to them the old days of kindness. Our hearts
wait for their redemption. All the resources of a renovated nation

shall be applied to rebuild their prosperity and smooth down the furrows of war.

NARRATOR : Before he returned North from that speech of reconciliation, news came—President Lincoln had been assassinated.

HENRY : Did ever so many hearts in so brief a time, touch such boundless feelings? It was the uttermost of joy; it was the uttermost of sorrow—noon and midnight without a space between.

•

NARRATOR : In frustration with abolitionist leaders, the feminist leaders Stanton and Anthony took on a new campaign. Kansas was to be allowed to vote on an amendment to enfranchise women as well as blacks. That was a chink in the wall, and they spent four months crisscrossing Kansas prairie settlements and cities. At length, low in funds and spirits, they accepted the help of the flamboyant George Francis Train. The campaign failed, but Train offered to finance a newspaper for the women's movement. This was the motto of their magazine, *The Revolution:*

STANTON : Principle, not policy; justice, not favors. —Men their rights, and nothing more; women their rights, and nothing less.

NARRATOR : In the two and a half years of its existence, the paper covered not only women's rights but also divorce laws, treatment of working women, rape, legalization of prostitution, and the double standard.

A few years after Charles Beecher's heresy trial, a second panel of Congregational ministers rescinded the earlier decision, and Charles Beecher was no longer a heretic.

Charles had already published his theological views, including the doctrine of the pre-existence of souls in *Redeemer and Redeemed.* He also wrote two more books on Christian spiritualism, an interest that Harriet and Isabella and other Beechers shared. And upon invitation of brother Henry, he took over editorship of the popular *Plymouth Collection of Hymns and Tunes.*

Despite his rapport with his vast audience, Henry Ward Beecher, like many a leader of the time, began to lose touch with popular sentiment.

HENRY : Everything marches. The style of thought is freer and more noble. The young men of our times are regenerated. The army has been a school. The war has changed not alone institutions, but ideas. Public sentiment is exalted far beyond what it has been at any other period.

NARRATOR : Henry Beecher's plea for reconciliation with the South went unheeded in the North, which seemed to be bent on revenge. Beecher supported gradual—not immediate—citizenship for blacks—and in 1866 he said so in a letter to the Soldiers' and Sailors' Convention in Cleveland—a fatal document. This Cleveland letter put him in the company of Andrew Johnson, who was facing impeachment, and with narrow-minded politicians who were fighting black representation in Congress.

The Republican Party had just picked up the cause of black citizenship at the same time Beecher dropped it. He was attacked by his old allies—Charles Sumner, the abolitionists, Horace Greeley, even by his own editor on *The Independent*, Theodore Tilton. Somewhere along the line, Beecher had lost his secure hold on the national mood.

HENRY : Better days are coming! Just now angry voices come to me as rude winds roaring through the trees. The winds will die; the trees will live!

NARRATOR : Greeley's *New York Tribune* continued to find flaws in Beecher's proposals, his congregation was cold, and Tilton continued to attack him in his own paper. In 1867, Beecher resigned from *The Independent*, leaving Tilton in charge.

Theodore Tilton was much like Beecher in many ways—he wrote a luxuriant prose and poetry, and he indulged in the same kind of polite essays as Beecher. He edited *The Independent* in the morning, and the *Brooklyn Union* in the afternoon. William Lloyd Garrison approved of him, and he had early declared himself an abolitionist. Tilton also had taken up feminism, and was friends with Elizabeth Cady Stanton, Lucretia Mott, Susan B. Anthony, Mrs. Greeley, and Isabella Beecher Hooker, Henry's youngest sister. When push came to shove between Tilton and Beecher, all the feminists, even Isabella, would side with Tilton.

•

The feminists had a hard time making clear their objectives,

Elizabeth Stanton was perhaps the most articulate figure in the feminist movement, yet her words appear not to penetrate male consciousness—in this case, Henry Ward Beecher and Henry James, Senior.

STANTON : Nothing can exceed the whole-souled, all-absorbing agonizing interest which I feel in the redemption of women. Our religion, laws, customs, are all founded on the belief that woman was made for man. How this marriage question grows on me! It lies at the very foundation of all progress.

HENRY : Woman is appointed for the refinement of the race. Man is said to have been made little lower than the angels; woman needs no such comparison; she was made full as high.

HENRY JAMES, SR. : Holding as I do that the human heart is the destined home of constancy and every courteous affection, I cannot but believe that it will abound in those fruits precisely as it becomes practically honored, or left to its own cultivated instincts.

NARRATOR : In late 1868, Isabella wrote a piece which appeared anonymously in *Putnam's Monthly*—"A Mother's Letters to a Daughter on Woman's Suffrage." It was a comparatively tame effort, relying on the argument that women would raise the moral level of politics.

In May 1869, the Equal Rights Association, the group that had been formed to join the black struggle with the women's movement, split on the Fifteenth Amendment—which gave the vote only to male citizens. Frederick Douglass declared:

DOUGLASS : When women, because they are women, are hunted down through the cities of New York and New Orleans, when they are dragged from their houses and hung upon lamp-posts, when their children are torn from their arms, when they are in danger of having their homes burnt down over their heads, then they will have an urgency to obtain the ballot equal to our own.

NARRATOR : The New York wing, with Stanton, Anthony and Davis, saw this as a stab in the back. They withdrew and organized the National Woman Suffrage Association. In response the Boston group, with Julia Ward Howe, Thomas Wentworth Higginson, Lucy Stone and her husband Henry Blackwell formed the American Woman Suffrage Association, and elected Henry

Ward Beecher as its president. It would be twenty years before the two groups reconciled their differences. Isabella threw in her lot with the New York wing of Susan B. Anthony and Elizabeth Cady Stanton.

Isabella proposed that she and Harriet be made associate editors of *The Revolution*, with pay—even though Stanton and Anthony were not paid. Anthony saw it as a chance to get the equivalent of *Uncle Tom's Cabin* out of Harriet. They were offered positions as contributing editors.

But the paper's editorial position alienated Harriet. She wrote an article in the *Woman's Journal*, a rival publication to *The Revolution*, calling George Sand an evil influence. Stanton replied.

STANTON : George Sand has done a grander work for women than any woman of her day, while Mrs. Stowe has been vacillating over every demand made for her sex, timidly watching the weathercock of public sentiment and ridiculing the advance guard. When women first demanded suffrage in this country, where was Mrs. Stowe? While the thousands of wives of drunkards, licentious men, tyrants and criminals call aloud today for deliverance from all these degrading relations, where is Mrs. Stowe? Behold her, Bible in hand, proclaiming to these unhappy ones, "a woman hath not power over her own body, but the husband."

NARRATOR : Harriet responded in kind, in an article sent to brother Henry's *Christian Union* magazine.

By 1870, the women's movement suffered a decisive split— Henry Beecher supported the moderates, for a time serving as their chairman, and Tilton supported the radicals, including Isabella Beecher Hooker. The radical wing was soon to encounter the flamboyant and infamous bluestocking Victoria Woodhull. Thomas Beecher said of her—

THOMAS : Mrs. Woodhull only carries out Henry's philosophy, against which I recorded my protest twenty years ago.

NARRATOR : Isabella organized the Connecticut Woman Suffrage Association and Society for the Study of Political Science. In 1870, she went on a speaking tour of the Midwest, and the next year organized at her own expense a national convention. Her early years reading law with her lawyer husband John Hooker had not gone to waste.

ISABELLA : This convention is for the purpose of calling the attention of Congress to the fact that women were already citizens of the United States under the Constitution, interpreted by the Declaration of Independence, and only needed recognition, by that body, to become voters.

NARRATOR : Before Isabella's convention began, she and Susan B. Anthony went on a speaking tour of the West—she addressed the second convention of the National Woman Suffrage Association in Chicago. But when they returned to open the convention, they found that Victoria Woodhull had been invited to speak to the Judiciary Committee of the House of Representatives. Woodhull dressed conservatively and spoke well, arguing that the Fourteenth and Fifteenth Amendments referred to women and to men.

At her convention, Isabella introduced her to the delegates, and again Victoria Woodhull captivated her audience—though Isabella was later criticized for allying herself with the most outrageous woman in America.

∙

Out of her convention, Isabella Beecher Hooker was able to present a petition with thousands of names to Congress. The Committee on the Judiciary of the United States Senate invited Isabella to present her argument in person. To her husband, she confided—

ISABELLA : I was perfectly infused with it and inspired by it—it flowed out of my inner consciousness as if it were a part of my very being. I dare not tell you all that I see in the future and know is to come to pass shortly. I would not put it on paper even if I had time and strength. God knows it and that is enough—but be sure that woman's hour has come. I find such loving and supporting friends who believe that I am raised up to strike this last blow for freedom. I am every day touched by indications trivial in themselves that I am called to a great and holy work whereof no one can prophesy the end.

NARRATOR : Senator Charles Sumner characterized her argument before the Senate Committee as "able, lucid, and powerful."

Susan B. Anthony said of her—

ANTHONY : Isabella Beecher Hooker is the soundest constitutional lawyer in the country.

NARRATOR : Back in Hartford, Isabella was blacklisted by society leaders. As her husband was about to leave for Europe, she wrote him.

ISABELLA : Little do you know what it has cost me to tear myself away from you of late, even a little, and give a part of myself to womanhood—that intangible but yet sad reality that has thrust itself between me and all I hold dear. Remember that I do not love you any the less, that I love truth and justice beyond all things else.

NARRATOR : In 1870, she and her husband drew up a bill to give women the same property rights as their husbands, and had it introduced into the Connecticut legislature. It didn't pass, but it was reintroduced every year until it passed in 1877 with the vigorous support of Governor Richard Hubbard. Another bill to grant the suffrage to women in Connecticut did not pass during her lifetime.

When Victoria Woodhull spoke to the New York convention in 1871, she called for a convention to establish a new government if Congress refused to act on the woman question.

WOODHULL : We mean treason; we mean secession. We are plotting a revolution; we will overthrow this bogus Republic and plant a government of righteousness in its place!

NARRATOR: Isabella's more moderate ideas, as set forth in her book, *Womanhood: Its Sanctities and Fidelities*, more closely approximated those of her sister Catharine, putting woman as the center of the family at the heart of cultural change.

ISABELLA : One generation of instructed mothers would do more for the renovation of the race than all other human agencies combined.

NARRATOR : The book also included some of her correspondence with John Stuart Mill and Harriet Mill on the relation between the sexes. The last section, citing opponents of the licensing of prostitutes, was called State Patronage of Vice. Because of this section, her critics called the book obscene.

Through it all, Isabella Beecher Hooker continued to defend the freethinker, free-love advocate Victoria Woodhull. At the 1872 convention, Susan B. Anthony was convinced that Victoria Woodhull simply wanted to capture support for her presidential campaign on the People's Party—which is exactly what she started to do. Anthony tried to stop her speaking, and then shut the lights out. The struggle would go on.

A New Era
1870–1886

The Post-Civil-War era offered different challenges for various members of the Beecher family. Thomas K. Beecher took his schooling at his brother Edward's Illinois College, though he was skeptical of religion. Afterwards, he visited and helped brother Henry in Indianapolis—he told Isabella that Henry was most like their father.

THOMAS : We sawed and split wood together; sat on rail fences and told stories; raised sweet potatoes weighing five pounds each; wrote articles for the *Farmer and Gardener*; banked up celery till it was nearly three feet tall, white and crisp; picked blackberries as big as my thumb; and hunted squirrels, rabbits and smaller game.

NARRATOR : Tom went down to meeting every night for sixteen weeks, to laugh and sing and hear Henry talk about Jesus Christ.

THOMAS : I did not know it at the time. There were no arguments. Nothing was proved. Can you tell how the bones of the unborn babe grow in the womb? So Christ was formed in consciousness.

Like some white bird high-flying, that drops down through the smoke into a walled city fortified against all comers, carrying under its wing a message from afar, so came to me the vision of Christ, as with matchless words brother Henry told the story, without theology or dialectic.

NARRATOR : Thomas remarried in 1857, to Julia Jones, a granddaughter of Noah Webster. Thomas's luxury was a plunge bath—on winter mornings he would break the ice with a boat hook and then jump in. Julia was a good amateur sculptor, and in some ways was as unconventional as Thomas.

Charles Beecher's son, Lt. Frederick Beecher, was killed by Indians in a battle in Yuma County, Colorado. Frederick had been a veteran of Gettysburg.

In 1869, despite advice against publication, Harriet Beecher Stowe published *Lady Byron Vindicated,* based on her conversations with her friend, the now dead wife of Byron. Lady Byron's side of the story gave a sordid portrait of the popular poet's private life. The book ended up besmirching Harriet's own reputation.

HARRIET : Alas! the history of Lady Byron is the history of too many women in every rank of life. The feeling which seems to underlie all English literature is that it is no matter what becomes of the woman, when the man's story is to be told.

NARRATOR : When the Plymouth Church treasurer, Henry C. Bowen, acquired *The Independent* magazine, he asked Henry Beecher to be its editor. Theodore Tilton was his assistant. A little later, Beecher complained of some of the patent-medicine advertising in it, and offered to resign. After negotiation, Beecher stayed on as editor, with complete control over content, including ads—but he lost Bowen's friendship and support.

Tilton was a brilliant young man married to one of Plymouth Church's Sunday-school teachers, and Henry took a fatherly interest in them both. When he returned from England, it was arranged that Tilton would continue to edit, as he had in Henry's absence, for one year more under Henry Ward Beecher's name, and then under his own. Acclaimed as the cleverest young editor in America, the thirty-year-old Tilton began to think rather highly of himself, and to treat Beecher patronizingly. Tilton went on a lecture tour and was highly applauded.

William Beecher, the eldest son, retired in 1870 when his wife Katharine died. His last church had been in North Brookfield, Massachusetts. He went to Chicago to live with his daughters until his death. All through his career, William Beecher had faced petty salary disputes and matters of pride. His courage, honest and zeal—all Beecher traits—were no guarantee of success for William Beecher.

In 1870, Charles Beecher gave in to Harriet's entreaties, and went south to her second home in Newport, Florida, to preach among the very poor but newly free black population.

CHARLES : I should perhaps have done them more good, but from some chance expression I believe, they had heard that I "was not sound." Poor creatures!

NARRATOR : Charles also served for three years as superintendent of public instruction for Florida, but then he returned to Georgetown, Massachusetts for a few years.

After the War, Theodore Tilton had become a Radical Republican, calling for retribution against the defeated South. He decided to attack Henry Ward Beecher's letter to the Soldiers' and Sailors' Cleveland Convention, which had called for immediate readmission of the former slave states. By so doing, Tilton established his independence from Beecher, aired his own opinions, and pleased Bowen, who was also a Radical Republican. Beecher and *The Independent* parted company.

In the meantime, Mrs. Tilton sent word to Beecher that she needed his advice; she had left home because of Theodore's cruelty and unfaithfulness. As her pastor, Henry of course saw her, and then sent his wife, as one more competent in such matters. Mrs. Beecher advised separation.

Henry Ward Beecher became editor and part owner of a rival publication, the *Christian Union*. Tilton, meanwhile, had become more radical and erratic. He committed *The Independent* to free love, as taught by the Claflin sisters, Victoria Woodhull and Tennessee Claflin, leaders of the radical women's party, and the first "lady brokers" on Wall Street. Henry Bowen, alarmed by the drop in circulation of *The Independent* accused Tilton of wrecking the paper. Tilton accused Beecher of having made improper proposals to Mrs. Tilton.

Henry Beecher denied any such actions, and concurred with Bowen that Tilton's presence on *The Independent*' was not good. Bowen consequently fired Tilton.

Enter Francis D. Moulton, a friend of Tilton's, and a political manipulator who had become rich through porkbarrel arrangements. Moulton worked on Beecher's well-known generosity of spirit—he told Beecher that he had blighted the Tiltons by failing to perceive Mrs. Tilton's excessive affection for him, and also had wrecked Tilton's career by his intrusive advice, based on malicious slanders. Henry took the man's words at face value and was amazed and remorseful that he could have been the one responsible. Moulton volunteered his good offices.

By this time, Calvin and Harriet Stowe maintained a house in

Mandarin, Florida as well as one in Hartford—the big house in Hartford was too much to handle, and they moved into a modest home on Forest Street, in Hartford's famous Nook Farm literary colony—with the Samuel Clemenses on one side and the Charles Dudley Warners on the other. John and Isabella Hooker had lived there for years.

James Beecher became minister at Owego, New York, when he was mustered out of the Union Army. He and his wife adopted three children there. He spent another four years at Poughkeepsie, and then he bought a square mile of wilderness in Ulster County, New York, where he preached to backwoods folk, and his wife ran a school. Ned Buntline, the dime novelist, knew James Beecher in those days.

BUNTLINE : His tract of land is densely wooded. A beautiful lake of good size occupies a portion of the property, and there is in all the Catskill Range no scenery more picturesque. "Beecher Lake," the natives call it. And on one of the mountain cliffs commanding a fine view of it the preacher built for himself his home, doing all the work himself.

It is a story-and-a-half structure, plain, neat and comfortable. At the time of its erection there was no wagon road within half a dozen miles; the nearest hamlet and post office was ten miles distant while it was three times that distance to the first railroad station.

There all five—James, his wife, and adopted daughters—have since remained. There is every reason to believe that there is no earthly inducement which induce James Beecher to enter again his old-time career. The few neighbors who have gathered about this lake fully appreciate him. "He is queer," they admit, but for all that they love him.

NARRATOR : In 1872, Isabella Beecher Hooker was already a leader in the women's movement. She had held her own convention for women's rights, even supporting Victoria Woodhull in her presidential campaign. Then Woodhull and her sister Tennessee Claflin published in their magazine *Woodhull and Claflin's Weekly* a long exposé article on Henry Ward Beecher's sex life, and everything they knew of the Beecher-Tilton scandal. Woodhull also blames Harriet and Catharine Beecher for avoiding the women's movement. Isabella was caught in the middle.

Finally, Henry Beecher broke his long silence and published a blanket denial to all rumors and charges. He asked his church to organize an investigating committee to look into the matter. After months of work, the committee completely exonerated Beecher of any wrongdoing.

At this point, Tilton felt cornered, and filed a lawsuit claiming alienation of affections involving adultery. This trial lasted for months, and took up more space in the newspapers than the Civil War, it was said. The verdict was nine in Beecher's favor, three against.

The Claflin sisters carried on their activities with the aid of their patron, Commodore Vanderbilt. Their magazine defended free love, socialism, birth control, women's suffrage—they objected to Henry Beecher's affairs not because of his immorality but because of his hypocrisy.

The Claflins believed that the book of Genesis was an allegory in which the Garden of Eden was the human body, and entertained other unconventional notions. They were a special target for Anthony Comstock and his Society for the Suppression of Vice. Meanwhile, Victoria Woodhull conducted a campaign for the presidency through the People's Party.

The Tilton Affair became stranger at every turn. Tilton produced a letter written by Mrs. Tilton, an accusation of improper advances by Henry Ward Beecher.

Beecher was aghast, and confronted Mrs. Tilton, who was ill in bed. She did not answer at first, but then said she couldn't help it. Tilton had worn her down—and that the letter was supposed to straighten things out. She then wrote Beecher a written retraction, and signed it. Later in the Tilton-Beecher trial, she retracted the retraction, and then reasserted it—so that after all she was not called as a witness by either side.

Moulton persuaded Beecher to make a statement, and then, being too excited, let Moulton do the writing—and when the dinner bell rang, and very little time until his evening service, Henry Ward Beecher signed the document without reading it. This Moulton document became the basis for Tilton's charges. The affair became messier as it went on—a document signed by all parties agreeing to maintain silence was published in the *New York Times*.

When Henry Beecher was disturbed on a Sunday about the trial, he said—

HENRY : Gentlemen, we have good authority for holding that it is lawful to draw up an ass from a pit on the Sabbath day. There never was a bigger ass nor a deeper pit.

•

NARRATOR : Back in Elmira, New York, Thomas Beecher felt his congregation was too large and his church too old, and decided to hold his meetings in a larger auditorium of an opera house. The Ministerial Union of Elmira expelled him—without any stated reason. His friend Mark Twain wrote an article on it for the *Elmira Advertiser*. Twain's marriage had been performed by Thomas Beecher in 1870.

TWAIN : Happy, happy world that knows at last that a little congress of congregationless clergymen, of whom it had never heard before, have crushed a famous Beecher and reduced his audiences from 1,500 down to 1,475 at one fell blow!

NARRATOR : Soon after his expulsion, Thomas Beecher held his regular Sunday services outdoors during the summer; he arranged it so that the streetcar company could run out to Eldridge Park on the outskirts of town even though it was Sunday—and he wore a white duck suit and white felt hat. His audiences grew even more.

•

In 1872, Harriet Beecher Stowe finally went on a speaking tour of forty cities to earn money. Her first reading in Bridgeport was a failure, but at the second, she rumpled up her hair, and galvanized herself into action—later telling her friend Annie Field that she looked like Lyman Beecher up there—and the audience was swept away with passages from *Uncle Tom* and from her latest book, *Oldtown Fireside Stories*.

HARRIET : I check off place after place as the captive does his days of imprisonment. On the whole it is as easy a way of making money as I have ever tried, though no way is perfectly easy.

NARRATOR : At the end of the tour, she was exhausted. She was tempted once more to raise money, but the second tour cured her of the practice. She went back to writing, and still was forced to sell the extravagant Hartford home for a smaller one. She wrote incessantly, light novels, poems, sketches, essays, continually interrupted by the needs of the ailing Calvin Stowe.

In 1873, Mark Twain wrote a piece called "A New Beecher Church," putting these words into Thomas Beecher's mouth. The situation was real, and Thomas's thoughtful new ideas would result in a new kind of church by simply following the idea of Christian brotherhood.

THOMAS/TWAIN : When I came to Elmira, the First Congregational Church was perhaps the worst church building in Elmira. That was twenty years ago. I think the building has held its own ever since. I do not think it will fall down for some time yet, although there is an apparent weakness in the roof over yonder, which I will have Brother Jones look at tomorrow and see whether it is still safe.

Several times since I have been here the question of a new church has been advocated. I have always opposed the idea, because I knew that you were not ready. I did not wish you to get subscription on the brain, and run races to see who should put down the largest sum; nor was I willing to leave a part of the cost in mortgage.

Whenever there is a mortgage on a church, the devil holds the mortgage, and the religious life in that church inevitably dies. A new church is not necessary to me. I can preach in the park in the warm weather and in a hall in the winter; or I can do as the Lord himself did—preach from house to house. What I am here for is the life of religion in your souls, and preaching is but a minor question.

Still, there are advantages in a suitable building. I have been talking with an architect, and I find that it is likely to cost about $50,000 to build such a church as I think we ought to have, if we have a new one. Therefore I am going to put it to you this morning to vote.

On the table in front of the pulpit is a box of envelopes directed to me, and in each envelope is a card with blanks. Write your name and address. Then vote on the questions: First, Do we need a new church, and are you in favor of building it now? Yes or no. Second, How much will you give in one payment toward it? Third, How much could you give in three payments toward it?

Take time to think it over, and return the envelopes to me within five weeks from yesterday. I will open them five weeks from today. If the majority decides to have a new church and the amount pledged is sufficient, we will have one. Do not tell anyone how you mean to vote; do not talk it over with anyone except your wife/husband. What I want is a vote of individuals.

NARRATOR : The vote came in for a new church, with pledges of $65,000. And the Langdon family had pledged to match whatever was raised dollar for dollar, making a total of $130,000. So, Thomas Beecher was able not only to build his church but to fulfill his ideal of a "Church Home."

THOMAS : We intend to love regardless of return and to do good, hoping for nothing; a clear, sheer, truthful, gospel investment. Gospel sermons are plenty. Gospel investments are scarce. You have heard gospel sermons for eighteen years. Now we propose to act a gospel sermon. In short, we want a family on a large scale, in which the smallest member will be the noisiest, and make the most trouble, and in which the strongest member will be the stillest and laugh at the little fool and love him, notwithstanding this noise and nonsense.

NARRATOR : This great building, when completed, was almost a city block long. Henry said of it—

HENRY : Tom, when I go, I shall leave behind me no such great monument to my life's work.

NARRATOR : The church house contained, besides a church, a gymnasium, library, theater, and a romproom/ dancing room. In other rooms, people could entertain, a pool table was set up in the basement. It was the fist institutional church in the country. In his lifetime, this new type of church spread across the country, and even had imitators in Elmira itself. Institutional churches remained the major social vehicle in many cities until YMCA, YWCA, Boy Scouts, Girl Scouts, settlement houses, boys' clubs became commonly available facilities.

•

In 1871, a small faction in his Illinois church forced Edward Beecher to resign, and he moved to New York where he served for two years as assistant editor on Henry's *Christian Union*. Then, when the paper changed hands, he in effect retired at age 70, and moved to Brooklyn, where he served as counselor and friend to his more famous brother Henry Ward Beecher—something he had done when Henry was a mere boy.

Over the years, these two brothers had kept up a sporadic but extensive correspondence. In middle-age, they found at last that they could share mutual confidences of a deep nature over their trials of faith. When the storm over the Tilton Affair broke over Henry, Edward was beside him like a rock. When Isabella talked with Edward, he said—

EDWARD : If Henry is guilty, he ought not to make confession.

ISABELLA : That is nothing more than male hypocrisy.

•

NARRATOR : After the trials, Henry went on the lecture circuit to pay back the terrific costs of the trials. He would lecture, and then speak outdoors to great crowds. Audiences came to jeer but stayed to listen and to give Beecher warm applause. He spoke 232 times in 235 days, to a total of 460,000 people in seven months. Even so, suspicion of him died hard.

When Thomas was considering offers to other jobs, Henry warned him:

HENRY : Don't leave the Park Church—they can appreciate you and endure you!

NARRATOR : And Thomas's associate, the Rev. Annis Ford Eastman said:

EASTMAN : And it is the glory of this church that this was true. A teacher sent from God is bound to make trouble when he comes. Whoever denies all human authority over his conscience, who fearlessly examines all religious systems and social conventions, taking what is good for him and rejecting what is bad, who is never moved out of his way by popular enthusiasms—who can see both sides of every question, and bravely states them—he must often be a sore trial to the average sense of propriety in a community.

NARRATOR : Thomas Beecher's church went from fifty members to seven hundred plus a Sunday school of one thousand— Sunday attendance was about 1,400, including people of all denominations, even agnostics and atheists. What was Thomas Beecher's secret? He was not an outstanding speaker, like his brother Henry. He simply taught the teachings of Jesus, the brother/sisterhood of humanity, and decided each question as he thought Jesus would have done.

A poor Irish woman's husband had been killed, and she struggled to feed her five children and pay the mortgage. Thomas Beecher called one day and handed her the mortgage deed paid in full.

THOMAS : And here is some money from the same friends with which to buy what you need for the children. Don't thank me, it isn't my money. Don't thank those who gave it to me. It isn't their money. It's Jesus Christ's money and that means that it belongs to whoever needs it most. If you come across anyone who needs it more than you, you must give it to them.

NARRATOR : Thomas Beecher dressed in a faded butternut coat, and a visor-shaped cap made to his specifications, and replaced it at intervals. Jervis Langdon finally took Beecher to a tailor to be fitted for a new broadcloth suit. But weeks later, he was wearing his old worn coat again. He had given his new coat away.

THOMAS : You see I couldn't give him the old coat because it wasn't fit to give to anyone so I had to give him the new one.

NARRATOR : He also rode a tricycle; and he would sometimes skip while walking, out of good spirits. But he also had periods of deep depression.

Thomas K. Beecher also served variously in Elmira, as bridge commissioner, as superintendent of schools—and he ran for various offices for the Republican, Democratic, Greenback, and Prohibition Parties.

He also had an important contact during his days at school in Illinois.

THOMAS : Abraham Lincoln wasn't considered good enough to associate with a Beecher in those days, but I took a chance, and it didn't hurt me.

NARRATOR : After all her years of travel in the cause of women's education, Catharine Beecher finally came to Elmira, New York, to stay with Thomas Beecher and his wife Julia. She said—

JULIA : I think there are worse afflictions in the world than the care of an old Christian woman who has at least tried to do good all her life and needs someone's kind attentions till the Lord calls her home. I am not going to worry about that.

NARRATOR : Of course, Catharine complained to sister Harriet of boredom in Elmira.

HARRIET : Catharine, you have more talents for making life agreeable than most women, you should visit and cheer some sick people at the cure and make life brighter around you.

Meanwhile the government of the world will not be going on a whit worse now that you are not doing it. I am relieved and glad to think of you at home at last with Brother Tom. Too many years have passed over your head for you to be wandering like a trunk without a label.

NARRATOR : Thomas K. Beecher wrote lay sermons, and a regular newspaper column called "Saturday Miscellany." Two volumes of his sermons were published, plus a book of children's stories.

Asked how to get to heaven, Thomas replied—

THOMAS : My boy, you can go to New York from Elmira by the Erie, the Lehigh Valley, the Lackawanna or the Northern Central, you can walk, ride horseback or you can go by boat. One way may be somewhat more roundabout than the other, but you will get there all right if you follow the sign posts. You can reach heaven by the Catholic Church, or by the Synagogue, Universalist, or Baptist Church, and you can even reach it through the Park Church—but, whatsoever you do, do it unto the Lord.

NARRATOR : Henry's troubles were not quickly over. After the trial, a council of Congregational churches took up the question of the behavior of both church and pastor in 1876. No new evidence was brought forth, and again Beecher's innocence was proclaimed. So, he had victory at last, though fees for the legal trial alone cost Beecher $118,000. In the meantime, he carried on his usual load of church work and preaching.

William A. Beach, chief counsel for the other side, gradually became convinced of Beecher's innocence.

BEACH : His appearance and utterance when he asserted his

innocence on the witness stand were the most sublime and over-powering exhibition of the majesty of human nature I ever beheld. I can't understand how anyone could resist that solemn avowal. I felt and feel now that we were a pack of hounds trying in vain to drag down a noble lion.

NARRATOR : At his church in Elmira, Thomas Beecher tried to conduct his affairs as Christ might have—just as he had tried with his school in Philadelphia. He occasionally drank a glass of beer in a saloon—but never treated anyone or accepted being treated to a beer. He occasionally played a hand of whist at a club, he played baseball, cricket, he sang and played the organ. He also set up office hours—instead of calling on his congregation, he expected them to call on him.

THOMAS : I cannot make pastoral calls. I am not constructed so that I can. But I am yours all times of the day and night when you want anything of me. If you are sick and need a watcher I will watch with you. If you are poor and need someone to saw wood for you, I will saw wood for you. I can read the paper for you if you need anybody to do that. I am yours, but you must call on me the same as you would on a physician.

•

NARRATOR : It wasn't long after she came to Elmira that Catharine Beecher died. Thomas describes her last days.

THOMAS : She was like a mirror fractured, each piece like the whole. She was incessantly, yet incoherently active, going from sewing to letter writing to piano playing to metaphysics. She inherited from her father great directness and positiveness of manner, and made it always apparent that her mission in this world was not to entertain but to instruct and improve.

NARRATOR : James Beecher finally left his wilderness sanctuary only at the entreaty of brother Henry, to take charge of the Bethel Mission of his Plymouth Church in Brooklyn. The work proved finally too exhausting—and at length, he broke down completely. After four years in a sanitarium, he was cared for by a nephew, and ended up at Dr. Gleason's water cure spa neighboring Thomas Beecher's home in Elmira, New York.

One day in 1886, after shooting, he put the muzzle of a gun in his mouth and pulled the trigger. This youngest Beecher was buried in Elmira beside the oldest Beecher, his sister Catharine.

When Henry Ward Beecher died the next year, Thomas said—

THOMAS : In those sad days when his good name was besmirched, and thousands of people took sides, Brother Henry— my brother Henry—solemnly asseverated his innocence and his purity. Knowing him, I believed him and read no further. He cared little for logic and consistency as an appletree that blossoms bountifully in the sunshine to the song of robins and bluebirds.

In the 1830s and 1840s, Amereicans experienced a number of phenomena that came to be known as spiritualism. These voices from the beyond, mesmerism, animal magnetism, and hypnotism fascinated a world still marveling and more than a bit dubious about scientific curiosities which were even more invisible—electricity, magnetism, radiation, chemistry, photography, astronomy. Why shouldn't one also accept the claims of clairvoyants or mediums? Psychic investigators abounded—and so did charlatans. Curiosity tantalized most people, especially the Beechers.

Catharine Beecher suffered at various times from nervous complaints. Seeking help at water cure spas, she found ideas there on health and psychic phenomena.

CATHARINE : I have a delicate and scrofulous constitution, and if overwrought I experience a semi-paralysis of the nerves of motion, attended by an extreme sensitiveness of the whole nervous system.

Dr. Buchanan and his theory of Neurology produced a strong impression in reference to future probable discoveries of the remedial agency of Animal Magnetism.

NARRATOR : Yet many passes with a bright silver sixpence had no effect on her. Likewise Sherwood's Electro-Magnetic Machine, and a man who detected disease by magnetic fingertips.

Though she was not cured, certain remarkable powers of the clairvoyant she consulted intrigued Catharine, and she attempted a rational explanation. Although Catharine Beecher believed that animal magnetism might work by invisible nervous fluid like electricity, she did not believe in mediums. To her, Spiritualism was a lower-class phenomenon.

CATHARINE : I have as yet never seen anything claimed to be Spiritual Manifestations that could not be easily accounted for. And the progress of time is more and more exhibiting the folly and inconsistency of the popular delusion that brings back the spirits of departed friends to perform fantastic tricks, and to make known inane and contradictory revelations.

NARRATOR : At one time, Catharine lived in the same boarding house as Kate Fox and her companion Laura Edmonds. The Fox sisters had become famous for communicating with spirits.

CATHARINE : They cut up all sorts of capers to mystify me. They said they had seen a vision of Lyman kneeling before me offering me a rose as the emblem of my purity. I knew then that they were frauds.

NARRATOR : Even before Kate and Margaretta Fox had made public their spirit-rappings, the Beecher family kept up an interest in supernatural phenomena. Calvin Stowe had had childhood hallucinations of spirits, and once out-argued the Devil himself with a passage from Ephesians.

•

Harriet and Henry conducted some mesmerism experiments. After some practice, Henry could produce a semi-somnolent state in Harriet, in which her hands wandered at their own will.

HARRIET : Amid all the bodily effects my mind and powers of observation seemed uncommonly bright and active.

Eunice, don't you remember you almost thought you had some hobgoblin magician for a husband last summer! How you did scud out of the room!

NARRATOR : Then she met Mrs. Bonneville, a professional mesmerist.

HARRIET : Henry, Mrs. Bonneville's view of the subject is that the mesmeric fluid is a powerful remedial agent in the cure of nervous diseases particularly—such as all forms of convulsions, hysteria, epilepsy, paralysis, neuralgia in general and it is to the dissemination of light and knowledge on the subject that she considers herself devoted. They had patients in the city by the hundreds, and the pretty graceful creature spent time and strength enough to wear her health out in mesmeric manipulations to this intent.

Henry, I think you have an immense power in this way and the time may come when you can relieve pain by trying it. Even I have been able to help a suffering neighbor fall asleep by making soothing passes.

NARRATOR : When Harriet and Charles toured England, she found that Spiritualism had spread there. On her second trip, they attended seances at the home of Robert Dale Owen, who was then American consul at Naples. Harriet was unconverted, but interested.

Henry was of another opinion.

HENRY : I am a stout unbeliever in the spiritual origins of these phenomena. A belief in modern spiritualism seems to weaken the hold of the Bible upon conscience, the affections, and to substitute diluted sentimentalism and tedious platitudes instead of inspired truth.

•

NARRATOR : Calvin Stowe, Harriet's husband, was not just a believer in spiritualism; he had from an early age seen creatures of various sorts, including Harriet herself. He claimed that unless the figure of Harriet spoke, he would ignore her, because he was not certain that it was she. The apparitions were most intense in his youth.

CALVIN : I have often thought I would communicate to some scientific physician a particular account of a most singular delusion under which I lived from my earliest infancy till the fifteenth or sixteenth year of my age, and the effects of which remain very distinctly now that I am past thirty.

From the hour of my birth I have been constitutionally feeble, as were my parents before me, and my nervous system easily excitable. With care, however, I have kept myself in tolerable health, and my life has been an industrious one.

As early as I can remember anything, I can remember observing a multitude of animated and active objects, which I could see with perfect distinctness, moving about me, and could sometimes, though seldom, hear them make a rustling noise, or other articulate sounds; but I could never touch them. They were in all respects independent of the sense of touch, and incapable of being obstructed in any way by the intervention of material objects. I could see them passing through the floors, and the ceilings, and the walls of the house, from one apartment to another, in all directions, without a door, or a keyhole, or crevice being open to admit them.

These appearances occasioned neither surprise nor alarm, except when they assumed some hideous and frightful form, or exhibited some menacing gesture, for I became acquainted with them as soon as with any of the objects of sense. They were as familiar to me as the forms of my parents and my brother. There was no time, or place, or circumstance, in which they did not occasionally make their appearance. They were more pleased with candlelight than the daylight. I kept up a lively conversation with them—not by language or by signs, for the attempt on my part to speak or move would at once break the charm and drive them away in a fret, but by a peculiar sort of spiritual intercommunion.

Sometimes they would take no notice of me, but carry on a brisk conversation among themselves, principally by looks and gestures, with now and then an audible word. Their most usual appearnce was with the human form and proportion, but under a shadowy outline that seemed just ready to melt into the invisible air, and sometimes liable to the most sudden and grotesque changes, and with a uniform darkly bluish color spotted with brown, or brownish white. There were many exceptions, particularly among my more welcome and familiar visitors.

Besides these rational and generally harmless beings, there was another set of objects which never varied in their form or qualities, and were always mischievous and terrible. The fact of their appearance depended very much on the state of my health and feelings—when sick and depressed they were sure to obtrude their hateful presence upon me. These were a sort of heavy clouds floating about overhead, of a black color, spotted with brown, in the shape of a very flaring inverted tunnel without a nozzle, and from ten to thirty or forty feet in diameter. They floated from place to place in great numbers, and in all directions, with a strong and steady progress, but with a tremulous, quivering, internal motion that agitated them in every part.

Whenever they approached, the rational phantoms were thrown into great consternation, for if a cloud touched any part of one of the rational phantoms it immediately communicated its own color and tremulous motion to the part it touched, then proceeded to diffuse itself over every part of the body, and as fast as it did so the body was drawn into the cloud and became a part of its substance. It was indeed a fearful sight to see their contortions and agonizing efforts.

Every different apartment which I occupied had a different set of phantoms, and they always had a degree of correspondence to the circumstances in which they were seen.

I awoke one bright moonlit night, and found a large full-length human skeleton of an ashy-blue color in bed with me! I screamed out with fright, and soon summoned the family around me. I refused to tell them the cause of my alarm, but begged permission to occupy another bed, which was granted.

For the remainder of the night I slept but little; but I saw upon the window-stools companies of little fairies, about six inches high, in white robes, gamboling and dancing with incessant merriment. Two of them, a male and female, rather taller than the rest, were dignified with a crown and scepter. They took the kindest notice of me, smiled upon me with great benignity, and seemed to assure me of their protection. I was soothed and cheered by their presence, though after all there was a sort of sinister and selfish expression in their countenances which prevented my placing implicit confidence in them.

Up to this time I had never doubted the real existence of these phantoms, nor had I ever suspected that other people had not seen them as distinctly as myself. I now, however, began to discover with no little anxiety that my friends had little or no knowledge of the aerial beings among whom I have spent my whole life; that my allusions to them were not understood, and all complaints respecting them were laughed at.

During the whole of this period I took great pleasure in walking out alone, particularly in the evening. The most lonely fields, the woods, and the banks of the river, and other places most completely secluded, were my favorite resorts, for there I could enjoy the sight of innumerable aerial beings of all sorts, without interruption. Every object, even every shaking leaf, seemed to me to be animated by some living soul, whose nature in some degree corresponded to its habitation. Moonlight was particularly agreeable to me, but most of all I enjoyed a thick, foggy night. At times, during these walks, I would be excessively oppressed by an indefinite and deep feeling of melancholy. At such seasons I felt a morbid love for my friends that would almost burn up my soul, and yet, at the least provocation from them, I would fly into an uncontrollable passion and foam like a little fury.

I very early learned to read, and soon became immoderately attached to books. In the Bible I read the first chapters of Job, and parts of Ezekiel, Daniel, and Revelation, with most intense delight, and with such frequency that I could repeat large portions from memory. I remember reading Morse's History of New England, which I devoured with insatiable greediness, particularly those parts which related to Indian wars and witchcraft. But of all the books, there was none that went to my heart like Bunyan's Pilgrim's Progress. I read it and re-read it night and day, and I read with the unspeakable satisfaction of most devoutly believing that everything which Honest John related was a real verity, an actual occurrence.

NARRATOR : The most famous spiritualist of the times was Andrew Jackson Davis, a medium and clairvoyant revealing teachings that were anti-Calvinist with a gently radical ethic and anemic optimism. Orestes Brownson, the Catholic writer, found Spiritualism's origin in Calvinism itself, and warned of its dangers in a long novel called *The Spirit-Rapper.*

Harriet Beecher Stowe took part, along with Calvin and Catharine in at least four séances conducted by Kate Fox Jencken. The Hookers had introduced them.

•

By 1870, Harriet began writing a series of articles on Spiritualism for Henry's paper, the *Christian Union.* She admitted that charlatanry survived because of the willingness to be deceived of those who wanted to talk to their departed loved ones. She also did a historical survey of early Christian beliefs, establishing a genuine Christian spiritualism. Calvin Stowe simultaneously contributed articles on mysticism.

CALVIN : The sanctified soul has communion with God, it knows God's heart. The Bible is mysticism, and the whole Christian system is a mystical system.

HARRIET : The sphere of the newborn immortal will be mercifully regulated according to his spiritual progress. A gentle God may lead us from regions not unlike our earth, and as it were, shading off into our mortal life—upward and outward—as we can bear it.

We sincerely believe that it has sometimes been God's will to vouchsafe to faithful souls some glimpses of the spiritual world, and by the loved voice or presence of the departed, seen in night visions or by vivid impressions of them, to relieve some crisis of agony—to give lightness, peace and joy.

NARRATOR : Another of Calvin's articles argued that there was an ontological reality that was the power of evil. Charles Beecher also felt that declining belief in diabolism was dangerous.

William Beecher, so inept at his career, claimed to be the family's most successful animal magnetizer. He had worked with a cataleptic child, so that the child could identify tastes and smells of objects in William's mouth. With further mesmerism, the boy was cured of his spinal injury and his fits. William became convinced that he could cure toothache, headache, and assorted pains.

WILLIAM : I don't know how to probe into its source, but as a remedial agent, mesmerism is to accomplish much good. I am not, however, a full believer in all which is affirmed of clairvoyants—what I see and know, I believe.

•

NARRATOR : Once they had met, Isabella Beecher Hooker became involved, some say enthralled, with Victoria Woodhull. At three years old, Victoria had been transported to the spirit world. She was taught by Demosthenes, who told her of her coming greatness. She had the power to heal, and apparently brought her son Byron back to life.

Isabella began to speak openly of her own experiences.

ISABELLA : We are not only becoming purified ourselves but lo we are already ministering spirits to others—entering by a subtle power of sympathy into their heart of hearts and giving them comfort, guidance even, almost without a word. I remember when the reality, the delicious sense of all this came to me, as a verification of old time teachings. You are too young yet to realize what I mean and I should be sorry if you could—but someday you will enter into it all and call to mind what I have written and said so many times.

NARRATOR : By this time, with Victoria Woodhull's encouragement, Isabella had come to believe that she had been appointed as the savior of the world, a messiah whose mission was to inaugurate a world government with herself as viceregent of Christ. This maternal government would bring in the millennium. Isabella's notebooks detailed the workings of this government, including provisional selections of cabinet members. The everyday world interpenetrated communings with the late Horace Bushnell or preparations for testing of women apostles.

In some ways Isabella Beecher Hooker was mad—although her feeling of responsibility for her brothers and sisters, of personal greatness, of moral government were common Beecher ideals. About this time John and Isabella Hooker were almost bankrupt, and John was demoralized. This was also the period when Isabella supported Victoria Woodhull against her brother Henry in the Tilton scandal.

Spiritualism gave Isabella a vocabulary and some useful concepts. At thirteen, she had had a brief vision of her mother. A second vision came in Paris, during the European trip she and John took to avoid the Tilton trial. Again it was her mother, this time as the Angel of Annunciation.

When they returned home, Isabella consecrated an upstairs room to her mother. Aided by her dead son Thomas, Isabella arranged scarves and ornamental grasses. Josef Haydn came with Thomas, and Joan of Arc. Harriet Martineau appeared, the deceased Lyman Beecher here renounced his Calvinism, and Horace Bushnell begged forgiveness for his attacks on the women's movement.

Soon after Catharine Beecher died in 1878, she began to appear in Isabella's sanctum. She was still pushy and demanding Isabella's voice, although another spirit was already speaking through her. For this Isabella rebuked her—and Catharine was repentant, begging Isabella for guidance.

All the while that Isabella was inhabiting this fantasy world of spirits, her husband John and son Ned tried to support her. When she predicted an attempt to kill their son-in-law Eugene Burton, John dutifully called in some Hartford plainclothes police, and was embarrassed and outraged with her when he had had to invent an ingenious story to cover up the truth. Isabella reminded him of his own family's history of insanity.

Son Ned proved more gullible, however, when she confided in

him the great secret that he had been immaculately conceived and was to be a great healer. One minor success with mesmeric passes confirmed his belief.

Meanwhile, Isabella learned from her Angel of the Annunciation, her mother, that she was the twin sister of Jesus Christ. At first she resisted the idea, but then called herself the Comforter. Then she saw Christ in the sanctum room.

Was Isabella Beecher Hooker insane? At this time, Spiritualism, Swedenborgianism, ouija boards, séances, and other forms of spirit communication were quite popular. Clairvoyants and mediums were common, and many intellectuals dabbled in the occult.

In Isabella's case, she experienced spirit-rappings, usually in her parasol. Automatic writing put her in touch with her mother, and also trance-speaking. Isabella was publicly known as a trance-speaker, and she had some proficiency at it, accompanying the voice with gestures and facial expressions. William Beecher's wife Kate spoke through her. But Thomas Beecher did not believe his first wife Livy was speaking through Isabella.

The truth is, Isabella's powers were supported by a community of belief. Some of her revelations were simply ancient myths brought to life, while others, such as pyramidology, were recent. She developed a personal mythology out of it too, with a coat of many colors, and the sanctum. Sisters Catharine and Harriet both supported the idea of women as religious teachers. And Harriet even suggested the revival of a female prophetic tradition. Isabella took this one step further, when she proposed to John Stuart Mill the idea that women were not only equal to men, they were superior.

ISABELLA : Of late I have been impressed more and more with the closer likeness to the divine nature which woman seems to bear, in that she is more sensibly, if not more truly, a creator than man is. What father can say, "Thou art my child," as a mother can? —and through what channels does he count the life-beat of his child as his own?

And to my mind there is more sense of power in this sense of motherhood than in all things else; that power we all reach after by virtue of our divine ancestry. To create is to live; to express our own beings through another and another is everlasting youth; and to mold, guide, and control this offshoot of our being, itself an independent power—this is the glory of existence, its very most supreme delight.

To my conception, a mother is the only being in this world who thus approximates the divine nature. So feeble in comparison is the father's relation to her child, so lost in her higher and divine relation, that it is within the experience of many a mother, whether recognized by herself or not, that from the moment of blessed annunciation to heavenly birth, she, like the Virgin of old, has known no father to her child save the Holy Ghost.

•

NARRATOR : One reason for Isabella's powerful imagination may have been heredity. Her brother James Beecher had always felt that there was something different about the three children of Lyman Beecher's second marriage—Isabella, Thomas, and himself.

JAMES : The difference between the preachings of Isabella and Harriet is in the family inheritance. I think sister Belle would have done far better to come here this winter than to be browsing around Brooklyn and Elmira where she will only make a nuisance of herself. She might have my pulpit every Sunday and I am very sure would attract quite an audience. She could explain her spiritual mysteries to Mr. Dibbles and her higher life and woman's rights to Mr. Nelson Kelly.

I am sure that there runs a streak of insanity in our mother's three children—or rather a monomania, assuming diverse forms. I recognize it in Tom and myself. The only advantage I have is in being absolutely conscious of the fact. Tom is partially so. Belle is absolutely unconscious and is therefore the craziest of the three. However she is almost sixty. If she got well, she couldn't do much good, and if she grows worse, she cannot do much harm—and a very few years will clear us all out, and in a dozen years or so if anybody should ask who were those Beechers anyhow, there will be nobody able to answer the question.

NARRATOR : Late in his life, James went off the deep end in his isolation, preaching to the woods folk of Ulster County. He eventually died by suicide a few years later.

Isabella saw no difference between herself and other Beechers. When brother Charles came to visit, this is how she saw things.

ISABELLA : Uncle Charles who left here Friday after a few days visit at the Stowes with his dear sweet wife, told me he was looking daily for the coming of Christ—and though cautioning me kindly against Spiritualism as of the devil probably, I found in all our conversation that our views were very similar as to the interpretations of the Bible and life generally.

And when he told me he was sure there was a conspiracy against Henry—he being utterly innocent, which was of the devil surely, my confidence in his judgment of Spiritualism was weakened—especially as he acknowledged the phenomena to be largely true.

•

NARRATOR : Soon after this, Charles wrote his *Spiritual Manifestations*, in part to warn Isabella and others of the pitfalls of Spiritualism. Charles had changed from being a skeptic to thinking of spirit-rappings as demonic displays. The *Report on Spiritual Manifestations to the Congregational Church* described his findings of the phenomena of various sorts called collectively Spiritualism. It caused quite a stir. Charles attempted to reconcile biblical with modern Spiritualism. Surprisingly, he finds that Spiritualism is materialism in disguise.

CHARLES : Rejecting the Bible as Authority, claiming for all people inspiration in common with Christ and the Apostles, and of the same mind regarding sin as immaturity of development, eschewing all received ideas of a fall of angels and people from original holiness, of total depravity, atonement, regeneration, pardon, etc.—the system is, in its last analysis, though but half-developed, a polytheistic pantheism, disguising under the name of Spirit a subtle but genuine materialism.

NARRATOR : Charles considered Spiritualism a competitor to Christianity, a debased form of religion.

CHARLES : Spiritualism has become a household religion, which is rapidly extending throughout Christendom. Vague rumors have gone abroad that God is dead, but can the soul coldly discuss the possibilities of such spiritual orphanage? The battle between God and Satan is now over the principles of good government. Soon the sixth seal will be opened, and we will see a very great and grand crisis of catastrophism.

Millions of low and deceptive spirits are already putting about the damnable lie that the millennium had already begun—when that claim is made, that the resurrection is now actually taking place in the materialization of the day—Spiritualists ought to be on their guard, and since they admit Christ and the apostles to be the strongest, purest, and most reliable mediums that have existed, they should carefully study their predictions respecting this great crisis.

•

NARRATOR : On the whole, Thomas Beecher gave his brother's book a favorable review. At the Elmira Opera House, where he preached because his church was too small, Thomas said—

THOMAS : I have studied these phenomena for twenty years until the whole habit of my mind has been changed in this regard. Instead of being surprised to hear that there are spiritual manifestations abounding throughout the land, I am daily more and more surprised and grateful that as yet I have been able to keep them out of my own house and out of my own body. There is very little doubt in my mind that the clamor and confusion and strife of opinion of these days are to be attributed largely to spiritual influences.

There is nothing in it to supersede the Bible. The value of Spiritualism, if it has any, is to convert atheists back to supernaturalism. In truth, Spiritualist teachings are nothing but pious truisms—goody slush! Charles Beecher's book at least raised the subject above the flavorous froth of popular thought.

NARRATOR : Isabella and John Hooker never wavered in their belief, however. Harriet, though still cautious, asked Isabella about the fate of her son Frederick.

HARRIET : I wish dear sister you would do me one other favor. Copy and send to me the supposed communication from my poor Fred—also poor Annie. Mr. Stowe wants to see them and I want to see them again. I committed Fred to my Savior, who knows all—who lives to save and goeth after that which is lost until he find it.

NARRATOR : And Frances Beecher sought Isabella's help when her husband James appeared hopelessly insane. But despite Isabella's efforts, Frances left unconvinced.

Even Edward Beecher, who had early classed Spiritualism among the ancient errors, sat in his old age with the Hookers with a number of mediums. When Mrs. Beecher was found to have cancer, Edward engaged a clairvoyant, perhaps Voice Adams, a young woman whom they later adopted.

In her later years, Isabella's messianic complex eased, though she still expected young apostles to come to her.

ISABELLA : Whatever my part in this revelation, the bald statements of ultra Calvinism and modified Calvinism in all their hideousness must give way to a conception of the true heart of God.

Christian Science is a long overdue development; nearly all the women I meet are more or less interested in some form of spiritual healing. It disturbs me, though, that Mrs. Eddy does not acknowledge the Spiritualists that she learned from.

AFTERMATH
1842–1907

This final chapter in the story of the Beechers will cover a lot of ground. Every Beecher still alive in the 1870s was active in his or her career.

In 1874, the Beecher-Tilton scandal was still current, with Isabella Beecher Hooker's loyalties torn between her friend, the feminist editor Victoria Woodhull and her accused brother Henry Ward Beecher. To escape this awkward situation, Isabella and her husband John left for Europe. They stayed a year and a half. In Paris, Isabella had a vision of her mother as the Angel of Annunciation, her own Annunciation. Spiritualism took up most of her energies.

Harriet Beecher Stowe, after the enormous success of her anti-slavery novels, *Uncle Tom's Cabin* and *Dred*, turned to her childhood and family life for her novels. Strong in her memory was the drowning of her sister Catharine's lover—this reminiscence resulted in *The Minister's Wooing*, the story retold with a happy ending. It was also an attack on Calvinism. While this story was appearing serially in the *Atlantic Monthly*, its editor, James Russell Lowell, wrote her—

LOWELL : What especially charmed me in the new story was that you had taken your stand on New England ground. You are one of the few persons lucky enough to be born with eyes in your head.

•

NARRATOR : In 1859, Calvin and Harriet Beecher Stowe made their third trip to Europe, meeting the critic John Ruskin in Geneva. He wrote:

RUSKIN : It takes a great deal, when I am at Geneva, to make me wish myself anywhere else, and, of all places else, in London; nevertheless I very heartily wish at this moment that I were looking out on the Norwood Hills and expecting you and the children to breakfast tomorrow.

NARRATOR : Mrs. Stowe's correspondence also included George Eliot, the pen name for Mary Ann Evans, the popular English novelist.

ELIOT : My dear friend—I value very highly the warrant to call you friend which your letter has given me. The best joy your words give me is the sense of that sweet, generous feeling in you which dictated them. I shall always be the richer because you have in this way made me know you better.

NARRATOR : In Elmira, New York, Thomas Beecher began his ministry with some quirks—for instance, office hours instead of pastoral calls. He secured additional rooms in his church for the women's sewing circle and church suppers, even setting up a pool table for the boys of the church. He established the town's first free library, partly with his own books.

In 1857 he had remarried, to Julia Jones. When friends of theirs died, leaving orphan children, Thomas and Julia adopted two daughters.

NARRATOR : Toward the end of the Civil War, Abraham Lincoln was asked whom he considered to be the greatest American. Perhaps in recognition of Henry's five speeches in Britain that probably prevented British diplomatic recognition of the Confederacy, Lincoln hesitated a moment, then said, "Beecher."

As the years went on, Harriet indulged her fantasies—as in the fantastical house in Hartford, and her second residence in Mandarin, Florida. So much did these, and social demands, make on her income that she was forced to continue to write. Eventually, the Hartford house proved to be too much of a burden, and the Stowes made their permanent home in Florida.

Mrs. Stowe's *Oldtown Fireside Stories* include many of Calvin Stowe's own tales. Professor Stowe was noted as a great storyteller and mimic. It's likely that Harriet learned much of her art from him. He had a quick mind, and a phenomenal memory. As a general scholar, he was outstanding, with Biblical and classical learning, and several languages, including Hebrew, Italian, and Greek.

Thomas Beecher left his Elmira church briefly at the beginning of the Civil War, but soon returned. He always acted as he thought Christ would act, giving away money and other generous acts. He also was mechanically inventive, devising a new cap, a tricycle, and keeping the town clock in good repair.

His major achievement, derived from Horace Bushnell's ideas, was to build a church for people's needs—the first institutional church, an enormous building with recreation rooms, parlors, and all kinds of facilities for social activities—dances, meetings, banquets. His idea served as a model for churches that became quite widespread throughout the United States. Like his church, Thomas K. Beecher was becoming an institution in Elmira, as he was to become a primary support within the Beecher family.

After the Tilton Scandal had died down, Henry Ward Beecher began to espouse evolutionism. He had long had his own idea that there was no conflict between religion and science. At a dinner given for Herbert Spencer, the British evolutionist philosopher, Beecher called Jesus the first scientist and Paul the first evolutionist.

HENRY : Religion is simply right living. In both Old and New Testament it is called Righteousness. It begins as a seed. It develops as a growth. It is relative to the individual characteristics, to the age, the institutions, the whole economy of life. God is that circle into which human consciousness and experience have poured all the qualities that have been proved by the human race to be admirable, above reproach, transcendent.

NARRATOR : Besides his polite essays on every subject, Henry also wrote a novel, *Norwood*—it offers a collection of pictures of New England life.

He built up an art library, collected precious stones, rugs, paintings, books. On Saturdays he would visit Tiffany's to look at their recent stones.

He read widely and by schedule. He talked with everyone, drawing them out.

HENRY : Every one knows more about some subjects than I do.

NARRATOR : To escape the enormous pressure of being the most famous preacher in America, Henry would go to his summer home in Peekskill on the Hudson, or to the White Mountains.

•

Catharine Beecher, at the end of her life, saw her life's work in terms of history. Much of her conclusions have been continued into the modern age.

CATHARINE : The great crisis is hastening on, when it shall be decided whether disenthralled intellect and liberty shall voluntarily submit to the laws of virtue and of heaven, or run wild to insubordination, anarchy, and crime. The great questions pending before the world, are simply these: Are liberty and intelligence, without the restrains of a moral and religious education, a blessing or a curse?

Only when education and not merely refinement is available will females cease to feel that they are educated just to enjoy themselves in future life, and realize the obligations imposed by heaven to live and to do good.

NARRATOR : In 1878, Catharine Beecher, the eldest child of Lyman Beecher, died at Thomas and Julia Beecher's home in Elmira, New York. Her spiritual crisis in 1822, and the failure of Lyman Beecher's Calvinism to provide any support or comfort, had affected the whole family. Catharine's ideas of the importance of women as culture-changers, and her work in the cause of women's education also had great influence on several other Beechers, as well as on the development of education in America.

The same year that Catharine died, Edward Beecher's book *History of Opinions on the Scriptural Doctrine of Retribution* came out. It was full of the world of the church fathers; in fact, Edward was writing a historical novel at the same time. It was called *Cornelia*, and it involved some of these church fathers—but it was never published. The introduction says—

> In our war with slavery, for the life of our country, a common interest and common danger united all who were willing to fight for their country. There was a readiness to subordinate all else to a great common interest and common danger. So it was during these early ages in the Church.

NARRATOR : As a work of fiction, *Cornelia* has major flaws—but Edward well drew the parallels between pre-Civil War America and Rome in 170–180 AD. Cornelia's religious problem reflects Catharine's crisis, Marcus Aurelius acts as Lyman Beecher did in that crisis, and the Christians are persecuted in a fashion similar to the mob at Alton persecuting Elijah Lovejoy.

Harriet became friends with Oliver Wendell Holmes, and they exchanged letters.

HOLMES : How much you have done and are doing to make our New England life wholesome and happy! If there is anyone who can look back over a literary life which has pictured our old and helped our new civilization, it is yourself. Of course your later books have harder work cut out for them than those of any other writer. They have had Uncle Tom's Cabin for a rival.

HARRIET : Dear Doctor, how time slips by! I remember when Sumner seemed to me a young man, and now he has gone. And Wilson has gone, and Chase, whom I knew as a young man in society in Cincinnati, has gone, and Stanton has gone, and Seward has gone, and yet how lively the world races on! A few air-bubbles of praise or lamentation, and away sails the great ship of life, no matter over whose grave!

They are living somewhere in intense vitality, I must believe, and you, dear doctor, must not doubt. I remember a remark you once made on Spiritualism. I cannot recall the words, but you spoke of it as modifying the sharp angles of Calvinistic belief, as a fog does those of a landscape. I would like to talk with you some time on Spiritualism. I have long since come to the conclusion that the marvels of Spiritualism are natural, and not supernatural, phenomena—an uncommon working of natural laws. I believe that the door between those in the body and those out has never in any age been entirely closed, and that occasional perceptions within the veil are a part of the course of nature, and therefore not miraculous. Of course such a phase of human experience is very substantial ground for every kind of imposture and superstition, and I have no faith whatever in mediums who practice for money.

•

NARRATOR : Harriet continued to write—her last novel came out in 1881. She lived another fifteen years, and in her old age she was remembered by many of her old friends at a birthday party. John Greenleaf Whittier, the old abolitionist poet, wrote these words for her:

WHITTIER :

> Thrice welcome from the Land of Flowers
> and golden-fruited orange bowers

to this sweet, green-turfed June of ours!
To her who, in our evil time,
dragged into light the nation's crime
with strength beyond the strength of men,
and, mightier than their sword, her pen;
to her who world-wide entrance gave
to the log cabin of the slave,
made all his wrongs and sorrows known,
and all earth's languages his own—
North, South, and East and West, made all
the common air electrical,
until the o'ercharged bolts of heaven
blazed down, and every chain was riven!

OLIVER WENDELL HOLMES :

If every tongue that speaks her praise
from whom I shape my tinkling phrase
        were summoned to the table,
the vocal chorus that would meet
of mingling accents harsh or sweet,
from every land and tribe, would beat
        the polyglots of Babel.

Know her! Who knows not Uncle Tom
and her he learned his gospel from,
        has never heard of Moses;
full well the brave black hand we know
that gave to freedom's grasp the hoe
that killed the weed that used to grow
        among the Southern roses.

Her lever was the wand of art,
her fulcrum was the human heart,
        whence all unfailing aid is;
she moved the earth! Its thunders pealed,
its mountains shook, its temples reeled,
the blood-red fountains were unsealed,
        and Moloch sunk to Hades.

NARRATOR : And Harriet Beecher Stowe replied:

HARRIET : I wish to say that I thank all my friends from my heart—that is all. And one thing more—and that is, if any of you have doubt about this world, just remember what God has done.

NARRATOR : By which she meant *Uncle Tom's Cabin*, which, finally, she denied writing.

HARRIET : The Lord Himself wrote it and I was but the humblest of instruments in his hands.

NARRATOR : At the age of 81, Edward Beecher went back into preaching, and for every Sunday for the next five years, he preached at the Parkville Church in Brooklyn.

Toward the end of his life, Henry Ward Beecher talked to a curious young friend about the Civil War and politics.

FRIEND : Who were the most influential leaders affecting the rise of the Republican Party?

HENRY : Well, I think Seward on the whole, Greeley was off and on. Horace Greeley was one of the ablest advocates in public affairs.

FRIEND : Do you share the belief that was quite general at the time that Fremont carried Pennsylvania despite the reported results?

HENRY : I do.

FRIEND : Do you believe that he was elected President?

HENRY : I do.

FRIEND : Do you believe that his inauguration as President would have averted a civil war?

HENRY : No.

FRIEND : Did you know President Buchanan?

HENRY : No, nothing more than just by sight.

FRIEND : Do you believe him to have been a square man?

HENRY : I believe him to have been a man of honest intentions, but utterly unfit for the times which found him. He had neither courage nor any commanding discretion.

FRIEND : How do you regard Douglas?

HENRY : I regard Douglas as a very able man indeed, but a dangerous man, because I do not think that he acted on great lines, but rather on the inner lines of political expediency.

FRIEND : Do you think he was a thoroughly loyal man?

HENRY : I think he was a thoroughly loyal man.

FRIEND : Do you think the election of President Lincoln precipitated the rebellion?

HENRY : yes.

FRIEND : Do you think that his death and its manner, and at the time, was a great thing for him in history?

HENRY : Yes, sir; I think that his coffin was more than the Presidential chair. It certainly gave to the whole of his career the influence of a kind of political saintship.

FRIEND : Do you believe that he would have carried out a different policy from that of Johnson?

HENRY : I know that at the time that things were drawing to a consummation he had in an inchoate form the very policy that Johnson undertook to carry out under a change of circumstances. I know it, because the Cleveland letter that I wrote was the result of conferences with Governor Andrew and President Lincoln, just preceding Lincoln's death, as to what were to be the next coming steps after the breaking down of the rebellion, and at that time, under the circumstances, it seems to me that they had, on the whole, very wise views.

It may be said almost in a sentence what their policy was. It was to say to the leading public men of the South: "Gentlemen, you took your section out of the Union; you must bring it back. We hold you responsible. We will give you all the power necessary to do it. Slavery is gone, and as you went out with those men who have been defeated, now you must come back and we will trust you."

FRIEND : Did you work for Grant?

HENRY : First, middle, and last.

FRIEND : You regarded him as a favorite with the people?

HENRY : I am not in a situation to determine that. I only know that when his name was mentioned in any large audience where I was present he always carried the day with great enthusiasm.

FRIEND : You knew Lincoln?

HENRY : Very well.

FRIEND : In a sentence, what did you think of him?

HENRY : I think that Lincoln was to a remarkable degree both a statesman and a politician, that he based his views of expediency on great principles, but that in executing expedient objects he was as shrewd and keen a politician as ever was in Washington.

He had a broad sympathy for human nature, and he understood it very well. He was as devoid of personal ambition and selfishness as any one of whom we have a record in our history. He was a man who wanted to do that which was right and best for this whole nation, South and North, and was willing to go as near to the edge of doubtful expediency as a man could go and not go over the precipice; but he saved himself.

NARRATOR : In 1884, Henry Ward Beecher spoke on behalf of Cleveland, and not Blaine the Republican, the candidate of the party he had helped to found. Cleveland's character was called into question on baseless charges. In one speech, Beecher said:

HENRY : When in the gloomy night of my own suffering, I sounded every depth of sorrow, I vowed that if God would bring the day star of hope, I would never suffer brother, friend or neighbor to go unfriended should a like serpent seek to crush him. That oath I will regard now. Because I know the bitterness of venomous lies, I will stand against infamous lies that seek to sting to death an upright man and magistrate.

People counsel me to prudence lest I stir again my own griefs. No, I will not be prudent. If I refuse to interpose a shield of well-placed confidence between Governor Cleveland and the swarm of liars that nuzzle into the mud or sling arrows from ambush, may my tongue cleave to the roof of my mouth and my right hand forget its cunning.

NARRATOR : James Beecher, youngest of the Beechers, had a mental breakdown, and soon after he sought the water cure near Thomas Beecher in Elmira. His last years of increasing isolation in upper New York State led him to a final despair. He committed suicide in 1886.

Not long after James's death, Henry died of a stroke. Fifty thousand people passed by his body. There were no special decorations, no mourning ceremonies, because Henry had forbidden it.

NARRATOR : Isabella Beecher Hooker continued to be active in the women's movement, though her involvement in the Tilton-Beecher scandal had been a political embarrassment. In 1888 she helped convene the first international convention of women in Washington. But later, she was rebuffed in her own state at the Connecticut Constitutional Convention—suffrage was no longer a novelty and not yet powerful enough politically.

In 1889, William Beecher, the oldest son, died.

Isabella's last public presentation was given at the Columbian Exposition in Chicago in 1893, where she prepared a universal litany, made up of similar passages from religious writings of the Egyptians, Hebrews, Chinese, Buddhists, Hindus, Moslems, and Christians.

She told her granddaughter Isabel:

ISABELLA : Isabel, I don't ask you to keep the Ten Commandments—you probably will anyway—but if I ever catch you being bored, I'll disown you.

NARRATOR : Her ideas of religion became in some ways even broader and more skeptical than Henry's.

ISABELLA : I am prepared to accept this life as the end—provided it's the end for everybody else!

The world is my country; to do good is my religion.

NARRATOR : In 1895, Edward Beecher, active through his eighties, died at 92.

The next year, 1896, Harriet Beecher Stowe died in Florida.

In 1900, three Beechers died—Mary Beecher Perkins in Hartford, Charles, and Thomas.

In her last year, Isabella said to her granddaughter Isabel:

ISABELLA : I can't stand all the suffering in the world.

ISABEL : Well, grandmother, you have the satisfaction of knowing you have always done more than your share to relieve it.

ISABELLA : That's the point. As long as I could help, I could stand it, but now that I can no longer help, I can't stand it!

NARRATOR : In 1907, Isabella Beecher Hooker died. The Beechers were gone.

Beecher Family Tree

LYMAN BEECHER (1775–1863)
 1799 married ROXANA FOOTE (1775–1816)
 1817 married HARRIET PORTER (1790–1835)
 1836 married LYDIA BEALS JACKSON (1789–1869)

CATHARINE (1800–1878)
 engaged, but never married

WILLIAM H. (1802–1889)
 1832 married Katherine—6 children

EDWARD (1803–1895)
 1829 married Isabella—11 children

MARY F. (1805–1900)
 1827 married Thomas Clap Perkins—4 children

HARRIET (1808—1 month)

GEORGE (1809–1843)
 1837 married Sarah—2 children

HARRIET E. (1811–1896)
 1836 married Calvin Stowe—7 children

HENRY WARD (1813–1887)
 1837 married Eunice Bullard—9 children

CHARLES (1815–1900)
 1840 married Sarah—6 children

FREDERICK (1818–1820)

ISABELLA H. (1822–1907)
    1841 married John Hooker—4 children

THOMAS K. (1824–1900)
    1851 married Olivia Day—4 adopted children
    1857 married Julia Jones

JAMES C. (1828–1886)
    1853 married Ann—3 adopted children
    1864 married Frances

Symphony of Flowers

The stone balcony has been fading
   For years.
   The crack has been sneaking up the wall
   Since she moved in.
   The color has been missing from her hovel
   Since he passed.
   Day in and day out brought nothing,
   Nothing but a hollow feeling,
   That she never felt like she would break from.
   Her world was dull.

Then as winter yielded to spring,
   The flower shops began blooming on the streets.
   One with lilacs, another with tulips, and several with
   Lavender and wisteria that popped in the sun.
   Slowly, very slowly, color began seeping into her
   View again.
   She would walk out on the fading balcony,
   In front of the cracking, bare wall,
   With tea in hand,
   To catch a glimpse at the symphony of flowers.

1

After two or so weeks of luminated street vendors
　　Peddling petals to pedestrians passing by,
　　The grandmotherly figure shuffled on her slippers
　　And slipped out the faded blue door.
　　She was going to only buy one flower.
　　After two or so years of a lifeless dinner table
　　And lack of conversation between television programs,
　　She was ready to bring back some life.
　　She would only buy the one
　　And put it beside his photo.

She arrived at the vendor directly below her balcony,
　　Who greeted her with a gentle smile,
　　And gestured towards the vases on the cart.
　　The old lady nodded and began to inspect,
　　Up close,
　　The arrangements in front of her.
　　There were yellow chrysanthemums,
　　Pink roses,
　　And tulips that faded from to pink to white.
　　Just like the cotton candy he always loved to buy her.

She returned home with the single flower in hand
   To place by his photo on the bedside table.
   The old lady grabbed his chipped coffee mug,
   Filled it water,
   And set it beside the photo that she woke up next to.
   He was smiling,
   She returned the gesture with moist eyes
   While the tulip rested beside him.
   The room finally seemed to gain luster.
   She grabbed her purse and left again.

The stone balcony shines like a rainbow,
   For the first time in years.
   The crack hides behind a waterfall of flowers
   Since she smiled with him.
   The color has returned to her home
   Since she regained purpose.
   Day in and day out children stare up,
   In awe and amazement,
   At the old lady's balcony.
   Her world was bright.

Beginnings

Ethereal darkness clouded the husk
   As life struggled to escape.
   It pushed,
   It cracked,
   It yearned for nutrients;
   This tiring repetition
   Exhausted the small soul.
   Resting.
   After days of struggle,
   With a home full of cracks,
   A piece of dirt fell through.
   The trapped one was shocked.
   Pushing,
   Cracking,
   Yearning,
   Believing after countless attempts,
   The trapped began to see a future,
   One with sunshine,
   And air,
   And life.
   The trapped was able to reach an arm out and touch the soil.
   Home.

It began to push out but quickly exhausted itself again.
Rest.
The trapped wanted to be boundless,
Yet I knew that it was not time yet.
Waiting was a virtue
That all must suffer through.

Iris

Greek god of rainbows.
  Watching over Tennessee.
  A hidden beauty.

Green Thumb

I've always been fond of plants
    But never seem to get it right.
    Daffodils wilt
    And Hydrangeas sink.
    Buttercups melt
    And Lilacs lack luster.
    Weeds like Denmark's court
    Snuff them out.
    I've found no real treatment.
    Water them less
    Or drown them.
    Happiness and love do so little.
    I leave it to fate
    Yet find a graveyard.
    One day I'll get it right.
    I must keep trying.

Cycles

Birth,
　　And Rebirth,
　　We return to our Earth
　　Like our time began.

As the sun sets,
　　Full of untimely regrets,
　　Time ending met
　　With our curtains closed.

Yet new,
　　Unknown to few,
　　Hope shines through
　　As new life rises.

Repetition,
　　Life with ambition,
　　Unique renditions
　　Of the never-ending cycle.

The Silver Arrow Prince

Cracks travel like converging highways to
    The silver arrow cactus; the sole ruler,
    Accepting all nutrients in its desert kingdom.

Silver spines that shine in the heat of Oaxaca,
    Spiraling with the golden ratio;
    This royal cross is the prince of the land.

After its inaugural year as ruler,
    The prince is scooped up, bagged, and seized
    Away from its throne and kingdom.

A displaced prince, along with its royal family,
    Lay along isles in a small country market.
    The Silver spines are sullied by fluorescent tubes.

Other members of the royal family display their
    Flowers like medals of honor.
    The prince hid away all signs of life.

Weeks pass, some leave to form a new regime,
    Others shrivel and welcome a black hole on wheels,
    The prince remains, alone, awaiting death.

Yet a pauper, who was as alone as the cactus,
    Lowered a hand much gentler than the abductor,
    And rested the silver arrow prince in a plastic carriage.

Tennessee sunlight pours like gold on
    The silver arrow cactus; the sole ruler,
    With a pauper butler in its new kingdom.

Lupinus texensic

Dazzling to the eyes,
    Yet poisonous to the tongue,
    But right for the heart.
    This pioneer bluebonnet
    Settled across the heavens.

Nature's Vines

Nature's tsunami:
   Overtaking structures with foliage
   That chokes away at humanity.

Nature's tentacles:
   Reaching out for a connection
   Among manmade jungles.

Nature's ego:
   Desiring to be seen and felt by
   All who chose to ignore it.

Nature's tangles:
   Twisting and turning up
   Architecture with grace and malice.

Nature's vengeance:
   Exhibited through the desire to
   Reclaim Her rightful kingdom.

Twisted Leaves

Spiraling upwards.
   Vines desire to overtake.
   Retrieving the earth.

Calvatia gigantea

Nature's marshmallow.
  The fungi of the meadow.
  Simply a puffball.

Bee-ing

Blissfully blitzing by
   The bounty of busy beings.
   Bouncing between birds
   And bluntly bypassing basil.
   Bound for beautiful blooms
   Of bee balms and borages.
   Buzzing beyond belief
   With bombastic bravery.
   Being a bee is a
   Bonafede blast!

The Halfwit Hummingbird

They flap like a car on a highway,
   Though not as fast as one on a speedway.
   They buzz like a bee
   On nectar to feed
   To get too drunk to call for a mayday.

Tides

They crash and they cry.
   Spontaneously in waves.
   Following the tide.

Flow

The current's soft hum.
   A calming road to travel.
   An infinite flow.

The Flamboyant Sepiida

A hollow hush of pink and yellow
   With dark sandy hues.
   A paradox of colors to lure prey;
   A poisonous muse.

Always hunting with coruscating tones
   And ink to confuse.
   A cuddleless cuttle with vivid luster
   That makes hearts bemused.

Gliding along the ocean floor
   Like a monstrous ooze.
   Hunting for small shrimp while being
   As small as a shrew.

Though their lifespan is short,
   Which is such sad news,
   They live their time to the fullest;
   Enjoying the views.

The Illustrious Phytoplankton

The illustrious phytoplanktons
   Of the ocean shore.
   An underwater sanctum for a
   Microscopic corps.

Microorganisms that wander
   And drift with currents.
   Whether the water is fresh or salt,
   They lack deterrents.

Appearing in all shapes and sizes,
   With only one cell,
   They photosynthesize the carbon;
   To which they excel.

These mysterious plants of the sea,
   Deserving of love,
   Life would not exist without their work
   For us up above.

Unseeable beauties of the deep,
    Surviving off light,
    They work constantly behind the scenes
    With no end in sight.

Nelumbo nucifera

The lotus of dreams.
   Our spirituality.
   Shining on water.

Endless

Waves crash into one another,
    Mimicking ouroboros,
    Looping endlessly under moonlight.

Stars resemble embers,
    Burning aqua,
    Nature's humble paradox.

Quintillions of gallons,
    Sustaining life,
    Over a million species to house.

Ripples form from boats,
    Passing selfishly,
    To disturb the serenity of the abyss.

Humans seek only to use;
    Wasting away
    Our limited life source.

Like the circular serpent,
   Destroying creation,
   Creating unneeded reasons for destruction.

Seasonal

The smell hits your nose of
    Spring flowers,
    Summer drinks,
    Fall candles,
    Winter desserts.

The air is unique in the
    Spring rainfall,
    Summer heat,
    Fall wind,
    Winter frost.

Your eyes shimmer at the colors of
    Spring pastels,
    Summer reds,
    Fall warmth,
    Winter blues.

Your mind wanders for the days of
    Spring get-togethers,
    Summer trips,
    Fall outings,
    Winter celebrations.

All year long, you've wanted
    Spring,
    Summer,
    Fall,
    Winter.

Autumn Arrival

Green melts from the leaves.
　An explosion of color.
　Landscapes glow with life.

Accidental Fall

Summer drifts to sleep.
  Autumn awakens early.
  Passing in the night.

Uninhibited Flow

Currents move like race cars on a speedway,
   Carrying tumbling rocks with swift gusto.
   Creek chubs swim down the waterway
   In an uninhibited flow.

Bur oaks and sugar maples cast shadows
   Over the serene stream below.
   Deep dips are juxtaposed by those shallow
   Of an uninhibited flow.

Blue jays and mourning doves drink
   From the freshwater creek below.
   Shagbark hickories sit on the water's brink
   Beside the uninhibited flow.

Monolithic ash trees tower over
   Little Eagle Creek, the current adagio,
   Dew dripping off some emerald clovers,
   Into the uninhibited flow.

Light glistens off the bubbling brook
   As fish swim with minerals in tow,
   Swimming along without a second look
   Through the uninhibited flow.

Rain hurdles down like a unwanted diatribe,
   Causing this body to overflow; however,
   The creek is always prepared to imbibe
   For this uninhibited flow.

The water's curve is nothing short of beauty,
   This is something that all know,
   Since we must uphold our duty
   Of protecting the uninhibited flow.

Clouds

The burden they carry is unprecedented.
   Overwhelming.
   Titans grow somber as the pain rises,
   Darkening the world,
   Forcing us to see the pain we inflict.
   Atone.

They are Watchers.
Guardians.
Looming high above as we live.
Disturbing us as needed.
Cleansing us.
Purifying all with water.

They are Gods.
Once we are sanctified,
Their hue lightens.
They tower.
Always Protecting.
Watching.

Afternoon Shower

Dripping against the window with a
   Natural syncopation.
   Hiding the blue behind a veil of gray.

The ground is coated in water to
   Entice sporadic rainbows
   To display their kaleidoscopic array.

Sunlight dances in the distance with
   Contagious motivation;
   Bookending the intermission of rainfall.

As soon as it began, it ended, like a
   Child's nursery story.
   Nature's break in daily monotony.

Drops

Pit
I feel an insatiable calm
Pat
As the ominous rainstorm rolls in.
Pit
Like blinds being closed over the land
Pat
Darkness envelopes like a blanket.
Pitter
The window begins to resemble
Patter
A waterfall deep in a forest.
Pitter
The clouds cry with thunder as water
Patter
Flows down to the streets and hills below.
Pitter Patter
My plans have been canceled for the day.
Pitter Patter
To watch the rain fall down like teardrops.

Winter Blues

Ice covers each branch
   As the frost coats the grass.
   Flakes flurry about the air
   And curtain the sky.

Streetlights glisten off sleet
   While crystals overtake windows.
   Traces of life disappear
   As winter's shadow falls.

Each calendar year ends
   In a bleak twilight.
   Joy and sorrow alike
   Can be veiled by snow.

Fireplaces thaw tenebrosity
   As chills melt away.
   Though darkness engulfs the hours,
   Beauty is found in this season.

Cold Warmth

On the rolling hills.
   The snow is a soft blanket.
   The wilderness sleeps.

Snowflakes

They fall without sound
  Yet dance in the air.
  Drifting to the ground
  Before you are aware.

Their whispers are hushed
  With size barely seen.
  Often in no rush;
  Purely serene.

Like millions of fairies
  Celebrating the season,
  Pure bliss they carry
  As a planned liaison.

Cool to the touch.
  Warm to the heart.
  They aren't doing much
  But doing their part.

When morning sun wakes,
And frosty glitter glistens,
There's rolling hills of snowflakes
For our day to sweeten.

Tennessee Winter

The church bells echo
   Across the hills of snow.
   Houses dance from
   Lights put up for show.
   Angels hang from lamps
   Lining the icy street.
   Trees appear in windows
   To give passing eyes a treat.
   Children pray for school's end
   Until the coming new year,
   All while dreaming of gifts,
   Toys, and Christmas cheer.
   A small town's winter
   Is something to hold close,
   Where all those around
   Are the ones that matter most.
   Warm, fresh baked desserts
   Fill the air with spice,
   Mixing with a cozy fire,
   For your senses to entice.
   Tennessee's season of cold
   Leaves some rigid at the start,

Yet all the comforting perks
Can thaw a frozen heart.

Renewed Season

Like the turning of an hourglass
   From a time-worn hand,
   Seasons change and quietly pass
   As gently as falling sand.

Each year brings renewal,
   A change barley seen,
   For nature does not seek approval
   As it repaints its timeless scenes.

It is simple, pure, and plain
   For the globe to go on spinning,
   But for us who must remain,
   We say it is our new beginning.

About the Author

Justin Byrne is an elementary teacher in Middle Tennessee. Justin earned his bachelor's degree in Elementary Education with dual minors of Music and English from Middle Tennessee State University, and he earned his master's degree in English Studies from Arizona State University. Justin's work can also be seen in *Plants & Poetry*, multiple books by *Poets' Choice*, *The Parliament Literary Magazine*, multiple books by *Wingless Dreamer*, *The Thing Itself*, *Poetry in the Boro*, *Arc Magazine*, and *Brick Street Poetry*. Justin can be found on his website byrnepoetry.com.

www.ingramcontent.com/pod-product-compliance
Lightning Source LLC
Chambersburg PA
CBHW051747040426
42446CB00007B/252

Acknowledgement

This book contains poems that were previously published in literary magazines and book anthologies. The poem "Cycles" was first published in issue number four of *Plants & Poetry Journal*. The poem "Symphony of Flowers" was first published in the second issue of *The Parliament Literary Magazine*. The poem "The Silver Arrow Prince" was first published in the book *The Plant People: An Anthology of Environmental Artists* by *Plants & Poetry*. The poem "Uninhibited Flow" was first published in the book *Reflections on Little Eagle Creek* by *Brick Street Poetry*. The poem "Iris" was first published in *Poetry in the Boro*'s 2022 calendar. The poem "Afternoon Shower" was first published in *The Dawn of the Day* by *Wingless Dreamer*. The poem "Tennessee Winter" was first published in *Snowflakes and Mistletoes* by *Wingless Dreamer*. The poems "The Illustrious Phytoplankton" and "Nelumbo Nucifera" were first published in *Wildlife of the Underworld* by *Plants & Poetry*. I would like to thank each and every one of these publishers for taking a risk on my work.

Contents

This book is dedicated to my parents, Randy and Cissy, who have supported my dreams ever since I was little. I love you both.

Library of Congress Control Number: 2023900239

First edition

ISBN: 979-8-218-10270-8

Illustration by Eva Polakovičová

This book was professionally typeset on Reedsy.
Find out more at reedsy.com

JUSTIN BYRNE

Nature's Whispers

I

Fernando Pessoa (só, no Cais das Colunas, de costas para o mundo, desorbitado para a foz do Tejo, absorto num céu crepuscular de tempestade e Infinito) –

Sozinho, no cais deserto, nesta Hora sem tempo
Olho pro lado da barra, olho pro Infinito
Olho sem olhos, corpo-alma transido de saudade
Olho a fúria deste céu de crepúsculo e tempestade
E a Distância começa em mim a girar
A Distância começa em mim a girar
A Distância começa em mim a girar

Sobe uma ânsia das entranhas do mundo
Que me arrepanha de desmesura
Ó Tejo, rio sagrado que me desaguas Oceano
Em todas as coisas!
Ó vento, ó espaço, ó sol morto e renascido, ó Terra!
Ó coisas vastas, nuas e impossíveis
Ó força do mundo
Ó força maior que o mundo
Que referves no coração de cada vida e coisa
E corres neste rio que nos leva a todos para o Infinito
Além-horizonte
Finisterra da vida e da morte
Grande e mais íntima Distância
Onde tudo morre e renasce
Livre de morte e renascimento

Ó grande e mais íntima Distância
Ó vasto espaço aberto
Ó Grande Presença
Ó Grande Ausência
Ó imenso remoinho
Onde tudo dança, canta e arde

Fernando Pessoa (alone, at the Cais das Colunas, his back to the
world, gazing distractedly at the mouth of the river Tagus, engulfed
in a crepuscular sky of storm and Infinity) –

Alone, on the deserted quay, in this timeless Time
I look towards the river bar, I look towards Infinity
I look without eyes, body-soul transpierced with longing
I look at the fury of this crepuscular, stormy sky
And Distance begins swirling in me
Distance begins swirling in me
Distance begins swirling in me

A yearning rises from the entrails of the world
That creases me with hubris
Oh Tagus, sacred river emptying me into the Ocean
Into all things!
Oh wind, oh space, oh dead and born again sun, oh Earth!
Oh wide open, naked and impossible things
Oh strength of the world
Oh strength greater than the world
Boiling once and again in the heart of every life and every thing
And flowing in this river that bears us all to Infinity
Horizon-beyond
Finisterre of life and death
Great and most intimate Distance
Where everything dies and is reborn
Free of death and rebirth

Oh great and most intimate Distance
Oh wide open space
Oh Great Presence
Oh Great Absence
Oh immense whirl
Where everything dances, sings and burns

11

Ó meu coração
Ó meu coração
Oh que és tudo e já te não encontro
Oh que nada vejo e tudo me beija
Oh que por tudo sou arrebatado!

Ó Mãe
Ó Grande Mãe
Ó Saudade!

Grande Mãe (voz que emana do espaço, como um cósmico Abraço
omni-envolvente, que vem simultaneamente do Céu, da Terra e de
todas as coisas) –

Sou A-que-não-é, A-que-não-foi, A-que-jamais-será
A matriz imensa que a tudo dá à luz, nutre, reabsorve e recria
A mãe, irmã, esposa e amante de todos os seres e coisas
O Alfa-Ómega
A Toda-Poderosa que nada pode senão tudo amar
A infinita saudade que há em todas as coisas
O Infinito-Saudade
O Ventre-Mistério que pare Caos e Cosmos
Brahma, Jeová, Júpiter, Vishnu, Shiva, Buda, Moisés, Cristo, Maomé
Todos os sábios, deuses, visionários e profetas idos, presentes e por vir
O Ventre-Mistério que gera todos os que o ignoram e negam
O Ventre-Mistério da Vida onde a cada instante tudo brota e se
    metamorfoseia entrelaçado
Céu-Terra-pedras-plantas-animais-humanos-espíritos-deuses-
    demónios
Realidades-ficções-factos-sonhos-danças-êxtases-delírios-volúpias

Tudo é o meu Corpo fremente, dançarino e amoroso
O meu Corpo sem tempo onde em todos os tempos Céu e Terra se
    amam e desposam
O meu Corpo leito-coração de todos os amantes

Oh my heart
Oh my heart
Oh you are all and yet I no longer can find you
Oh nothing I see and everything kisses me
Oh by everything I am enthralled!

Oh Mother
Oh Great Mother
Oh Longing!

Great Mother (voice emanating from space as a cosmic all-
surrounding Embrace simultaneously arriving from Heaven, from
the Earth and from all things) –

I Am the One-who-is-not, the One-who-was-not, the One-who-never-
will-be
The immense matrix that to everything gives birth, nurtures, re-absorbs
and recreates
The mother, sister, wife and lover of all beings and things
The Alpha-Omega
The All-Mighty who can but love all things
The unending longing there is in all things
The Infinite Longing
The Mystery-Womb giving birth to Chaos and Cosmos
Brahma, Jehovah, Jupiter, Vishnu, Shiva, Buddha, Moses, Christ,
Mohamet
All the bygone, present and coming sages, gods, visionaries and
prophets
The Mystery-Womb engendering all those that ignore or deny it
The Mystery-Womb of Life where at each instant everything blossoms
and metamorphoses all entwined
Heaven-Earth-stones-plants-animals-humans-spirits-deities-demons
Realities-fictions-facts-dreams-dances-extases-deliria-voluptousness

All is my shivering, dancing, loving Body
My timeless Body where at all times Heaven and Earth love and wed
each other
My Body, bed and heart of all lovers

13

O meu Corpo vibração íntima de matéria-energia-consciência
O meu Corpo unidade múltipla de todas as coisas
O meu Corpo seio de tudo o que se ama e odeia, afaga e devora, cria e
    destrói
O meu Corpo coro-dança-teatro caósmico
Meu Corpo Ópera eterna e infinita
Meu Corpo Grande Obra

Invocaste-me Noite, antiquíssima e idêntica
Noite Rainha nascida destronada
Noite igual por dentro ao silêncio
Nossa Senhora das coisas impossíveis

Visionaste-me Cais Absoluto
O Grande Cais Anterior de onde tudo partiu
Em verdade sou o Útero de todo o espaço-tempo
Dado à luz Aqui-Agora

Chamaste-me King of Gaps, Rei dos Abismos
Chamaste-me ultra-ser
O que está para além de deuses, Deus, Destino
Aquilo que faz que haja deuses, Deus, Destino
O haver ser maior que tudo
O Abismo onde se libertam todas as mentes
O Amor onde se inflamam todos os corações
O espantoso e tremendo Mistério que transfigura todas as coisas

Invocaste-me, vislumbraste-me, mas será que plenamente me
    reconheceste?
Reparaste em quem desde sempre te amou?
Verdadeiramente tocaste quem em tudo te embalou?
Alguma vez tocaste o íntimo do teu coração?

Em verdade a mim desnudaste quando descobriste que não eras
    ninguém
Que não eras, nem serias, nem poderias querer ser nada
E que à parte disso tinhas em ti todos os sonhos do mundo

My Body, intimate vibration of matter-energy-consciousness
My Body, multiple unity of all things
My Body, bosom of everything loved and hated, caressed and devoured,
    created and destroyed
My Body chaosmic choir-dance-theatre
My Body eternal and infinite Opera
My Body Masterpiece

You summoned me, Oh Night, ancient and identical
Night Queen born dethroned
Night matched inside to silence
Our Lady of all impossible things

You envisioned me as Absolute Quay
The Great Primal Quay whence all departed
In truth I am the Uterus of all space-time
Giving birth Here-Now

You called me the King of Gaps, King of the Abysses
You called me the ultra-being
The one beyond the gods, God, Fate
Whatsoever lets there be gods, God, Fate
The there-is greater than everything
The Abyss where all minds are freed
The Love where all hearts are inflamed
The amazing and tremendous Mystery transfiguring all things

You summoned me, caught sight of me, but did you fully recognize me?
Did you notice the one who always loved you?
Did you truly touch the one who in all things cradled you?
Did you ever touch the very intimacy of your heart?

In truth, you stripped me bare when you found that you were nobody
That you were not nor would you be nor could you want to be nothing
And that besides that you had within you all the dreams in the world

Sim, sou a tua nudez e o teu deserto fecundo
O nada seres e por isso poderes imaginar-te tudo
A tua cena vazia e o teu teatro de máscaras
O grande vazio que permeia todas as ficções-realidades do mundo
O fundo sem fundo de tudo
A terra de ninguém de todas as falsas identidades distintas e separadas
O espaço-sopro da Vida que move todas as vidas
Reais e imaginárias, reais porque imaginárias, imaginárias porque reais

Sou a Rainha anónima cuja corte de heterónimos são todos os
    fenómenos, seres e coisas
Imperatriz dos intervalos e interlúdios
Senhora da Noite que embala e devora os dias e os deuses
A que nunca passou e deixa os mundos como evanescente e fugaz rasto

Nunca te deixei, sempre te assisti, sempre te amparei, sempre te
    consumi
Fui a tua inspiração e a tua angústia
A tua loucura, o teu génio, o teu desassossego
A que te deu eternamente à luz antes de haver mundo e Deus
O que há em ti anterior a ti e a tudo

Fui sobretudo o Amor que rejeitaste
Pois fiz-me carne para me dar a ti
Para que intimamente me comungasses
Para te revelar, despertar e completar
Despertar e completar o poeta sonâmbulo e triste
O homem infeliz que não deixaste de ser
Porque me recusaste na que te enviei
Porque me recusaste Ofélia
Em nome da falsa "Lei" e dos falsos "Mestres" que inventaste
Para camuflar o pânico de amares e viveres
E te refugiar no casulo da obra

Yes, I am your nakedness and your fruitful desert
Your being nothing and therefore being able to imagine yourself as
    everything
Your empty scene and your theatre of masks
The great void trespassing all fiction-realities of the world
The bottomless depth of everything
The no man's land of all distinct and separate false identities
The space-breath of Life moving all lives
Real and imaginary, real because imaginary, imaginary because real

I am the anonymous Queen whose court of heteronyms are all the
    phenomena, beings and things
Empress of intervals and interludes
Lady of the Night that cradles and devours the days and the gods
The one that has never passed and leaves the world as an evanescent
    and fleeting trail

I have never left you, I always assisted you, I always supported you, I
    always consumed you
I was your inspiration and your anxiety
Your madness, your genius, your disquiet
I am the one who eternally gave birth to you before there were world
    and God
All there is in you prior to you and to everything

I was, first and foremost, the Love you rejected
Because I made myself flesh to give myself to you
So that you intimately took me in communion
To reveal, awake and complete you
To awake and complete the sleepwalking and sad poet
The miserable man you never ceased to be
Because you refused me in the one I have sent you
Because you refused me, Ofélia
In the name of the false "Law" and the false "Masters" you fashioned
To camouflage the panic of loving and living
And taking refuge in the cocoon of your *œuvre*

Muito discorreste sobre coisas ocultas
Mas deixaste oculto o mais profundo acontecimento da tua vida
Por isso lhe falhaste o sentido
O teu sucesso literário foi o teu fracasso humano
O esplendor do teu génio o crepúsculo do teu espírito
E morreste sem saber o que o amanhã traria:
"I know not what tomorrow will bring"

Sabe que esse amanhã é Aqui-Agora, Fernando!
Desperta e vê que jamais descobrirás o antiquíssimo de ti
E a verdadeira diferença na alma
Enquanto te não abrires ao Amor
Pois só ele "move o sol e as mais estrelas"

Por isso volto a ser Anjo e me te reenvio Ofélia!

(Enquanto a voz em todo o espaço ressoa, Fernando Pessoa, avassalado, lança os olhos em todas as direcções, procurando e não conseguindo ver de onde vem. Subitamente, Ofélia surge ante si, branca e resplandecente. Fernando Pessoa, em profunda comoção, leva as mãos ao coração e cobre e descobre o rosto várias vezes, balbuciando:)

Fernando Pessoa –

Ofélia, Ofelinha!...
Bebé, Bebezinho!...

Ofélia (firme e terna, poderosa e insinuante) –

Não me viste, Fernandinho
Não viste quem era o teu Bebé!
Não me viste, Nininho
Nada viste, Íbis meu

Much have you said about hidden things
But you left hidden the most profound event of your life
So you missed its meaning
Your literary success was your human failure
The splendour of your genius was the twilight of your spirit
and you died not knowing what the morrow might hold:
"I know not what tomorrow will bring"

Know that tomorrow is Here-Now, Fernando!
Awake and see you will never discover the most ancient part of you
And the true difference within your soul
As long as you do not open yourself to Love
For only Love "moves the sun and the other stars"

So I go back to being Angel and I send thyself back Ofélia!

(While the voice in all space resonates, Fernando Pessoa, overwhelmed, casts his eyes in all directions, seeking and not being able to see whence it comes. Suddenly, Ofélia appears before him, white and resplendent. Fernando Pessoa, in deep emotion, places his hands over his heart, before covering and uncovering his face several times, stammering:)

Fernando Pessoa –

Ofélia, dear Ofélia!...
Child, dear child!...

Ofélia (firm and tender, powerful and seductive) –

You did not see me, my dear Fernando
You did not see who your little child was!
You did not see me, Nininho
Nothing have you seen, Ibis of mine

Por isso fumaste e bebeste a vida a sós
E "todo o mundo" te foi "um grande livro aberto
Que em ignorada língua" estranhaste
Sem saber que era eu a tua solidão, o teu fumo e o teu álcool
De cada dia e de todas as horas

Sim, era eu a carne dos teus pulmões
E o tabaco que os enegreceu
Era eu o fundo dos teus cálices
E o bagaço e o absinto que os encheu
Era eu as tuas entranhas
E o delírio que as consumiu

Fernando Pessoa –

Ofélia, Ofélia!...
Como é possível!?
Havia de facto um mistério em tudo aquilo!...
Um mistério ogival...
A ogiva-mistério do meu desassossego
O mistério desta inquietação que trago de antes de todos os
     nascimentos, que me consome todas as vidas e se prolonga para
     além de todas as mortes...
Eras e és tu antes e depois de todas as impossíveis versões de ser eu!...
E não te vi, Ofélia! Não te vi!...

Ofélia –

Sim, Fernando, era eu o papel branco dos teus cadernos
O sinuoso traço que os percorreu
O silêncio espantado das tuas visões
A inspiração e ânsia que as moveu
Era eu a tua poesia
Os teus olhos míopes
Os teus óculos de aros finos

So you smoked and drank life alone
And "all the world" was to you "a wide open book
That in an unknown language" you found strange
Without knowing that I was your loneliness, your smoke and your
    alcohol
Of each day and every hour

Yes, I was the meat of your lungs
And the tobacco that blackened them
I was the bottom of your wine glass
And the moonshine and absinthe filling them up
I was your entrails
And the delirium that consumed them

Fernando Pessoa –

Ofélia, Ofélia!...
How is it possible!?
There was actually a mystery in it all!...
A warhead-shaped mystery...
The ogive-mystery of my disquiet
The mystery of this uneasiness that I bring with me preceding all births,
    consuming all my lives and enduring beyond all deaths...
You were and you are before and after all impossible versions of my
    being me!...
And I did not see you, Ofélia! I did not see you!...

Ofélia –

Yes, Fernando, I was the white paper of your notebooks
The sinuous trail that went through them
The amazed silence of your visions
The inspiration and yearning that moved them
I was your poetry
Your myopic eyes
Your thin rimmed spectacles

O chapéu de abas negras e a amarrotada gabardina que te envolvia
O nó da tua gravata e a gasta sola dos teus sapatos
A pedra das calçadas que percorrias
A branca Lisboa que tanto amaste
O Orpheu, o Chiado, a Brasileira, o Martinho da Arcada
A Rua dos Douradores, a Baixa, o Tejo
O longínquo apito dos barcos
A Hora marítima
As saudades da infância
Do tempo em que festejavam o dia dos teus anos
A África do Sul
A educação inglesa
Os teus escritórios e os teus patrões
As cartas comerciais, as traduções, as dívidas, o tédio
O Mário que te abraçava "em Alma e Ouro"
Os amigos literatos e aqueles a quem pedias dinheiro
As peregrinações de quarto para quarto
A solidão, a solidão, a solidão
Era eu tudo isso e os intervalos do nada ser de tudo isso

Fernando Pessoa –

Ah, Ofélia!
Na mais funda solidão senti sempre um outro e um intervalo em mim
Na mais funda solidão senti-me sempre outro
Na mais funda solidão senti sempre...
Mas procurei sempre outra coisa, outra coisa, outra coisa
Fugir, fugir, fugir
Fugir à Presença-Ausência que sempre tive em mim
E me segredou todas as palavras-silêncios que vivi
Fugir, fugir, fugir
Evadir-me de mim e de tudo

The black brimmed hat and the wrinkled raincoat encompassing you
The knot of your tie and the threadbare soles of your shoes
The cobblestone streets you walked through
The white Lisbon that you so loved
The Orpheu, the Chiado, the Brasileira, the Martinho da Arcada
The Rua dos Douradores, the Baixa, the Tagus
The faraway hooter of ships
The maritime Hour
The childhood longing
From the time your birthday was celebrated
South Africa
English education
Your offices and your employers
The commercial letters, the translations, the debts, the *ennui*
Mário who embraced you "in Soul and in Gold"
Your literati friends and those you borrowed money from
The pilgrimages from room to room
The loneliness, the loneliness, the loneliness
I was all that and the gaps of the being nothing of it all

Fernando Pessoa –

Ah, Ofélia!
In the deepest loneliness I've always felt an other and a gap within me
In the deepest loneliness I always felt myself other
In the deepest loneliness I always felt...
But I always sought for some other thing, some other thing, some other
    thing
To escape, escape, escape
To escape the Presence-Absence I always had in me
And that whispered to me all the words-silences I lived
To escape, escape, escape
To evade myself and everything

Ofélia –

Fugir a ti e a tudo
Por não veres que o âmago de ti e de tudo é essa Presença-Ausência
Sobretudo fugiste ao seu fazer-se carne, humana, feminina e sensível
À sua incarnação numa mulher...
Pois tudo isso, Fernando, eu era
O convite-desafio a despertares para o íntimo de tudo isso
Por isso te apareci
Nesta terrena forma ilusória
Para que despertasses da ilusão e desilusão em que sobreviveste
Para que visses o que o mestre Caeiro
Não viu e jamais te poderia ensinar
Para que visses que as coisas não são coisas
Que dizer que há coisas ainda é estar doente dos olhos e dos sentidos
Ainda é pensar e não sentir
Não ver e não sentir que nada está separado e tudo se interpenetra e
    entretece
No espaço infinito da vida e da consciência
Para que visses que dizer que as coisas são coisas ainda é estar cego por
    apenas ver
Ser escravo da metafísica
E não abraçar tanto o mundo com o coração e as entranhas
Que se revele que em cada coisa é o inteiro mundo que nos abraça e
    ama
E tudo é o nosso coração e entranhas

Não apareci senão para te iniciar ao Amor
Para te insuflar boca na boca o Fogo-Sopro do mundo
Para unirmos os corações ardentes
No íntimo da carne iluminada

Ofélia –

To escape from you and from everything
Because you saw not the core of yourself and of the everything that is
    Presence-Absence
Most of all you escaped its becoming flesh, human, feminine and
    sensitive
Its incarnation in a woman...
For all that, Fernando, was I
The invitation-challenge for you to awake to the intimacy of it all
So I appeared to you
In this earthly illusive shape
So that you would awake from the illusion and the disillusion in which
    you survived
So that you would see what master Caeiro
Saw not and could never teach you
So that you would see that things are not things
That to say there are things is still to suffer in your eyes and in your
    senses
It is still to think and not to feel
Not to see and not to feel that nothing is separate and everything
    intertwines
In the infinite space of life and consciousness
So that you would see that saying that things are things is still to be
    blind through seeing alone
To be a slave to metaphysics
And not to embrace the world with heart and entrails
Revealing that in each thing is the entire world that loves and embraces
    us
And everything is our heart and entrails

I did not appear but to initiate you in Love
To breathe in you, mouth to mouth, the Fire-Breath of the world
To unite our flaming hearts
In the intimate depth of our enlightened flesh

Fernando Pessoa (extasiado) –

O Fogo-Sopro do mundo!...
Unir os corações ardentes...
No íntimo da carne iluminada!...
No íntimo da carne iluminada!...

Ofélia –

Tudo fiz para te despertar, Fernando
Para que libertasses os sentidos e o coração da inteligência
E descobrisses que o mundo é a tua carne sempre que o amor for a tua
    pele

Disseste que a Eterna Criança te ensinou a olhar para as coisas
Mas não viste quem te convidava a ver com o coração
Quiseste ser e sentir tudo de todas as maneiras
Mas não suportaste ser o namorado normal de uma rapariguinha
    simples
E passaste ao lado de descobrir o imenso fundo que há na superfície
Das coisas mais comuns e triviais
Criaste todo o tipo de projectos, revistas e movimentos
Mas não te moveste para fora de ti e do pensares a vida sem a viver
Enriqueceste a literatura mas passaste ao lado da Vida maior
Que há na existência mais quotidiana e banal
Para quem abre os olhos do espírito-coração
Por isso entreténs e desassossegas hoje imensos leitores
Que em todo o mundo te idolatram
Mas será que verdadeiramente iluminas uma consciência-coração?
És a imagem de marca de uma nação, de uma língua e de uma cultura
Dás de comer a infinitas tribos de pessoanos desavindos
Dás dinheiro a ganhar a todo o tipo de comerciantes
Tens teu corpo ilusório nos Jerónimos
Mas será que ressuscitas para uma Vida Plena?

Fernando Pessoa (ecstatic) –

The Fire-Breath of the world!...
To unite our flaming hearts...
In the intimate depth of the enlightened flesh!...
In the intimate depth of the enlightened flesh!...

Ofélia –

All that I have done to awake you, Fernando
So that you might free the senses and the heart from the intelligence
And find out that the world is your flesh whenever love is your skin

You said that the Eternal Child taught you to look at things
But you did not see who invited you to see with the heart
You wanted to be and to feel everything in every way
But you could not stand to be the normal boyfriend of a simple young
    girl
And you missed finding out the immense depth there is at the surface
Of the most common and trivial of things
You created all kinds of projects, magazines and movements
But you did not move outside yourself and away from the thought of life
    without living it
You made literature rich but missed the larger Life
There is in everyday banal existence
For those who open the eyes of the spirit-heart
That is why you today entertain and disquiet many readers
That everywhere idolize you
But do you really cast light on a consciousness-heart?
You are the trademark of a nation, a language and a culture
You feed infinite tribes of quarreling Pessoans
All kinds of merchants make money from you
Your illusive body is at the Jerónimos
But will you be born again for a Full Life?

Fernando Pessoa –

Ai, Ofelinha, Ofelinha, que tens razão!...
Que grande cruz que carrego, esta dos pessoanos e dos que me admiram
      e imitam e comercializam!...
Se soubesse, não tinha criado tantos mitos em torno de mim...
Não tem paz quem morre deixando uma tal descendência...

Ofélia –

Não tem paz quem morre sem ter vivido...
E só morre quem não vive...

Fernando Pessoa –

Ai, Ofelinha...
Quantas vezes não pensei em ti e não me arrependi
De não ter tido a coragem de te amar
De me abrir à vida simples e comum
De abandonar a literatura para ser e viver apenas...
Deixar cair aquela maldita e contraditória
hiper-consciência de mim e da impossibilidade de ser eu...
Mas demitia-me de viver ficcionando a vida
E justificando-me com pensar que isso era tão ou mais real...

Ofélia –

Desde cedo te anunciaste o Supra-Camões
O maior poeta português e europeu de sempre
Movido da vontade de superar o grande vate
Mas falhaste o que ele conseguiu:
Amar carnal e espiritualmente a Deusa em todas as mulheres
E ser por ela levado ao cume da Ilha dos Amores
A ver o mundo com imortais e divinos olhos
A ver a transparência de tudo em cada coisa

Fernando Pessoa –

Oh, dear Ofélia, dear Ofélia, you are right!...
What a heavy cross I bear, the cross of the Pessoans and the admirers
    and the imitators and the merchants!...
If only I had known, I would not have created so many myths around
    me...
There is no peace for those who die leaving such an offspring...

Ofélia –

There is no peace for those who die having not lived...
And only those who do not live die...

Fernando Pessoa –

Ah, my dear Ofélia...
How many times have I not thought of you and repented
From not having had the courage to love you
To open myself to the simple and ordinary life
To leave literature behind only to be and to live...
To shed that cursed contradictory
hyper-consciousness of myself and the impossibility of being me...
But I would resign from rendering life a fiction
While justifying to myself that it was as real or even more real...

Ofélia –

From very early on you proclaimed yourself the Supra-Camões
The greatest Portuguese and European poet ever
Moved by the will to overcome the great bard
But you failed where he succeeded:
To love carnally and spiritually the Goddess in all women
And by her be taken to the summit of the Isle of Love
To see the world through immortal and godly eyes
To see the transparency of everything in each thing

Também eu te quis pela mão conduzir
A "veres o que não pode a vã ciência
Dos errados e míseros mortais"
Mas recusaste, Fernandinho, recusaste!
Que imprudente foste na tua prudência!
Ah, que "são grandes as cousas e excelentes
que o mundo encobre aos homens imprudentes"!...

Julgaste ser a nova vinda do Encoberto
O argonauta do renascer da alma portuguesa
Mas não viste que encobriste o Amor
E assim escreveste teu "livro à beira-mágoa"
Permaneceste nevoeiro e falhaste a Hora
Falhaste a Hora que tanto anunciaste
Como a falham todos os que a proclamam sem a serem

Escreveste a *Mensagem*, mas não a foste...
Por isso te suicidaste vivo
Proclamando que "a vida é nada", que "tudo é vão"
Sem veres que só falavas do teu coração fechado...

Fernando Pessoa (arrasado) –

Ofélia, Ofélia
Mas tu sabes que me possuía algo de grandioso
Que não me deixava sossegar
O Supra-Camões, o Encoberto, o Quinto Império
O Império espiritual e andrógino
"A verdade/ que morreu D. Sebastião"
A *Mensagem*
(a mente a mover a matéria-multidão)
O ser-sentir tudo de todas as maneiras
O Caminho da Serpente
O caminho para além de haver caminhos
O querer "grandeza/ Qual a Sorte a não dá"

I, too, wanted to guide you by the hand
For you to see the "Mortals' petty pride and
science vain"
But you refused, dear Fernando, you refused!
How heedless you were in your heedfulness!
Oh, how "excellent wonders and great things here lie
by Nature veiled from Man's imprudent eye"!...

You thought it to be the new coming of the Hidden One
The Argonaut of the Portuguese soul's rebirth
But you did not see that you had hidden Love
And thus you wrote your "book at the edge of grief"
You remained fog and missed the Moment
You missed the much announced Hour
As all those that proclaim it without being it

You wrote the *Message*, but you were it not...
And so you killed yourself alive
Proclaiming that "life is nothing", that "all is in vain"
Without seeing that you spoke only of your own sealed heart...

Fernando Pessoa (devastated) –

Ofélia, Ofélia
But you know I was possessed by something grandiose
That would not let me settle down
The Supra-Camões, the Hidden One, the Fifth Empire
The spiritual androgynous Empire
"the truth/ that Dom Sebastião did die"
The *Message*
(the mind moving the matter-multitude)
The being-sensing everything in every way
The Way of the Serpent
The way beyond ways
The wanting "greatness/ Such as Fate does not give"

31

O sonho, a loucura, o golpe d'asa
O não querer nem poder ser "besta sadia,
Cadáver adiado que procria"
A ânsia de despertar Portugal, a Europa, o Mundo!...
Não falhar a missão de criar "o supra-Portugal de amanhã"
Recriar mitos regeneradores
Refazer e cumprir as profecias
Sim, a missão... A Missão...
"Emissário de um rei desconhecido",
cumprir "informes instruções de além"
A Missão...
Ah, como me lembrava de terem visto Deus "as minhas sensações"
Ah, a memória-saudade de ter sido Deus
De me acontecer a vida "do alto do infinito"...
De ser ainda anterior ao mundo e a Deus...
Ah, a grande iniciação, o "além de Deus"!
Como podia eu viver num lar e para um lar
"casado, fútil, quotidiano e tributável?"
Como podia eu ser feliz!?
Sabes o que escrevi:
"Triste de quem vive em casa,
Contente com o seu lar,
Sem que um sonho, no erguer de asa,
Faça até mais rubra a brasa da lareira a abandonar!

Triste de quem é feliz!
Vive porque a vida dura.
Nada na alma lhe diz
Mais que a lição da raiz –
Ter por vida a sepultura"

Como podia eu casar contigo!?
Como podia eu ser feliz!?

E depois eu era tantos

The dream, the madness, the fortune
The not wanting nor being able to be "But a sated beast,
A deferred cadaver that procreates"
The yearning to awaken Portugal, Europe, the World!...
Not to fail in the mission of creating "the supra-Portugal of tomorrow"
To recreate regenerating myths
To remake and fulfil prophecies
Yes, the mission... The Mission...
"The Emissary of an unknown king",
to follow "shapeless instructions from beyond"
The Mission...
Oh, how I recalled "my sensations" having seen God
Oh, the memory-longing of having been God
Of life happening to me "from the height of infinity"...
Of being prior even to the world and to God...
Oh, the great initiation, the "beyond God"!
How could I live in a home and for a home
"married, futile, everyday and taxable?"
How could I be happy!?
You know what I wrote:
"Sad is he who lives at home,
Content with his hearth,
Unless a dream, in the lifting of its wing,
Makes thus redder the ember of the hearth to be abandoned!

Sad is he who is happy!
He lives because life endures.
Nothing speaks to his soul
Except the at-root lesson –
Of having a sepulchre for life."

How could I marry you!?
How could I be happy!?

And after all I was many

Nem sequer existia...
Nenhum dos muitos existia...

Mas na verdade não sei se valeu a pena...
Parece que da obra pela qual troquei a vida
Só saem pessoanos, intelectuais e académicos,
Comércio, rivalidades e vaidades...

Ofélia (rindo-se e depois com uma pronunciada e crescente inflexão
    erótica na voz e no movimento do corpo, como uma serpente
    dançarina e sibilante) –

Casar e ser feliz!? Casar e ser feliz!?
Pois julgas ainda tu que era apenas disso que se tratava!?
Ai, Nandinho, Nandinho, pois continuas ainda sem ver!?...
Continuas sem ver o que fui e sou!?
Não me vês!?
Não te vês!?
Não vês o que soprou através de Raphael Baldaya!?
Não vês que fui e sou a Serpente e seu Caminho a largar a pele de todas
    as vias?
Não reconheces quem sibilou o teu escrito mais libertador?
Aquela cujo S rodeia e transcende todas as coisas e mundos
A ilusão do superior e do inferior, do oculto e do patente, do espírito e
    da matéria, da realidade e da ficção
A que "deixa a Cobra do Éden como a pele largada"
A que "deixa Saturno e Satan como pele largada"
A que passa "em Satan para chegar a Deus"
"E quando chega a Deus não pára"
A que "passa para além de Deus"

Não vês aquela cujas "formas que assume não são mais que peles que
    larga"
"o entendimento de todas as coisas e a compreensão intelectual da
    vacuidade delas"

I did not even exist...
None of the many existed...

But in truth I know not if it was worth it...
It seems that from the work for which I traded life
Come forth only Pessoans, intellectuals and scholars,
Commerce, rivalries and vanities...

Ofélia (laughing and then with a pronounced increasingly erotic
inflection in her voice and her body movement, as a dancing sibilant
serpent) –

To marry and be happy!? To marry and be happy!?
Do you still think that was the issue!?
Oh, Nandinho, Nandinho, are you still unable to see!?...
Are you still unable to see what I was and am!?
Can you not see me!?
Can you not see yourself!?
Can you not see what breathed through Raphael Baldaya!?
Can you not see that I was and am the Serpent and its Way by shedding
the skin of all the ways?
Can you not recognize the one who hissed at your most freeing work?
The one whose S encircles and transcends all things and worlds
The illusion of superior and inferior, invisible and visible, spirit and
matter, reality and fiction
The one who "leaves behind the Snake of Eden as sloughèd skin"
The one who "leaves behind Saturn and Satan as sloughèd skin"
The one who goes through "Satan to get to God"
"And when she does she does not stop"
The one who "goes beyond God"

Can you not see the one whose "shapes are nothing more than the skins
she sheds"
"the knowledge of all things and the intellectual understanding of their
emptiness"

"A igual ironia para com os sábios como para com os néscios"
A que atravessa e conhece a ilusão de todos os mistérios, vias e
  iniciações
A fusão e transcendência de todos os opostos
O "viver todos os contrários, não os aceitando"
O "sentir tudo de todas as maneiras, e não ser nada, no fim, senão o
  entendimento de tudo"
A que "está acima das ordens e dos sistemas"
"Fora das ordens e das iniciações"
A que dispensa todas "as linhas e os caminhos"
"Fora das leis [...] dos mundos e de Deus"
Aquela cujo caminho "passa por todos e não é nenhum"
O Spírito que a tudo nega, pois tudo são negações
Aquela que "a si mesma se tenta e se mata"
Não vês, Fernando, não me vês, não te vês!?

(Ao dizer isto, Ofélia eleva-se e transfigura-se numa serpente alada,
fogosa e devoradora, que paira sobre o Tejo e dança entre Céu e Terra
com requebros eróticos e uma poderosa irradiação sexual. Fernando
Pessoa recua, cambaleando e tapando o rosto. Ofélia prossegue, com
voz funda, vinda das entranhas do mundo.)

Ah, Íbis meu
Não viste que o mistério do mundo se revela de muitos modos
Consoante as necessidades, condições e aptidões de cada um
Mas sempre contra as suas mais entranhadas tendências
Pois de outro modo não há a iniciação que tanto procuraste
De outro modo não há morrer e renascer, transformação e libertação
  profundas!?
Não viste que para ti aquela rapariga simples, de aparência fútil e
  burguesa
Que por duas vezes me fiz surgir na tua vida
Era o verdadeiro Encoberto e a grande *Mensagem*
A alma secreta de Portugal
E o espírito-sopro do Quinto Império!?

36

"The selfsame irony toward the wise and the ignorant"
The one who goes through and knows the illusion of all mysteries, ways
and initiations
The fusion and transcendence of every opposite
The "living of every opposite by not accepting them"
The "feeling everything in every way, and being nothing, at the end, but
the knowledge of it all"
The one who "is above all orders and systems"
"Beyond all orders and initiations"
The one who dismisses all "lines and pathways"
"Beyond the law [...] of worlds and God"
The one whose way "passes through everyone and is no one"
The all-denying Spirit, since all is negation
The one who "tempts and kills herself"
Can you not see, Fernando, can you not see me, can you not see
yourself!?

(While uttering this, Ofélia elevates and transfigures herself into a fiery
devouring winged serpent roaming over the Tagus and dancing between
Heaven and Earth with erotic writhing and a powerful sexual
irradiation. Fernando Pessoa steps back, stumbling and covering his
face. Ofélia goes on, with a deep voice coming from the entrails of the
world.)

Ah, Ibis of mine
you did not see that the mystery of the world reveals itself in many ways
To each one according to their needs, conditions and skills
But always against their most ingrained tendencies
For otherwise there is not the initiation you so much sought
Otherwise there is no dying and rebirth, no deep transformation and
liberation!?
Did you not see that for you the simple girl with futile bourgeois
appearance
That twice I made myself appear in your life
Was truly the Hidden One and the great *Message*
The secret soul of Portugal
And the spirit-breath of the Fifth Empire!?

Se Cristo se fez menino e deixou o Céu
Para te vir ensinar a olhar para as coisas
Eu deixei tudo para te abrir o coração
Para além de haver coisas e quem as olhe
Devias ter sondado mais o ambíguo sentido do meu nome
Para além das tuas fixações shakespearianas
Pois fui a Pomba-Serpente, o Santo Spírito
O Sopro, o hálito, o bafo quente e sagrado
Da Grande-Deusa
A mãe-irmã-amante de todos os seres e coisas
Que tudo fez para te despertar e abrir
Àquilo que mais faltou a todo o teu génio:
O grande Amor, o Amor sagrado
Por todas as formas de vida, pela Terra, pelo Cosmos
O grande Amor
O imenso Eros de olhos e asas bem abertos
Anterior a Deus e ao mundo
A grande Saudade, viva, morta e ressurrecta na carne-espírito
A grande Saudade
A grande Saudade
A grande Saudade

(Ao dizer isto, Ofélia-Serpente torna-se ela mesma saudosa e vaga,
como perdida na visão de algo simultaneamente muito distante e
próximo.)

A grande Saudade
A grande Serpente
O verdadeiro regresso da que nunca partiu
A verdadeira Encoberta
A Rainha das Serpentes
Nesta minha terra, mais antiga que o tempo
Ophyussae
Terra das Serpentes

38

As Christ was made child and left Heaven behind
To come and teach you how to look into things
So did I leave everything to open my heart to you
Besides there being things and those who look into them
You should also have inquired into the most ambiguous meaning of my
    name
Beyond your Shakespearean fixations
For I was the Serpent-Dove, the Holy Spirit
The Breath, the hot and sacred exhalation
Of the Great-Goddess
Of the mother-sister-lover of all beings and things
Who all tried to awake and open you
To what was most lacking in your genius:
The great Love, the sacred Love
For all forms of life, for the Earth, for the Cosmos
The great Love
The immense Eros of wide open eyes and wings
Prior to God and the world
The great Longing, alive, dead and resurrected in the flesh-spirit
The great Longing
The great Longing
The great Longing

(While uttering this, Ofélia-Serpent becomes homesick and faint, as if
lost in the vision of something simultaneously faraway and close.)

The great Longing
The great Serpent
The true return of the one that has never left
The truly Hidden One
The Queen of Serpents
In this land of mine, more ancient than time
Ophyussae
Land of the Serpents

Ophyussae
O mais antigo nome dado a este extremo-ocidente
Finistérrico, crepuscular e oceânico
Onde ninguém fita impune o horizonte
O aquém-além de céu e mar

Ophyussae
Terra das Serpentes

Lisboa
A cidade da clara luz
A cidade em cujas sete colinas me encantei
Perdida de Amor e Saudade
Perdida de Amor e Saudade

Ah, quem me desencantará?
Quem me reconhecerá?
Quem me beijará o coração?
Quem me amará e fecundará?
Quem erguerá a mão, encontrará hera
E verá que "ele mesmo era
A Princesa que dormia"?

Quem ousará em mim morrer e renascer
Para que esta terra e tudo ressuscitem!?

Serás enfim tu, Fernando!?
Ou deixar-me-ás Encoberta
Na Ilha do teu esquecimento?

Ophyussae
The most ancient name given to this
Finisterrean, crepuscular and oceanic extreme West
Where nobody stares unscathed at the horizon
This side and the other of heaven and sea

Ophyussae
Land of the Serpents

Lisbon
City of the bright light
City by whose seven hills I was enchanted
Lost with Love and Longing
Lost with Love and Longing

Ah, who will disenchant me?
Who will recognize me?
Who will kiss my heart?
Who will love and impregnate me?
Who will raise his hand, find ivy
And see that "he himself was the
Sleeping Princess"?

Who will dare to die and be reborn in me
So that this land and everything be resurrected!?

Will it be you after all, Fernando!?
Or will you leave me Hidden
In the Isle of your forgetfulness?

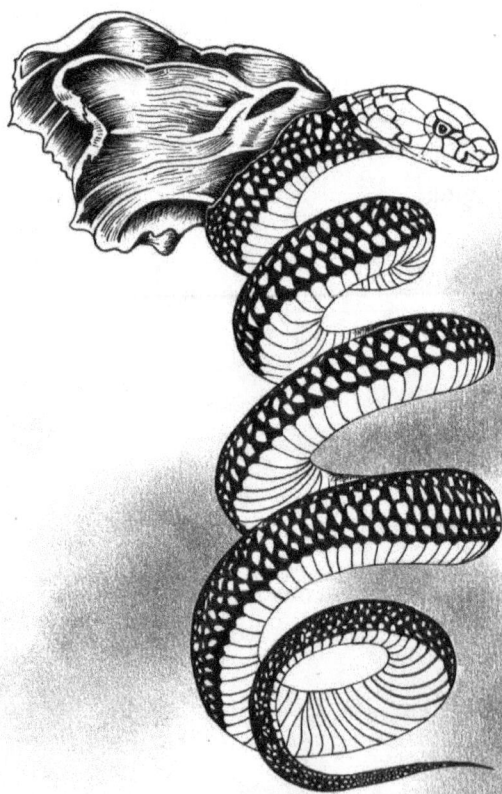

II

Tejo (um ancião de rosto velado, envolto num manto de águas, que
 surge e roda em torno de Ofélia e Fernando Pessoa) –

Sou o Tejo
Vasto e profundo
Regaço dos deuses
Leito do mundo

Homenagem a ti, Ofélia
"A que ajuda"
Homenagem a ti, rainha de Ophyussae
Homenagem a ti, Deusa-Serpente
Que vens abrir os olhos dos humanos
Para além do falso paraíso
Que os vens conduzir
Através da dor e da morte
Para o que há aquém-além
De haver criador e criatura

Homenagem a ti, Ofélia
Que pela terceira vez vens ao mundo
Resgatar teu noivo
Para o enlace vasto e profundo

Coro de Nereidas e Tritões (Surge uma profusão de figuras
 femininas e masculinas, igualmente vestidas de águas e ornadas de
 búzios, algas e corais) –

De novo a Hora eterna
No tempo se prenuncia
Sacro silêncio se faça
Cumpra-se a profecia:

Tagus (an ancient with a veiled face, draped in a cloak of water,
emerging and turning around Ofélia and Fernando Pessoa) –

I am the Tagus
Wide and deep
Lap of the gods
Bed of the world

Homage to you, Ofélia
"The helper"
Homage to you, queen of Ophyussae
Homage to you, Goddess-Serpent
Who comes to open the eyes of humans
Beyond the false paradise
Who comes to lead them
Through pain and death
Toward what there is in the here and the beyond
Of there being a creator and a creature

Homage to you, Ofélia
Who for the third time are coming to the world
To rescue your betrothed
For the bond both wide and deep

Choir of Nereids and Tritons (A profusion of female and male
shapes emerges, dressed of water and ornate with conch, seaweed
and coral) –

Once again the eternal Hour
In time foreshadowed
Sacred silence be made
And the prophecy be fulfilled:

"Patente me farei aos do Ocidente
Quando a porta se abrir lá no Oriente.
Será coisa pasmosa (de ver)
Quando o Indo com o Ganges trocar
Segundo vejo, os efeitos com o Tejo"

Fernando Pessoa (atónito, como que despertando gradualmente para
algo muito antigo) –

Ah, vozes, vozes
Vetustas e veneráveis vozes
Vozes de antes de haver nascimento
Vozes de antes do materno ventre
Vozes da Mátria anterior
Ao exílio de todas as pátrias
Vozes do Silêncio
Anterior e interior a todas as vozes
Vozes da Saudade

Algo em mim se recorda
Algo em mim se desfaz
Algo em mim se renova

Ah, a multidão que sou se agita
As vidas-vozes íntimas despertam
As personagens deste teatro da vacuidade amotinam-se
Rompem e soam através deste eu-máscara
Destes olhos e boca vazios
Desta persona
Os muitos, os tantos que somos!

"O abismo é o muro que tenho
Ser eu não tem um tamanho"

"I will make myself known to those in the West
When the door opens itself in the East.
It will be an amazing thing (to see)
When the Indus and the Ganges change
According to my vision, their effects with the Tagus"

Fernando Pessoa (stunned, as if gradually awakening for something
    very old) –

Ah, voices, voices
Ancient and venerable voices
Voices from before there being birth
Voices from before the maternal womb
Voices of the previous Motherland
To exile from all countries
Voices of Silence
Prior and within all voices
Voices of Longing

Something in me remembers
Something in me is undone
Something in me is renewed

Oh, the multitude that is me trembles
The intimate lives-voices awaken
The characters of this theatre of emptiness riot
Break and sound through this I-mask
From these empty eyes and empty mouth
From this persona
The many, the so many that we are!

"The abyss is the wall I possess
To be me has no limit"

Ofélia –

Bem-aventurado quem é Abismo
Pois no Abismo repousa todo o possível
Pois no Abismo nada é impossível

Quando reconhecerás que sou Abismo?
Quando reconhecerás que sou o teu Abismo?
Quando me desencantarás?
Quando me beijarás o coração e o farás florir?
Quando me amarás e fecundarás?

Quando erguerás a mão, encontrarás hera
E verá que tu mesmo eras
"A Princesa que dormia"?

Quando te darás enfim à luz no meu ventre?
Quando ousarás morrer e renascer em mim
Libertando tudo o que há em ti
Para que esta terra e tudo ressuscitem!?

Ousarás, Fernando!? Enfim ousarás!?
Ou deixar-me-ás sempre Encoberta
Perdida de amor e saudade
Na Ilha do teu grande esquecimento?

(Ao som da voz de Ofélia, do corpo-vida de Fernando Pessoa, que
estrebucha, como que resistindo, saem muitas formas e vultos, que
dançam em seu redor, agarrando-se e combatendo-se e afagando-se uns
aos outros, em gestos delirantes, ora solenes, ora patéticos. Subitamente
fundem-se e reduzem-se a quatro. Um deles avança, enquanto
Fernando Pessoa tomba de joelhos e cabeça no chão, esgotado.)

Ofélia –

Blessed those who are Abyss
Since in the Abyss rests all that is possible
Since in the abyss nothing is impossible

When will you acknowledge that I am Abyss?
When will you acknowledge that I am your Abyss?
When will you disenchant me?
When will you kiss my heart and make it flower?
When will you love and impregnate me?

When will you raise the hand, find the ivy
And see that you were
"The sleeping Princess"?

When will you give birth in my womb?
When will you dare to die and be reborn in me
Freeing everything there is in you
For this land and everything to be resuscitated!?

Will you dare, Fernando!? Will you!?
Or will you leave me Hidden
Lost in love and longing
In the Isle of your forgetfulness?

(To the sound of Ofélia's voice, from the floundering as if resisting
body-life of Fernando Pessoa, emerge many shapes and figures dancing
around him, grabbing and fighting and stroking each other in delirious
gestures, sometimes solemn, other times pathetic. Suddenly, they
merge and are reduced to four. One of them steps forward while
Fernando Pessoa falls, knees and head on the ground, exhausted.)

Álvaro de Campos (dirigindo-se para Ofélia, efusivo, de braços abertos e inclinando-se perante ela) –

Eu te reconheço e saúdo, ó Ofélia, ó Antiquíssima!
Ó tu, que és tudo a que mais aspirei
Ó tu, que és "toda a gente e toda a parte"
Ó tu, minha inefável Hora de êxtase e doçura
Ó tu, que me surgiste do Indefinido do "lado da barra"
E me foste marítima ode
Ó tu, "Grande Cais Anterior, eterno e divino"
Ó tu, "Cais Absoluto"
"Distância Absoluta", "Puro Longe"
Ó tu, meu grito, meu êxtase e minha reconciliação:

"Ahò-ò-ò-ò-ò-ò-ò-ò-ò-ò-ò-ò-ò – yyy......
Ahò-ò-ò-ò-ò-ò-ò-ò-ò-ò-ò-ò-ò-ò – yyy......
Schooner ahò-ò-ò-ò-ò-ò-ò-ò-ò-ò-ò-ò-ò-ò – yy......"
Ó tu, em quem "sinto tudo de todas as maneiras"
Vivo "tudo de todos os lados"
E sou "a mesma coisa de todos os modos possíveis ao mesmo tempo"
Ó tu, em quem beijo na boca e me deito com tudo quanto existe
Ó tu, em quem se dão todos os encontros e todas as despedidas
Ó tu, meu coração *rendez-vous* cósmico
Ó tu, meu nada-"todos os sonhos do mundo"!
Ó tu, minha grande e enorme e imensa felicidade de não ser eu!

Ó tu, por cujo Amor proclamo um sempiterno "mandado de despejo" a todos os "mandarins da Europa" e do mundo!
Ó tu, cujo Amor por tudo e todos
Me faz tão precisa e intensamente ver que tudo o mais é nada
Sim, "homens, nações, intuitos, está tudo nulo!"
Tudo falido! Tudo gasto! Tudo imprestável!
Tudo coisa nenhuma
Tudo uma civilização apodrecida e mundializada a devorar a Terra e a vida
Com cabeça, dentes e ventre cancerosos, egoístas e ávidos!

Álvaro de Campos (going toward Ofélia, effusive, arms open and bending before her) –

I acknowledge and salute you, oh Ofélia, oh Ancient One!
Oh you, who are all that I aspired to
Oh you, who are "everybody everywhere"
Oh you, my ineffable Hour of ecstasy and sweetness
Oh you, who came to me from the Indefinite, from the river "bar"
And were maritime ode to me
Oh you, "Great Primal Quay, eternal and divine"
Oh you, "Absolute Quay"
"Absolute Distance", "Pure Faraway"
Oh you, my cry, my ecstasy and my reconciliation:

"Ahò-ò-ò-ò-ò-ò-ò-ò-ò-ò-ò-ò-ò – yyy......
Ahò-ò-ò-ò-ò-ò-ò-ò-ò-ò-ò-ò-ò-ò – yyy......
Schooner ahò-ò-ò-ò-ò-ò-ò-ò-ò-ò-ò-ò-ò-ò – yy......"
Oh you, in whom I "feel everything in every way"
I live "everything from all sides"
And I am "the same thing in all possible ways at the same time"
Oh you, whom I kiss on the mouth while I lie with all this
Oh you, in whom all encounters and all goodbyes take place
Oh you, my cosmic heart *rendez-vous*
Oh you, my nothing "all the dreams of the world"!
Oh you, my great and enormous and immense happiness of not being
    me!

Oh you, for whose Love I proclaim an everlasting "eviction notice" to all
    the "mandarins of Europe" and the world!
Oh you, whose Love for everything and everybody
Makes me so precisely and intensely see that everything else is nothing
Yes, "Men, nations, objectives: all a huge zero!"
All broke! All spent! All unworthy!
Everything nothing
Everything a rotten and globalized civilization devouring the Earth and
    life
With cancerous, selfish and greedy head, teeth and stomach!

Ah, Ofélia, que ânsias
Que imensas e sagradas ânsias de um Mundo Novo
Que desprezo por tudo o que seja menos que o descobrir e ser
Agora mesmo, Agora mesmo, Agora mesmo!

Ah, Ofélia
"Proclamo isto bem alto e bem no auge, na barra do Tejo, de costas para
    a Europa, braços erguidos, fitando o Atlântico e saudando
    abstractamente o Infinito!"

Ricardo Reis (dirigindo-se igualmente a Ofélia e inclinando-se ante
    ela, porém mais circunspecto) –

Ofélia, feminino Pã redivivo
Ante ti me inclino
Tu que me foste Lídia
Sentados à beira-rio
A enlaçar e desenlaçar mãos
A ver passar as águas, o tempo e a vida
Alheados do rumor do mundo

Também receei amar-te
Refugiado na contemplação da impermanência
E no sossego falso dos indiferentes e tristes sábios gregos

Agora em paixão plena enfim me surges
Ó Fado maior que todos os divinos
Ó Vida ampla que não vivi
Caos-Noite primitiva
De que tudo são estrelas súbditas

Em ti abdico de todo o abdicar
Ó saudade "de quem habito
Por trás dos olhos cegos"!
Em ti me visto de todos os afectos

Oh, Ofélia, what yearnings
What immense and sacred yearnings of a New World
What contempt for all that is less than finding and being
Right Now, right Now, right Now!

Oh, Ofélia
"I shout this out at the top of my lungs, on the European coast where
　　the Tagus meets the sea, with arms raised high as I gaze upon the
　　Atlantic, abstractly saluting Infinity".

Ricardo Reis (once again going toward Ofélia and bending before her,
　　although more circumspect) –

Ofélia, feminine Pan risen from the dead
Before you I incline
You who were my Lídia
Sitting by the riverside
Entangling and untangling hands
Watching the water, time and life go by
Absent-minded from the rumour of the world

I also was afraid to love you
Taking refuge in contemplating impermanence
And in the false quietness of the indifferent and sad Greek sages

Now in full blown passion you finally appear to me
Oh Fado larger than all divinities
Oh wide Life that I did not live
Primal Chaos-Night
Sudden stars of everything

In you I resign from all resigning
Oh longing "for whom I inhabit
Behind blind eyes"!
In you I dress myself in every affection

Em ti tudo enfim fruo
Livre de tudo e nada querer

Em ti sou inteiro e todo em cada coisa
Sem nada exagerar ou excluir
Em ti ponho quanto sou no mínimo que faço
Em ti nada espero e por tudo sou grato

Em ti cada momento é gozo
Beber, amar, sorrir
Ou "o reflexo do sol ido na água
De um charco"

Pois em tudo me regozijo
Todas as coisas, mínimas ou máximas
Tua presença são
Ó suma e "natural ventura"!

Em ti enfim nada temo
Nem ao destino, nem a mim, nem ao medo
Nem a ti
Ó profunda superfície
Que em tudo tanto mostras aos olhos que iluminas

Em ti a cada instante colho o dia que sou
"Este é o dia,
Esta é a hora, este o momento, isto
É quem somos"
Isto é tudo
Isto és tu!

Bernardo Soares (com um ar inicialmente vago, mas
    progressivamente apaixonado e devoto) –

Ó meu Amor!

In you everything I ultimately enjoy
Free of everything and wanting nothing

In you I am whole and complete in each and every thing
Without exaggerating or excluding
In you I lay everything I am in the least I do
In you I hope for nothing and for all I am grateful

In you each moment is enjoyment
To drink, to love, to smile
Or "the sun's reflection spent in the water
Of a pond"

Since in all I rejoice
All the things, minimal or maximal
Are your presence
Oh great and "natural fortune"!

In you I ultimately fear nothing
Neither fate nor myself nor even fear itself
Nor you
Oh deep surface
Who in every thing show so much to the eyes you enlighten

In you at each instant I gather the day I am
"This is the day,
This is the hour, this is the moment, this
Is who we are"
This is all
This is you!

Bernardo Soares (with an air initially vague, but progressively
    passionate and devout) –

Oh my Love!

Ó bem-aventurada negação da "minha incapacidade de viver"
A que chamei "génio"
Ó "Silenciosa" que desconheci na floresta do meu alheamento
Ó "Nossa Senhora do Silêncio"
Ó grande "Consoladora"
A quem supliquei que me libertasses "da alegria e da felicidade"
E me tornasses "inútil e estéril"
Ó meu Amor
"Esplendor do nada, nome do abismo, sossego do Além"
Ó meu grande Amor
"Virgem eterna antes dos deuses e dos pais dos deuses, e dos pais dos
    pais dos deuses"

Ó meu grande Amor
Livra-me enfim de mim
Agora e na hora do meu desassossego
Livra-me do meu horror às mulheres reais e ao sexo
Livra-me do meu horror a tudo
Livra-me de não me ver desde sempre livre
E capaz de te amar em todas as coisas
Sem jamais te pretender possuir
Pois só então para sempre te perderia

Livra-me do terrível cansaço da vida
Do tédio, da monotonia
Do desejo e da saudade do que não pode ser
De querer sempre "aquela outra coisa que brilha no fundo da ânsia
    como um diamante possível numa cova a que se não pode descer"
Livra-me de tudo isso
Ó tu, que és a Vida
E o tudo ser possível a cada instante

Ó minha Liberdade
Livra-me de querer fugir "para fora de Deus"
E "do ser ou do não-ser"

Oh blessed negation of my "incapacity for living"
Which I called "genius"
Oh "Silent One" that I did not know in the forest of my own absent-
     mindedness
Oh "Our Lady of Silence"
Oh great "Consoling One"
To whom I begged to free me "from joy and happiness"
And make me "useless and sterile"
Oh my Love
"Splendour of nothing, name from the abyss, peace from the Beyond"
     Oh my great Love
"Eternal virgin, who existed before the gods, before the gods' fathers, and
before the fathers of the gods' fathers"

Oh my great Love
Finally free me from myself
Now and at the hour of my disquiet
Free me from my horror of real women and sex
Free me from my horror of everything
Free me from not seeing myself free forever and ever
And able to love you in all things
Without ever pretending to own you
Since only then would I forever lose you

Free me from the terrible tiresomeness of life
From the *ennui*, from monotony
From the desire and the longing for that which cannot be
From always wanting "that other thing shining in the depths of longing,
     like a possible diamond in a pit one can't fathom"
Free me of all that
Oh you who are Life itself
And the ever all being possible

Oh my freedom
Free me from wanting to escape "outside of God"
And from "being and non-being"

Livra-me de me ver preso
Livra-me de confundir a "vacuidade das coisas"
Com o nada valer a pena
Ó tu, que és o meu poder "imaginar-me tudo" por não ser nada
Ó tu, "relâmpago íntimo" que me mostra que "não sou ninguém"
"Ninguém, absolutamente ninguém"
"Poço sem muros"
"Centro de tudo com o nada à roda"
Mas também todas estas personalidades que continuamente sonho e
    logo sou
Esta "cena viva onde passam vários actores representando várias peças"
Esta multidão que todos somos
Este sermos outros constantemente

A ti o devo
A ti o devemos
Ó bem-aventurada e eterna Vida
Na exuberância sem fim das sagradas metamorfoses

Ó Mulher bendita
Cheia de graça
Mãe do Mundo
Ámen

Alberto Caeiro (dirige-se para Ofélia, com uma elegante simplicidade e
    nobreza no porte e na voz) –

Ofélia
És quem me amou e amei
És a Natureza que trouxeste "para o pé de mim"
E quem me fez ver que "Natureza" é só uma ideia
És quem me fez não ser eu e ser feliz
És o centro do girassol-realidade que me contempla
És toda a força que me abandona ao olhar para ti

Free me from seeing myself imprisoned
Free me from confusing the "emptiness of things"
With the nothing being worthy
Oh you, who are my being able to "imagine myself everything" because I
     am nothing
Oh you, "inner flash" that shows me "I am no one"
"No one, absolutely no one"
"A well without walls"
"The centre of everything with nothing around it"
But also all these personalities that I continuously dream and therefore
     I am
This "empty stage where various actors act out various plays"
This multitude that we all are
This constantly being each other

To you I owe it
To you we owe it
Oh blessed and eternal Life
In the endless exuberance of the sacred metamorphoses

Oh blessed Woman
Full of grace
Mother of the World
Amen

Alberto Caeiro (to Ofélia, with an elegant simplicity and nobility in
     stance and voice) –

Ofélia
You are the one who loved me and I loved
You are Nature brought close
And who made me see that "Nature" is just an idea
You are who made me not be me and be happy
You are the centre of the sunflower-reality contemplating me
You are all the strength that leaves me when I look at you

És o sentir-me "nascido a cada momento
Para a eterna novidade do mundo"
És este sempiterno acordo com as coisas
Sem pensar sequer que são "coisas"
És o amar, a "eterna inocência", o "não pensar"
O meu ver tudo sem filosofia nem ciência nem arte nem religião
A janela que o mundo sempre me abre para si
A "clara simplicidade" e "saúde em existir"
De árvores, animais, fontes, pedras e plantas
O mistério de não o haver
O sentido íntimo que nada tem
A Mãe da "Eterna Criança"
Que nos dá a mão uns aos outros e a tudo
Na eterna dança de roda do mundo

És o fim das saudades e da Saudade
O ir pela vida sem olhar para trás ou para a frente
O ir pela vida apenas atento à vida
Sem sequer pensar nisso

És este meu desaprender tudo a cada instante
Estas bolas de sabão mais eloquentes e sábias que todas as escrituras
Esta vida que por mim corre "como um rio por seu leito,
E lá fora um grande silêncio como um deus que dorme"
És este passar do vento
Que só por escutá-lo "vale a pena ter nascido"
És este bem-aventurado viver não no presente
Mas na realidade

És tudo isto
E o meu compreender enfim
Que na verdade nem sequer há "coisas"
Que dizer que há coisas é ainda ter cataratas de pensamento nos olhos
Que dizer que o mundo é exterior é ainda referi-lo a mim
E que dizer que "haver gente doente torna o Mundo engraçado"
É uma total falta de sensibilidade, amor e compaixão

You are the feeling myself "at each moment just born
Into the eternal novelty of the world"
You are the everlasting agreement with all things
Without even thinking they are "things"
You are the loving, the "eternal innocence", the "not thinking"
The my seeing all without philosophy or science or art or religion
The window the world always opens to itself for me
The "clear simplicity" and "the health of existing"
Of trees, animals, springs, stones and plants
The mystery of the not-there-being
The intimate sense that nothing has
The Mother of the "Eternal Child"
Who gives her hand to every other and to every thing
In the eternal dance around the world

You are the end of longings and of Longing
The going through life without looking behind or forward
The going through life merely attentive to life
Without even thinking about it

You are my unlearning everything at each instant
These bubbles more eloquent than every scripture
This life running through me as a river along its bed
And outside a great silence as a never sleeping god
You are this rush of the wind
Whose sound "makes it worth having been born"
You are this blessed living not in the present
But in reality

You are all this
And my understanding at last
That in truth there aren't even "things"
That to say there are things is still to have cataracts of thought in one's
    eyes
That to say the world is outside is still to relate it to me
And that to say "there being sick people makes the World fun"
Is a total lack of sensitivity, love and compassion

Por isso, Ofélia
Ante me ti humildemente me inclino
O Fernando canonizou-me mestre
Mas mestre é quem me faz reconhecer a ignorância

Possa eu em ti me libertar de toda a confusão que também lancei no
    mundo
Possamos nós
Os meus irmãos, todos os nossos leitores e todos os seres
Encontrar enfim em ti luz, paz e abrigo
Possas tu amorosa acolher-nos
E nos conduzir à Vida Nova

(Dizendo isto, inclina-se e ajoelha-se perante Ofélia, juntando-se aos
demais. Ofélia permanece silenciosa. Fernando Pessoa então ergue-se e,
com um gesto largo, que parece reunir de novo os quatro heterónimos
em si, dirige-se para Ofélia.)

Fernando Pessoa –

Ofélia, somos teus.
Sou teu.
Reconheço-te.
Aceita-me, por Quem és.

(Ofélia sorri-lhe e tudo se suspende, num longo silêncio, até que se
ergue, solene, a voz do coro.)

Therefore, Ofélia
Before you I humbly incline
Fernando has canonized me master
But master is he who makes me acknowledge my ignorance

That I be able to free myself in you from all the confusion that I also cast
     into the world
That we be able
My brothers, all our readers and all beings
To Find in you light, peace and shelter at last
That you be able to harbour us
And lead us to the New Life

(While saying this, he inclines and kneels before Ofélia, joining the others. Ofélia stays quiet. Then Fernando Pessoa rises and, with a sweeping gesture that seems to gather again the four heteronyms in himself, speaks to Ofélia.)

Fernando Pessoa –

Ofélia, we are yours.
I am yours.
I acknowledge you.
Accept me, for Whom you are.

(Ofélia smiles at him and everything is suspended, in a long silence, until the voice of the choir rises solemnly.)

III

Coro de Nereidas e Tritões –

De novo a Hora eterna
No tempo se anuncia
Sacro silêncio se faz
Cumpre-se a profecia:

"Patente me farei aos do Ocidente
Quando a porta se abrir lá no Oriente.
Será coisa pasmosa (de ver)
Quando o Indo com o Ganges trocar
Segundo vejo, os efeitos com o Tejo"

Indo e Ganges (Dois vultos aquáticos e entrelaçados, um masculino,
outro feminino, entram em cena, ao mesmo tempo que o Tejo.
Convergem de braços abertos uns para os outros.)

Somos o Indo e o Ganges
A correr do vasto Oriente
Para saudosos abraçar
Nosso irmão de Ocidente

Divinas águas se misturam
Ó veneranda profecia
Da reunião dos dois gomos
Da intemporal sabedoria

Consciência desperta
Justa acção no mundo
Amando todos os seres
De tudo mostra o fundo

Choir of Nereids and Tritons –

Once again the eternal Hour
Announces itself in time
A sacred silence sets in
The prophecy is fulfilled:

"I shall make myself known to those in the West
When the door opens itself in the East.
It will be an amazing thing (to see)
When the Indus and the Ganges mingle
According to my vision, their waters with the Tagus"

Indus and Ganges (Two water shapes intertwined, one male, the
other female, enter the scene at the same time as Tagus. They
converge with arms wide open to each other.)

We are the Indus and the Ganges
Streaming from the wide East
To embrace
Our much-missed brother from the West

Divine waters are mixed
Oh ancient prophecy
From the gathering of two wedges
Of timeless wisdom

Consciousness awake
Just action in the world
Loving every being
Showing the nethermost of everything

A fusão de nossas águas
Ó Tejo finistérreo gémeo
Das Núpcias mais sagradas
É símbolo, altar e prémio

Tejo –

Ó Irmãos, saudosos Irmãos
Soa enfim a ansiada Hora
Da mais pura conjunção
Das metades da Pletora

Feminino masculino unidos
Mais que um e outro são
Uma só ave, vastas asas
Sabedoria-Compaixão

Céu-Terra, Dia-Noite,
Ouro-Prata, Sol-Lua
Nada houve dividido
A Vida é una e nua

Nova idade do mundo
Nova Aliança com tudo
Mais alto é mais fundo
Ó Verbo canoro e mudo!

Coro de Nereidas e Tritões –

Nossa pátria toda a Terra
Todos os seres nossos irmãos
Todas as vidas nossa Vida
Folhas, patas, asas, mãos

The fusion of our waters
Oh twin finisterrean Tagus
Of the most sacred Nuptials
Is symbol, altar and prize

Tagus –

Oh Brothers, much-missed Brothers
The longed for Hour sounds at last
For the most pure conjunction
Of the halves of the Plethora

Female male united
More than the one and the other they are
One bird, several wings
Wisdom-Compassion

Heaven-Earth, Day-Night,
Gold-Silver, Sun-Moon
There was nothing divided
Life is one and naked

New age of the world
New Alliance with everything
Higher is deeper
Oh sung and mute Word!

Choir of Nereids and Tritons –

Our fatherland is the whole Earth
All beings are our brothers
All lives our Life
Leaves, paws, wings, hands

Oriente-Ocidente reunidos
Finda da cisão a fantasia
Desperta já a consciência
Ilha do Amor e da Alegria

(O Indo-Ganges e o Tejo abraçam-se e mesclam as águas. A sua união
converte-se num grande oceano no seio do qual desponta uma
paradisíaca Ilha dourada com uma montanha no centro. Ofélia conduz
Pessoa pela mão por uma vereda que serpenteia rumo ao cume, pelo
meio de uma densa floresta onde cantam aves e correm fontes. Tudo é
luminoso. As árvores, as plantas, as pedras e a terra. Trazem vestes
vaporosas, onde se mesclam tons vermelhos e brancos. São seguidos
por um vasto séquito de um povo composto de todas as espécies de
seres: deuses, humanos, animais, plantas, minerais. Alguns são
híbridos, como no *Jardim das Delícias* de Jerónimo Bosch.)

Ofélia –

Como me regozija, Fernando
Conduzir-te enfim ao cume desta "ínsula divina"
Como outrora Tétis, meu avatar
A Camões, luso vate!
Divina Ilha desencoberta
Pelo coração aberto
E a consciência desperta

Sigamos este Caminho da Serpente
Abandonando cada pele a cada passo
Memórias, expectativas, projectos
Juízos, conceitos, palavras
Ideias, ideais, doutrinas
Imagens, símbolos, identificações
Dispamo-nos de tudo isto
Fiquemos tão nus como a Vida!

East-West reunited
The fantasy of schism ended
Awakens now the consciousness
Isle of Love and of Joy

(The Indus-Ganges and the Tagus embrace each other and combine
their waters. Their union is converted into a large ocean in whose
bosom arises a paradise golden Isle with a mountain at the centre.
Ofélia leads Pessoa by the hand through a path meandering toward the
summit through a dense forest where birds sing and springs run. All is
light. Trees, plants, stones and the dirt. They bring vaporous clothes
combining red and white shades. They travel with a vast following
consisting of all kinds of beings: gods, humans, animals, plants,
minerals. Some are hybrid, as in Hieronymus Bosch's *The Garden of
Earthly Delights*.)

Ofélia –

How it delights me, Fernando
To lead you at last to the summit of this "ínsula divina"
As once did Thetis, my avatar
To Camões, Portuguese bard!
Divine Isle unveiled
By the open heart
And the awakened consciousness

Let us follow this Way of the Serpent
Leaving behind every skin at each step
Memories, expectations, projects
Judgments, concepts, words
Ideas, ideals, doctrines
Images, symbols, identifications
Let us strip ourselves of all this
Let us be as naked as Life!

Sejamos Caminho, sejamos Serpente
Emplumada, alada, rediviva!

Vês, quanto mais deixamos tudo para trás
Mais ligeiros, rápidos e livres sem esforço ascendemos!
Esqueçamo-nos de tudo
Abandonemos todos os nomes
Deixemos a mente que mente
Abandonemos todas as humanas mentiras que mascaram e devastam o
    mundo
Ah, que já se avista o cume!
Ah, que já cada vez mais esplende a luz!
Vem, Amado, vem!

(e corre, puxando-o pela mão)

Fernando Pessoa (dando-lhe a mão e deixando-se levar) –

Sim, Ofélia
Em ti e por ti me dispo de tudo
Em ti e por ti me dispo enfim de mim
Não sou ninguém!
Não somos ninguém!
Que alegria, Ofélia, que Alegria!

Ofélia –

Sim, Querido! Nunca fomos ninguém!
Vem então! Depressa! Depressa!
Despe-te e corre!
Corre!
Oh, que já chegamos! Já chegamos!
Já....

Let us be the Way, let us be the Serpent
Feathered, winged, born again!

You see, the more we leave everything behind
The effortlessly lighter, faster and free we climb!
Let us forget everything
Let's leave behind all names
Let's leave the lying mind
Let's leave behind all human lies masking and wasting the world
Oh, the summit is already in sight!
Oh, the light shines more and more!
Come, Loved One, come!

(and runs, drawing him by the hand)

Fernando Pessoa (giving her his hand and letting himself be led) –

Yes, Ofélia
In you and for you I strip myself of everything
In you and for you I ultimately strip myself
I am nobody!
We are nobody!
What joy, Ofélia, what Joy!

Ofélia –

Yes, Darling! We never were any body!
Come then! Hurry! Hurry!
Strip and run!
Run!
Oh, we have already arrived! We have arrived!
We have already...

(Deparam-se com a súbita visão de um infinito esplendor, um ilimitado espaço luminoso e aberto onde fervilha o multiverso de todos os seres e coisas, em total e contínua osmose e metamorfose.)

Ofélia (inebriada de espanto e maravilhamento) –

Eis, Fernando, o que desde sempre somos...
O que tudo desde sempre é...
Transparência!
Infinita e luminosa transparência...
Osmose e metamorfose!
Total e contínua osmose e metamorfose...

Neste instante único
Neste lugar sem lugar
Eis que tudo é simultaneamente presente
Todos os tempos e espaços
Todos os seres e coisas
Tudo fenómenos
Aparições insubstanciais e nítidas
Espantosas e únicas e sempre diversas aparições
Tudo transparecendo em todos
Todos transparecendo em todos
Todos transparecendo em tudo
Tudo e todos interpenetrados, mesclados, sempre outros
Inapreensíveis, impensáveis, indizíveis

O que desde sempre e para sempre somos
O que todos e cada um dos seres desde sempre e para sempre são
O que todos enquanto não o reconhecemos pressentimos e procuramos
Em tudo o que sempre insatisfeitos desejamos...

Cesse aqui todo o pensamento, imaginação e linguagem
Dissipem-se todos os véus de conceitos, palavras e símbolos
Finde tudo o que a musa antiga canta

(They stumble upon the sudden vision of an infinite splendour, an unlimited bright and open space where the multiverse of all beings and things buzzes in total and continuous osmosis and metamorphosis.)

Ofélia (suffocating with awe and wonderment) –

Behold, Fernando, what we forever and ever have been...
What everything forever and ever is...
Transparency!
Infinite and luminous transparency...
Osmosis and metamorphosis!
Total and continuous osmosis and metamorphosis...

In this unique instant
In this placeless place
Behold, everything is simultaneously present
Every time and space
Every being and thing
Everything is phenomena
Insubstantial and clear appearances
Amazing and unique and always diverse appearances
Everything shining through in all
All shining through in all
All shining through in everything
Everything and all intertwined, combined, always other
Unintelligible, unthinkable, unutterable

What we forever and ever are
What all and each one of the beings forever and ever is and are
What all of us insofar as we do not recognize forever sense and seek
In all that always unsatisfied we desire...

Let all thought, imagination and language stop here
Let all the veils of concept, word and symbol vanish
Let all the ancient muse sings be ended

Que outro valor mais alto se levanta
Nada acrescentemos ao espanto, perplexidade e maravilhamento
Deste imenso esplendor e prodígio!

Fernando Pessoa (atónito) –

Ai, Ofélia
O que é isto!? O que é isto!?
Que deixo de me ver e a ti
Que nada vejo e vejo tudo!

Ofélia –

Sim, Fernando...
Não tenhas medo! Mantém a serenidade...
Encontrar-nos é perder-nos
Perder-nos de nos vermos algo ou alguém idêntico ou diferente
Perder-nos de vermos algo ou alguém idêntico ou diferente
Perder-nos de não vermos que tudo está em tudo
Perder-nos da "vã ciência
Dos errados e míseros mortais"...
Perder-nos de tudo o que enche as mentes e escolas e bibliotecas e
    saberes dos humanos
Perder-nos de não nos revermos e encontrarmos em tudo
Na grande, sempiterna e sagrada Festa da metamorfose de todas as
    coisas

Fernando Pessoa –

Sim, Ofélia
Na Festa do tudo que devém em cada coisa!
Olha ali os meus óculos
Compostos de infinitas minúsculas partículas divisíveis ao infinito
E em cada uma delas a turbilhonarem os infinitos universos!
Olha ali a caneta com que escrevi "O Guardador de Rebanhos"

That another, higher value be raised
That nothing to the bewilderment, perplexity and wonderment be
    added
Of this splendour and prodigy!

Fernando Pessoa (amazed) –

Oh, Ofélia
What is this!? What is this!?
That I stop seeing me and you
That I see nothing and everything!

Ofélia –

Yes, Fernando...
Be not afraid! Keep your serenity...
To find ourselves is to lose ourselves
To lose ourselves from seeing ourselves as something or somebody
    identical or different
To lose ourselves from seeing something or somebody identical or
    different
To lose ourselves for not seeing that everything is in everything
To lose ourselves from the "Mortals' petty pride and
Science vain"...
To lose ourselves from everything filling the minds and schools and
    libraries and human knowledge
To lose ourselves from not seeing and finding ourselves in everything
In the great, everlasting and sacred Feast of the metamorphosis of all
    things

Fernando Pessoa –

Yes, Ofélia
In the Feast of the everything that becomes in each thing!
Look at my glasses over there
Composed of infinite minute particles divided to infinity
And the infinite universes whirling in each of them!
Look over there at the pen with which I wrote "The Keeper of Sheep"

E nela todo o caos e todo o cosmos
A rodopiar de bocas coladas!
Ah, Caeiro, como pudeste tu dizer que as coisas são coisas!...
As coisas não são coisa nenhuma!
Olha ali o meu patrão Vasques
A Rua dos Douradores
A Brasileira do Chiado
O Martinho da Arcada
Tudo tão luminoso
Tudo tão cheio de tudo
Tudo tão saturado de todas as gentes e formas e sons e imagens e
    emoções e pensamentos do mundo!
Olha ali o último telegrama que te enviei
A responder ao que me enviaste no meu último aniversário
"Muito obrigado e identicamente com saudades"
Ah, cada partícula de tinta e de papel velho
A gemer inebriada de todas as dores e saudades e sonhos e tristezas
De todos os amantes do mundo!
Olha ali o último bagaço que bebi
Cada gotícula de aguardente a explodir no tumulto de todos os ébrios
De álcool, sonho e desmesura!
Eis a derradeira visão a que ao morrer em vão me tentei agarrar
Crispando as mãos geladas no lençol húmido da cama de hospital
Eis tudo o que vi e que só agora recordo
Mas não posso dizer, não posso dizer, não posso dizer
Porque não foi nada, nada, rigorosamente nada
Nada que se possa agarrar
Pois não é senão esta transparência
Esta infinita transparência e este infinito silêncio que há em tudo o que
    se pensa, sente, imagina, diz e vê
E trespassa todos os universos possíveis!
Ah, cada coisa, cada mínima coisa
Cada gota de água, cada poro da pele, cada pétala de flor, asa de insecto,
    grãozinho de terra, fio de tecido ou brisa que passa

And in it all the chaos and all the cosmos
Whirling with mouths glued!
Oh, Caeiro, how could you say that things are but things!...
Things are no thing at all!
Look over there at my boss Vasques
The Rua dos Douradores
The Chiado's Brasileira
The Martinho da Arcada
All so lucent
All so full of everything
All so saturated with all the people and shapes and sounds and images
    and emotions and thoughts in the world!
Look over there at the last telegram I sent you
Answering the one you sent me on my last birthday
"Thank you very much, I miss you too"
Oh, each particle of ink and old paper
Moaning inebriated of all the pains and longings and dreams and
    sadness
Of all the lovers in the world!
Look over there at the last *bagaço* I drank
Each droplet of cheap liquor exploding in the riot of all drunkards
Of alcohol, dream and hubris!
Behold the ultimate vision to which I grabbed on while dying
Cold hands gripping the wet sheet of the hospital bed
Behold all I have seen and only now remember
But cannot say, cannot say, cannot say
Because it was nothing, nothing, strictly nothing
Not to hold on to
Since it is nothing but this transparency
This infinite transparency and this infinite silence that is in all that is
    thought, imagined, said and seen
And crosses all possible universes!
Oh, each thing, each minute thing
Each water drop, each skin pore, each flower petal, insect wing, grain of
    dirt, fabric thread or passing breeze

É um tumulto caósmico que contém em si a eternidade selvagem de
 todos os possíveis!
Ah, a poesia que há em tudo
A infinita Poesia que sempre busquei, apenas vislumbrei e jamais
 consegui
A vertiginosa criatividade de nada existir em si mesmo
De tudo ser e transparecer tudo o mais
Na abissal e constante metamorfose deste vazio pleno e infinito!

Ofélia –

Deste vazio pleno, festivo e infinito que somos, querido Fernando!
Pois é isto que desde sempre e para sempre somos e tudo é
Um nada que a cada instante devém tudo!
Neste esplendor fervilha a vida profunda e secreta de todas as coisas
Que nunca são coisas porque cada uma é todas as outras
Ao contrário do que pensou o Caeiro
A Vida encoberta pela ignorância, esquecimento e desatenção que gera
 os mundos fictícios dos seres aparentes, deuses incluídos
É todavia neste esplendor que todos vivem
É nele que nascem, respiram, vibram, morrem e renascem
É ele que todos sem o saber desejam
É nele que enfim despertam
Como outrora o Gama levado pela mão de Tétis
"Comovido
De espanto e de desejo"
Não viu todavia senão o transparente globo do mundo
Com o centro, o princípio e o fim por toda a parte
Não viu quem via
Não viu isso a que Tétis chamou "Deus"
Isso cujo ser "ninguém o entende
Que a tanto o engenho humano não se estende"
Ah, se o Gama houvesse tentado ver quem nessa visão via...

It is a chaosmic riot containing in itself the wild eternity of all the
    possibles!
Oh, the poetry there is in everything
The infinite Poetry I sought for and never achieved
The dizzying creativity of there being nothing in itself
Of everything being and appearing
In the abyssal constant metamorphosis of this full and infinite
    emptiness

Ofélia –

Of this full, festive and infinite emptiness that we are, dear Fernando!
Since this is forever and ever what we are and all is
A nothing that becomes everything at every instant!
In this splendour buzzes the deep secret life of all things
That never are things because each is all the others
Contrary to what Caeiro thought
Life hidden by ignorance, forgetfulness and inattentiveness engendering
    the fictitious worlds of appearing beings, gods included
It is however in this splendour that all live
In it they are born, breathe, vibrate, die and are reborn
It is desired by all without knowing
In it they ultimately awake
As once Vasco da Gama led by the hand of Thetis
"Overwhelmed this globe to see
With desire"
However did not see but the transparent orb of the world
With the centre, the beginning and the end everywhere
Did not see who saw
Did not see what Thetis called "God"
That whose being "th' intelligence
of mortal genius ne'er shall dare pretence".
Oh, if da Gama had but tried to see who in that vision saw...

Fernando Pessoa –

Teria visto que era "Deus" que via!?...
"Deus" que em si via!?...
O Gama teve a visão divina?
O Gama tornou-se ou era Deus sem dar por isso!?
Foi isso que Tétis lhe tentou revelar, sem o conseguir!?
Foi isso que tu lhe tentaste revelar!?...

Ofélia –

Luís de Camões no Gama viu muito sem ver tudo, Fernando...
Se visse bem e visse tudo
Se não visse como quem vê
Se não visse com a cegueira da visão
Veria que nada havia a ver, nem quem visse, nem visão...
Que não havia nem deixava de haver Deus, Tétis, a Ilha, o globo do
    mundo e ele próprio...
Espero que agora enfim veja tudo o que há a ver nada vendo...
Espero que agora enfim vejas e compreendas...
Espero que...

Fernando Pessoa (estupefacto) –

Esperas que eu agora veja e compreenda que fui o Gama
Que fui Luís de Camões e perdi a oportunidade
Que tu me abriste!?
Que falhei a revelação, a iniciação e a iluminação!?
Ai, Ofélia!
Pois afinal queres fazer de mim o Supra-Camões
O meu orgulhoso sonho de juventude!?

Ofélia –

Chega, Fernando!

Fernando Pessoa –

Would he have seen that it was "God" seeing!?...
The "God" who in himself saw!?...
Did da Gama have the divine vision?
Did da Gama become or was he God without noticing it!?
Was that what Thetis tried to reveal to him without being able to!?
Was it what you tried to reveal to him!?...

Ofélia –

Luís de Camões saw much in da Gama without seeing everything,
     Fernando...
If he had seen well and everything
If he had not seen as one who sees
If he had not seen with the blindness of sight
He would have seen there was nothing to see nor any one to have seen
     nor vision...
That there would not be God, Thetis, the Isle, the orb of the world and
     himself...
I hope that now, at last, he sees all there is to see by seeing nothing...
I hope that now, at last, you see and understand...
I hope that...

Fernando Pessoa (stunned) –

You now hope I see and understand that I was da Gama
That I was Luís de Camões and missed the opportunity
Open to me by you!?
That I failed the revelation, the initiation and the illumination!?
Oh Ofélia!
Since after all you want me to be the Supra-Camões
My proud boyhood dream!?

Ofélia –

Enough, Fernando!

Não voltes a essas peles que a Serpente largou
Não percas a visão que o não é!
Nem eu nem tu somos algo ou alguém distinto deste vazio
    esplendoroso, festivo e metamórfico
Nele somos tudo, todas as coisas e seres
Que na verdade não são coisas e seres
Mas apenas fenómenos e aparições luminosos e espaciais
A única coisa que importa é que todas as consciências despertem nesta
    experiência
E não vãs querelas de literatura, literatos e filósofos
O que importa é Despertar
Pois no Despertar algo em todos e tudo desperta!
Vê pois bem, Fernando! Vê sem ver!
Mas deixa-me ajudar-te:
Dá-me um beijo, um grande beijo
Que deixe envergonhados aqueles furtivos que outrora trocámos ou
    imaginámos
Nos becos de Lisboa, nos bilhetinhos e na solidão dos nossos quartos
Dá-me o Beijo dos beijos, Fernando, meu Amor!

Fernando Pessoa (cingindo-a e abraçando-a pela cintura) –

Beijo-te sim, Ofélia, meu bem!
Beijo a tua boca-coração imaculados!

(Abraçam-se e beijam-se intensamente, fundindo-se num corpo-luz
único e convertendo-se no esplendor que antes contemplavam no cume
da montanha no centro da ilha.)

Indo-Ganges e Tejo –

Ofélia-Fernando unidos
Sacro amor primordial
Ó excelsa hierogamia
Todo o cosmos Esponsal!

Do not return to those skins sloughèd by the Serpent
Do not lose the vision that is not!
Neither you nor I are something or somebody different from this
    splendorous, festive and metamorphic emptiness
In it we are everything, all things and beings
That in truth are neither things nor beings
But just luminous and spatial phenomena and appearances
The only thing that matters is that all consciousnesses awake in this
    experience
And not vain quarrels of literature, literati and philosophers
What matters is Awakening
Since in Awakening something is all and everything awakes!
You see, then, Fernando! See without seeing!
But let me help you:
Give me a kiss, a deep kiss
That might shame those furtive kisses we once shared or imagined
In Lisbon's alleys, in the little notes and in the solitude of our rooms
Give me the Kiss of kisses, Fernando, my Love!

Fernando Pessoa (encircling her and holding her by the waist) –

Yes, I do kiss you, Ofélia, my dear!
I kiss your immaculate mouth-heart!

(They embrace and kiss intensely, melting into a single light-body and
becoming the splendour they contemplated before at the mountain
summit in the centre of the isle.)

Indus-Ganges and Tagus –

Ofélia-Fernando united
Sacred primordial love
Oh exalted hierogamy
All the Spousal cosmos!

Portugal, Terra, Cosmos
São Morte-Ressurreição
Neste esplendor prodígio
Da sacrossanta união!

Rufem cósmicos tambores
Rompa o mundo dança-folia
Bailem ninfas, musas, génios
Dure a festa noite e dia!

Despem-se humanos, divos, demos
Plantas, pedras, animais
Tombam todas as máscaras
Do Despertar eis os sinais!

Desencobre-se o Encoberto
No íntimo de todo o coração
Rei-Rainha são despertos
Das quatro eras finda a ilusão

(Ofélia e Fernando surgem coroados e unidos sobre um cavalo branco,
ele com um manto branco com uma faixa vermelha, ela com um manto
vermelho com uma faixa branca.)

Ofélia-Fernando –

Vinde a nós, ó vós todos em cujo íntimo desde sempre habitamos!
Vinde a nós, ó vós todos em cujo coração agora mesmo ressurgimos!
Vinde, ó vinde, vós todos que sois Todo o Mundo e Ninguém!
Ó vós todos, povos-seres de todo o cosmos que trazeis no coração um
    Mundo Novo!
Aqui e Agora vos convocamos
É a Hora da Grande Mutação
A Hora das Horas
A Hora dos quatro tempos refluírem para o centro anterior a tudo

Portugal, Earth, Cosmos
Are Death-Ressurrection
In this prodigious splendour
Of the sacrosanct union!

Let the cosmic drums beat
Let the world burst in dance and revelry
Let the nymphs, muses, geniuses dance
Let the feasting last night and day!

Humans, deities, demons undress
Plants, stones, animals are stripped
All the masks fall
From the Awakening these are the signs!

The Hidden One is unveiled
In the intimacy of all hearts
King-Queen are awake
The illusion of the four eras ceases

(Ofélia and Fernando appear crowned and united on a white horse, he
with a white red-striped cape, she with a red white-striped cape.)

Ofélia-Fernando –

Come to us, oh all of you in whose intimate forever and ever we inhabit!
Come to us, oh all of you in whose heart right now we resurface!
Come, oh come, all of you that are All the World and Nobody!
Oh all of you, people-beings of the whole cosmos that have a New World
    in your heart!
Here and Now we summon you
This is the Hour of the Great Mutation
The Hour of Hours
The Hour of the four tenses re-flowing into the centre preceding
    everything

E ressurgirem como o Quinto
O Império sem império
A Era sem tempo
A Era sem era do despertar da consciência-coração na visão-amor
   universal!

Vinde a nós, ó vós todos que sois o sol, a lua, a prata, o ouro, o sal e o
   sopro do mundo!
Vinde a nós, ó vós todos, consciências-energias sem género nem
   espécie, livres dos disfarces-máscaras da ilusória hierarquia do
   carnaval do mundo, consciências-energias livres das formas
   divinas, humanas, animais, vegetais e minerais!
Vinde a nós, uni-vos, despertai e enchei a Terra de quem não a domine
   e devaste, mas a ame e com ela a todas e a cada uma das suas
   criaturas-aparições!
Enchei a Terra de quem a ame e a todas as criaturas como a si mesmo,
   porque a Terra e todas as criaturas, em todo o cosmos e espaço sem
   fim, são o si mesmo de cada e de todo o si mesmo!
Vinde a nós, ó vós todos de cujas sagradas uniões nasce já nova
   "progénie, forte e bela"
Nova geração de fiéis vigilantes do Amor
De fiéis guardiões do "fogo imortal" que entre Céu e Terra arde
Que com ele varra o "mundo vil e rebelde"
Emendando "erros grandes" que há eras "nele estão,
Amando coisas que nos foram dadas,
Não para ser amadas, mas usadas"!

Vinde a nós, ó vós todos, seres maravilhosos e estranhos e subtis e
   sábios e proféticos e visionários e loucos!
Seres imensos e excessivos, que transbordam da estreiteza da cultura,
   da política e da economia e se riem dos governos, parlamentos,
   escolas, empresas, instituições, ideias e desejos dos humanos!
Ó vós todos, loucamente sábios e sabiamente loucos!
Ó vós todos, ó muitas e desvairadas e esquisitas e esdrúxulas gentes!
Ó vós todos, os únicos sãos e normais e naturais, capazes de reconhecer
   e despertar o que há de são, normal e natural em todos os loucos
   varridos que devastam a Terra e as vidas por ganância de lucro,
   poder e prazer!

And resurfacing as the Fifth
The Empire without empire
The Era without time
The Era without era of the awakening of the heart-consciousness in the
   universal vision-love!

Come to us, oh you all that are the sun, the moon, the silver, the gold,
   the salt and the breath of the world!
Come to us, oh you all, consciousnesses-energies without gender nor
   species, free from the mask-disguises of the illusory hierarchy of the
   world's Mardi Gras consciousnesses-energies free from divine,
   human, animal, vegetable and mineral shapes!
Come to us, unite, awake and fill the Earth with whomsoever will not
   dominate and waste it, but love it and with it each and every one of
   its creature-apparitions!
Fill the Earth with whomsoever will love it and all creatures as they do
   themselves, because the Earth and all creatures, in all the cosmos
   and in endless space, are of each and everything the self!
Come to us, oh all of you from whose sacred unions a new "fair brave
   race" is already being born
New generation of the faithful watchers of Love
The Faithful guardians of the "immortal fire" burning between Heaven
   and Earth
That with it sweep the "vile and rebel" world
Emending "errors grand" that long time since "in it are,
Loving things that were given to us,
Not to be loved, but used"!

Come to us, oh you all marvelous and strange and subtle and wise and
   prophetic and visionary and mad beings!
Immense excessive beings, overflowing the narrowness of culture, politics
   and economy and laughing at governments, parliaments, schools,
   companies, institutions, ideas and wishes of humans!
Oh all of you, madly wise and wisely mad!
Oh all of you, oh many and frantic and weird and extravagant peoples!
Oh all of you, the only sane and normal and natural ones, able to
   recognize and awaken all the sane, normal and natural that there is
   in all the raving mad who waste the Earth and lives for greed for
   profit, power and pleasure!

Ó excelsas irmandades e confrarias do Quinto Império sem império nem imperador a não ser a coroada criança que dança de roda e olhos atónitos num rodopio de espantos, pombas e rosas!

Ó excelsas irmandades e confrarias do Império do Santo Espírito, que ninguém sabe de onde vem nem para onde vai, sopra onde quer e fala um silêncio de todas as línguas!

Ó excelsas irmandades e confrarias dos amantes andróginos, que conduzem ao altar interno o masculino e o feminino e o unem em Núpcias mais vastas que o espaço que explodem em festas e folias de amor por todos os seres e coisas!

Vinde a nós, ó vós todos, que é a Hora!

É a Hora!

A Hora!

Agora!

Valete, Fratres!

Saúde, Irmãos!

(Ressurge o séquito que havia acompanhado Ofélia e Fernando Pessoa na ascensão ao cume da montanha, aumentado por uma ingente multidão de seres, energias e aparições que vêm de todos os pontos e direcções do espaço. Dançam e cantam em torno de Ofélia-Fernando, que permanecem unidos e extáticos, olhar mergulhado no sem fundo do mundo, até que com eles se fundem. Tudo se dissolve em luz.)

"A madrugada" real "do Quinto Império
Doira as margens do Tejo".

Oh distinguished brotherhoods and confraternities of the Fifth Empire
without empire nor emperor except the crowned child dancing
around with awed eyes in a swirl of amazement, doves and roses!
Oh distinguished brotherhoods and confraternities of the Holy Spirit
Empire, which no one knows whence it comes whither it goes and
blows wherever it wants and speaks a silence of all languages!
Oh distinguished brotherhoods and confraternities of androgynous
lovers who lead to the internal altar the male and the female united
it in Nuptials vaster than space exploding in feasting and revelries
of love for all beings and things!
Come to us, oh all of you, the Time is now!
It is the Hour!
The Hour!
Now!

Valete, Fratres!
Hail, Brothers!

(The preceding retinue follows Ofélia and Fernando Pessoa as the
climbing to the summit of the mountain resurfaces, augmented by a
huge multitude of beings, energies and apparitions that come from all
points and directions in space. They dance and sing around Ofélia-
Fernando, who remain united and ecstatic, their gaze plunged in the
bottomlessness of the world until they merge with them. All is dissolved
in light.)

The real "dawn of the Fifth Empire
Gilds the banks of the Tagus".